Boilerplate

Boilerplate

The Fine Print, Vanishing Rights,
and the Rule of Law

Margaret Jane Radin

Princeton University Press

Princeton and Oxford

Library of Congress Cataloging-in-Publication Data

Radin, Margaret Jane.
Boilerplate : the fine print, vanishing rights, and the rule of law / Margaret Jane Radin.
p. cm.
Includes index.
ISBN-13: 978-0-691-15533-3 (cloth : alk. paper)
ISBN-10: 0-691-15533-X (cloth : alk. paper)
1. Standardized terms of contract—United States. I. Title.
KF808.R25 2012
346.7302'2—dc23
2012017290

British Library Cataloging-in-Publication Data is available

This book has been composed in Sabon LT Std
Printed on acid-free paper. ∞

Printed in the United States of America

1 3 5 7 9 10 8 6 4 2

....

In memory of

C. Edwin Baker

(1947–2009)

CONTENTS

Acknowledgments   ix

Prologue: World A (Agreement) and World B (Boilerplate)   xiii

Part I. Boilerplate, Consumers' Rights, and the Rule of Law   1

Chapter One • An Overview of Worlds A and B   3

Chapter Two • Normative Degradation:
Deleting Rights without Consent in the Name of Contract   19

Chapter Three • Democratic Degradation: Replacing the Law of
the State with the "Law" of the Firm   33

Part II. Boilerplate and Contract Theory: Rationales and Rationalizations   53

Chapter Four • A Summary of the Philosophy of Contract:
The Theories of World A   55

Chapter Five • Can Autonomy Theory (Agreement, Consent)
Justify Boilerplate Deletion of Rights?   82

Chapter Six • Can Utilitarian-Welfare (Economic)
Theory Justify Boilerplate Deletion of Rights?   99

Part III. Boilerplate and Contract Remedies: Current Judicial Oversight and Possible Improvements   121

Chapter Seven • Evaluating Current Judicial Oversight   123

Chapter Eight • Can Current Oversight Be Improved?   143

Chapter Nine • Improving Evaluation of Boilerplate: A Proposed Analytical Framework   **154**

Part IV. Escaping Contract: Other Remedial Possibilities   187

Chapter Ten • "Private" Reform Ideas: Possible Market Solutions   **189**

Chapter Eleven • Reconceptualizing (Some) Boilerplate under Tort Law   **197**

Chapter Twelve • "Public" and Hybrid Regulatory Solutions   **217**

Afterword: What's Next for Boilerplate?   **243**

Notes   **249**

Index   **313**

ACKNOWLEDGMENTS

T HIS BOOK HAS BEEN a number of years in development. It probably began when I first started teaching contract law at Stanford Law School in the late 1990s, and, of course, noticed that boilerplate fits very uneasily with contract theory. So my first acknowledgment should be to Stanford, and to former Dean Paul Brest, for allowing me to switch from property to contract at that point in my career, and for underwriting the research and writing I did beginning in 2000. Thanks for institutional support of my research is also due to Princeton University, where I was the inaugural Microsoft Fellow in Law and Public Affairs in 2006–2007; at that point I began work on the book that eventually metamorphosed into this one. The institutional support of the University of Michigan from 2007 onward has been indispensable; thanks especially to the Wolfson and Cook funds, and to Dean Evan Caminker and Associate Dean Mark West.

As it developed, this project benefited from numerous workshops at other schools and the active engagement of workshop participants. Thanks to workshop participants at Duke University, Cornell University, the University of Wisconsin, and the University of Michigan, and to the Georgetown Contract and Promise Workshop organized by Gregory Klass. Thanks to Capital University Law School for inviting me to deliver the 2011 Sullivan Lecture. Very special thanks to the University of Toronto and to Dean Mayo Moran for sponsoring an all-day workshop on a version of this book in March 2011, for which many faculty members read the manuscript and presented their views and critiques. I am grateful for such extraordinary colleagueship. I am also grateful to the Centre For Innovation Law and Policy at the University of Toronto for inviting me to deliver the Grafstein Lecture in March of 2011.

A great many colleagues have read all or portions of the drafts of this book and significantly improved it. I owe special recognition to the generosity of Michael Trebilcock, who read the entire manuscript in at least two and perhaps three stages of development, and wrote astute comments on many of its pages. For reading through the manuscript and offering helpful critiques and suggestions, thanks also to the ideal colleagueship of Ariel Katz, Abraham Drassinower, Catherine Valcke, Bruce Chapman, Stephen Waddams, Peter Benson, Jennifer Nedelsky, Arthur Ripstein, Brian Langille, Lisa Austin, Ian Lee, Mariana Mota Prado, Simon Stern, Denise Réaume, John Pottow, Bruce Frier, Aditi Bagchi, and Ethan Leib. Thanks to Stephen Poppel, an amateur musician like me, an acquaintance from summer music camp, who read the entire manuscript in an early version and made numerous suggestions for how to make it suitable for nonlawyers to read.

Thanks to Jay Feinman, Arti Rai, Andrew Gold, and Jeffrey Ferriell for commentary on portions of this project presented at workshops and lectures. I also appreciate suggestions made by Andrew Coan, Kim Krawiec, Bernadette Meyler, Edward Parson, Jill Horwitz, Scott Hershovitz, Robert Hillman, Daniel Schwarcz, Brian Bix, and Daniel Markovits. Special thanks to advocates who offered advice from the field: Paul Bland, John Richard, David Arkush, and Theresa Amato. I am very much indebted to the talented and diligent law students who have worked on this project as research assistants: Stephen Woodcock, Eli Best, Rory Wellever, Bryn R. Pallesen, Aqsa Mahmud, James Ray Mangum, Ankit Bahri, Jennifer Tanaka, John Patrick Clayton, and especially Meera El-Farhan and Shannon Leitner, both eleventh-hour lifesavers. Finally, thanks to Michigan Law Review veterans Adam Teitelbaum and Charles Weikel, who checked the citations on all the notes. Thank you all. I hope I have not forgotten anyone.

Chuck Myers, my acquisitions editor at Princeton Press, contributed invaluable expertise and critical help. He is very good at what he does! Thanks to Wayland J. Radin for the photos and for help in preparing the manuscript for submission. Finally, thanks to my husband, Phillip Coonce, thanks that I really cannot write with adequate eloquence. Phil's personal support has been more than "the reasonable person" could ever have wished for. In addition, he read the manuscript twice from cover to cover, and he improved it significantly with comments ranging from small "noodges" on almost every page to overarching big questions.

This book is dedicated to the memory of C. Edwin Baker, my close friend for more than thirty years and my worst (that is, my best) critic for that long. I have no doubt that if Ed were still here, his gracious and tenacious critique would have made this a better book.

Margaret Jane Radin
Ann Arbor, Michigan
December 2011

PROLOGUE: WORLD A (AGREEMENT) AND WORLD B (BOILERPLATE)

Agreement, the traditional basis of contract (an invented story):

Sally says to John, "I really like your bicycle. Will you sell it to me for $100?" John says, "Well, I couldn't part with it for $100, but how about $125?" Sally says, "OK, I really do like it, so how about $120?" John says, "It's a deal. I'll go get the bike." Then Sally hands over $120.

But John never delivers the bike. After John fails to perform his side of the bargain, Sally can bring John to court in a place convenient for her and ask that John be found in breach of contract. If the court finds that John breached a contract with Sally, John will be ordered to compensate Sally. Probably John will be ordered to pay Sally whatever amount she has lost by not receiving the bicycle, which could include not only the amount it would cost her to buy an equivalent bicycle from someone else, but whatever amounts she has lost as a consequence of the broken contract, such as being unable to deliver her packages of handmade chocolates to her customers, and having her customers go to other chocolate sellers.

Boilerplate, our nonideal "contract" in practice (stories based on real cases):

Arbitration Clause: *Garrit S., age eleven, a boy who cared deeply about animals, went to Africa with his mother on a fantasy safari vacation. Before it booked the trip, the tour company had Garrit's mother sign a form. The form waived (cancelled) the right to sue the company for injury to either the mother or the son. Instead, the form said, if there was any complaint against the company, the mother would be limited to arbitration. Such a waiver of legal rights to remedies in court is known as an arbitration clause. (Examples of arbitration clauses appear on pages 111, 116.) A terrible tragedy happened. Hyenas dragged Garrit away from the camp where the tourists were sleeping. The boy was mauled to death. Garrit's father, who did not sign the pre-tour paperwork, brought suit in court charging the tour company with negligence that caused the death of his son. The company asked the court to halt the suit and instead compel arbitration. This case went all the way to the state supreme court. Garrit's father was defeated. The state supreme court upheld the trial court's order to compel arbitration. It held that when the mother signed the paperwork containing the arbitration clause, she signed away her son's right to jury trial in court as well as her own.[1]*

<u>Another Arbitration Clause</u>: *Tonya C. was offered a job as manager of a fast-food restaurant at a salary of $7,000 per year. In order to get the job, Tonya was asked to sign some forms. One of the forms contained an arbitration clause that waived Tonya's right to bring a legal action in court against the franchise owners for any reason, including sexual harassment. Unfortunately, later Tonya did feel she had to bring a sexual harassment claim against her employer. She brought suit under the federal civil rights law that prohibits discrimination on the basis of race, sex, religion, or national origin. The employer filed with the court a motion to dismiss her suit on the ground that the arbitration clause contained in the paperwork Tonya had signed eliminated her right to sue in court. The federal district judge who made the initial decision on Tonya's claim ruled in her favor. He thought it obvious, despite the arbitration clause in the employer's form, that a civil rights action based on federal antidiscrimination law belongs in federal court before a jury.*

But on this point the trial judge was overruled by the federal court of appeals. The appellate court was not at all troubled by Tonya's exclusion from federal court and jury trial. The federal appellate court that reviewed Tonya's case, along with other federal appellate courts, holds that once an employee (or anyone) is held to have acceded to an arbitration clause, the right to jury trial "vanishes."[2]

Choice of Forum Clause: *Jeffrey K. filed a lawsuit against an Internet service provider on behalf of himself and the class of all other customers of the service provider who were similarly situated. Jeffrey alleged that the service provider had behaved illegally toward its customers by unjustifiably charging an extra fee of $5.00 per month for paying by check instead of by credit card. It would not be worthwhile for one customer to sue for a refund of the $5.00 (multiplied by the number of months he had been a subscriber), and yet the company, if indeed it was behaving in bad faith or unjustly enriching itself at its customers' expense, was illegally raking in millions of dollars because of the number of customers affected. In a different jurisdiction, two other customers filed a class action against the same Internet service provider, alleging that the service provider had behaved illegally by including in its hourly charges the time it took for customers to view pop-up ads.*

The service provider's online equivalent of paperwork was its five-page Terms of Service, which subscribers could access by clicking a link, and to which subscribers had to click "Agree" before proceeding. Jeffrey did not sign anything, but because he became a customer, it could be inferred that he clicked "Agree," though of course it was unknown whether he actually clicked the link to the document and read it. The Terms of Service contained a clause saying that lawsuits had to be brought in the state of Virginia. This term is known as a choice of forum clause. Choice of forum clauses are most often coupled with choice of law clauses, in which the parties choose whose law will govern. The state of Virginia does not allow class actions, and this was probably the main reason that the service provider chose Virginia as the only place in which it would allow itself to be sued. Both of these suits were dismissed and the claimants were told to go and sue in Virginia, even though the courts realized that that would be useless.[3]

Exculpatory Clause: *Michael J., a landscaper, rented a Bobcat truck loader from an equipment company. He paid $185.87 to rent the equipment, and in conjunction with the rental, he was given paperwork to sign. The paperwork included a term stating that the company "is not responsible for injuries or damages sustained in the use of these items whether the damages are due to neglect,* *mechanical failure or any other cause."*[4] *This term is known as an "exculpatory clause," because its purpose is to render the firm not culpable; that is, not legally liable for its harm-causing behavior. (An example of an exculpatory clause appears on page 114.) Michael had asked the advice of the employees of the equipment company before he rented the Bobcat. They told him it was the right equipment for what he wanted to do, which was to transport loose materials to the top of a slope, and they instructed him in how to operate it. Unfortunately, while Michael was using the Bobcat it flipped over. Michael suffered permanent injury to his spinal cord.*

Michael brought suit against the equipment rental company, seeking to hold it liable for causing his injury, because, he alleged, its employees were negligent in their recommendation and instructions. The trial court granted summary judgment for the company, which means that even if everything Michael said were true, he would not have any legal right to hold the company liable. The state supreme court affirmed. Michael had no legal right to hold the company liable even if the company was at fault in causing his injury. The company, the court said, was protected against liability for its own fault by the contract it had had the renter sign.[5]

What happened to Garrit's family and the other people in these World B stories was a deletion of legal rights that are otherwise guaranteed by the political order—by the constitution, or by legislation, or by other sources of law. Instead of the set of rights belonging to each of these people under the legal system, they had only the constricted set of legal rights allowed by the firms who delivered paperwork (or its electronic equivalent) to them. Businesses use forms such as those received by the people in these vignettes, and such as most of us receive almost every day, to change the legal infrastructure applicable to us. Businesses use such forms to create their own legal universe. Because we cannot change them, these forms are called "boilerplate." *

---

* According to Wikipedia: "The term dates back to the early 1900s and refers to the thick, tough steel sheets used to build steam boilers. From the 1890s onward, printing plates of text for widespread reproduction, such as advertisements or syndicated col-

All of the clauses in the stories I have recounted above will figure in this book, as will other common clauses occurring in boiler-plate. The main project of this book is to consider the following questions: To what extent should firms be permitted to create their own legal universes in this way? What justifications can be brought forward in favor of firms creating their own legal universes? What limits exist on such universe-creation, and what limits should exist? How can such limits best be implemented?

---

umns, were cast or stamped in steel (instead of the much softer and less durable lead alloys used otherwise) ready for the printing press and distributed to newspapers around the United States. They came to be known as 'boilerplates.' Until the 1950s, thousands of newspapers received and used this kind of boilerplate from the nation's largest supplier, the Western Newspaper Union. Some companies also sent out press releases as boilerplate so that they had to be printed as written."

PART I

. . . .

Boilerplate, Consumers' Rights, and the Rule of Law

. . . .

An Overview of Worlds A and B

O NCE UPON A TIME, it was thought that "contract" refers to a bargained-for exchange transaction between two parties who each consent to the exchange. This once-upon-a-time story is the ideal of contract. The story of bargained-for exchange represents contract as it is imagined to be in a world of voluntary agreement, the world I am calling World A (for Agreement). In this book I am referring to contracts, such as the one between Sally and John (in the invented story in the prologue), that actually look like the free exchanges imagined in liberal theory as contracts of World A.* This is still how many people understand contract (with good reason). And it still animates contract theories. Contract is supposed to involve consent by each party to give up something of his or her own to obtain something he or she values more. Sally values the bicycle more than she values her $120; John values $120 more than he values his bicycle. Contract, at least in this paradigm case, is typified by a process of negotiation that results in a bargain satisfactory to both parties. The paradigm case involving negotiation is not the only kind of contract that can be valid under the basic commitment to freedom of contract; but, as we shall see, the elements of the paradigm case involving a bargain and free choice or consent are indispensable.

---

* Liberal theory refers to the dominant strain of political theory stemming roughly from the time of the Industrial Revolution. Political liberalism is not "liberal" in the popular sense of opposed to "conservative." Political liberalism is the theory that underpins much of our traditional legal structure, including contract law; and I will often use "liberal" interchangeably with "traditional" in this sense.

Once upon a time, it was also thought that when a contract is broken, there will necessarily be a remedy available to the aggrieved person. If Sally hands over her $120 but John fails to deliver the bicycle, Sally can bring John to court in a place convenient for her, and ask that John be found in breach of contract and have the court order John to make it up to Sally for his breach. Depending on the circumstances, the court will simply order John to refund Sally's money, or perhaps even to hand over the bicycle. What is important to understand is that the ideal of contract has as an important component the idea that if a contract is breached, there must be the opportunity to seek a remedy. The aggrieved party must have her day in court, and so must the party who allegedly breached. Courts, as an arm of the state, enforce contracts so that all of us may have confidence in dealing with one another. In order for the system of contract to function, there must be a viable avenue for redress of grievances in cases where the bargain fails; otherwise the trust that the ideal of contract imagines would be weakened and perhaps collapse.

The Stories of the Prologue: Issues for the Basis of Contract

The Vanishing Right to Jury Trial

Tonya and Garrit's father both attempted to bring lawsuits to try their grievances before a jury. By using paperwork to shunt them to arbitration, the companies automatically cancelled their right to a trial before a jury of their peers. Jury trial vanishes in such cases, even if the claimant has not been informed that this will happen—in spite of the fact that most people don't know what arbitration is and have no idea that their right to jury trial is so fragile. In arbitration, the claimant must appear instead before one or more arbitrators, who are widely believed to be more favorable to businesses. No public record is made of the arbitrators' decision, and no class actions are permissible.

The holding in Garrit's father's case meant that henceforth in his state, at least, all parents can sign away the remedial rights of their children as well as their own. It also meant that almost all tour companies would include this clause in their pretrip paperwork in the future, as indeed they now do. Companies are also trying the same thing in other states. Although other states are not bound by one state's holding, judges in other states often take opinions of sister states into account.

The appellate court in Tonya's case recited governing law in its jurisdiction suggesting that Tonya could have overturned the effect of the paperwork on her right to try her civil rights claim in federal court before a jury of her peers if she could have proved that she was not able to obtain some other job that did not force her to sign this paperwork. (It seems judges in many jurisdictions actually think that a $7,000-per-year wage earner can look around for another job with less onerous clauses in its paperwork, and perhaps find such an employer if she does look.) Dismissals based on paperwork shunting those with grievances to arbitration are routinely upheld, though in rare cases (as I will describe later in this book) some lucky claimant may be able to overcome the loss of rights accomplished by the paperwork.[1]

It is reasonable to infer that many claimants simply do not try to challenge the paperwork. Most people do not know what an arbitration clause is. Moreover, given the state of the law, lawyers would be remiss if they did not inform a client who is subject to an arbitration clause that very likely he or she should not bother to bring a wrongful death action or a civil rights action in federal court, unless there is something very special about the case.

Once one business firm finds that courts will enforce dismissal of suits such as these, other businesses will use the same forms. Terms that are favorable to businesses will spread, because they serve the firms' economic interests. Any term that a court (in a rare case) finds questionable will disappear. All of which means that most people in Tonya's position would indeed be unlikely to find another employer that did not use the same type of waiver of legal grievance rights that she encountered, or one even more robust. Likewise, most parents wanting to avoid the unhappy position of Garrit's father in case an unimaginable loss were to befall them would be unlikely to find another tour company that did not impose an arbitration clause.

Making Redress Remote

A legislature provides for class actions when it intends for people in its jurisdiction to have the opportunity to seek a remedy, even if the harm to each person is too small to make it worthwhile for that individual to bring suit alone. Class action remedies also are intended to deter companies from reaping large profits by unjustly extracting small overages from large numbers of customers. In the case of Jeffrey K., it is reasonable to infer that the legislature's intent was thwarted by a choice of forum/choice of law clause that forced the plaintiff into another state.

Another means whereby a choice of forum clause can effectively deny a remedy to injured parties is by limiting claimants to bringing suit in a jurisdiction that is very far away.[2] Federal courts are very favorable to choice of forum clauses, based on a famous US Supreme Court case of 1991, *Carnival Cruise Lines v. Shute*,[3] which validated a choice of forum clause forcing injured claimants to bring suit in Florida. In that case, Mrs. Shute was injured on a cruise ship and tried to sue the company in her home state of Washington. The Shutes did not sign anything. The choice of forum clause that prevented Mrs. Shute from suing in Washington was in fine print on the last page of her ticket, which she received after booking the cruise, and which was nonrefundable. Nevertheless, the reasoning upholding the choice of forum clause was based on the assumption that the claimants had willingly accepted the clause. In their enthusiasm for choice of forum clauses, federal courts routinely cite *Carnival Cruise* as precedent for upholding choice of forum clauses, even in situations where consent by recipients is problematic.

Escape from Fault

Michael J., who was injured by the rented Bobcat, was subject to an exculpatory clause. This type of clause waives (cancels) the usual legal rights an injured party would have against a company that was at fault in causing the injury, thus exculpating the company from its own fault. An exculpatory clause goes even further than an arbitration clause, because instead of merely depriving the injured party of a remedy in court, it deprives the injured party of all remedies. Many tour companies, as well as many other proprietors of activities such as camping trips or physical fitness training, are using exculpatory clauses instead of, or in tandem with, arbitration clauses. At this point, parents wanting to escape what happened to Garrit's father if such a terrible loss were to befall them would be unlikely to find a tour company, or a sports camp, or a training facility, that did not have a clause exculpating itself from liability for any harm suffered by the child while participating in its program, no matter how that harm was caused.

In some cases a court can hold an exculpatory clause unenforceable (as I will describe later in this book).[4] In such a case, an injured party would have to litigate, perhaps all the way to a state supreme court or a federal appellate court, before knowing whether he would have the right to hold the company responsible for his injury if he could prove the company was at fault. A litigant could only succeed in achieving this result if he could afford the time and money to litigate or, more likely, if the situation were extreme enough that lawyers who work on a contingency fee basis were willing to take the case. We may safely assume that in cases where the injury is not serious enough (or the injured party is not rich enough), exculpatory clauses will prevail. In general, in situations without the kind of special circumstances that might ultimately persuade a court that the case is exceptional, many people injured through the fault of a business they deal with are precluded by the company's paperwork from holding the company legally accountable.

Alternative Legal Universes Created by Forms

Like the injured parties in the stories of the prologue, most of us are used to receiving paperwork (or its electronic equivalent) during transactions. We are given forms to sign when we rent an automobile or an apartment, and piles of forms to sign when we buy an automobile or a house. Most of us don't read them, and most of us wouldn't understand them if we did. We are given forms to sign when we get a job, when we join a gym, when we send our kids to camp. We click "I agree" to buy products or services on the Internet, after being shown lists of fine-print terms that we don't read. We receive forms even though we don't sign them or click "I agree," such as the fine-print terms of service interior to websites, or the fine print on everything from parking lot tickets to theater tickets to sports events tickets. Illustrations of some of these commonly used forms are shown on pages 117–119.

Arbitration clauses, choice of forum/choice of law clauses, and exculpatory clauses, such as those that figured in the stories in the prologue, are common components of the alternative legal universes created by firms. Most readers, I expect, are subject to one or more of them. But there are many other ways in which fine print has the effect of deleting recipients' legal rights. One common provision limits remedies for losses caused by a defective product or service to the replacement, repair, or reimbursement for the cost of the product itself, thus eliminating damages for injurious consequences of the product's failure. Another deletes ("disclaims") warranty coverage. Another says the firm will continue billing you forever for whatever you have purchased unless you notify it that you wish to terminate. Yet another waives recipients' user rights in information not protected by the law of intellectual property and otherwise free for public use; and still another waives information privacy rights. (These practices are widespread in the US. Countries other than the US do not make as ubiquitous use of such clauses against consumers. Later in this book I will consider some solutions to boilerplate issues that prevail outside the US.)

In short, if you are like most US consumers, you enter into "contracts" daily without knowing it, or at least without being able to do anything about it. The purported contracts come in the form of paperwork that you receive and are asked to sign, or that contain terms supposedly binding without your signature, and sometimes even without their your knowing this is happening. This paperwork is boilerplate, or, less colloquially, standardized form contracts. These are the contracts—the *purported* contracts—that belong to World B.

Standardized form contracts, when they are imposed upon consumers, have long been called "contracts of adhesion," or "take-it-or-leave-it contracts," because the recipient has no choice with regard to the terms.[5] "It's my way or the highway," says the firm to the recipient. Such paperwork is often called boilerplate, because, like the rigid metal used to construct steam boilers in the past, it cannot be altered. I have been calling boilerplate "paperwork" because "paperwork" is a neutral term, but you will have noticed that courts most often treat boilerplate as if it were a contract. The law considers boilerplate to be a method of *contract* formation. World B is the expanding universe of purported contracts that don't look or act like those of World A.[6] World B is the world of boilerplate.

Some of you may belong to firms that impose boilerplate on their customers. But even if you are the CEO, you are subject to boilerplate from other firms, just like everyone else. I myself am subject to many of these clauses. Even though I know more about their legal significance than most people, I can't do anything about them, so, just like almost everyone else, I don't read them.[7] I must, like everyone else, accept them or forego the transaction. I can't employ a financial manager for my retirement account without accepting an arbitration clause. I can't use iTunes without clicking "I agree" to its terms of service. I can't proceed with an exercise class until I've signed a form that exculpates the provider for any injury to me no matter how caused. Once I tried to tell a person presenting paperwork to me that the exculpatory clause would be unenforceable if her studio harmed me intentionally or through gross negligence rather than mere negligence. I took out a pen and offered to emend the clause, but the person presenting the form would not hear of legal niceties. It was take it or leave it.*

---

*Actually she had no idea what the form was for. She told me that her insurance company requires her to use the form and that she is required not to allow clients to change it in any way. As I will mention later in this book (in chapter 7), the effect of such an exculpatory clause is to incentivize recipients to buy their own insurance rather than relying on the firm's insurance, which according to economic theory may (or may not) be deemed efficient.

Varieties of World B (Purported) Contracts

Here is an overview of the varieties of World B contracts we are seeing in practice. (I will stop calling them "purported" contracts, but please understand that labelling something a "contract" does not necessarily make it one.)

1. <u>Standardized Adhesion Contracts</u> of the traditional variety: An example is the parking lot ticket. (See examples on page 117.) It's a contract of adhesion because either you "adhere" to it by taking hold of it and then driving your car into the lot, or else you don't park there. The ticket often says, "This contract limits our liability. Read it." Hardly anyone does so. The on-line analogue is clicking on-screen buttons to signify receipt of contractual terms. By clicking, it says, you are saying that you've read the terms and "agree" to them. It is doubtful that many people are truthful in saying this, though, because very few people read them.*

2. <u>Offsite Terms</u>: Refers to terms that are a part of standardized adhesion contracts but that are not stated in the document you can see. An example is the airline ticket. It says you are bound by the set of terms that make up the airline's tariff and that you can find them somewhere else—in the airline's office, perhaps, or online. Who knows what background legal rights have been given up in favor of the airline?

3. <u>"Shrink-wrap Licenses"</u>: So called because they originated with the shrink-wrapped commercial software products that you buy in a box. The idea is that if you break the wrapper you are bound to the terms that are printed below it. By tearing cellophane you have "agreed" to a bunch of boilerplate.

---

*To test this assumption, a software company named PC Pitstop inserted a reference to "financial compensation" midway through its nine-hundred-word boilerplate, along with an invitation to contact the company for more information. After four months and over three thousand sales, the company received its first inquiry. The company rewarded the lone customer's reading of its boilerplate with a check for $1000. Jeff Gelles, "Don't Ignore Those Click-and-Agree Contracts," *Philadelphia Inquirer*, Sept. 15, 2005, at C01.

A later variant, sometimes called "shrink-wrap of the second kind," seeks to bind you to terms that you can't see *until* you run the software and look at the first screen. An online analogue to the standard adhesion contract, sometimes called "click-wrap," is also considered shrink-wrap of the second kind; it refers to terms that you adhere to by clicking a box onscreen that says "I agree." Here the recipient affirms that she has read the terms—but, again, most likely she has not.

4. "Rolling Contracts" (also called "money now, terms later"): Perhaps the earliest example of this variant is the insurance contract. The agent sells you a policy, but when the pages of fine print arrive, they contain (if you read and can understand them) a lot of exclusions and wrinkles that you didn't know about. You are still bound to the purported contract, even though you signed it *before* the terms were delivered to you.

Another example is ordering a product by telephone or online. You select the product and give the seller your credit card information, the company charges your card, receives the funds, and ships the product. When the product arrives, you open the box and a piece of paper with a lot of fine print falls out. It informs you that you have relinquished background legal entitlements, such as the right to sue the seller (by limiting you to arbitration), the right to copy material that is not under copyright, and so on.

A parallel example in the software world is the set of terms often called EULA ("End User License Agreement"); you see this (purported) contract when you fire up the product, which is *after* you've paid for it, not before. That is, these terms are often received under the "shrink-wrap of the second kind" procedure.

5. Then there is the Unwitting Contract: Most websites have a small link called something like "terms of service" (TOS). If one were to click on it, which most users don't (in fact, most probably don't even notice the link), one would see pages of boilerplate open out, telling the user that she is bound to these terms, that she has "agreed" to them simply by the act of looking at the site, and, moreover, that the owner may

change the terms from time to time and that the user will then be bound by the new terms as well. This strategy has been dubbed "browsewrap." With browsewrap you are clueless unless you find and click on the link that opens it.

I am sure that most readers will recognize many of the contract varieties listed in the foregoing typology. (Some examples appear on pages 111–119.) It should be clear now that many interactions that are called "contracts" these days are very far from the traditional notion of a contract, the idea of bargained exchange by free choice, that still holds sway in our imaginations. Contract reality belies contract theory in many situations where consumers receive paperwork that purports to alter their legal rights. In these situations, contract theory becomes contract mythology.

Why Don't We Read Boilerplate?

Given that firms regularly use boilerplate to transport us into an alternative legal universe, why don't we read these things? Here are seven answers: (1) We wouldn't understand the terms if we did read them, so it isn't worth our time. (2) We need the product or service and have no access to a supplier that does not impose onerous clauses, so reading the terms wouldn't make any difference. (3) We are not even aware that we are becoming subject to these terms, so we don't know that there is anything to read. (4) We trust the company not to have included anything harmful. (5) We suppose that anything harmful would be unenforceable. (6) We think that the company has power over us, so that we are simply stuck with what it imposes on us. (7) Yet another reason, and an important one: we don't believe that we will ever need to exercise our background legal rights. We don't expect misfortune to befall us. As psychological research has shown, we are not able to make accurate assessments of risks. All of these issues will be explored in the course of this book.

Boilerplate and Contract Formation

Because the law considers boilerplate to be a valid method of contract formation, the law usually holds that a contract has been formed between the firm and the boilerplate recipient, and that the terms of the contract are the fine print in the boilerplate. Garrit's mother, Tonya, Michael, and the others were held to have relinquished their legal rights by contract with the firms whose terms they tried to contest. (The question of what these people may have received as bargained-for exchange for giving up their legal rights will be difficult to answer, as we shall see.)

Even when there is no signature, as when we simply click "I agree," courts are likely to find that a contract has in fact been formed. Firms use other procedures online that are even further removed from the kind of consent we normally suppose is required for contract. Consider the declaration, "By using our e-mail server, you have agreed to all of the rules we have placed in a separate document that you can access by clicking here." Courts may be somewhat less likely to find that these procedures result in an enforceable contract, but firms today are hopeful that courts will rule in their favor when and if the procedures are challenged, hopeful enough that they use such procedures very widely. Of course, even if a firm is less than confident that a court would enforce its clauses if they were challenged, it might reason that the attempt was worth trying: "It can't hurt to stick this in. It might prevent someone from suing us, if indeed someone were to read it. And nothing bad is going to happen to us if we use an unenforceable term. At worst, some court will declare it unenforceable, but it will still probably work against other recipients. Might as well give it a try."

The ultimate use of "By doing X you have agreed . . ." was received by an academic author friend of mine a few years ago after he had an article accepted for publication in a prestigious journal and transferred his copyright to the publisher. The publisher sent him a PDF copy of the article with an accompanying list of terms and conditions. The terms included permission to use copies only for his own teaching and research, disallowed his reselling the copies, and disallowed updating the PDF. At the bottom of this list appeared, in boldface type: "Upon reading of this page, you agree to be bound by these terms and conditions."

"By reading the above you have agreed to it" doesn't really fulfill what most people think of as the main prerequisite of an agreement. That is, for something to count as agreement, whatever you are agreeing to has to be presented to you as a matter for your decision before, not *after*, the agreement takes place. Declaring that you've agreed to something before you could have known that that is what you were doing has an Alice-in-Wonderland quality to it. The fact that the sender thought it was creating a contractual obligation for the recipient speaks volumes about the state of contract in our legal system. "Agreement" has become a talismanic word merely indicating that the firm deploying the boilerplate wants the recipient to be bound.

Our conventional understanding of contract is at odds with this reality. Most people still think that a contract is a voluntary transaction, a consensual exchange. Indeed, contract law is itself based on the idea of free exchanges between willing parties. "Freedom of contract" is a revered ideal underlying World A, the world of voluntary exchanges, the world of Agreement. World B is another world, the world of Boilerplate. In practice some contracts reflecting voluntary exchanges between willing parties may nevertheless consist partly or wholly of a collection of form clauses, yet belong to world A. Nevertheless the archetypes of World A and World B will be useful for analysis, if only because of the large realm of purported contracts that do consist entirely of nonnegotiated boilerplate.

World B, the world of boilerplate, doesn't fit the theory, the rationale, of contract law. Many people are surprised when they find out that boilerplate is treated as a contract. Even incoming law students, who are college graduates and curious about law, are astonished when they find out that everything they have signed, clicked "I agree" to, or otherwise been deemed to accede to in the week before our class starts is supposedly a contract between them and the firm deploying the form.

One task of this book is to think again about whether boilerplate should be considered contractual. Indeed, I want to urge that it should not, at least not in all of its manifestations. Meanwhile, however, as long as boilerplate *is* considered contractual, as it is in our current legal system, it is regulated under contract law. Why "regulated"? Because not everything that is *called* a contract actually *is* a contract, and the law needs to be able to distinguish between those that are valid (and therefore enforceable) and those that are not. A purported contract obtained by coercion or fraud is not an enforceable contract, for example. Because boilerplate is regulated by—that is, evaluated under—contract law, those who defend boilerplate must argue that boilerplate somehow meets the requirements of contract law. Thus, they must argue that recipients somehow agree to or consent to its terms.[8]

Normative and Demographic Degradation
Normative Degradation

Boilerplate is, to say the least, problematic when it comes to the issue of agreement or consent. In this book I am going to call this problem of consent a "normative degradation" for our legal system. "Normative degradation" refers to the fact that our system is committed to the moral premise that justifies our legal structure of contract enforcement, that premise being that people who enter contracts are *voluntarily* giving up something in exchange for something they value more.[9] Moreover, a legal system that would allow people to take away the rights of others without their consent, even if compensation is paid, is contrary to another basic premise of our own system: "private eminent domain" is normally not allowed.

If boilerplate were not regulated by contract law, that would not mean either that boilerplate should be unregulated or that boilerplate should be entirely eliminated. If boilerplate were not regulated at all but could be used freely by firms to divest people of legal rights, we would not be living under the rule of law. Indeed, as things stand, we risk losing our claim to being a society observant of the rule of law when our courts permit too free a rein to boilerplate. Yet, if all attempts to use boilerplate were to be declared unenforceable, that would cause a considerable disruption of current commercial practice.

Businesses that use forms to construct their own legal universe, and others who argue in defense of this practice, usually say something like this: "We need to constrict recipients' legal rights in order to contain costs. When we reduce costs, recipients benefit with lower prices. Furthermore, recipients, if given a choice, would choose lower prices over legal rights. So we are not really interfering with people's freedom of choice."

This argument should not be ignored. But it should be reconsidered, not only in light of the varying market circumstances that can make its premises true or untrue, but also in light of the nature of the various legal rights that firms are negating by using boilerplate, together with the questionable normative premise that hypothetical choice is as good as real choice. These questions are considered in chapters 2 and 3, and indeed throughout this book.

Democratic Degradation

There is a second problem with some form contracts, one that, although it has so far been less noticed than the problem of normative degradation caused by the question of agreement or consent, is in my view equally serious. This is the problem I will call "democratic degradation." Mass-market systems of form contracts that restructure the rights of users of products and services operate to undermine or cancel the rights of users granted by legislatures. In other words, these systems of contracts can delete rights that are granted through democratic processes, substituting for them the system that the firm wishes to impose.

In this book I will refer to this deletion of recipients' rights as the problem of boilerplate rights deletion schemes. The terms of such schemes are imposed by firms. Just as the law requires us to obey its dictates if we wish to live where it holds sway, these terms require us to be bound by them if we wish to engage in a transaction with the firm. Mass-market boilerplate rights deletions, when the courts uphold them, replace (supersede) the law of the state with the "law" of the firm. The boilerplate received by Tonya, Garrit's family, Michael, and the others, operated to supersede their legal rights. A firm supersedes the right to jury trial, a basic right underwritten by the polity, when it deploys a different scheme in which jury trial "vanishes" and those with grievances against it must use arbitration. By deploying an arbitration clause, a firm also deletes recipients' right to bring a class action suit. By deploying an exculpatory clause, it supersedes their right to bring suit for harm caused by another, a right underwritten by the polity for situations that satisfy legal parameters such as causation of the harm by fault of the defendant. Instead of the set of rights given to each of the recipients by the legal system, recipients have only the constricted set of legal rights as rearranged by the firms who deliver boilerplate to them. Recipients must enter a legal universe of the firm's devising in order to engage in transactions with the firm.

Reconsidering Theory and Practice

In order to think about how to respond to the issues I have posed in this introductory chapter, I will begin (in chapter 2) with the normative degradation caused by the apparent lack of consent to boilerplate, or at least by the problematic nature of recipients' consent to boilerplate. Then (in chapter 3) I will describe the democratic degradation that may be caused by the apparent replacement of the law of the state with the "law" of the firm when boilerplate is deployed in mass markets.

In Part II, I will consider matters of a more theoretical nature. As one might expect, there is a legal and philosophical literature focusing on contracts. Many theorists do not take heed of the existence of World B. In their writings we might imagine boilerplate as a philosophical elephant in the room. But some legal scholars do attempt to use traditional theory to justify firms' imposition of boilerplate on consumers. I will review the main theories of contractual ordering, and I will explore to what extent boilerplate's alternative legal universes can be justified under those theories. I will argue that attempts to bring boilerplate rights deletion schemes under the aegis of traditional contract theories by and large fail. In reviewing these attempts to justify boilerplate, I will consider different boilerplate procedures—such as clicking "I agree" versus merely visiting a website that posts "Terms of Service"—and consider to what extent the procedures make a difference in justification and enforceability.

In Part III, this book will come to grips with the issues posed in practice by the widespread deployment of boilerplate rights deletion schemes. What is being done about mass-market systems of boilerplate deletion of rights? I will consider how the legal system now treats boilerplate, reviewing judicial oversight of boilerplate through the legal doctrines of unconscionability and voidness as against public policy, among others. (A court may invalidate a contract as unconscionable if it finds that one party lacked meaningful choice and the terms unreasonably favor the other party. A court may find a contract void if it transgresses a specific and important public policy.) I will consider as well whether the current system of judicial oversight could be improved, and I will offer an analytical framework that might be helpful to courts faced with questions of the validity of rights deletion by means of boilerplate.

In Part IV, I will leave contract and its oversight doctrines behind. I will consider other alternatives that might alleviate some of the problems posed by mass-market boilerplate. When and how might the market alleviate some of the problems raised by boilerplate rights deletion schemes? Is regulation by legislatures or administrative agencies on balance necessary, and if so, can such regulation transcend the categories of contract and individual bargaining? Can common-law courts themselves make improvements in the current situation? I will look at solutions such as rating organizations and filtering systems; consider the advantages that might be achieved by evaluating some types of boilerplate under tort law rather than contract law; and review varieties of regulatory solutions from piecemeal to comprehensive.

Agreement or consent of the parties is the bedrock principle of contract, so that is where we will begin.

Normative Degradation

DELETING RIGHTS WITHOUT CONSENT IN THE
NAME OF CONTRACT

O
UR LEGAL SYSTEM ADHERES to an ideal of private ordering and its importance to individual freedom. Within this system, freedom of contract is a core value, and "involuntary" or "unfree" contract is a contradiction in terms. Involuntary divestment of one's entitlement (to money, to property, or to a legal right) is simply *not what "contract" means*. The notion that a coerced or deceptive or completely covert divestment of an entitlement might qualify as a "contract" is paradoxical. Thus, if the purported contracts of World B, which are widely enforced in the US, cannot be justified by the traditional justification of contract enforcement—freedom of choice, or consent—then our legal system is suffering from a widespread normative degradation.

Consent is not the only requirement for an enforceable contractual obligation, but it is a major one.[1] In this chapter I will begin by considering consent as it functions in contractual obligation. Then we can move on to look at how those who wish to defend World B procedures as contractual attempt to shoehorn them into the paradigm of contractual consent.[2]

We should begin with the understanding that consent, even when it is contested, is primarily viewed as consisting positively of the specific words or actions of a person (in conjunction with a particular context), but not negatively; that is, not as a lack of words (silence) and a lack of action. Situations in which there is sheer ignorance that something is happening are instead treated under fields of law other than contract, primarily tort or criminal law. One way to couch a survey of this field as it bears on the legal infrastructure of contracts is to consider what consent is *not*.

Varieties of Nonconsent

A system based on consent, as is our institution of contract, must also be based on nonconsent. Why? Because the system must have the basic commitments and procedures that will enable a decision-maker to conclude that observed physical and verbal behavior (or lack of such behavior) amounts to nonconsent rather than consent. The legal system must be able to distinguish those allegedly agreed-upon transfers of entitlements that are actually agreed upon from those allegedly agreed-upon transfers of entitlements that are not actually agreed upon. The legal system must therefore contain rules and principles for courts to use in deciding to which category a purported contract belongs. Unless a purported contract would result in a trade that is disallowed (such as murder for hire, for example), in deciding whether a purported contract is enforceable a court will be called upon to make a decision regarding consent versus nonconsent.

What are the varieties of nonconsent to which consent is contrasted? First among them is coercion and its allied conceptions of force and duress. In some legal doctrines pertaining to contract, the concept of coercion (or force, or duress) expands to a broadened and controversial scope, so as to encompass economic duress, oppression, undue influence, and perhaps unconscionability. (Unconscionability is a legal doctrine under which judges may exercise their conscience to invalidate purported contracts that they deem too unfair to enforce.[3])

Second among the varieties of nonconsent is fraud, with its allied conceptions of misrepresentation and deception. In some legal doctrines pertaining to contract, the concept of fraud (or deception, or misrepresentation) also expands into more contested areas, such as failure to disclose, mistake, and perhaps bad faith.[4]

The reason that these doctrines are very important in contract law is that they delimit the interactions that can count as valid contracts. The notions of coercion and fraud are relevant in other areas of law, particularly in tort and criminal law, because, of course, contracts is not the only body of law premised on freedom of choice and action. Coercion and fraud are also important in classical liberal theories of the state, for reasons that parallel their appearance in contract law.[5] Indeed some of these theories are called social contract.

Sheer Ignorance

In addition to coercion and fraud, a third variety of nonconsent is sheer ignorance; that is, the situation where a person's entitlement is being divested, but the person does not know that it is happening, or indeed, that anything is happening. (This is not the same as deceit; a person who is being deceived knows that something is happening, but is mistaken about what it is.) Sheer ignorance is illustrated by the case of John Moore, who brought a lawsuit against the University of California because doctors employed by one of its hospitals used a cell line derived from Moore's body without his knowledge, and made money from it.[6]

Perhaps this variety of nonconsent is best contrasted with its opposite, the notion of "informed consent." Before consent to something relating to a person's entitlements can be acceptable, the person must at least be informed that something is happening. The notion of "informed consent" means more than that, however; informed consent is judged on the basis of how much and what specific information a person (who *does* know that something is happening) must have in order to be held to have consented to what is happening. This notion of informed consent is relevant, for example, to the "consent" we give when we sign information forms that are given to us while attendants are placing an IV in our arm and we are about to be wheeled into the operating room.

Sheer ignorance is similar in one sense to lack of informed consent. Both lack of informed consent and sheer ignorance result when the information needed in order to understand significant parameters of a situation is not available to a person, and both refer to perception by others with regard to whether the person had the needed information. Informed consent differs from sheer ignorance in that it is usually invoked to describe situations in which information is presented to a person. The notion of informed consent is also used in the analysis of the situation and in making a judgment with regard to whether the information presented was enough.[7]

By contrast, sheer ignorance describes a situation where we either don't know that something is happening or do know that something is happening but do not know the significance of what is happening. Suppose, for example, that we know we are being wheeled along on a gurney but have no idea we are headed for the operating room; or that we know we are headed for something called the "operating room" but have no idea what happens in operating rooms; or, indeed, that we really do not know that anything is happening because we are unconscious. Sheer ignorance describes such situations. It often characterizes recipients' lack of awareness of (purported) contracts known as "browsewrap," and it also may characterize recipients' lack of awareness in many instances in which boilerplate is received after the fact of exchange, as in the case of "rolling contracts."

A subset of the purported contracts represented by boilerplate belongs to this category of nonconsent, i.e., sheer ignorance, because there are many situations in which recipients of boilerplate do not even know that it exists and therefore certainly do not know that they are being divested of important legal rights, such as the right to sue for damages for harm inflicted by a product or service. For example, many (perhaps most) people don't know that the fine print that appears in light type on a FedEx or UPS or Post Office receipt is a contract, as is the fine print in light type on the back of Apple Computer's repair invoices. Likewise, many (perhaps most) people don't know that there are boilerplate terms internal to websites that can only be seen by noticing a link and clicking on it.

I am introducing the category of sheer ignorance to refer to situations where even less information is supplied than in cases lacking informed consent. Most people who find themselves in a hospital know they are in a hospital, and they know about the kinds of things that generally go on in hospitals. But many people who find themselves recipients of boilerplate do not even know that they are receiving boilerplate purporting to impose obligations or to remove background rights.[8]

Sheer ignorance is a category of nonconsent that, to my knowledge, has not been treated by philosophers or other theorists under the rubric of consent. Most likely this is because it is obvious that sheer ignorance is not even arguably consent. Nor has sheer ignorance become one of the doctrines in contract law that is penumbral to the categories of coercion and fraud. There is a contract rule holding that silence is not consent (except in very particular circumstances), but this might be the only doctrine that comes at all close to the sheer ignorance category.[9] That rule covers situations in which a person knows that something is happening (for example where a product arrives that she did not order but that the sender now expects her to pay for), but it could also be interpreted to apply to situations where a person does not know that something is happening.

In cases where a recipient's situation with regard to boilerplate rights deletion constitutes sheer ignorance of the sort I am describing here, it is possible that the situation should not be dealt with by contract law, but rather by tort law.[10] Tort law is brought into play when someone is injured, out of the blue, by the unexpected actions of another,[11] which may come close to what a recipient of boilerplate experiences when she wants to sue someone and finds out what the boilerplate has done to her.

Problematic Consent

Consent is a contested and problematic area in many fields of law. The difficulty stems in part from the fact that consent depends on processes internal to a person, but it must be observed by others who cannot fully know those processes. Observers outside the thought and feeling processes of a person can only with difficulty interpret the behavior (both physical and verbal) of that person in context, so as to decide whether he did or did not consent to, for example, waive a right. Moreover, the expression of consent also can involve conventional behavioral signals embedded in culture, such as nodding the head, and these cues are not infrequently contested. An observer may say that he is entitled to interpret such behavior as consent, while the allegedly consenting party asserts that she did not intend consent. For these reasons, there have been many intense but inconclusive controversies regarding interpretations of consent. Consider, for example, the notion that "No" could sometimes mean "Yes" in the context of consent to sexual relations or that a failure to protest might amount to consent. (In regard to this particular example, I believe—or at least hope—that the contemporary consensus is that "No" does mean "No," and silence is not consent.)

I have said that consent is absent in many instances when the deployment of boilerplate results in situations of sheer ignorance for recipients. But sometimes, boilerplate instead gives rise to a situation of problematic consent, as, for example, when recipients click "I agree" to terms presented online, most often without reading the terms. In this situation consent becomes contested. In chapter 5 I will consider in more depth how this behavior might be interpreted. But meanwhile, we should note that in situations where firms impose boilerplate on consumers, one party (the firm) has an immensely more thorough understanding than the other (the consumer) of what the boilerplate says and is supposed to accomplish. This imbalance is called "information asymmetry."

Information Asymmetry

Information asymmetry is a fancy way of saying that recipients of boilerplate have a lot less information about what the clauses in boilerplate mean and what their effects are than do the firms that deploy them. The short way of saying this is that even if recipients did try to read the clauses, most often they wouldn't understand them. For example, most people without legal training do not know what an arbitration clause is, and even if they take the time to read the clause and parse the words, the words themselves don't convey the effect of the clause, which is not only to eliminate trial in court, but also thereby to eliminate class actions. Similarly, most recipients of a parking lot ticket do not understand that the entity holding the car might have the responsibility to care for it, a responsibility known as "bailment." Therefore, when the ticket says that "no bailment is created," what the parking lot firm is really saying is that it disclaims responsibility for caring for your vehicle.

Most people probably would understand the literal meaning of some of the exculpatory clauses that now appear with regularity (where a firm declares itself not liable for any and all harms, no matter how caused), but few would understand the extent to which such a statement over-reaches, since they will most likely be unaware that firms cannot legally exculpate themselves for intentional harm or for criminal or grossly negligent acts. Also, most people would understand a clause that says legal disputes must be resolved in Virginia under the laws of Virginia (a choice of forum/choice of law clause), but few would know that a big reason the clause exists is because Virginia does not provide for consumer class actions. Many purported contracts contain language such as "waiver of so-called moral rights" or "waiver of consequential damages," or indeed terms such as "integration" or "merger," which have legal meanings that are opaque to nonlawyers.

If someone who receives boilerplate does read the clauses, but doesn't understand their meaning or effect and nonetheless clicks "I agree," does that amount to consent? It seems not to be "informed consent" as that concept (contested as it is) is understood. For informed consent a recipient is supposed to understand what she is getting into, at least at a rudimentary level. (One cannot be understood to be consenting to surgery just by saying, "I realize you're planning to operate on something, so go ahead and operate on anything with any side effects or aftermath.") Because information asymmetry is so prevalent in the context of deploying and receiving boilerplate, it would be problematic to assimilate the kind of nonunderstanding behavior that occurs in a context of clicking "I agree" to the ordinary conception of consent. Perhaps in some cases it would be appropriate to view this as consent—a kind of "as if" consent—but it is a consent that is at best problematic, not clear-cut. Even though the recipient does not understand what she is allegedly consenting to, the firm does.

Moreover, by far the large majority of recipients do not read the forms they receive. It may be quite rational not to try to read clauses that one knows he will not understand, as long as he believes that the firm will not do anything really bad, and as long as he believes that the legal universe governing his transaction doesn't matter. But why do people trust a firm to be fair? Why do they think it doesn't matter what the clauses say about their legal rights? (Even if they read them, and even if they understand them?) The main answers to those questions require us to consider the issue of "heuristic bias."

Heuristic Bias

Psychological research has determined that human beings reason and choose for themselves in ways that are not fully rational (at least as economists would define rationality).[12] Sometimes this is called "bounded rationality." Important features of bounded rationality include the following: We are not good at assessing risk; we tend to stay with the status quo; and we make choices according to particular surrounding circumstances that are salient to us, ignoring others that may be more pertinent.

We are not good at assessing risk.* For example, we tend to be afraid of airplane crashes, which are very infrequent, but we tend not to fear car crashes, which are very frequent. We wouldn't get into a plane if we thought it was improperly maintained, but we do drive on poor tires.

Moreover, even when we know we are engaging in risky behavior, we tend to think that the risk will materialize for another person, not for ourselves. We know that 50 percent of marriages end in divorce, but we are sure that our own will not. People know the horrendous death toll from smoking, but they imagine that lung

---

*We are not good at assessing probability generally. Many people think they might actually win the lottery.

cancer, emphysema, stroke, and other smoking-related illnesses will strike others but not themselves.[13]

Assuming that a recipient reads a boilerplate clause stripping her of the right to sue, and assuming that she understands that this is what the clause does, she would nonetheless be unlikely to take it seriously, because she is unlikely to think the risk applicable to her. Most of us don't take seriously the risk that we will ever need to sue anyone. All of which is to say that we don't take seriously the risk that any grievous harm will befall us through the fault of a firm we are dealing with.

We are also prone to a status quo bias. We tend to keep what we have. A bias called the "endowment effect" makes us value a thing more when we already have it than when we have only the opportunity to acquire it. And we tend to stick with what we've done before. (When I was a teacher of property law I always wondered why US property law has retained so much of the estate system we inherited from the common law of England, especially since England abolished it in the mid-twentieth century. One answer is that we stick with what we have.) Then there is brand loyalty. Once we are accustomed to dealing with a particular firm, we tend to stay with that firm. Marketers know that it is hard to get consumers to switch; so much so that whole theories of marketing are devoted to establishing or disrupting brand loyalty.

Given our tendency to stick with what we've done before, it is hardly surprising that after we've received boilerplate many times without having any negative repercussions, we will persist in our acceptance of it. Once we are used to clicking "I agree," we'll keep clicking "I agree." It would take some extraordinary event, some real change in the context, to make us stop doing what we're used to doing when it seems to work.[14]

Another aspect of heuristic bias or bounded rationality that may be relevant to World B is the psychological phenomenon known as "framing." People's choices are often related to some known quantity called an "anchor point." If the anchor point changes, so does the preference. When offered a pen costing, say, $1.00, or a pen costing $2.00, experimental subjects chose the cheaper one, but when there were three to choose from, priced at $1.00, $1.50, and $2.00, they tended to choose the middle one. Restaurants have started placing possible tip amounts at the bottom of their bills: 15 percent, 20 percent, and 25 percent. This pushes customers to tip 20 percent when most would otherwise have tipped the 15 percent that used to be customary. In other words, restaurants are trying to overcome the status-quo bias (tip 15 percent) by framing around 20 percent. (I can report that this scheme has succeeded with me—even though I understand the strategy!)

Another example: If a firm's boilerplate disclaims warranty coverage, but warranties can be purchased for three months, six months, or twelve months, recipients are likely to take the six-month option. The default warranty would often not have been time-limited. (A "default" rule is a background rule of the legal system that parties can contract out of. This terminology entered legal doctrine, probably sometime in the 1980s, by way of computer parlance in which default settings are the ones your machine comes with, but which you can change.) Depending on market circumstances, an option of this type may induce recipients to pay extra for less than they would have gotten with the default rule; and the fact that the option is offered may make the warranty disclaimer (the status quo) more palatable, assuming anyone reads it.

The choice of whether or not to purchase a product that comes with boilerplate perhaps will not normally be anchored to what is in the boilerplate, but rather framed by what other products are on offer. Nevertheless, it is possible that a particular firm might become notorious for extremely onerous boilerplate, in which case merely somewhat onerous boilerplate would seem like an appropriate alternative (at least to that rare recipient who understood what was in the boilerplate). In fact, some software firms are known for their extremely onerous boilerplate,[15] and their boilerplate may be making other firms' boilerplate look better by comparison. Because of the phenomenon of framing, a firm's product will look good if the comparison set looks worse.

The pervasive effects of heuristic bias, which are apparently very difficult to escape even when people understand them (and more so when they don't), tend to render consent problematic. Consent is problematic, for example, in cases in which a recipient characteristically underestimates a risk that people consistently underestimate and that the firm knows that people will consistently underestimate. Some theories of consent would consider that this situation vitiates consent, and some would not, but that is to note again that consent is a contested concept. The idea of informed consent, at least, does suppose that people can generally understand the level of risk they are facing, and heuristic biases tend to undercut that possibility.

Strategies of Assimilating World B to Consent: The Devolution of Voluntary Agreement

Various commentators and scholars have accepted the challenge presented by a desire to bringing World B—the boilerplate world—within the parameters of valid contract by extending the meaning of consent to cover adhesion contracts. Many of the contracts in World B use the word "agreement," because that is the traditional word used for a contract; but in a World B context the word is only being used as a label, or a wish: "Dear Judge, and Dear Consumer: We wish that you would treat this as a contract." But one-sided wishes do not agreement make. Although the acronym EULA stands for "End User License Agreement," the typical software EULA is nothing like what speakers would normally mean when they use the word "agreement." If we need to use Windows, we become subject to Microsoft's EULA with no dickering or negotiating, and that is that.

Procedures construed as acceptance have also been transmogrified. It has always been possible in traditional contract law to signify voluntary acceptance by a specified procedure, such as, perhaps, signifying agreement to purchase by retaining or modifying a product sent on approval. But what are we to make of: "By looking at this website, you have agreed [to a bunch of internal boilerplate you don't know is there, as well as whatever changes the website owner might make from time to time]."[16] Or what about, "By walking past my sign, you have relinquished all your rights to control my use of photos of you, including in advertisements for anything, anywhere and forever."[17] And recall my academic friend who received a list of Do's and Don'ts, followed by "Upon reading the above, you have agreed to it." These items push the traditional notion of contract-formation by specified agreement procedure to an absurd length. One cannot (except in Humpty-Dumpty's world) make something into an agreement just by using the term "agreement," at least not in the ordinary meaning of the word.

The gerrymandering of the word "agreement," along with various other strategies for fitting World B into the World A paradigm of voluntary transfer by agreement can be viewed as a process of devolution or decay of the concept of voluntariness. In this process, consent is degraded to assent, then to fictional or constructive or hypothetical assent, and then further to mere notice (i.e., something that tells recipients that terms are there), until finally we are left with only a fictional or constructive notice of terms. The ultimate result of this process is the contention by some scholarly apologists for boilerplate that if a recipient of boilerplate could reasonably have found out that terms existed, that is enough to constitute consent. And in some sense they are right, not by any measure of justice or fairness or philosophical validity, but simply because some US courts will accept this rationale.

As I will explain in more detail in chapter 5, apologists for the sort of purported contracts that are very problematic on the issue of consent have resorted to arguments such as the notion that "blanket assent" to unknown terms constitutes assent, provided the terms are what a consumer might have expected; or even to the argument that the very receipt of boilerplate (though perhaps only when the recipient clicks "I agree"?) amounts to consent to anything and everything in the fine print, as long as the terms could be "reasonably expected," or, perhaps, "not radically unexpected." This notion that expectation somehow amounts to consent to particular terms is also very problematic. Given that in our experience boilerplate consistently shrinks legal rights to the vanishing point, a loss of rights via boilerplate might well be empirically expected. Because an expectation is widespread, however, doesn't necessarily make it right. Recipients have a right to expect justice, even in an unjust system. When injustice exists, normative expectation of justice conflicts with empirical expectation.

The final stage in the degradation of "consent" (by scholarly apologists and the courts that adopt their reasoning) is the mere (allegedly efficient) rearrangement of entitlements without any actual consent or assent. This is indeed a more honest position than either attempting to gerrymander the meaning of "agreement," or finding that because a recipient should have known there were terms, he is therefore (*therefore*??) bound by them. But this honest position leaves the firm with power to change consumers' entitlements without their consent or even knowledge. Businesses and their lawyers who rely on the argument endorsed in the *Carnival Cruise* case discussed in chapter 1, and judges who accept this argument, ask us to assume (without evidence) that deleting consumers' rights saves firms money, that firms pass on those savings to consumers rather than just pocketing them, and, moreover, that consumers "would" choose (if economically rational?) to sell those rights to the firm in return for lower prices. The case for rights deletion put forward by business writers often includes the idea of a "deal" whereby consumers trade off their legal rights for lower prices and employees trade off their legal rights for higher wages.[18]

In sum, to conclude our initial exploration of the normative degradation caused by boilerplate: Recipients cannot be said to have consented to, and thereby become subject to, purported contracts when they don't know that they exist, i.e., in circumstances of sheer ignorance. Consent is problematic even when recipients click a box that says "I agree," because it remains unclear what they could actually be said to be agreeing to. Evasion of the issue of consent by arguing (more honestly) that although recipients do not consent, they "should" have, and "would" have (if economically rational), skirts the basic premise of contractual exchange; namely, that a free decision is made to engage in an exchange beneficial to both parties.

Moreover, this evasion of consent assumes that peoples' rights can be sold to a firm without their actual consent if the price is somehow right. To the contrary, our legal system adheres to a fundamental premise that one private party (for example, a firm) cannot divest another private party (a consumer) of any right belonging to her, even if compensation is paid. (For example, I can't swipe your bicycle and make it all right by paying you the going market price for that particular used bicycle.) A system in which rights could be taken from people without their consent if they were paid the alleged market price for those rights would be a major departure from our own. If our system is tending in that direction because millions of people are without their consent being made subject to boilerplate that erases important legal rights, then surely our system of contract law, in which consent is essential, is being degraded. Each time problematic consent, or indeed nonconsent, is treated as if it were real consent, the normative idea of consent inherent to contract is being degraded. Moreover, if millions of people are being held to have sold important rights, such as their rights to meaningful legal redress of grievances, then surely our political system, along with its support of equality before the law, is being degraded. Which leads me to an exploration of democratic degradation, and the next chapter.

. . . .

Democratic Degradation

REPLACING THE LAW OF THE STATE WITH THE

"LAW" OF THE FIRM

W HEN A FIRM'S MASS-MARKET boilerplate withdraws a number of important recipients' rights—such as rights of redress granted by the state, or user rights that are free of owner control under intellectual property regimes—it is displacing the legal regime enacted by the state with a governance scheme that is more favorable to the firm. It is transporting recipients to a firm's own preferred legal universe. I am not referring here to all "contracts of adhesion." Rather I mean to focus on mass-market boilerplate rights deletion schemes: the deployment of boilerplate to rework a system of recipients' rights that are guaranteed by the polity in order to divest recipients of those rights, or of some substantial portion of them, for the benefit of a firm.

When such boilerplate comes into widespread use, as it has in current practice, it causes democratic degradation in various ways. It threatens the distinction between public and private ordering, and indeed the ideal of private ordering itself. In addition to undermining or bypassing the system of rights structures enacted and guaranteed by the state, the degradation of our commitment to democratic political ordering includes several other interlocked deficiencies. Widespread boilerplate undermines the rationale that justifies the state's power to organize the polity; it undermines the rule of law; and it converts rights enacted and guaranteed by the state into rights that can be "condemned" by private firms. The state is enlisted to enforce purported "contracts" that undercut rights supposedly guaranteed by the state, thus undermining the basis of contract itself.

Private Law

Our theory of private ordering presupposes that there exist distinct and stable entitlements (property), underwritten by the state, that belong to individuals but can be detached and exchanged; and that there exist distinct and stable rules of exchange (contract), underwritten by the state, that regulate private exchanges to keep them within the bounds of freedom of the parties, and thus justify interpreting private exchanges as free rather than as not-free. The main legal infrastructure of the liberal notion of private ordering traditionally known as "private law," consists of the legal rules of property and contract.*

Exchange transactions in the aggregate are considered private ordering in that they are initiated by individuals according to their own individual will and individual subjective valuations. They are not initiated by government or some agency of central planning; they result in no preordained pattern of distribution. Property rights and control over resources end up wherever the collective workings of exchange freedom take them, according to no preexistent plan—or so the theory goes. In a commonly used metaphorical shorthand, private ordering is viewed as "bottom-up," the result of myriad activities by individual actors, whereas public ordering is conceived as "top-down," imposed by the polity through its authoritative entities such as legislatures.

The system of private ordering is a treasured centerpiece of liberal political thought, and freedom of contract is a revered ideal.

---

* "Legal infrastructure" is the term I use for the necessary ordering rules for setting up and maintaining an appropriate market so as to foster a realm of private ordering. Legal infrastructure includes baseline rules of property—that is, entitlements, meaning the allocation of power over scarce resources. These rules are supposed to make clear who justifiably "has" something before it can be traded justifiably to someone else. Legal infrastructure also includes rules of contract—that is, means of enforcing appropriate exchanges of entitlements and of preventing or punishing inappropriate ones, and means of deciding which is which.

The traditional liberal understanding of freedom of contract portrays individual freedom as effectuated by individual voluntary agreements, with the concomitant understanding that unfreedom will thereby be avoided. Liberal conceptions of freedom (in most guises) have a bedrock commitment to the market—an understanding that freedom involves at least the freedom of individuals to engage in exchange transactions with one another. Contract refers to the aggregate of these individual transactions as well as to each separate transaction, thus forming a system of private ordering. In traditional liberal theory, enforcement of contracts by the state is a basic reason for the existence of the state; that is, a basic justification for the state's existence is its exercise of state power to enforce contracts that uphold and instantiate the ideal of freedom of contract and a realm of private ordering, while disallowing purported contracts that fail to do so.

So much is commonplace, reflecting the core commitments (some would consider them ideological) of political liberalism. In the past decades there has been vigorous critique of these basic liberal commitments, particularly of the "public" vs. "private" distinction. Nevertheless, the ideal of a realm of private ordering protected by the state still holds substantial sway, as it must if we are to believe in such revered ideals as freedom of contract and its connection with freedom of the will.

Undermining the Distinction between Public and Private Ordering

Mass-market form contracts that amount to boilerplate rights deletion schemes undermine the distinction between public and private ordering, and thereby undermine the ideal of private ordering itself. The erosion of the distinction leads to degradation of the democratic political order in so far as it relies on the idea of private ordering.

Private ordering refers to ordering controlled by individuals—bottom-up, relying on freedom of contract. Public ordering refers to ordering initiated by the state—top-down, through legislative and administrative decisions. The traditional distinction between private and public ordering has been vigorously critiqued in recent decades. Yet our society's underlying commitment to the idea of private ordering, which is embedded in our legal infrastructure of contract, unequivocally relies on the existence of a distinction between the realms of public and private action and ordering—a public/private distinction. Entitlements are granted and/or maintained by public ordering, and they are exchanged by private ordering. The exchanges by private ordering are legitimate only within a polity that underwrites a background "public" legal infrastructure by which contracts that lack consent or are obtained by force or fraud will be denied enforcement, and by which contracts that are legitimately made will in fact be enforced.

Excessive "privatization" of those functions that are situated in the public realm—whether by private armies, private prisons, or private police—erases the safeguards that are afforded by the polity. Establishing and maintaining these safeguards is the reason that those functions were situated within the control of polity in the first place. In the same way, excessive "privatization" of the legal infrastructure of contracts (deleting the background rules of legal rights to redress in case of breach, for example) undermines the possibility of private ordering by contracts as envisioned in the basis of liberalism, and as it must exist in actuality if it is to justify the state that is established to facilitate it. *Firms that deploy boilerplate in order to erase the legal rights that form the infrastructure that makes contractual private ordering possible are using contract to destroy the underlying basis of contract.* They are deploying contract against itself.

Destabilizing the Public/Private Distinction

It is easy to deconstruct (or at least destabilize) the public/private distinction if it is viewed as consisting of two hard-and-fast conceptual categories or as consisting of a pure binary opposition. As the legal realists of the first half of the twentieth century pointed out, property and contract as the legal infrastructure of private ordering must (as must all legal infrastructures) stem from the polity, the public realm. In the latter part of the twentieth century, the "crits" of the Critical Legal Studies movement mounted a similar critique. To the extent that one adheres to legal positivism,* it is apparent that "public" law, the law of the state, controls the content and process of "private" transactions, the realm of private ordering. But even if one is an ardent antipositivist who believes that all of the details of a property system and a contract system are conceptually or metaphysically delineated without any admixture of evolving cultural commitments or positive law (the activities of legislatures), it is still the case that those systems cannot function without state enforcement. State enforcement means, as the legal realists argued, that the state is involved willy-nilly in the functioning of private ordering, because the state must sustain and police its constitutive rules.

To be functional state enforcement must meet certain criteria. It must follow the liberal ideal(s) of the rule of law reasonably closely, with predictable and even-handed application of the law to keep transactions within the bounds of free exchange.[2] Moreover, public oversight must be in place as an ever-present deterrent against players who might otherwise transgress. All private transactions are carried out in the shadow of the law. In short, as the legal realists realized, law is public and pervasive, even when it is used to undergird a system of private ordering.

The Rule of Law

The ideal that people should be governed by law instead of arbitrary power was historically stated as "the rule of law, not of men." It is the law that should rule, in other words, not a monarch or a group of nobles. The rule of law is central to liberal political thought. It incorporates the idea that we exit the state of nature to enter a structure of binding rules which grants to the state a monopoly on force, and insists upon the further idea that the monopoly of force must be legitimated by a juridical structure, a specifically

---

*Legal positivism, roughly defined, is the philosophical doctrine that the law consists of what is authoritatively posited, whether or not that is morally justified. *See* Leslie Green, *Legal Positivism*, THE STANFORD ENCYCLOPEDIA OF PHILOSOPHY (Edward N. Zalta, ed., fall 2009 edition), http://plato.stanford.edu/archives/fall2009/entries/legal-positivism (last modified Aug. 10, 2009).

legal regime of reciprocal rights and duties. Today the ideal of the rule of law is primarily invoked in urging the reform of property and contract in developing and nonwestern countries with the aim of facilitating the organization and functioning of free markets. So it is often said that what is needed is stable property entitlements and rules of contract, together with impartial courts to administer and enforce them. But the ideal of the rule of law is historically broader than the notion of an appropriate market infrastructure of property and contract; it is the elaboration of the notion of what it means to be governed by law as opposed to arbitrary rule, and as opposed to no rule at all in a state of nature (anarchy).

Almost all important western political theorists have analyzed the rule of law.[3] I will recapitulate here some of the main characteristics they regard as essential to effective legal directives, then explain why boilerplate rights deletion schemes undermine the rule of law when they undermine the basis of contract.

Legal directives should exist in advance of the conduct they are supposed to regulate. Retroactivity is contrary to the rule of law, because in order for an action to be governed by law, the law must at least preexist the action. Where there is extensive retroactivity, we have passed out of a society governed by law; that is why the US Constitution disallows ex post facto laws, and why courts are careful when dealing with retroactivity.

Legal directives should be knowable by those who are supposed to follow them. A lack of notice can be caused not only by secrecy but also by the instability that results when legal doctrines are too much in conflict with one another or change too quickly.

Legal directives should not be impossible for human beings to follow, and they should not be irrational or useless for human well being.

Legal directives should be enforced fairly and impartially, not capriciously and arbitrarily. The entities that declare the directives (such as legislatures) should address them to citizens as a whole or to rationally determined groups, and should neither single out individuals nor unfairly target subgroups. The entity with the power to set directives (such as a legislature) should, at least as it is usually argued, be separate from the entities (such as courts) that over-see enforcement against individuals. The courts should enforce the directives impartially and according to preexisting law and legal principles, rather than arriving at results arbitrarily and ad hoc. The law on the books should correspond to the law in practice (a virtue that Lon Fuller called "congruence"[4]). Judges should be guided by law and legal principles, not by their personal political commitments or monetary interests, and not by arbitrary proce-dures such as flipping a coin.

All of the precepts of the rule of law are related to the governed being able to know the law and able to follow the law, as well as to the governed being equal before the law and benefitted by the law. Interpretations that were not predictable at the time plans were made or businesses were structured or acts were done are prob-lematic for the rule of law, in the same way that retroactivity is. Consider, for example, the retroactive aspect of the US copyright term extension act that the US Supreme Court upheld in *Eldred v. Ashcroft*.[5] People who relied on the expiration of copyright terms had their businesses disrupted; rights were "taken" from those who relied on the content of the public domain under existing law, and "given" to those who had not previously possessed these rights.[6]

But prior to these precepts of know-ability, do-ability, equality, and benefit in the rule of law, there is an underlying notion of com-mitment to law itself, to the sovereignty of the political constitu-tion set up and maintained for the very reason of underwriting a government by law (rather than by arbitrary power). Firms that use contract to destroy the ideal of contractual ordering are effec-tively undermining the rule of law and contributing to democratic degradation.

Erasing Legal Rights

Boilerplate rights deletion schemes undermine the significance of political debate and procedures. That is the most obvious way they degrade democracy. Many of the entitlement regimes that boiler-plate erases have been enacted through democratic processes, often after extended debate and fierce political struggle, whereas erasing them only requires drafting boilerplate (or indeed just copying someone else's boilerplate).[7] Why does Congress debate reform of the Copyright Act for years if the resulting legislative regime can be restructured in minutes by a firm deploying a boilerplate scheme? When firms can easily divest recipients of entitlements that are part of a legislative regime arrived at only with much difficulty, debate, and compromise, it makes a sham of the apparatus of democratic governance. All of the public input and hard-fought compromises and trade-offs seem like an ironic form of kabuki theatre. Worse, well-funded interests lobbying in the legislative arena may be merely feigning legislative horse-trading and may be entering into compromises just for show. These firms may reasonably expect that whatever political compromises they make can be easily rescinded with boilerplate.[8]

Democratic ordering as we know it is certainly not ideal. Why, then, should we care about this particular sort of democratic degradation?[9] Well, democratic procedures at least give us a voice in the structuring of the regimes we must live under; not in the ideal sense, but not wholly theoretically either. We can "vote 'em out" if we don't like what "they" enact. When a boilerplate rights deletion scheme replaces the legal rights regime maintained by the state with the scheme desired by firms, we have a means of exit (we can refuse to buy the product or service) but we have no voice.[10] That is why they are called "take-it-or-leave-it" contracts.

Exit from a boilerplate scheme is frequently thought not to be difficult: "What's the problem? Just don't buy the product or service to which the form contract is attached." But in reality, exit often is almost impossible. Recipients most likely will not read the terms of boilerplate, because of heuristic biases and other reasons (mentioned in chapter 1); a leading reason being that the recipient would not understand the terms if she did read them, so why waste the time?[11] Exit may be almost impossible for market structural reasons, too. Many products that consumers need to purchase are sold by only one supplier, or by a group of suppliers who all use the same set of terms.

Copycat Boilerplate: A Form of Tacit Collusion?

Boilerplate proliferates. The situation in which exit is impossible because all suppliers of a needed product or service use the same boilerplate is common. Once one tour company deploys a form purporting to exculpate itself from all kinds of liability for any injury, whether to the recipient or his children, no matter how caused, forms with almost identical wording pop up everywhere. Once the terms of service of one website say, "To the fullest extent permissible pursuant to applicable law, we disclaim all warranties, express or implied, including warranties of merchantability, fitness for a particular purpose, accuracy, completeness, availability, security, compatibility and noninfringement," a host of other websites will decide to use the very same language. Once one firm prints on its invoices, "To the maximum extent permitted by law, [Seller] will under no circumstances be liable for any special, indirect, incidental or consequential damages," we begin to see this clause everywhere.

One way in which boilerplate could possibly become uniform in an industry or trade is by old-fashioned collusion, the kind that antitrust law is designed to target. We normally think of price-fixing when we think of the collusion that antitrust law prohibits, but it is possible that all of the sellers using the same boilerplate have colluded to fix the terms of their transactions with customers as well as, or perhaps instead of, their prices. If so, this would be a contract in restraint of trade under the Sherman Antitrust Act, which can result from tacit collusion as well as overt agreement.[12] Such a situation is perhaps not likely to happen very often.

What is more likely is that firms will copy boilerplate from other firms, which will often lead just as surely to identical boilerplate occupying the territory in which a consumer is participating. Proliferation is especially easy in the online environment. Copycat boilerplate should be evaluated as a possible form of tacit collusion. It is not exactly the kind of tacit collusion that antitrust law already understands, collusion in which an actual "contract" in restraint of trade is tacitly made; but it can have a similar effect of restricting the choice in a market. Industry-wide standardization of a boilerplate scheme prevents consumers from choosing terms they would prefer. They have no exit from onerous terms. Moreover, industry-wide standardization may result in a market in which firms offer the least favorable terms they can get away with.[13]

Standardization and Privatization

The mere fact that a form is standardized is not in and of itself problematic. Sometimes standards promote knowledge and ease of use, reduce uncertainty, and lower transaction costs for all parties. An example is the standardized bond contract or insurance policy, which may well facilitate commercial transactions because everyone knows how courts will interpret the clauses contained in such contracts. Not all copycat boilerplate is necessarily pernicious or a form of tacit collusion, either. A firm that uses a "fair" set of terms with its customers might find its terms copied by others, in many jurisdictions, and could find its terms widely validated. That would be an example of the kind of beneficial network externalities that can accompany standardization in certain circumstances.[14] Not all standardization, even if resulting in widespread uniformity, contributes to democratic degradation.

In the abstract standardization is neither good nor bad. Nor does it seem to matter, at least in the abstract, how a standard comes into being; whether bottom-up through market emergence or top-down through regulation or the actions of a standard-setting entity. How does this general premise about standards apply to boilerplate sets of terms? If a "fair" set of terms occupies a market, in a setting in which it makes sense to think that consumers understand the terms and are choosing to buy the product with the terms, it might seem, at least at first, that the normative acceptability of the terms need not turn at all upon whether the standard came about through "bottom-up" market forces or through "top-down" legislation or administrative order.

Courts, nevertheless, have sometimes looked askance at the legal standardization that results from "bottom-up" market forces while deferring readily to the legal standardization implemented by means of governmental ordering. This may not seem to make sense if viewed through the lens of welfare maximization (efficiency), because it would seem, at least through that lens, that a situation should be judged by its social results rather than by its origins.[15]

I suggest that judges who make this distinction may in fact be reenacting the traditional public/private distinction. In that traditional view, whatever becomes law-like belongs to the public realm and not to the private realm. Therefore, standardization of terms, especially industry-wide standardization, may be seen as fine if the government does it (that is the point of safety regulations, and much else); but not fine—and, in my terms, a form of democratic degradation—if it comes about by operation of the market (private ordering).

Note, however, that standardization is—or should be—more troubling when it amounts to privatization of an arena of social ordering whose parameters and oversight are properly the duty and exclusive province of the polity. Some legal systems outside the US rely on constitutional or charter values, or indeed on general legislative regimes, to limit the extent of rights deletion by boilerplate schemes. In Germany in particular, scholars and legal actors have recognized the dangers of democratic degradation: contracts that impinge on particular rights that belong to the ordering of the state, such as redress of grievances, are no longer considered private, but must instead meet the constitutional standards of the state.[16] US constitutional law turns in the opposite direction: the US Supreme Court over time has made it more and more difficult to find "state action" (that is, government action) in a transaction so that constitutional values will apply.[17]

Undermining the Public/Private Distinction from the Right

Although the legal realist critique of the public/private distinction that I mentioned earlier has been primarily a critique (a dissolution of this distinction) from the Left, at the same time—and I think this is just as significant, if not more so—there has been a dissolution of this distinction from the Right. This dissolution, although it has been less explicit, has been no less effective, and indeed is probably more far-reaching.

Theorists belonging to the school of thought known as political economy or public choice theory, along with numerous nontheorist followers, reason in exactly the same terms about the purchase of legislation or agency regulation by market actors as they reason about the purchase of contractual obligations or of any other good advantageous to the actor. To the public choice way of thinking, a firm would ask itself whether to purchase contractual obligations (in the private "marketplace") or to purchase legislation (in the governmental "marketplace") just as it would ask itself which firm it should buy its inputs from, or whether indeed it should produce them in-house. All such decisions are economic decisions, to be based on cost-benefit calculations. For example, the firm would ask itself, "Shall we purchase legislation that bars class actions for certain types of transactions and makes it impossible for consumers to get into court with such actions, or shall we deploy a boilerplate scheme waiving recipients' entitlement to bring class actions?" In this calculus, there is no distinction in kind between political (public) action and market (private) action. The premises on which political economy theory is based have obliterated the public/private distinction central to the traditional liberalism upon which our political system is based.

In spite of the various avenues that lead to a dissolution of the public/private distinction, unless some version of that distinction remains applicable to current institutions and practices, the notion of private ordering cannot reasonably characterize those institutions and practices. I am not denying at this point that these ideals might well exist as an attractive mythology, even though they do not now describe actual practice. But unless we have a functioning regime of private ordering *in practice*, the justification of the state itself is undermined, for the traditional liberal justification of the state depends upon the state's ability to structure and maintain a realm of private ordering. Liberal ideal thought holds, that is, that the state is justified by the necessity of establishing and maintaining a background infrastructure by means of which private actors can realize and exercise their freedom through private ordering. This ideal thought does not map onto actual practice if in practice we cannot maintain a distinction between the public and private realms of action and ordering. How can the realm of private ordering be maintained by the public order in a way that enhances the freedom of individuals, if the public order is itself dissolved into the private?

Political economy, in particular by considering that firms and interest groups purchase legislation when it is of benefit to themselves, undermines the liberal justification of the state, which supposes that the state is justified because it can restrain the war of all against all by establishing rules that are in the public interest; that is, in the interest of everyone. To organize and justify a state, each firm is supposed to give up its untrammeled quest for profit at the expense of society as a whole, provided that all other firms will also do so. It is hard to mesh this kind of justification of the state with the common public choice reasoning that legislation is purchased for self-interested reasons by firms or interest groups.[18] If all legislation is considered to represent such self-interested purchases, then the state has not distanced itself much from the war of all against all that is envisioned as taking place in the state of nature. Thus, the traditional liberal justification of the state, the notion that the state enables an exit from the prepolitical anarchy into a realm of governance in the public interest, is undermined.[19] In a sense, the prevalence of political economy theory itself contributes to democratic degradation.

Can the Ideal of Private Ordering Be Salvaged?

It is possible to reinterpret the public/private distinction as pragmatic rather than formal or conceptual. In a pragmatic interpretation, the distinction is a contextual characterization that tends to work in practice most of the time. In the past, it seemed possible to distinguish what was appropriately labeled "public" vs. "private" in a way that was functionally understandable, in spite of difficult borderline cases. But in a pragmatic understanding, the borderline cases must be exceptional, not run-of-the-mill, in order for the pragmatic interpretation to work well enough to keep viable in actual practice the liberal ideal of a functioning regime of private ordering under the aegis of a public infrastructure supporting the rule of law. To what extent has the ubiquitous use of boilerplate rights deletion schemes in contemporary markets undermined the distinction between how the state undergirds the social environment with public ordering, on the one hand, and the structuring of the social environment by means of private ordering, on the other? Perhaps the theory of traditional liberalism no longer describes our practice even in a pragmatic way, if indeed it ever did. If a theory does not describe a practice, to what extent (if any) can it be useful as a justification of that practice? That is perhaps a deep philosophical question; but prima facie it would seem that if the ideal of private ordering and the role of public ordering in structuring it and upholding it does not describe World B, then the transactions in World B stand in need of some other justification. If the transactions of World B cannot be justified, then we are in a situation of democratic degradation.

The Threat to Legal Infrastructure Posed by the Advent of Technological Protection Measures

An important development taking place in the digital environment is the implementation of technological protection measures (TPMs) for digital information goods. (Note that some people call these technological mechanisms DRMs, for "digital rights management," but I think that label is misleading. To assume that these mechanisms manage "rights" begs the baseline question of whose rights they are and whether the manager has any right to manage them. Moreover, "TPM" is closer to the term "technological measures," which is used by an international treaty in referring to these mechanisms.[20])

The TPM as Successor to Boilerplate

TPMs, which are being deployed more and more widely, have the effect of enlarging a realm of self-help that replaces the public legal infrastructure of oversight and enforcement. For example, sophisticated copy protection that disables a program or makes a document unviewable if the user tries to copy it can replace boilerplate that has the recipient "agreeing" not to copy, which itself has been deployed in order to supersede the prevailing legal background intellectual property regimes.

TPMs may at first seem to give rise to the same issues that I have already mentioned with respect to the boilerplate rights deletion schemes that they replace. Content owners can, and often do, deploy privately implemented technological resources instead of privately deployed boilerplate terms to foreclose activities and rights that the baseline public legal infrastructure has allocated to the user.

TPMs institute a form of "machine rule." Common among the activities foreclosed by machine rule are the copying of material that is not covered by copyright and uses of material that is covered by copyright but could have been adjudicated "fair use." A prominent example is the attempt to prevent the copying of internal programs that would enable a competitor to reverse engineer a firm's product. This is a form of copying that is widely considered to be fair use, but individual firms widely want to get rid of it (unless they need to use it themselves).[21] (The evaluation of boilerplate that cancels user rights under intellectual property regimes will be considered in more detail in chapter 9.)

In spite of the fact that TPMs may substitute for boilerplate in so far as they attempt to accomplish more or less the same goals as boilerplate, the issues for traditional liberal theory posed by machine rule are more serious, or at least clearer, because TPMs more clearly bypass contract. Indeed, TPMs bypass the state's structuring of the legal infrastructure of exchange. Boilerplate rights deletion schemes also bypass legal infrastructure to some extent, since no one reads them and it is difficult to bring them before a court. Even so, in the case of boilerplate we at least still have a juridical structure to which those purported contracts might ultimately be referred for interpretation and validation, which means that those contracts exist (however tenuously) in the shadow of that potential referral. TPMs, by contrast, bypass the juridical structure.[22] TPMs work automatically. They do not turn disputes over to adjudication by neutral disinterested courts that operate as a branch of sovereign power within a juridical system. They are deployed by one private party against another; usually against many others. Moreover, they subject parties to their control but deprive those subjected parties of the juridical structure that they are entitled to expect in a political state, a structure that provides for juridical interpretation, balancing the equities, review of what parties have done in their contractual transactions and the ability to withhold as well as grant enforcement.

A TPM, in sum, is like a self-enforcing injunction controlled completely by one party. Unlike governance under the law of contract, the recipient has no option to breach and pay damages. Unlike governance under the law of copyright, the recipient has no option to infringe and then argue fair use before a court. Unlike governance under the law of contract, the recipient has no option to plead to a court that there are sufficient grounds to keep the injunction from issuing. No entity of the state will balance the hardships and look for irreparable harm before issuing the injunction. (Under some circumstances irreparable harm caused by a TPM seems very possible; consider licensed software running a heart-lung machine.) Unlike governance under the law of contract, a TPM recipient cannot ask a court to reinterpret what the terms mean; cannot question whether the level of consent is appropriate; and cannot ask a court to consider defenses such as reasonable expectation or economic duress. In other words, TPMs can make even nonwaivable user rights—such as the right to seek redress in court—irrelevant.[23]

Self-Help

TPMs are usefully viewed not as contract substitutes but rather as technological self-help. Their operation is analogous to the way that landlords were once allowed to lock out tenants who had failed to pay rent and cart off their furniture; or to the way that landowners wishing to defend their property against trespassers used to set up spring guns that would automatically shoot anyone who stepped over the boundary line.

The topic of how much self-help is permitted under a regime

devoted to the rule of law rather than anarchy, the hypothetical state of nature, is a difficult one.[24] Building a high fence could be considered self-help, and yet it might well qualify as a version of self-help that is consistent with the liberal ideal of freedom and safely within the appropriate bounds of property ownership. Some kinds of self-help are more problematic, but have been allowed to a limited extent, usually with a backdrop of regulatory safeguards. For example, the repossession of some chattels for failure to make payment is allowed under such a scheme (the repossession of automobiles, for example) but not of others. The legal action of unlawful detainer has superseded any self-help right of a landlord to repossess a rented apartment by locking out tenants and seizing their furniture. A landlord who thinks she has a right to recover her rental unit must take her case to court.

The relationship between self-help and the legal system is complex. Sometimes self-help is not merely permitted by the legal system, but required. Thus, parties often must build fences around their property in order to receive protection from trespass, and they must deploy appropriate systems to keep information confidential in order to prevent the loss of their trade secrets.[25] In contract law, nonbreaching parties are required to engage in self-help by mitigating damages.[26] The question of when self-help is required, when it is permitted, and when it is precluded, is unclear.

TPMs vs. the Ideal of the Rule of Law

If TPMs are appropriately regarded as self-help mechanisms, the question emerges whether widespread deployment of TPMs is consistent with a functioning version of the ideal of the rule of law.[27] If it is not, and I believe that it is not, then TPMs also create democratic degradation. Courts and legislatures in the past which made decisions to exclude self-help in property disputes understood the connection between self-help and the rule of law. At worst, self-help can degenerate into vigilante "justice," which might better be described as a partial retreat from the liberal ideals of civil society. Too much self-help "invite[s] disorderly scrambles"[28]; that is, a return to the war of all against all in which it is every man for himself, the condition that the state is supposed to supplant with its peaceful juridical order of mutual reciprocal rights and obligations.

Is the automatic injunction implemented by a TPM more like a high fence, a trade secret protection, an auto repossession, an apartment repossession, or a spring gun? Or should the proper characterization vary depending upon the nature and purpose of the TPM? It might be that the ideal of individual freedom under the rule of law should be interpreted to include the right to build high fences as a component of property entitlements in light of their role in the fulfillment of individuality and freedom; whereas it might be that deployment of landlord self-help repossession is too invasive of the individual freedom of tenants and too likely to cause violence (between the tenant's friends and the landlord's friends) to be compatible with the rule of law. Sorting out these questions in detail is a necessary investigation, but I will not undertake it here. That would, I think, necessitate a separate book. Suffice it to say that I do not think the needed elaboration is going to be self-evident or uncontested.

As I mentioned earlier in this chapter, the basis of the rule of law is a commitment to law itself, to the sovereignty of the political constitution set up and maintained for the very reason of underwriting a government by law rather than by arbitrary power. Widespread deployment of TPMs, without any legal limits, would be contrary to that underlying basis of the rule of law. The widespread and unchecked use of TPMs would bypass the public character of contract law—that is, its characteristics of legality rather than merely private power. TPMs would go further than mass-market boilerplate rights deletion schemes do in undermining the public legal infrastructure that supports and justifies the ideal of a realm of private ordering As they exist today, TPMs are inimical to the rule of law, and therefore a cause of democratic degradation. As they exist today, they are accorded stringent protection by treaty and by US legislation under the Digital Millennium Copyright Act, even though they are subject to no legal limits on what they can accomplish by their machine rule.[29] Whether in the future they can be pulled back into an appropriate juridical structure remains to be seen.

Bringing TPMs within the Rule of Law?

What kinds of measures might help to make TPMs less problematic from the point of view of the rule of law? First, it may help to require those who deploy a TPM to give recipients actual notice of its existence and of how it operates. Other possible courses of action, such as evaluating TPMs under tort law, or using regulation to disallow TPMs for mission-critical systems, might be considered as part of a reassignment of mass-market rights deletion schemes to tort law (see chapter 11) or to regulation (see chapter 12). I would at least note here that the deployment of TPMs could be pulled back toward a juridical structure by providing an opportunity for recipients to seek a judicial declaration invalidating them, something analogous to a declaratory judgment action. The grounds for invalidating a TPM might be that the TPM is illegally locking up information or precluding activities that are available to the recipient under her legal background rights.

Of course, TPM recipients might be asked—or required, depending on circumstances—to accept boilerplate that would have them agreeing to the TPM and waiving whatever the rights were that the TPM was disabling. Thus, it is likely that an attempt to regulate TPMs in the manner suggested above would push us back toward the core issues posed for the rule of law by the deployment of boilerplate rights deletion schemes.

PART II

Boilerplate and Contract Theory

RATIONALES AND RATIONALIZATIONS

. . . .

A Summary of the Philosophy of Contract

THE THEORIES OF WORLD A

To RECAPITULATE THE BACKGROUND structure upon which the philosophy of contract is built: When a court enforces a contract, it uses the power of the state to order a transfer of rights (property, money, etc.) from one party to another. Something the party breaching the contract was previously entitled to becomes an entitlement of the nonbreaching party. The use of state power must be justified, if we are to assert that we live under the rule of law (i.e., under a justifiable legal system, rather than unjustified arbitrary state power). To put this another way, because contract enforcement is a transfer of entitlement, it is a form of redistribution of property rights.[1] The justification for using the force of state power to accomplish such a transfer stems from the traditional justification of the state itself, the justification usually known as liberal ordering.

According to the traditional political theory that still articulates the background commitments of our legal system, the rationale or justification for setting up the state (that is, the polity) is to set up rules, limitations, and structures that make free action by individuals possible, or enhance their possibilities for freedom of action; and, in particular, to set up such rules, limitations, and structures as make possible an orderly market. A situation in which no deal can be enforced (when it fulfills the requirements that justify enforcement) and no deal can be overturned (when it does not fulfill those requirements) is not a free market; it is anarchy.

Because our legal system adheres to the ideal of private ordering and asserts its importance to freedom, freedom of contract is a core value. "Involuntary" or "unfree" contract is a contradiction in terms: involuntary divestment of one's entitlement is just not what "contract" *means* within the system of private ordering. Within our legal system it seems paradoxical to try to think of coerced or deceptive or completely unknown divestments of entitlements as being nonetheless "contracts."

This chapter will sketch the main streams of contract philosophy. The purpose of the sketch is to facilitate further investigation of the extent to which boilerplate is a permissible means of creating contractual obligation. In particular, I mean to demonstrate the deep embeddedness—the ineradicability—of the notion of voluntariness, which is not dependent on the type of theory one favors. The other main goal of this sketch is to compare and contrast the economic efficiency theory of contract with the various theories based more directly on freedom of the will.

After the overview of contract theory in this chapter, the following two chapters will explore the extent to which the main forms of contract theory can (or cannot) be deployed in justification of boilerplate.* In chapter 5, I will explore the question(s) whether the procedures of World B (the Boilerplate World)—including clicking "I agree"—can be justified by interpreting them as in fact the kind of consent that is needed for contract; and whether, indeed, we should accept the argument put forward by businesses that say recipients must be understood to be trading off their legal rights for lower prices. In chapter 6, I will explore the economists' "the-contract-is-part-of-the-product" theory (the "contract-as-product" theory for short).

With the contemporary exception of social welfare (utilitarian, economic) theory, mainstream philosophy of contract tends not to confront the issue of whether state enforcement of World B contracts is justifiable. Boilerplate is largely absent from writings

---

* Readers who prefer not to examine at this point the theory of contract and how it applies (or does not apply) to boilerplate may proceed directly to Parts III and IV, where I explore what the law is now doing about boilerplate and what might be done in addition or instead.

on contract theory. The philosophy of contract is thus somewhat divorced from the particular reality of practice that is the focus of this book. In the end, the body of writing that constitutes the philosophy of contract may incline us to wonder whether World B might not be better regulated by some part of the legal infrastructure other than contract law.

An Introduction to Contract Theory

There is a vibrant literature on philosophy of contract, with a number of interesting and vigorous debates ongoing within its theoretical confines. Those theoretical confines are, by and large, the parameters of World A (the Agreement world). This chapter will not lay out those debates in detail or weigh into them, but I do mean to sketch the contours of the different theories and at least to establish the point—an obvious one, I hope—that all streams of philosophy of contract depend on a basic premise of voluntariness. These streams of philosophy are supposed to delineate the normative universe in which contract is justified; that is, the extent to which transfers of individual entitlements can be justifiably considered contracts, enforceable by the state by means of legal remedies against those who breach them. Insofar as contract theories do define the limits of enforceable transfers, they reveal the root of the normative degradation suffered by the legal system on account of the myriad entitlement transfers in practice whose voluntariness is seriously in doubt, or indeed whose lack of voluntariness is not in doubt.

Philosophy of contract has two main branches: welfare theories and autonomy theories. Welfare theories, stemming from Bentham, involve the maximization of social welfare based on subjective individual choices; autonomy theories, stemming from Kant, involve individual rights derived from the nature of freedom of the will.[2]

Traditional autonomy theory, when applied to contracts, focuses on an exchange of promises, or on agreement. In theories based on exchanges of promises, the focus is on the bindingness of each party's promise, when it is given in return for a promise from the other side. Promise-based theory serves the purpose of validating purely executory contracts; that is, those that are not to be performed by either side until some time after the bargain is struck. Promise-based theory is still the basis of much of contract philosophy, and is also ensconced in US legal doctrine.[3] In autonomy theories based on agreement rather than on exchange of promises, the commitment of each individual to do something is less the analytic focal point than it is with theories based on promising, and the idea of each party committing to the same thing is more the focal point. Central to both promise-based theories and agreement-based theories is reciprocity—the commitments of both parties to a bargain. Those who engage in reciprocal promises necessarily are each consenting to give up something in return for what the other is delivering. Those who enter into agreements with one another are also necessarily consenting to give up something in return for what the other is delivering.

We have inherited the two main streams of theory, autonomy and welfare, from the late eighteenth and early nineteenth centuries. They are both artifacts of political liberalism that reached their flowering in the era of laissez-faire. Two other theories more recently developed (or resurrected) suggest different ways to look at contract: reliance theories (based on justifiable reliance on a promise); and equivalence of exchange theories (neo-Aristotelian and other theories based on virtue ethics and/or human flourishing).[4] A third recent theory, intended to validate libertarian premises, seeks to base contract explicitly on consent only.[5]

Theories based on autonomy and welfare are at present still the primary and best-developed justificatory theories we have for the enforcement of contracts, even though not all aspects of contract law fit comfortably into either of them, and efforts to combine them present significant challenges.

Autonomy (Rights) Theories

Autonomy theories of contract derive from the moral imperative to manifest and extend freedom of the will by establishing and maintaining the situation of reciprocal rights and duties in a juridical state, thus forming an ethically just society. In such theories, contract becomes necessary in order to assist freedom of the will in expanding to its furthest reaches. Freedom of the will would be curtailed or thwarted, in other words, if entitlement holders could not justifiably exchange their entitlements.

In autonomy theories, in order for any entitlement to be transfered (assuming it is justly held in the first place),[6] voluntariness of transfer is an indispensable premise of justice. Involuntary transfers or transfers that are not matters of free choice for the transferor are affronts to the autonomy of the transferor. The basic premise justifying enforceable contract is that a juridical system of private property and free contract must exist in order to implement the moral law with regard to autonomy. The moral law with regard to autonomy holds that one person may not use another person; persons may freely use objects but not other persons. Involuntary transfers can be characterized as "using" the transferor rather than treating her with the respect due to persons. A transfer that amounts to one person's using another is thus contrary to the moral law with regard to autonomy.

Kant, in his Doctrine of Right (*Rechtslehre*), and Hegel, in his Philosophy of Right (*Grundlinien der Philosphie des Rechts*) each argued from the moral law of freedom to the requirement that contract law exist. Charles Fried, in *Contract as Promise*, was one of the first contemporary writers to take up this strand of philosophical thought. In the US, as I mentioned earlier, contract is most of the time considered to be rooted in the concept of promising,[7] in which a promise creates a moral obligation on the part of the promisor. This US promissory basis may be part of the reason why Fried chose to base his Kantian contract theory on promising.[8]

Fried argues that promising is a special kind of moral obligation, whose parameters, broadly speaking, are convention, reciprocity, and will. According to Fried, promising is an institution, a very general convention, which, to have force in a particular case, must be assumed to have force generally. The purpose of the convention of promising is to facilitate the projects of others so that they will facilitate one's own projects. This reciprocity is the principle that makes possible the greatest possible range of free will for one individual consistent with the similar will of others. It is clear that the idea of a reciprocity of obligation that enables the great possible range of free will for each in the context of everyone is Kantian. So is Fried's identification of himself as a "moralist of duty," committed to respect for individual autonomy and the need for trust in order to make the reach of individual will greater, and so is his conviction that promise-breaking is "using" another person. But the idea of finding moral meaning in the existence of convention is not Kantian (perhaps it is Humean), and it is unclear that these two features can satisfactorily coexist in one theory.

Although Fried popularized (at least among contracts professors, and therefore among their students) a species of Kantian contract theory, later writers on Kantian autonomy theory as it applies to contracts have been more philosophically sophisticated. Much of the criticism of Fried—and there has been a great deal of it—is aimed not at his marrying of convention to Kant, but rather at how he reasons from a moral obligation to keep promises to the obligation of contract (legal enforcement of promises).[9] What turns a moral obligation into one that is legally enforceable? Fried refers to the obligation of contract as a special case of the general obligation of promising, "in which certain promises have attained legal as well as moral force."[10] It is unclear how a "moralist of duty" would determine which promises have "attained legal . . . force." Even more of the criticism of Fried revolves around how one might use a general theory of promising (in the special case where legal force has been "attained") to justify particular institutional features of the law of contract that we have at present—or other institutional features that we ought to have instead.[11]

Some writers on autonomy theory think of contract formation as the transfer of a property right (in the promise of performance, or in the object promised). For them, the transfer of entitlement takes place immediately upon formation of the contract and not later when performance is due or after breach when the contract is enforced.[12] Among these writers is Peter Benson, who argues that the transfer must take place upon formation in order for the accepted expectation damages remedy to be properly considered compensatory. Benson's view is in some respects Hegelian rather than strictly Kantian, but he relies (as indeed does Hegel) on Kantian categories of right and characterizations of juridical activity: "Contract is a relation of two wills."[13]

Unlike Fried, Benson thinks that not only promising, but also the doctrines of consideration and the modern doctrine of unconscionability are inherent in the law's conception of contract.[14] About unconscionability, Benson says:

> [W]hat the doctrine of unconscionability does is to ensure that parties can acquire rights against each other only in a way that respects the other throughout as an equal owner with a capacity for rights. This is an essential condition of it being reasonable to construe the parties' voluntary interaction as a transfer of right. Indeed, the doctrine of unconscionability implies a conception of the person that makes salient only a party's capacity for ownership and for voluntary action.[15]

Benson's conception of unconscionability is intended to be nondistributive. As he makes clear, bargains can certainly be one-sided (if, for example, one party assumes the risk of unequal treatment, or if the risks associated with dealing with one party justify the other party in charging a price that is higher than that charged to others). In his discussion of offer and acceptance, Benson makes clear that his conception of voluntariness is formal and quite minimal; voluntary action is any action that a person wills, under whatever circumstances. If I sign a paper under threat of serious bodily harm, as long as I moved the pen myself, that is voluntary action under this definition; coercion must be dealt with elsewhere in the theory. In the passage quoted above on unconscionability, I am assuming that the conception of voluntariness is the same minimal, formal one, which is why unconscionability in this theory stands for the importance of equal treatment but yet is nondistributive.

Although the issue of unconscionability almost always arises in the context of adhesion contracts, Benson does not discuss adhesion contracts explicitly. Thus it is unclear whether in his theory an adhesion contract would fulfill the requirements for being a contract. Perhaps it would, because Benson does say that equal value in exchange, which is required by his theory, can be measured by market value when the subject matter of a contract consists of commodities;[16] and he also says that a gross lack of equivalence can be valid if it "has objectively been willed by a party, whether in the form of an assumption of risk or by a donative intent."[17] Would Benson argue that recipients of form contracts have willed to assume the risk of loss of their rights? That argument would perhaps be more applicable if the contract had actually been signed by the recipient (even if he did not read it and would not have understood it if he had read it), because that would seem to comport with Benson's conception of voluntariness. Perhaps Benson would not want to call "browsewrap" a contract, however, and perhaps not even the procedure of "money-now-terms-later."

In general, defenders of form contracts can argue that those who receive form contracts, whether or not they know anything about what rights they are giving up—and therefore even if they have willed nothing about giving up rights—might still have willed to assume the risk of giving up rights. (In the next chapter we will see examples of this argument.) This type of argument tends to demonstrate that philosophical treatment of contract stemming from autonomy simply cannot relinquish the idea of voluntariness. Indeed, perhaps that is one reason why philosophers tend not to treat the subject of mass-market contracts where voluntariness on the part of the recipient is seriously problematic. Another reason could be that philosophical theories of contract proceed at a high level of abstraction and do not detour very often into the specific phenomena of practice.

Welfare Theories

The other main theory of contract is welfare theory, otherwise known as utilitarianism or economic theory. Theories of this type often do have something to say about form contracts (though perhaps what they say should not be considered philosophy of contract) and I will reserve space for that subject in chapter 6. Meanwhile, although we must keep in mind that welfare theories,

perhaps even more than autonomy theories, come in many different sub-species, I nonetheless think that the following (simplified)
review of basic premises will be useful.[18]

Basic Premises of Economic Theory of Law

First of all, we should take note of the characteristic distinction
between positive and normative economic theory. Positive theory
aims to observe and explain; normative theory aims to justify.
Economic theories of contracts, at least as espoused by law professors, are most often of the normative variety. The normative underpinning of the economic analysis of contracts, as indeed of all
economic analyses of law, is the philosophical ethical premise by
which the goodness or badness of actions and rules are to be evaluated by their results in practice. This type of philosophy is called
consequentialist, because it is the consequences that render actions
and rules good or bad.

In this worldview, results are better if they result in greater aggregate maximization of something important and worse if they
result in less. The important something to be maximized (the "maximand") was "happiness" for Jeremy Bentham, the founder of this
type of philosophy, which he named utilitarianism. For today's utilitarian analysts—and economic analysis of law, to the extent that it
is normative, is utilitarian[19]—the maximand is often "welfare," or
"preference satisfaction," or indeed "wealth." Maximization is an
aggregative procedure, so the "welfare" to be maximized is aggregate "social welfare," or the "wealth" to be maximized is aggregate
"social wealth," and so on.

Utilitarian/economic/welfare theories of contract, of whatever
sub-species, adhere to, elaborate, debate, and refine a set of premises ultimately stemming from Bentham:

(1) Consequentialism, which means that from an ethical point of
    view, results are what matter. This premise results in a charac-
    teristic primary focus on incentive structures.

(2) Aggregation and maximization of the sum of welfare (or
    whatever the maximand is that is sought; for Bentham it was

"happiness"), which means that from an ethical point of view, the summation of something is what matters. Or as economic theorists often say, it is the "size of the pie" that matters, not the individual slices thereof;[20] and as economic theorists also often say, "distributional considerations" do not come into their theory.*

(3) Individualism: Community values that do not reduce to the values of individuals do not have a place in this theory.[21]

(4) Subjectivism: The input into the social sum that is to be maximized is the actual subjective value of the maximand to *individuals*. Since subjective value cannot be accurately ascertained by an observer, normative economic analysts must rely on proxies to reveal how individuals actually value things. An important proxy is "revealed preference": what can be thought to be revealed to the observer by the behavior of individuals. Another important proxy tends to be an assumption that individuals' behavior is "rational," where rationality refers to self-interested maximization.

(5) Self-interest: Utilitarianism has a distinctive premise of self-interest. Roughly stated, the premise is that individuals are motivated by self-interest as subjectively experienced by themselves; and that self-interest so experienced impels indi-

---

*Richard Craswell in his "Ballade of Distributional Considerations" makes this recurring statement into a refrain:

What do economists study today?
Anything anyone wants to pursue:
Monarchs of all that they care to survey,
Subjects beyond their dominion are few.
Still, there is one that they often eschew,
Leaving this caveat standing astride
Much of what legal economists do:
"All distributional issues aside."

. . .

Sir, if I earned just a dollar or two
Each time I heard that expression applied,
Life would be bliss with the wealth I'd accrue
(All distributional issues aside).

—R. B. Craswell, JOURNAL OF LEGAL EDUCATION, vol. 39, no. 1, 54 (March 1989).

viduals to maximize welfare (or personal wealth, happiness, preference-satisfaction, or "utils"—or whatever the maximand is for the particular version of theory).[22] Thus, the premise has two aspects: one being the nature of self-interest (it equals maximizing something that one desires to possess or experience); and the other the core function of self-interest (self-interest is what motivates individuals). The self-interest premise may be regarded as behavioral, or as psychological, or as theoretical. When an analyst treats the premise as theoretical, he will say that people are not in real life solely self-interested maximizers, but that this is the proper premise to use when doing political or ethical theory; and the analyst will often call this premise "rationality." Many utilitarians, however, including many economists, believe that people actually are self-interested maximizers in real life. In this case, the premise is more psychological if the analyst thinks that individual psychology creates the motivation, and more behavioral if the analyst is more interested in the objective observation and characterization of behavior, whatever the psychology behind it.[23]

(6) Empiricism: Utilitarianism has an important empirical aspect, stemming from its consequentialism. To know whether an action (or rule) is good, we need to know how much of the aggregate maximand it produces; and we need to be able to compare alternatives to see which will produce the highest aggregate sum.

(7) Commensurability: Utilitarians (including economic analysts) tend to accept that there is only one kind of value, so that everything we want to evaluate can be arrayed on a scale as yielding more or less of that maximand. For many lawyer economists, the unit of value is money.[24]

(8) Economic efficiency and the allied concept of externality: Both these concepts are famously difficult to define.[25] Roughly (very roughly) speaking, "efficiency" refers to a situation in which scarce resources are allocated to the actors who value them

the most and/or will create the most social value by controlling their use (often by propertization). "Externality" refers to costs or benefits that are not within the scope of the segment of the social world of resource allocation otherwise chosen for evaluation of efficiency; and the statement that externalities should be internalized means (roughly) that the scope of the segment of the social world chosen for such evaluation should be expanded to include the costs and benefits that are otherwise seen as externalities.

(9) Rule-utilitarianism: Most welfare theorists in legal realms, including contract law, are rule-utilitarians rather than act-utilitarians, meaning that instead of evaluating individual acts by their consequences they evaluate existing or possible legal rules as incentive structures, to see which rules or rule-sets will result in social welfare maximization.

Beyond Autonomy and Welfare Theories

As I mentioned at the beginning of this chapter, there are at least two contemporary attempts to move beyond autonomy and welfare theories, rather than just to critique them. One, reliance theory, is elaborated primarily in the work of Patrick Atiyah, who argues that a better normative basis for contract should refer to restitution and reliance, rather than to expectation or promising. The other, neo-Aristotelian theory, has been elaborated primarily by James Gordley, who argues that both prevalent theories of contract are mistaken in seeking to ground contractual obligation in freedom of choice alone (whether it is called free will, as in autonomy theory, or preference satisfaction, as in welfare theory). Instead, although contract must be consensual, it must also be in the service of further ends, ends that serve the good life for human beings.

Reliance Theory

In contract law, "reliance" refers to the circumstance in which one party has expended money or otherwise changed position in anticipation of the other party's fulfillment of her promise. Premodern legal systems did not enforce contracts based entirely on promises to be performed in the future. (Those are the contracts that we now call purely executory: each party promises to do something in the future.) Various modern writers have considered justification for enforcement to be weak when one party breaches a contractual promise before the nonbreaching party has changed position in reliance on that promise. The primary contemporary champion of this position was Patrick Atiyah. Atiyah found no convincing justification for awarding damages for breach of contract absent reliance by the nonbreaching party, and consistently argued that contemporary legal practice in fact only rarely awards damages absent such reliance.

With regard to justification, Atiyah held that enforcing purely executory contracts was "only justifiable on the assumption that we have already distributed a property-like entitlement to the promisee: the promisee is entitled to the benefit of the promise, and the promisor is not entitled to change his mind."[26] Contrary to the position of writers such as Peter Benson and Stephen Smith, Atiyah firmly rejected the assumption that a property-like entitlement passes to the promisee upon the making of a contract, finding no moral principles upon which such an assumption could be based.[27] With regard to damages in practice, Atiyah said that regardless of traditional liberal theory, which holds otherwise, executory contracts without reliance are only rarely enforced.[28] Interesting philosophical debates are joined between those who share Atiyah's position and those who hold that purely executory contracts are justifiably enforceable, but neither side endorses enforcement of obligations that are imposed by one party upon the other without consent.

Neo-Aristotelian Theory

James Gordley has contributed a thorough scholarly overview of the Aristotelian theory of contracts that evolved out of Aristotle's ethics as mediated through Roman law and the writings of Thomas Aquinas and other scholastic writers.[29]

From an Aristotelian point of view, contracts are justified to the extent that they foster the virtues that enable people to realize the good life for human beings. Gift transfers are justified to the extent that they foster the virtue of liberality, and exchange transfers are justified to the extent that they foster the virtue of commutative justice. Prudence is the virtue that leads people to make the right choices in light of the best life for human beings. Neo-Aristotelian philosophy starts from "the idea that human beings have an end, a manner of life in which their human potentialities are realized."[30] The Aristotelian virtues represent "an acquired capacity to choose rightly."[31] Human actions and social structures, such as contract law, should be justified by looking to the extent that they promote development and exercise of these virtues. According to Gordley, "the details of contract law must be understood in terms of the purposes served by contract, which must themselves be understood in terms of the ends of society and of human life itself."[32] Thus, contract law should be constructed and evaluated in light of its role in fostering the virtues of liberality, commutative justice, and prudence.

Gordley offers strong critiques of both welfare and autonomy theories, the primary theories that we have inherited from the rise of liberal political thought in the seventeenth and eighteenth centuries. Both of these theories are empty, according to Gordley, because they glorify choice for its own sake, rather than taking into account the question of which choices foster the good life for human beings.[33] Welfare theory glorifies choice for its own sake by honoring mere preference-satisfaction, rendering off limits the question, a preference for what? Autonomy theory does something similar by declaring autonomy to depend upon exercise of the will in the abstract rather than focusing on what it is that the will is directed toward doing.

In spite of the commitment of most contract theorists to either autonomy or welfare theories, Gordley finds that contract doctrines and enforcement practices do sometimes exemplify or foster neo-Aristotelian principles, though not explicitly. The neo-Aristotelian idea of "just price" (equality of exchange), derived from the principles of commutative justice and just distribution, can fit cases of unconscionability. Implied terms in contracts can also be explained by the principle of equality in exchange.

More on Welfare (Economic) Theories
The Role of Incentives

In light of its premises, summarized above, how does welfare/utilitarian/economic theory view contracts? Basic economic contract theory, as regards individuals, can be simply stated in terms of the facilitation of gains from trade via exchange. If two individuals each possess an entitlement that the other would value more highly, then each has an incentive to exchange with the other, and the result will be an increase in social welfare. Usually this can be put in terms of monetary value: if you have a table that you value at $100, and I would value it at $120, there will be a gain from trade if you and I enter into a contract whereby I pay you a sum more than $100 and less than $120 in exchange for the table.

The theory is more complex when we try to look at contract law from a rule-utilitarian point of view. From that point of view, we must ask, What are the rules of contracts that will maximize social welfare; that is, the sum of individuals' welfare? This endeavor requires looking at rules as creating incentives for actions by individuals (or, indeed, firms) and trying to determine which incentives will create the best outcome overall. The endeavor is further complicated because incentives interact with each other, and we are really looking for the entire set of incentives that will maximize social welfare.

Welfare theories explaining or justifying the infrastructure of contractual ordering and its particular doctrines and institutional practices focus on the aggregate benefit to society of having a system of enforceable exchanges, as well as on the particular rules that will best serve to structure such a system. Once it has been determined (by whoever has authority to do so) that a particular rule providing for enforceable contract (for such-and-such subcategory of promises, or for such-and-such subcategory of voluntary relinquishment of entitlements, etc.) has social benefits that outweigh its social costs, and indeed greater net social benefit than alternative rules that could be imagined, then it follows that it is a justifiable rule. When it is made binding on actors (by whoever has authority to do so), actors must follow the rule instead of reconsidering it case by case.

Given the premises of utilitarian ethical systems, especially the centrality of the role of incentives on rational actors provided by any particular governing rule, welfare theorists characteristically take an "ex ante" perspective. That is, they attempt to predict the results of implementing a particular rule. As they attempt to predict how legal rules will serve as incentives to actors, welfare theorists have the goals of deterring actors from breaching contracts (unless possibly a breach would be efficient), incentivizing actors to draft contracts that are well written (but not inefficiently over-detailed), and incentivizing actors to take care with whom they enter into a contract (without being too inefficiently over-fussy). In light of these interests, welfare theorists have been particularly interested in determining appropriate remedies for breach of contract and deciding what circumstances should trigger the use of any particular remedy.

An inquiry into the incentive effects of available legal remedies can get quite complicated. Under-compensation will be costly in light of the welfare rationale for instituting any particular rule of contract performance by, for example, deterring actors from entering into contracts that would result in net welfare gain because of risk-aversion due to the ineffective remedy available in case of breach. But over-compensation will also be costly in light of the underlying welfare rationale for the particular rule by, for example, encouraging actors to sue for breaches when performance would have resulted in more net welfare gain. The rub is that it is extremely difficult for a welfare theorist to determine what is "under" and what is "over" in this regard.

This kind of theory depends upon numerous predictions about how incentives will strike the class of actors governed by the rule. Assumptions need to be made about their risk-aversion, their state of knowledge (and the expense of acquiring it), and so on and so forth. Such assumptions, if they are ad hoc and not empirically based, are often known (pejoratively) as armchair economics. As the reader will observe in chapter 6, too often the economic justification for enforcement of boilerplate amounts to armchair economics.

Efficiency and Contract Law

Early law-and-economics theorists tended to assume that all the rules we already have are efficient. Therefore, they tended to explain (and also at the same time to justify) our current rules of contract law (such as consideration, expectation damages, and many more arcane doctrines) in terms of efficiency.[34] Early law-and-economics theorists also developed a "theory of efficient breach," which held that a party that could pay damages to its contractual partner and still come out ahead would contribute to aggregate social value by breaching the contract.[35]

Later theory moved away from the mere assumption that current doctrines are efficient into a more complex analysis of the effect of contract rules (and especially of rules regarding remedies for breach) on parties' incentives.[36] Ian Ayres and Robert Gertner, in an influential article published in the late 1980s, examined how the legal system's "default rules" (the background rules that govern transactions unless parties contract around them) provide varying incentives for parties to reveal information and thereby affect the efficiency of results.[37] Alan Schwartz examined the remedy of specific performance, in which a court orders a breaching party to deliver the performance promised, and concluded that the common-law system of using expectation damages (monetary compensation) as the remedy for breach of contract is likely to be inefficient if the parties themselves would prefer specific performance.[38] Richard Craswell examined the range of possible remedies and showed how they implicate a very complex set of incentives, including incentives to seek and investigate possible contractual partners, incentives concerning how much to rely on performance by the other party, incentives to take precautions against difficulties that might inhibit one's own performance, and many more.[39]

There is indeed a very rich literature on the economics of contract, but it is not my purpose to review it in depth.[40] For my purposes here, the main issue to examine is where (if anywhere) in economic theory the issue of voluntariness of transfer of entitlements is located. Where, if anywhere, do we find the relevance of consent and free choice? Unlike autonomy theorists, economic theorists do not often speak explicitly about voluntariness. Nevertheless, to be true to the premise of individual welfare-maximization or preference-satisfaction, there must be an assumed element of choice by individuals in accordance with their own welfare or preferences. Efficiency theorists must be assuming that those who transfer their entitlements to another in return for something else are voluntarily choosing to do so because they consider that they will be better off after the trade than before.

In light of this core assumption, there is always an information issue in economic theories of contract: how much information must a party have before it can be concluded that the contract is efficient, that it will result in gains from trade for the parties?[41] This information problem we could also call a problem of informed consent. What does a party have to know about the proposed trade before we can conclude that she is choosing to trade? (I will say more about this information issue in chapter 6.)

Property Rules and Liability Rules

To conclude this overview of welfare theory, it will be useful to take note of the theory of "property rules" and "liability rules" introduced by Guido Calabresi and A. Douglas Melamed in 1972.[42] Property rules permit an entitlement owner to choose whether or not to transfer his entitlement and to set the price for that transfer. Liability rules allow a third party (the government, or a court, or an agency . . . or indeed [perhaps?] a firm) to divest the owner of an entitlement without the owner's consent upon payment of compensation determined by the third party. The reason I want to take note here of Calabresi and Melamed's theory and terminology is this: *Much of the economic argument in favor of enforcing boilerplate tacitly assumes that it is perfectly acceptable to turn recipients' property rules (as holders of legal rights) into liability rules (rights that can be divested by a firm in return for compensation to the rights holder, such as a cheaper price for the product).*

In introducing the notion of entitlements protected only by liability rules, Calabresi and Melamed proposed that exceptions to the requirement of consent are appropriate in particular circumstances, provided compensation is paid. Consider, for example the recurring species of real property dispute in which a party mistakenly becomes a trespasser by building something that encroaches on neighboring land. If the normal property rule is applied, the trespasser will be enjoined to remove the building. In some cases, however (which may make their way into law school textbooks because they are exceptional), courts decide to let the building stand and simply charge the defendant a reasonable price for the land under it. In other words, plaintiff's normal property rule becomes a liability rule in this particular case.

Calabresi and Melamed theorized that property rules are the norm, and liability rules are literally the exception that proves (in the original sense of "tests") the rule. The general argument that property rules are best has two parts. The first, to which most of Calabresi and Melamed's attention was devoted, is that property rules are prima facie efficient because, since individual valuation is subjective and not easily ascertainable, the fact that an exchange has taken place at whatever price was agreed upon by the parties to the transaction signifies that the trade is welfare-enhancing (between the two parties, leaving externalities out of account).

The second argument, to which Calabresi and Melamed alluded more tentatively, is that property rules are superior from the viewpoint of individual autonomy—and this is of primary interest for my discussion here. Calabresi and Melamed took note of the accepted idea that when persons relinquish entitlements out of free choice, that action is autonomy-enhancing in a way that having entitlements "condemned" is not, even if compensation is paid. The exceptional cases put forward by Calabresi and Melamed, in which liability rules would be preferable, involve circumstances where property rules will not be efficient, and perhaps circumstances where property rules will not serve distributional goals.[43] In other words, Calabresi and Melamed suggested that there are exceptional cases in which the core value of autonomy should not trump serious inefficiency.

Calabresi and Melamed mainly elaborated one class of circumstances that render property rules inefficient: market failure caused by the high cost of coordination in situations where either buyers or sellers are numerous—cases involving the notorious "freeriders," who want to use a benefit without paying, and the equally notorious "holdouts," who want to be the last to sell and thus get an exorbitant price. This coordination problem in fact is the primary economic justification of eminent domain (condemnation with payment of just compensation) by the government. Governmental eminent domain belongs to the public realm; the justification for condemning houses to build roads, for example, is that holdouts would otherwise prevent the polity from providing physical infrastructure beneficial for all, or at least greatly raise the cost of doing so to all taxpayers.

By suggesting that private eminent domain could also be acceptable, in certain special circumstances when certain conditions hold, the work of Calabresi and Melamed may mark the beginning of a dissolution of the traditional public/private distinction by economic theorists, a topic I discussed in chapter 3. In the realm of private ordering, one private party is not supposed to be able to take the property of another, even with compensation. As Calabresi and Melamed noted, there have been sporadic exceptions where one private party has been allowed essentially to condemn the entitlement of another. If the exceptions were to become widespread practice rather than exceptions, however, they would sweep away the traditional rationale for the system of private ordering.

A Collapse of Property Rules into Liability Rules

As a result of widespread boilerplate schemes, are we now seeing a wholesale collapse of property rules into liability rules? The purported contracts in World B, in which agreement or free choice or consent is not present, except in some gerrymandered or problematic sense, seem to present a widespread practice in which entitlements of the recipient of boilerplate terms have de facto turned into liability rules.[44] Many welfare theorists do accept the assumption that in exchange for the onerous terms that recipients are made subject to by form contracts, recipients receive compensation in the form of a lower price for the product. In effect, this argument turns the recipient's rights, which we thought were covered by property rules requiring consent of the holder to accomplish divestment, into liability rules which can be condemned by a firm if compensation is paid.

Suppose we accept the economic argument that the divestment of entitlements that these boilerplate schemes effect is what recipients "would" have chosen, because the firm saves money and passes the savings on to the recipients. Unless we conflate hypothetical consent with actual consent, a topic I will take up in chapter 5, we must simply concede, using the terminology of Calabresi and Melamed, that the compensation argument turns recipients' property rule entitlements into liability rule entitlements. That is, divestment takes place without consent, but compensation is paid in an amount determined by the other party.[45] Calabresi and Melamed thought that liability rules would be appropriate only in exceptional circumstances, and the examples they cited involved coordination problems. But the argument that those who are subject to boilerplate are trading their rights for cheaper prices assumes that it is appropriate to allow property rules to decay into liability rules very generally.

What exactly is wrong with allowing property rules to decay into liability rules more generally, even if liability rules can be justified in the exceptional circumstances described by Calabresi and Melamed? The answer involves the conception of individual entitlement to which we remain committed, a commitment that is fundamental to our legal system. It is the conviction that an individual is in control of her entitlements for the purpose of advancing her own ends, a conviction that stems from the commitment to individual autonomy, at least in the sense of noncoercion.

Control over how and when one's entitlements are divested seems key to this embedded conception. From an economic perspective, entitlements enable me to plan my own wealth-maximization strategy. Beginning with my own subjective valuation of my entitlements, I am able to deploy them as I think best to enhance my position. From a noneconomic perspective, entitlements enable me to maintain a stable context of goods and services in my environment, against which I can constitute myself as a person and live my life. If all my entitlements—or even a considerable number of them, or even some few important ones—can be divested at any time without my consent, this disrupts the economic function of individual entitlement by ignoring my subjective valuation and the strategies I want to pursue to maximize my wealth in light of that valuation. From a noneconomic perspective (though this argument does not apply to firms considered as purely economic entities), these divestments unjustly invade personhood.

In sum, the Calabresi and Melamed argument for cautious implementation of liability rules in some situations involving deals between private parties was meant as an exception to a governing normative structure about private ordering, and not as a new general structure. Surely they did not imagine or countenance a sweeping transformation of property rules into liability rules.[46]

The Expanded Use of Liability Rules

Richard Craswell has shown that the implementation of liability rules could be useful in certain classes of contracts where courts would consider rewriting the terms when they declare a contract unconscionable.[47] Even if the recipient of the boilerplate did not consent to the terms, Craswell argues, there are cases in which it does not make sense to treat the recipient's entitlement as a property rule; that is, to hold that no contract is formed and unwind the entire transaction, allowing the recipient to retain his entitlement. It does not seem efficient or fair, for example, to create a situation in which poor people are unable to enter into enforceable contracts because they are recipients of onerous terms that can be found unconscionable.

To avoid this problem Craswell argues that in certain cases—but by no means across the board—it makes sense to treat a recipient's entitlement as a liability rule. But, significantly for the present discussion, rather than arguing that the recipient is automatically being appropriately compensated for the loss of his entitlements worked by the onerous terms, Craswell argues that at least sometimes an appropriate result will be that a contract is formed, but on the terms set by the court (*not* by the firm). In other words, under a liability rule entitlement for recipients, the court would enforce only those terms in the contract that are deemed reasonable, or import some other terms deemed reasonable to replace those written but not consented to. Because terms will the enforced against the recipient without her consent, Craswell's reasoning thus makes an exception to the general idea that recipients' rights are held under property rules. But his reasoning definitely does *not* endorse the idea that the amount to be "paid" under the liability rule can be entirely determined by the very firm that is "condemning" the recipients' rights.

Moreover, Craswell's reasoning supplying a liability rule applies only to a class of cases in which the firm deploying the boilerplate cannot inexpensively correct the lack of consent. If it can, the property rule in recipient's favor forms an incentive to do so, and under a welfare theory that incentive should be retained, because of the social value created by a system of individual consent. Thus, the firm has an incentive to correct the lack of consent because otherwise its contract waiving the recipient's baseline rights will be completely unenforceable and the recipient will retain her rights (for example, the right to sue the firm).

Some of the terms in contracts that inhabit World B, in particular many of the "clickwrap" and "browsewrap" schemes in use online, are not good candidates for liability-rule enforcement under Craswell's criteria. For one thing, sometimes it might not be costly to make clear the meaning of the term and so get actual consent. Even if a firm cannot easily correct the lack of consent, thus invoking potential liability-rule analysis, it is possible that when the reason lack of consent cannot be easily corrected is that a term is extremely difficult to explain, such as what it means to "warrant that all so-called moral rights have been waived,"[48] it is possible that such a term is a candidate for being judicially replaced by a reasonable term under the Craswell analysis. It is also possible that such terms should simply be excised, under the theory that it would be efficient to deter their use. In any case, the decision with regard to how to implement the liability rule is up to a court. The decision is not up to the firm, so the court should not simply defer to the firm. The court certainly should not simply assume that recipients are being compensated for loss of rights through cost savings.

Craswell identified another consideration that might lead to the enforcement of some contracts without consent—"institutional competence" of the courts. This is an argument that firms deploying boilerplate rights deletion schemes would like to advance if they can.

The argument goes like this: At least from the point of view of welfare theory, if it would be too hard for a court to come up with a reasonable set of terms to replace the unconscionable ones, it should not try. Rather, even where consent is lacking, the court should enforce the terms as written, because the injury to welfare from enforcement would likely be less serious than the injury to welfare from the court's intervention. Here Craswell joins forces to a limited extent with those who argue that from an economic point of view, boilerplate should almost always be enforced. For example, according to economic theorists, price regulation is difficult, so we should (they say) assume that it would be difficult (and lead to inefficiency) for a court to come up with a reasonable price to replace what is seen as a monopoly price. Rewriting warranties and other nonprice terms is thought to be equally difficult. For the economist, of course, the inquiry is comparative: the question is whether the difficulty encountered in arriving at the court-enforced price would result in that price deviating from an ideal competitive market price even more than the contract price does.

The suggestion Craswell makes here is a species of nonideal theory, a risk-of-error rule. The rule he suggests is: If our estimates of institutional competence tell us that a systemic admonition for courts to substitute reasonable terms for unreasonable ones will yield results that are worse for total welfare, on balance, than a systemic admonition for courts to let unconsented-to contracts (but only of the type where the seller cannot readily correct the nonconsent) be enforced as written, then we should let the suspect contracts be enforced as written. Autonomy in our nonideal world—however threatened it may be by such contracts—might be even more seriously undermined if courts intervene than if terms are enforced as written. Craswell suggests that this could happen, for example, if (accepting the assumption that firms pass on the savings that accrue from their use of onerous terms) court intervention on balance caused a rise in prices for essential products, so that some consumers were priced out of the market and could no longer obtain those products at all.

Craswell's attempt to explain why some enforcement of contracts lacking consent can be justified is the best attempt known to me, but it does not pretend to justify all of World B. Indeed, it applies only to a small subset of World B schemes. And, like all nonideal arguments, this one has weaknesses. One problem is that in each case someone must decide whether, and to what degree, courts are "institutionally competent" to replace unreasonable terms, or specific classes of unreasonable terms, with reasonable ones. That "someone" might be the court itself if it is asked to intervene in a particular suspect scheme. But courts may not be the best arbiters when it comes to evaluating themselves; courts might, for example, be reluctant to declare themselves institutionally incompetent.[49]

Autonomy is threatened by enforcement of unconsented-to obligations. But, as Craswell and others argue, autonomy is also threatened if no such obligations are ever enforced, because then those who are forced by circumstances to grant questionable consent (for example, those under economic duress) will be unable to enter enforceable contracts to buy what they want and need. The marketplace will in effect punish them by excluding them from opportunities to participate. Craswell wants us to see that autonomy may also be threatened if courts try to save unconsented-to contracts from being unenforceable by rewriting terms to make them reasonable, but it turns out that judges are not good at this task.

Now the question becomes which alternative is best (or least worst) for the cause of autonomy. It is a question that does not seem readily answerable in the abstract. Judges may be better at the task of rewriting terms than Craswell fears. Courts faced with questions like this may indeed be inclined to investigate, even if the investigation is nonideal, rather than merely deleting terms on a haphazard basis, or else presuming that boilerplate instantiates freedom of contract.*

Conclusion: The Persistence of the Core Notion of Voluntariness

This chapter has provided an overview of contract theory, especially of its main branches, which are based either on autonomy or welfare, as well as an overview of some aspects of welfare (economic) theory. These overviews are intended as background to the following chapters, in which I consider to what extent boilerplate can be understood and evaluated within prevalent views of contract. As is evident, contract theorists (except for welfare economists) do not for the most part investigate whether or not boilerplate can be justified under their theories; and welfare economists often adopt a summary argument (the widespread metamorphosis of recipients' property rules into liability rules) the empirical basis and normative basis of which both remain dubious. (The empirical basis is dubious because we don't really know whether savings to the firm are passed on to recipients, and in the proper amount sufficient to "compensate" them. The normative basis is dubious because a wholesale metamorphosis of property rules into liability rules organized by the very parties that benefit from the metamorphosis is contrary to the commitments of our legal system regarding individual rights.)

I have offered this chapter because I believe that before investigating further (in the next two chapters) how the attempted justifications for boilerplate play out, it is important to have in mind what contract theory in general does and does not do with

---

*In chapter 9, I will develop an analytical framework which should be helpful for courts in performing this scrutiny.

regard to boilerplate. Accordingly, I have not tried to convey in detail the philosophical controversies surrounding the institution of contracts, but rather to show that boilerplate has largely not been incorporated into the theories of contract; and moreover, that the prospects for incorporating boilerplate appear quite dim because the philosophical theories of contract we now possess depend on the core notions of voluntariness, freedom of choice, or consent.

In sum, almost all contract theory is theory about World A. Economic theory is the only theory that takes serious cognizance of World B and tries to justify enforcement of its purported contracts, but, as I have already mentioned in chapter 2, and will pursue in more detail in the following chapters, those efforts depend on a distorted notion of voluntariness, or even on mere hypothetical rather than actual consent. If we reject autonomy theory per se, because of its central understanding of free will and reciprocity, and instead think about reliance or neo-Aristotelianism, we still cannot justify enforcement in World B. Reliance theory does not reject freedom but instead hopes to describe practice in a way that honors it. And it is hard to imagine a neo-Aristotelian construing a divestment of entitlements without the consent of a recipient as somehow contributing to the development of virtues in the recipient.

. . . .

Can Autonomy Theory (Agreement, Consent) Justify Boilerplate Deletion of Rights?

Strategies for Assimilating World B to Consent: The Devolution of Voluntary Agreement

Various commentators and scholars have accepted the challenge of trying to annex World B—the Boilerplate World—to the realms of justifiable contractual ordering by expanding the meaning of consent to cover boilerplate deployment procedures. Many of the transactions in World B use the word "agreement" because that is the traditional word used for a contract, but, as I mentioned in chapter 2, one cannot (except in Humpty-Dumpty's world) make something into an agreement merely by using that word. At least, the term "agreement" is not used with its ordinary meaning when applied in this way.

The gerrymandering of the word "agreement," along with various other attempts to fit World B into the World A paradigm of voluntary transfer by agreement can be viewed as a process of devolution or decay of the concept of voluntariness. Agreement gets reduced to consent, then further reduced to assent. Next assent becomes "blanket assent" to unknown terms, provided they are what a consumer—an abstract general construct of a "consumer"— might have expected. This idea was apparently introduced by the great contract reformer, Karl Llewellyn. Llewellyn described "blanket assent" as follows:

> Instead of thinking about "assent" to boilerplate clauses, we can recognize that so far as concerns the specific, there is no assent at all. What has in fact been assented to, specifically,

are the few dickered terms, and the more broad type of the transaction, and one thing more. The one thing more is a blanket assent (not a specific assent) to any not unreasonable or indecent terms the seller may have on his form that do not alter or eviscerate the reasonable meaning of the dickered terms. The fine print which has not been read has no business to cut under the reasonable meaning of those dickered terms which constitute the dominant and only real expression of agreement, but much of it commonly belongs in.[1]

Llewellyn excluded "unreasonable" or "indecent" terms from enforceability under blanket assent. Leaving aside the question of what is meant by "indecency," blanket assent plays out in subsequent attempts to provide for exceptions to enforceability for unknown terms not within the recipient's "reasonable expectations," or for unknown terms not "radically unexpected." Assent then devolves to fictional or constructive assent, then further to fictional or constructive opportunity to assent, then to notice that the terms are there, then to fictional or constructive notice of terms. And, finally, to mere (allegedly efficient) rearrangement of entitlements without any consent or assent.[2]

What is the difference between agreement and the notions of consent or assent? Agreement seems to imply more of a two-sided process (the idea of two parties coming to an agreement, the idea of discussion or negotiation, what contracts scholars tend to call "dickered terms"). Consent seems to imply instead a one-sided process, in which one party proposes and the other says OK. Assent seems similar but still more passive. It may also carry less of an implication regarding the information that the recipient is required to have before the assent is valid (we speak of "informed consent" but not of "informed assent").[3]

Insurance contracts were the first in which scholars took notice of the issue of "adhesion."[4] A recurrent problem with insurance contracts is that the agent describes the coverage to the insured and the insured purchases the policy, but then when the policy comes in the mail it is full of fine print that may severely undercut the coverage that the insured thought she was buying. The courts developed a "reasonable expectations" doctrine to provide the coverage that the insured expected (if she expected "reasonably," of course, an "if" that poses a serious problem for the court charged with decided what it is that is reasonable to expect).[5]

The development of the "reasonable expectations" doctrine in insurance contracts can be viewed as a subsequent incarnation of Llewellyn's "blanket assent." In the 1970s there was movement in academic circles to extend to a wider range of transactions the limitation of enforceable boilerplate to terms that are within recipients' reasonable expectations.[6] This idea found its way into the second Restatement of Contracts, in which the American Law Institute suggested to courts that a recipient should not be held to be "bound to unknown terms which are beyond the range of reasonable expectation."[7] With very rare exceptions, courts have not taken up this suggestion, and the doctrine of "reasonable expectations" remains limited to insurance contracts.

"Reasonably Expected" or "Not Radically Unexpected"?

Some contemporary contracts scholars wish to justify enforcement of boilerplate by arguing that actions (or inactions) and mental states assumed to be typical of recipients can be interpreted as actual (not fictional or constructive) consent. Perhaps the best-known advocate of such a position is Randy Barnett. Barnett argues that people can consent to be legally bound even if they don't know what the terms are, so long as the terms are not "radically unexpected."[8] This reasoning, which, if you are not a contract theorist, might remind of you of buying a pig in a poke, is claimed to work equally well for terms that come later (after you have ordered the product and your credit card has been charged) as for terms that are presented with the product but which you don't read. Barnett understands consent to include willingly purchasing something that presents a risk, or purchasing something the value of which is unknown. According to Omri Ben-Shahar, another writer adopting this view, an analogy would be purchasing a lottery ticket.[9]

But the lottery analogy is inapt. In buying a lottery ticket you hope to win a prize, but your possible loss cannot exceed the price of the ticket, whereas a boilerplate rights deletion scheme may involve significant unknown losses of your entitlements (for example, your right to sue a firm for consequential damages if the product destroys your computer and your data). The theorist who wants to endorse this type of argument has to assume that those who receive boilerplate must realize that it probably contains divestment of significant entitlements.[10] (That assumption may well be wrong. For example, recipients of arbitration clauses typically don't know that the clauses erase the legal availability of jury trial and class actions.)

Of course, the notion of radical unexpectedness creates a big problem for courts. When a recipient who has been harmed by an unread boilerplate clause presents the purported contract to a court and asks that the clause be excised, invoking unconscionability or some other oversight doctrine of contract law, what principles or procedures can the court use to decide whether the term is radically unexpected? Judges are ultimately pretty much on their own here.[11] For a recipient wishing to excise an onerous clause, "*radical unexpectedness*" seems to be a more stringent standard than "not reasonably expected," but either way, these expectation theories do not make for a predictable jurisprudence.

Moreover, it is important to realize that reasoning in terms of expectation can itself often obscure an important point. If a draconian form of governance prevails in which many bad practices exist that unjustly allow harm to citizens, citizens will empirically come to expect the harm. Nevertheless, from a normative point of view, they are still being unjustly treated. The issue is, or should be, exploitation, rather than expectation.

Confusion is very likely here, because the term "expectation" can be ambiguous. It can mean normative rather than empirical expectation; that is, "expectation" can be used to characterize the just practices that a citizen has a *right* to expect. Some courts intuitively interpret expectation at least partly in this normative sense, whereas others are resolutely empirical in their interpretation ("surely everyone knows by now that unpleasant clauses lurk in boilerplate"). The ambiguity of "expectation" makes for murky and unpredictable jurisprudence.

The Search for Actual Consent
(by Means of the Objective Theory of Contract)

The objective theory of contract holds that a person in the position of offeror (and would-be promisee) is entitled to understand the person in the position of offeree as agreeing (promising) to enter into a contract on the terms proposed, if a "reasonable" person in the position of the would-be promisee would understand the words and conduct of the offeree as signaling consent or agreement to the terms proposed by the offeror. When applied to the deployment of boilerplate by a firm, let's say Apple, the objective theory of contract would ask whether a "reasonable" party in the position of Apple would be entitled to understand my words and behavior with regard to the AppleCare boilerplate as acceptance on my part of its boilerplate terms. (For a sample of this boilerplate, see page 112.)

In my view, the objective theory of contract is akin to the objective theory of language. If someone utters certain words, his meaning depends upon social understanding, not whatever he intended inside his mind—always assuming that relevant features of immediate context are taken into account, not merely words alone. (For example, "Yeah, right," uttered in a certain tone of voice, does not mean "Yes, that's true.") Analogously, the objective theory of contract holds that if a "reasonable" person would understand the words and actions of another, in context, to be consent to a deal, the deal is deemed consented to, no matter what was actually inside the mind of the other.

In my view, the "reasonable" person in this formulation should be interpreted as one socialized into a particular form of life that is relevant under the circumstances. So, can we say that Apple and I are socialized into a particular form of life such that Apple is entitled to conclude that, in the circumstances of my receipt of its boilerplate, I am agreeing to the terms in it? Such an assumption cannot be lightly made, to say the least. Yet that is what Barnett (and others) do in their attempts to convince us (and courts) that boilerplate is objectively consented to.

In my view, it doesn't make much sense to consider firms that deploy boilerplate as having been socialized into a common form of life with those who receive their boilerplate. The objective theory of contract applies more readily to a situation in which there are mutual understandings among a community of traders; that is, for situations where established usages in commercial trading prevail. It makes sense to assume that such a community's members are speaking a common language, and that, moreover, inferences to be drawn from behavior as well as words are mutually intelligible, whereas in consumers' dealings with firms that deploy boilerplate that assumption does not make sense. The objective theory of contract therefore is not applicable to boilerplate. (It works better for the way commercial trades may have existed at the time this theory developed; and it works better for interpreting commercial contracts in light of usages of trade that are common to those who participate in a particular trading community.)

As I have described in chapters 1 and 2, the circumstances in which boilerplate is received differ. In cases in which recipients do not know of the existence of the boilerplate—a circumstance that I call "sheer ignorance"— certainly we cannot say that recipients are objectively consenting because the firm can reasonably believe that they are doing so. On what grounds could the firm reasonably believe that? If I have no idea that there are terms interior to a website—regardless of whether or not a judge would consider that it would not have been excessively difficult for me to click on some small link to access them, and that I therefore had an opportunity to see them—then the firm cannot understand my lack of knowledge as signaling that I am consenting. Similarly, in so-called rolling contracts (also known as "money-now-terms-later" contracts) no theory of joint socialization could credibly conclude that someone who doesn't know that terms are coming later is signaling that he means to be bound by the terms that haven't arrived yet and that he doesn't know will arrive. Firms know that recipients do not see these terms, so even if we did think that firms were socialized into a common form of life with recipients, a firm would not be "reasonable" in concluding that by not protesting against the unseen terms, recipients are signaling consent.

Because of the possibility of sheer ignorance, "browsewrap" and "rolling contracts" cannot be assumed to yield obligation by invoking the objective theory of contract. The same conclusion applies to idiosyncratic procedures, such as "By walking past this sign you have agreed. . . ." The primary social meaning of such actions is not "signaling agreement," so a "reasonable" party in the position of the firm that put up the sign (or otherwise declared some arbitrary procedure to signal consent), even if socialized into a common form of life with recipients, cannot purport to understand such behavior as constituting consent to its terms.

Clicking "I Agree"

Now consider the more difficult case of the recipient who clicks "I agree" on her computer screen before being allowed to proceed with a transaction. Here we do not have sheer ignorance that there are terms that the firm wants the recipient to be bound to; and clicking "I agree" is not an idiosyncratic procedure. Nevertheless, is a firm justified in concluding that by clicking "I agree" the recipient actually is consenting to be bound to its terms?

Those who click are almost certainly not thinking about, or intending to consent to unread—or, even if read, not understood—terms that may deprive them of important legal rights that they might not know they have and probably don't consciously think they will ever need. Heuristic biases, which apparently are powerful and not readily escapable, tend to make us underestimate risks to ourselves and fail to consider situations that may result in future harm.

Can we retreat to a more objective standard characterization of receipt of boilerplate, positing what it is that a "reasonable" recipient should be deemed to have understood by his own act of mindless clicking? If so, how should a court construct this reasonable recipient? One could say that a reasonable recipient in this culture would be likely to know (if she did think about it) that firms are in the habit of exploiting consumers with boilerplate terms and thereby depriving them of important legal background rights. To assume that such hypothesized *knowledge* would ipso facto amount to *consent* to a waiver of such rights is, at best, a very uneasy assumption. (Hypothetical consent is further discussed below.)

Proponents of boilerplate might want to support their case with the objective theory of contract discussed above rather than trying to analyze what recipients "really" are thinking. But the objective theory of contract does not help in the attempt to construe clicking "I agree" as consent to the terms of boilerplate, because that theory of contractual consent does not relate to the reasonable understanding of the party who is (or is not) going to be deemed to be consenting,[12] but rather to the reasonable understanding of the other party, the one who is going to rely on the consent to claim that there is a deal. The objective theory of contract would have us look at the reasonable understanding of the firm, not the recipient. It seems unlikely that firms are socialized in the same language/behavior community with recipients to such an extent that firms are justified in believing that clickers are consenters in the way that they would need to believe this (reasonably) in order for a court to hold that a recipient consented under the objective theory of contract.

The Tension between Objective Theory and Autonomy

The objective view of consent traditionally used in legal analysis of contractual contract—the objective theory of contract—relies on the nature of language and communication. This language theory is in tension with the autonomy theory of contracts, which relies on the free will of the individual. Autonomy theory has a subjective basis (or better, a basis internal to personhood); that is to say, free will is not a matter of community acquiescence and is not understood as dependent on community attribution.[13]

By contrast with contractual consent, the notion of informed consent (to surgery, for example) relies squarely on autonomy theory, which is why the information required about what is happening to the patient must be detailed and understood by the patient before consent will be deemed to exist.[14] The objective theory of contracts does not require the subjective understanding that informed consent requires. Nevertheless, autonomy theory is the primary theory for fostering exchange transactions in which the state is justified in divesting a breaching promisor of a property entitlement. Because the institution of contract is still justified primarily on the basis of free will (individual autonomy), the objective theory of contract causes a fissure in contract theory, roughly between internal and external views of intention. Although I believe this fissure has been known to contracts theorists, it has been latent. Boilerplate focuses our attention on that fissure and brings it to the fore.

Leaving aside this fissure, however, and supposing that objective theory—basically the theory of meaning in its behavioral and social context—is the right way to look for consent in the case of clicking "I agree," it nevertheless is true that we do not have a clearly understood meaning of clicking "I agree," a fully socially accepted meaning, such that any hearer socialized into our form of life could be expected to take that meaning at face value. Rather, the meaning of clicking "I agree" is more analogous to a contested concept. It is something that can have different meanings. In other words, one reason that a firm cannot "reasonably" understand all of its recipients to be consenting to its terms is that no one can. Especially in the light of the effect of prevalent (and well known) heuristic biases,[15] the firm that deploys boilerplate cannot, as a "reasonable" hearer, rightfully understand that all of its recipients' clicking *means* that those recipients are accepting everything that is inside the firm's boilerplate.

It is on the contrary well known, for example, that we do not properly estimate risks of harm to ourselves, so we (and a reasonable person in the position of the firm) should be able to infer that recipients would *not* properly evaluate cancellation of legal rights. I interpret the exceptions developed by scholars and courts for "indecency" or "unexpectedness" (whether or not "radical") as ways of groping for this conclusion. But would it not be better to face outright the fissure between autonomy theory and language theory inherent in contract discourse? Until we take that step, the arguments that clicking "I agree" amounts to actual consent fail to address our normative degradation.

Relational Boilerplate?

The fissure in contract theory may be evident even to some of the theorists who wish to validate boilerplate by claiming that clicking "I agree" does amount to contractual consent to boilerplate terms. Is there another arrow in their quiver, another way to achieve their desired result? Some boilerplate defenders are attracted to the idea that boilerplate is relational. They claim that those who click "I agree" are actually agreeing to a *relationship* with the firm, which relationship has the indicia of taking on whatever alternative legal universe the firm is propagating as part of the relationship.[16] Under such a relational theory, my relationship with my cell phone service provider, for example, has the indicia that the firm may fine me if I wish to end the service before two years have elapsed, while the firm may take advantage of provisions allowing it (but not me) to modify the terms unilaterally on its own initiative at any time and in any way that it wishes.[17] If we do decide to view a contract as a kind of relationship we should keep in mind that relationships are not necessarily beneficial, nor are they necessarily based on some sort of equality. Indeed, contractual relationships have the potential to be as dysfunctional and injurious as any other species of human relationship.

In discussions about agreements to enter into a relationship, and thereby all of its indicia and obligations, I have heard theorists analogize to the relationship of marriage. Whatever the indicia and obligations of marriage, one takes them on, known or unknown, when one says "I do." Nevertheless, the marriage analogy is inapposite here precisely because the relationship of marriage is considered risky enough and important enough that it is structured by the state.[18] Certain relationships must be juridical, because they involve human interests that are important enough to be placed in the care of the polity, and indeed their care is among the reasons why the polity is established: examples of such relationships include citizenship, parenthood, and (perhaps) marriage.

There are also juridical limits. One could not agree to a relationship of enslavement or vassalage, for example. Some of the indicia and obligations of the supposed "relationship" between recipients and the firm deploying boilerplate may fail the test of what is permissible in relationships between private parties. I believe, for example, that allowing the firm unrestricted modifiability while the recipient remains bound by the original terms of a contract may well fail that test, and I also believe that deleting all remedies (in practical effect) for a firm's misbehavior, which is what the contracts of many camps and tour companies claim to accomplish, does fail that test.[19]

If we are to consider the contract between the firm and the recipient as establishing a relationship, we must not forget that the relationship is one of power. It is not a relationship of equals, as contract mythology imagines, but rather more akin to a new kind of serfdom. When I gave a talk to some very capable law students about these matters, one of them said, "Even if a representative of AT & T came on my screen and negotiated with me about their terms, I would still be screwed," and the rest of the class nodded approval to his comment. Some recipients feel that they will inevitably be badly treated in their dealings with firms. That is not a good basis for finding a relationship that would presumptively and unquestioningly validate (almost all of) the firm's constricted legal universe.

The situation is complicated by the fact that in certain cases we are able to deal with firms more relationally after the fact. Banks impose fees for this, that, and the other, but the customer (if she is persistent and has the time to stay on the telephone) can often succeed in getting the charges reversed. A similar situation prevails with mistaken cell phone charges. It seems that cell phone service providers make mistakes in their favor sometimes, but the customer (again the customer who is persistent and has the time to spend on the telephone) can sometimes get the charges reduced if not reversed. One reason that this relation-after-the-fact situation complicates the picture is that it divides boilerplate recipients into two classes—those in the know who have time to spare for messy dickering, and everybody else. Those who can negotiate after the fact have a better relationship than those who cannot. The upshot is that the firm makes a lot of its money from those who cannot.

Constructive (As-If) Consent

So much for attempting to find actual consent in the actions associated with the receipt of boilerplate. The next stages in the progressive decay of voluntariness are "assent" and then "reasonable opportunity to assent." Opportunity to assent serves as fictional or constructive assent: a recipient can be held to terms *as if* he had passively assented to them, if he had a reasonable opportunity to be less passive and to read the terms (even if he did not do so).[20] When this issue comes before a court, it involves the learned judges in a debate about exactly what the website of the deploying firm looked like, and how likely the recipient was to see the link to the terms, and how many times the recipient would have had to click on different links in order to see them.[21] Here the notion of consent (or assent) has devolved to a species of mere notice. This species of notice is not *actual* notice, something the recipient did know, but rather fictional or constructive notice, something the recipient (in the judge's view) could or should have known but in fact did not.

It seems true enough that when terms in boilerplate divest recipients of important legal entitlements, having an opportunity to read the terms is better than having no opportunity to read them.[22] But "having an opportunity" does not come near to consent to the divestment. Even actual notice of something you don't approve of does not amount to consent. (Unless failure to object, or some other particularity of circumstance, can be understood to amount to acquiescence, which would take more evidence than the mere unknown presence of the offending term.) A fortiori, it would at least take a lot of mental gymnastics to argue convincingly that constructive notice is really tantamount to consent. I suspect that this cannot be accomplished. At least it hasn't yet been.

Hypothetical Consent: To the State, to Laws, to Boilerplate?

Many liberal political theories rely on hypothetical consent to arrive at justification of the political state based upon consent of the governed. (John Rawls's theory of justice is an example.*) It is disputed, of course, whether hypothetical consent is a proper procedure for arriving at the parameters of a just political state. But even if hypothetical consent is an appropriate procedure for justifying a form of political state, we are left with the question, can hypothetical consent also be an appropriate procedure for justifying individual contracts under the enforcement rules of the state?

Our consent to the state is hypothetical or weak at best, and our consent to the operation of the laws of the state upon us is also hypothetical or weak at best. It might be thought that because consent to boilerplate is dubious but allegedly no weaker, there is no problem, or no greater problem, with holding such contracts to be just as binding on us as are the laws of the state.

I question this line of thought. There is no easy parallelism between (on the one hand) consent to the state and consent to the bindingness upon us of the laws of the state, and (on the other hand) consent to terms imposed by firms using boilerplate. In a democracy, we have little opportunity to exist apart from the state, but we have voice to try to change the character of the state and the laws of the state. This is difficult in practice, but it is the bedrock commitment of democracy. By contrast, in boilerplate schemes that replace the entitlements of the state with the entitlements desired by firms we have exit (we can refuse to buy the product or service) but we have no voice. That is why these are called "take-it-or-leave-it" contracts.

A more important distinction between consent to the state and its laws and consent to boilerplate is inherent in the difference between public and private ordering. The laws of the state are supposedly established in the public interest and not in the private interest of a particular firm. Boilerplate schemes by their nature are in the interest of a firm and its market strategy and profits. We

* John Rawls, A THEORY OF JUSTICE (1972). By "liberal" I don't mean here the opposite of "conservative," but refer rather to the traditional western theories of political thought, based on the rule of law, consent of the governed, and private ordering by individuals exercising freedom of contract under a system maintained by the state.

should not routinely justify private schemes established by boiler-plate in the same way we justify public regimes established by the state. We cannot analogize from one to the other. (To do so leads to democratic degradation.)

Finally, at least in modern theories, the notion of consent when we are talking about justification of the state and its laws functions only as metaphor, a device to facilitate political reasoning. For example, John Rawls does not suggest that his "original position" exists in real life, but rather explains that it is merely a heuristic device intended to help us reason about the proper general principles applicable to a justifiable political state.* By contrast, the features of the state that are supported and justified by this sort of heuristic reasoning are justified only if they actually exist in practice, and not if they merely can be posited as a metaphor to assist reasoning. The rule of law, for example, is supposed to exist in practice in a justified state, not merely as a metaphor or a reasoning device; and to the extent that states fail to follow the precepts of the rule of law, they may be considered unjustified.[23]

The background theory that justifies exchanges under consensual transfers (contracts) is another example. A liberal state that failed to set up proper rules for enforcing those contracts that are instantiations of freedom of contract and for refusing to enforce those that are not, would not, at least in that respect, be a justified state.[24] The underlying theory of contract that indeed is derived from the general notions of the parameters and functions of a liberal state, particularly the notion of individual freedom, involves consent to divestment of individual entitlements by means of contract; and that consent is still meant to be real. Freedom of contract is not metaphorical, a heuristic reasoning device. It must exist in real life. Hypothetical consent does not substitute for real consent when it comes to freedom of contract.

---

*Rawls's "original position" is a situation in which we imagine that people come together to reason about justice under circumstances in which no one knows what his status in life would be in the hypothetical state under consideration. It is supposed to make it easier to formulate general principles applicable to all, whether well or poorly endowed, lucky or unlucky in life, etc. *Id.* at 3–5.

So, using the terms "agreement," "consent," "freedom of contract," and so forth for procedures that are not actually consensual in any normal sense causes normative degradation of the system. Efforts to assimilate World B procedures to the consent envisioned in World A remain unconvincing. Without mental sleight of hand—which, being a mental activity, we should perhaps call sleight of brain—delivery of boilerplate just does not ipso facto become freedom of contract.

But Should We (Must We Nevertheless) Settle for Less Than Real Consent?

US courts have validated as enforceable contracts many kinds of entitlement transfers that are prima facie seriously questionable on the issue of consent. I suppose we could conclude that the US courts, in so ruling on various kinds of adhesion contracts, have simply defined consent to mean a different thing in these situations than consent means in other contexts.[25] Otherwise one must conclude that US positive law is in the wrong.

In this book I start from the position that we should not conclude easily or unreflectively that our current situation is the best US positive law can do about this problem and that we must simply accept the normative degradation that the current situation is causing. In a thoughtful essay,[26] Brian Bix correctly observes that consent in the "robust sense expressed by the ideal of 'freedom of contract'" is arguably "absent in the vast majority of the contracts we enter into these days, but its absence does little to affect the enforceability of these contracts."[27] True. And I would add, this "robust sense" of consent expressed by the ideal of freedom of contract *is the sense upon which justification of enforcement is based.* But Bix says that we should live with this "shortfall in consent," because, "[a]mong other problems, making too many commercial transactions subject to serious challenge on consent/voluntariness grounds would undermine the predictability of enforcement that is needed for vibrant economic activity."[28]

I disagree with Bix and others who assume that the commercial importance of the present US regime means it must be accepted in toto. I think, rather, that the normative degradation the present regime is causing in the legal system is serious enough to necessitate careful analysis of the question before we decide that this is the best our legal system can do with the problem (i.e., that the US has the best of all possible legal regimes). One should not just assume, in other words, that any regime of coping with mass-market arrangements other than the one now in effect in the US would result in loss of predictability of enforcement and therefore diminution in "vibrant economic activity." These are empirical questions, after all. Other solutions might indeed result in *more* predictability in the operations of the system in practice. Other countries use solutions that differ in some respects, and their economic activity has not suffered from a lack of vibrancy on this account.

Although it has been a popular endeavor, the attempt to jigger the understanding of agreement or voluntariness or consent in order to sweep into its linguistic purview the vast majority of the items in World B cannot ultimately suffice. To be sure, the law has often in the past found a way to keep doctrinal categories in place by using the word "constructive" to assimilate the orange to the doctrinal apples.[29] If there are too many such doctrinal fixes, however, the law begins to look silly, unduly out of touch with reality, and perhaps full of traps for the unwary nonlawyer who just might want to take words at face value.

The law has so far survived a fair number of critiques of this nature. Nevertheless, the large scope of World B and the normative degradation it causes for the justification of enforcement when consent is lacking or seriously problematic is a much broader and deeper problem than most of the legal doctrines shored up by constructive fictions. It is ethically unsatisfactory, and therefore prima facie unjustified, to rest the legitimacy of the myriad contracts in World B on a constructive version of consent. Efforts to assimilate World B procedures to the consent envisioned in World A remain unconvincing. They remain at odds with the underlying commitment to a realm of private ordering instantiating the individual freedom that, according to traditional liberal theory, justifies the state's existence.

Boilerplate alternative legal universes simply do not assimilate to freedom of contract. They lead us instead to normative and democratic degradation.

Can Utilitarian-Welfare (Economic) Theory Justify Boilerplate Deletion of Rights?

The Contract-as-Product Theory
(the Law-and-Economics View of Boilerplate)

Hill v. Gateway 2000 is a well-known decision in which recipients of a boilerplate rights deletion scheme tried to persuade a court to declare an arbitration clause invalid so that they could bring a class action against a computer company. (Recall that arbitration clauses eliminate the possibility of aggregative remedies, primarily class actions.[1]) In holding against the recipients, dismissing them from court, and compelling arbitration, Judge Easterbrook of the US Seventh Circuit Court of Appeals said that the plaintiffs were objecting to the "bundling of hardware and legal-ware"—a practice to which the judge not only had no objection but which he, on the contrary, heartily endorsed.[2] "Bundling of hardware and 'legal-ware'" refers to the idea that from an economic point of view, *the terms that come with a product are part of the product itself.*

This is the view that I call contract-as-product. The contract-as-product view attempts to sidestep the issue of consent by denying that a particular set of contracted terms is an individual transaction requiring consent in the traditional sense. This view instead argues that whatever adhesion terms accompany the purchase of a product should actually be conceived of as part of the product. This is now the prevailing contemporary view among US proponents of law and economics—that is, the view of a substantial sector of the welfare branch of contract theory.[3] It is espoused, for example, by

Douglas G. Baird, a former Dean of the University of Chicago Law School, who argues as follows.[4] (This view causes Baird to think that the debate surrounding lack of consent to boilerplate terms is puzzling.)

> The warranty that comes with your laptop computer is one of its many product attributes. The laptop has a screen of a particular size. Its microprocessors work at a particular speed, and the battery lasts a given amount of time between recharging. The hard drive has a certain capacity and mean time to failure. . . . Then there are the warranties that the seller makes (or does not make) that are also part of the bundle. Just as I know the size of the screen, but nothing about the speed of the microprocessor, I know about some of the warranty terms that come with the computer and remain wholly ignorant of the others. . . . To say that a product comes with boilerplate is to say that one of its attributes, along with many others, is partially hidden and is one over which there is no choice on the part of the buyer. But why should any of this raise special concern? . . . Hidden product attributes over which sellers give potential buyers no choice are a commonplace, necessary and entirely unobjectionable feature of mass markets.[5]

The contract-as-product view originated in work by Arthur Leff[6] (who called it "contract as thing") in 1970 and Lewis Kornhauser[7] in 1976. As Baird makes clear, this view rejects the idea that standardized form contracts should be considered in terms of "the rights of A against B," as in traditional contract law, because that framework "is out of touch with how mass markets work."[8] As I have noted in chapter 4, however, the paradigm of two individuals with rights against each other is still paramount in contract philosophy and still forms the basic rationale of contract law. It is still the reasoning by which contractual divestment of entitlements is justified.

Baird suggests that the traditional focus of contract theory upon individuals and their bargains is not applicable to boilerplate. He proposes, instead, that if boilerplate is over-reaching, the legislature can prohibit specific clauses that are deceptive and/or exploitive, just as it might regulate other practices that are deemed deceptive or exploitive, such as payday lending or door-to-door sales.[9] He also suggests that the legislature can make waivers or the curtailment of recipient rights more difficult to accomplish in certain cases, for example in the attempted curtailment of warranties,[10] a topic that I will discuss in chapter 9. Baird implies that the way to manage World B is to implement piecemeal legislative remedies for clauses that seem abusive, a topic I will take up in chapter 12.

We could also, taking seriously the idea that these clauses are really part of the product, regulate them under tort law as potentially defective or dangerous products. In other words, we could consider onerous or oppressive "legal-ware" as posing product safety issues instead of as posing issues of contractual consent under a system of private ordering. I will consider this possibility in chapter 11.

Meanwhile, let's continue exploring the notion of contract-as-product.

The Role of Choice (Consent)

How does choice or consent by the recipient enter into the contract-as-product view, if at all? Here the assumption seems to be that the choice to purchase a product in a free market assimilates to a choice to be bound by the terms inside the product, and thereby to a choice to relinquish baseline legal rights without knowing specifically what those rights are. According to the reasoning espoused by Baird (and many other adherents of the prevalent law-and-economics view of boilerplate), relinquishing one's right to bring a class action in court, without knowing that that is what one is doing, is conceptually indistinguishable from purchasing a computer without knowing that its hard drive will fail in two years.

Thus, the contract-as-product view has apparently not relinquished consent *in theory*—this it cannot do and still purport to be in the realm of contract—but it has attenuated the idea of consent. It diverts us into asking questions about what it means to choose to purchase a product in a free market rather than what it means to perform an individual act of choice about divestment of entitlements. For contract-as-product proponents, the main question about "legal-ware" bundled with a product becomes an efficiency question: is a boilerplate scheme of standardized terms internal to a product efficient? In trying to answer the question, the problem of information available to recipients, at least in some segment of the market, becomes important, as I will discuss shortly. And therefore, lurking in the background, the problem of consent is in some sense still present; but it is deflected.

How does the information available to recipients mesh with the problem of consent? Knowledge on the part of an individual recipient that his or her rights are being divested does not by itself amount to voluntary transfer or consent, but it certainly seems to be a necessary precursor to it, because divestment of rights without information that divestment is happening—the scenario that I called sheer ignorance in chapter 2—seems to preclude description of such a transaction as one that involves individual consent. The general problem is: How much information, and what kind of information, must a recipient possess in order for passive behavior to be adjudged consent?

In pursuing the goal of efficiency (that is, welfare maximization), economic theories of contracts, in particular the contract-as-product theory we are examining here, tend to submerge the issue of autonomy in transfer by collapsing the requirement of actual choice to hypothetical choice. That is, the economist tends to view what the (properly informed, economically rational) consumer "would" have chosen to maximize his welfare as being equivalent in analytical procedure to what real people do choose. (Indeed, as I discussed in chapter 4, some economists eliminate the topic of choice by endorsing, usually implicitly, the substitution of liability rules for the recipients' property-rule entitlements, on the ground that economically rational recipients would have chosen this scheme.)

In order for a consumer to make a free choice, that consumer must have some level of information. Even if autonomy is collapsed to hypothetical choice or to liability-rule nonchoice, these stand-ins still relate to what a properly informed consumer would have chosen, so the problem of information as precursor to choice does not disappear. Thus, a major problem for economic theories of form contracts is how to address the issue of information, the idea that market demand is supposed to represent choice by consumers based on knowledge, even if we are to look at consumers in the aggregate rather than one at a time. Appropriate market functioning depends upon an acceptable understanding of the basis of demand. A market is not functioning properly if demand is based on completely erroneous notions about what the product is.

The Role of Information Asymmetry and Heuristic Bias

The expression "information asymmetry" refers to the fact that consumers often have very little information to go on when making choices in markets. (Information is asymmetrical because the firm has much more of it than the recipient.) Because information asymmetry is so prevalent in the context of imposing and receiving boilerplate, it is problematic to equate this nonunderstanding behavior and context to the ordinary conception of consent. It may be quite rational for someone not to try to read clauses that she knows she will not understand, and by far the large majority of recipients do not read the forms they receive. This means that there is very little information about the clauses in boilerplate that gets through to even a subset of consumers.

Moreover, as I discussed in chapter 2, we are prone to pervasive heuristic biases. An important one is our inability to assess future risks in ways that would be considered economically rational. Even if a recipient reads a boilerplate clause stripping him of his right to sue, and even if he then understands that this is what the clause does, he still would be very unlikely to take it seriously, because he is very unlikely to think the risk applicable to him. We don't take seriously a risk that we will ever need to sue anyone. These two problems—heuristic bias and information asymmetry—render erroneous the assumption of economic rationality.[11]

The Role of Market Assumptions

Adherents of the contract-as-product theory, to the extent they use it to declare boilerplate rights deletion schemes valid and enforceable, most often rely on the presence in the market of at least some recipients who can and will read and understand the terms of boilerplate.[12] These knowledgable consumers will drive the market; that is, their correct evaluation of the "product" will set the appropriate price for all purchasers, and cause the market to function properly. This is an assumption about the amount and kind of information available to some sector of the market. Because of pervasive information asymmetry and heuristic biases, however, the assumption that information available to some segment of the market will influence demand for the "product" (i.e., decisions to purchase the product based on informed choice by individuals in this segment), is likely to be false for a large number of World B composite "products."

In addition, the contract-as-product theorist must also assume that the firm cannot segment the market, charging one price to those who do understand the terms that are part of the "product" and another price to those who do not. This assumption too may be false for a substantial portion of World B schemes. Another way of putting this is that if the market is to function efficiently we must suppose that at least some subset of "enough" marginal consumers must properly evaluate the quality of the bundled product and then use this information to drive an appropriate structure of market demand. But this assumption may be false.

Actually, then, we must make four assumptions in order to validate contract-as-product theory. (1) At least some appropriate subset of consumers must be well enough informed to understand (in Baird's computer example) the nature of the hard drive and the nature of the clauses that are being purchased, and this subset must factor that information into their demand for the product. We must also suppose that (2) other consumers are piggybacking on the knowledge of those who have the information needed for informed choice, which requires the further assumption that (3) the firm must charge the same price to all buyers. We must then further assume that (4) the market is structured such that demand influenced by consumer information can actually drive the efficient, welfare-maximizing provision of bundled hardware and "legal-ware."

Each of these four interlocking assumptions may or may not be true in practice in a given market. Thus, it is an empirical question, and not a matter of theory, in which cases the type of argument endorsed by contract-as-product theorists to validate World B transactions could be validly applied.[13] In spite of these welfare theorists' belief that they are being more attentive to the realities of practice than those contract philosophers who are still engaged with the rights of individual A against individual B, it seems likely that these welfare theorists are themselves focused on an ideal world that has only a tenuous relationship to much of actual practice.

To explicate this point, let's consider the contract-as-product proponents' necessary assumptions about market structure in a little more detail. The question whether a scheme of boilerplate terms is efficient must be explored in varying market contexts. In one set of contexts we assume that the scheme operates in a situation of market failure of some kind. In another set of contexts we assume that the boilerplate scheme is operating in a competitive market.

Entrenched information failure, due to information asymmetry and heuristic biases, is more likely than other kinds of market failure. Nevertheless, I would like to take the contract-as-product theorists' assumptions seriously and consider old-fashioned market failure as well; that is, we should consider monopolization and cartelization in addition to issues of information failure, even though monopolization and cartelization may be uncommon in markets governed by boilerplate rights deletion schemes.[14] If a boilerplate scheme is imposed by a monopolist or a cartel, or if for some other reason there is only one scheme available, it can be argued that its terms are not what the recipients would have chosen (or what those marginal well-informed consumers did wish to choose), and it becomes harder to argue that the terms, considered in conjunction with the product, maximize value or welfare to society.

If recipients cannot find out what the terms mean because of entrenched information failure (that is, information asymmetry that would be very difficult to correct), it is easy to argue that the terms are not what the recipients have chosen—they have not chosen anything—and probably not what they would have chosen if they were economically rational.

In the case of a boilerplate rights deletion scheme that waives the background rights granted and/or maintained by the state, it seems at the very least that the recipients' democratically chosen regime, in which they did have a voice (ideally), is being overridden by the scheme imposed by the firm, in which they do not have a voice. And where competing terms are not available, recipients do not have the usual market exit of "voting with their feet" since they cannot (still assuming a monopoly or cartel) turn to a competitor. In this case the argument for democratic degradation is apt: the firm has replaced sovereign power—the law of the state—with its own. It has done so for its own benefit, perhaps at the expense of the public. At minimum, it cannot be assumed that benefit to society as a whole is coextensive with benefit to the firm, so it cannot be assumed that such a scheme is efficient. Instead, boilerplate rights deletion schemes, in cases of less than competitive market structure, tend to create democratic degradation. At least, they cannot be assumed *not* to, so they pose more of an issue than contract-as-product theorists will admit.

Turning to the other set of market contexts, let's posit that the market in which a boilerplate rights deletion scheme appears is actually competitive. In that case, would a boilerplate rights deletion scheme be presumptively efficient? Proponents of contract-as-product theory certainly seem to think so; recall that Baird wonders what the fuss is all about. But, even ignoring information failure, an analysis of the efficiency of a boilerplate rights deletion scheme in a competitive market would be more complex than Baird's unpuzzled attitude implies. The analysis would entail different starting points depending upon whether the competing firms each deploy a different boilerplate EULA ("End User License Agreement") or they all deploy the same one (industry-wide standardization).

If each of the competitive firms within a market has a different EULA, i.e., a different standardized scheme, recipients can reject one scheme in favor of another that they like better. In this scenario the scheme is chosen by the recipients, and thus the question whether they value it more than its competitors is not much at issue, assuming that we are confident that recipients (or at least an appropriate segment of them) can acquire and understand the information about the scheme and its effects on them. This still assumes, of course, that the firm must charge the same price and use the same terms with all.

Even so, such a scheme nevertheless supersedes one aspect of the law of the state; namely, the infrastructure of background rights recognized by law. Therefore, in this scenario we face the question (to be taken up in chapter 9) of to what extent the infrastructure of baseline entitlements (such as the right to redress of grievances) should be understood to consist entirely of rules waivable at will by those to whom their enactment is directed. There are strong non-economic arguments against treating all baseline entitlements as easily waivable. Even for the political economist, as I also discuss in chapter 9, an understanding of the legal infrastructure as consisting entirely of waivable rules could lead to inefficiency if the legal infrastructure represents a solution to a coordination problem. In that case, each firm wishes to "defect" for its own advantage, yet the coordination solution maximizes welfare.

Still assuming a competitive market, what if all the firms have the same EULA—that is, what if we see industry-wide standardization and not merely firm-specific standardization? In this circumstance, the recipient has a choice of firm but not a choice of scheme; the scheme is ubiquitous in its domain. There still may not be a clear-cut problem with choice, however, because since we are supposing that competition prevails, it may be that this is the set of terms that has won out in a competitive market. If it has won out, that means that if a different set of terms were offered, either in a previous stage of this market or hypothetically, the users and customers chose or would choose this set of terms, thereby forcing all firms to offer this set of terms in order to maintain their market share. In these circumstances we might not be too worried about choice, because we would suppose that choice has caused this set of terms to become the standard.

But once we raise the possibility of information failure, this conclusion is brought into serious doubt. Is it possible that imperfect information has caused market participants to choose an inefficient set of terms as the standard?[15] (That is, should we fear that the market has reached a "lemons equilibrium"?*) In such a case, choice would not imply an efficient outcome, and the normative persuasiveness of choice would be undermined by information failure. That is why, ultimately, the problem of information failure is more significant than the problem of old-fashioned cartelization or monopoly. Even in a competitive market, industry-wide standardization is likely to reflect a "lemons equilibrium" rather than what recipients "would" (if they had had sufficient information) have chosen. The "lemons equilibrium" is the result of a race to the bottom, in which, given information failure on the part of recipients, competition forces firms to offer progressively worse and more onerous terms.

At what point does information asymmetry vitiate choice? How much information a chooser must have before we consider his activity to be free choice is a difficult philosophical question, but at some point lack of information does vitiate free choice, as does the prominent problem of heuristic biases. We most likely don't understand that an arbitration clause causes our right to jury trial to vanish, and even if we do understand that, we think we will never experience injury because of a product or service, and never need to take the seller to court. Empirical studies—and amusing experiments—demonstrate that in fact people don't read form contracts.[16] Anecdotal evidence convinces me that even if people did read form contracts, most would not understand them.† There is plenty of evidence as well that even if people understand a risk, they fully expect that it will not materialize for them.[17]

---

* A "lemons equilibrium" occurs when no (or not enough) buyers can accurately assess the value of a product through examination before sale. Some sellers will be able to pass off lower quality as higher quality products, in which case buyers will choose the cheaper priced product and all firms will have to cut prices and lower quality in order to maintain market share. *See* George A. Akerlof, *The Market for "Lemons": Quality Uncertainty and the Market Mechanism*, 84 Q.J. ECON. 488 (1970).

†For example, I begin my contracts course with a packet of contracts and purported contracts, including a lot of boilerplate examples. Incoming law students have no idea that they have entered into these contracts. When they do read them because I've assigned them, it becomes clear they have no idea what an arbitration clause will do, or what a choice of forum/choice of law clause will do, or the possibility of a severe limitation of remedies, or that it is possible to eliminate user rights available under copyright law, etc.

The contract-as-product view holds that not everyone has to make the choice to buy a product under appropriate information in order to create the effect that product demand is structured to result in welfare maximization, but a significant subset must do so. In practice, however, such a subset of knowledgeable recipients may be hard to come by, even in markets we can determine to be competitive.

Conclusion

Contract-as-product is a theory subject to many parameters that will vary from market to market. It cannot suffice, therefore, to validate boilerplate in general, or even presumptively. We cannot assume that all markets in which boilerplate appears are competitive. We cannot assume that all markets in which boilerplate appears have a sufficient subset of consumers whose knowledge of the attributes of the composite product (terms plus functionality) will set the market price appropriately for all. Moreover, because we cannot assume that enough consumers are knowledgeable about the composite product, a competitive market may reach a "lemons equilibrium" in which firms must compete by offering their worst contract, not their best.

It would be very difficult for a court to try to evaluate the empirical assumptions upon which contract-as-product theory rests in order to see whether it should validate any particular boilerplate scheme. A blanket assumption that markets are competitive is unwarranted in any case. More important, however, is the probable falsity of any assumption of economic rationality and information acquisition by a subset sufficient to drive the market to efficient structure. The fact that it would be difficult for courts to evaluate boilerplate schemes empirically cannot mean that courts should conclude that they are all efficient. Rather, it means that contract-as-product theory does not provide the easy answer it claims.

your choice to your Financial Advisor. We will provide you with the specific Program Agreement ("Program Agreement") and any applicable descriptive brochure disclosure document for the Advisory Program that you have selected, and confirm in writing the fee for that program or service. Delivery of the specific Program Agreement to you will serve to confirm your direction to retain MSSB in accordance with all of the terms and provisions of that Program Agreement for your advisory account ("Account"). **By signing this Agreement, you agree to all of the terms and conditions of this Agreement. You also agree that all of the terms and provisions of the Program Agreements that you receive are incorporated by reference into this Agreement as though they were fully set forth herein when you signed this Agreement.** Thus, all of the terms of this Agreement, any specific Program Agreement that you receive from us for the Advisory Program that you have selected, and the Client Agreement for your Account (including the arbitration provisions contained in the Client Agreement and set forth in Section 7 below), will detail our mutual obligations regarding the Advisory Programs for Accounts that you open with SB.

For example, notwithstanding any language in the Program Agreements for the Advisory Programs listed in paragraph 4 to the contrary, where available and at our discretion, you hereby authorize us to accept your verbal authorization to close an Account or to change: (i) asset allocation investment models, third-party or affiliated portfolio Managers or Sub-Managers or investment products; (ii) between discretionary and non-discretionary versions of an Advisory Program (and between discretionary versions) where applicable; (iii) to/from a discretionary rebalancing version of an Advisory Program; (iv) investment styles within the Advisory Program; (v) the amount of the fee charged on an advisory account; or (vi) the investment objectives or suitability profile information for an advisory account. We will confirm in writing your verbal authorization to make these changes.

You hereby agree to indemnify and hold harmless MSSB, and their officers, employees, agents, successors and assigns against any and all claims or liabilities by virtue of their acting on your instructions. This indemnity shall be binding upon your heirs, successors and assigns.

You agree that all claims or controversies, whether such claims or controversies arose prior, on or subsequent to the date hereof, between you and MSSB and/or any of its present or former officers, directors, or employees concerning or arising from (i) any account maintained by you with MSSB individually or jointly with others in any capacity; (ii) any transaction involving MSSB or any predecessor firms by merger, acquisition or other business combination and you, whether or not such transaction occurred in such account or accounts; or (iii) the construction, performance or breach of this or any other agreement between us, any duty arising from the business of SB or otherwise, shall be determined by arbitration before, and only before, any self-regulatory organization or exchange of which MSSB is a member. You may elect which of these

Excerpts from a financial services contract.

5. Limitation of Liability

TO THE EXTENT PERMITTED BY LAW, APPLE'S LIABILITY UNDER THESE TERMS AND CONDITIONS IS LIMITED TO THE AMOUNTS PAID BY YOU FOR THE SERVICE PLAN YOU ORDERED. IN NO EVENT SHALL APPLE HAVE ANY LIABILITY FOR ANY INDIRECT, SPECIAL, INCIDENTAL OR CONSEQUENTIAL DAMAGES, INCLUDING BUT NOT LIMITED TO DAMAGES FOR LOST PROFITS, LOSS OF DATA, LOSS OF USE OF EQUIPMENT OR FACILITIES, INTERRUPTION OF BUSINESS OR FAILURE TO MAINTAIN THE CONFIDENTIALITY OF DATA ARISING IN ANY WAY OUT OF THESE TERMS AND CONDITIONS UNDER ANY THEORY OF LIABILITY, WHETHER OR NOT APPLE HAS BEEN ADVISED OF THE POSSIBILITY OF SUCH DAMAGE. APPLE SPECIFICALLY DOES NOT WARRANT THAT IT WILL BE ABLE TO (i) REPAIR OR REPLACE COVERED EQUIPMENT WITHOUT RISK TO OR LOSS OF PROGRAMS OR DATA, AND (ii) MAINTAIN THE CONFIDENTIALITY OF DATA. IF YOU ARE COVERED BY CONSUMER PROTECTION LAWS OR REGULATIONS IN YOUR COUNTRY OF PURCHASE OR, IF DIFFERENT, YOUR COUNTRY OF RESIDENCE, THE BENEFITS CONFERRED BY THESE TERMS AND CONDITIONS ARE IN ADDITION TO ALL RIGHTS AND REMEDIES CONVEYED BY SUCH CONSUMER PROTECTION LAWS AND REGULATIONS. SOME COUNTRIES, STATES AND PROVINCES DO NOT ALLOW THE EXCLUSION OR LIMITATION OF INCIDENTAL OR CONSEQUENTIAL DAMAGES OR EXCLUSIONS OR LIMITATIONS ON IMPLIED WARRANTIES OR CONDITIONS, SO THE ABOVE LIMITATIONS OR EXCLUSIONS MAY NOT APPLY TO YOU. THESE TERMS AND CONDITIONS GIVE YOU SPECIFIC LEGAL RIGHTS, AND YOU MAY ALSO HAVE OTHER RIGHTS THAT VARY BY COUNTRY, STATE OR PROVINCE.

An excerpt from a computer warranty.

Equitable Remedies.

You hereby agree that Blizzard would be irreparably damaged if the terms of this License Agreement were not specifically enforced, and therefore you agree that Blizzard shall be entitled, without bond, other security, or proof of damages, to appropriate equitable remedies with respect to breaches of this License Agreement, in addition to such other remedies as Blizzard may otherwise have available to it under applicable laws. In the event any litigation is brought by either party in connection with this License Agreement, the prevailing party in such litigation shall be entitled to recover from the other party all the costs, attorneys' fees and other expenses incurred by such prevailing party in the litigation.

An excerpt from an End User License Agreement (EULA) for an online role-playing game.

INSTRUCTIONS FOR USE

⚠ WARNING

For climbing and mountaineering only. Climbing is dangerous. Understand and accept the risks involved before participating. You are responsible for your own actions and decisions. Before using this product, read and understand all instructions and warnings that accompany it and familiarize yourself with its capabilities and limitations. We recommend that every climber seek qualified instruction.* Failure to respect any of these warnings can result in severe injury or death!

* A list of guides, guide services and instructional programs may be obtained through local or national mountain guide associations. In the USA, contact the American Mountain Guide Association, (303) 271-0984 or www.amga.com.

The only printed material accompanying a mountaineering device.

By entering these premises, you, on behalf of yourself and any minor accompanying you (collectively, "you") (i) understand that you will be engaging in activities that may involve risk of injury, which might result not only from your actions, inactions, or negligence, but from the actions, inactions or negligence of others, the condition of the premises, or any equipment used at the event; (ii) VOLUNTARILY ASSUME ALL RISK AND DANGER of personal injury (including death) and all hazards arising from, or related in any way to, this event, whether occurring prior to, during, or after this event, however caused and whether by negligence or otherwise; (iii) release, waive and discharge HSBC Bank USA, N.A., JWT U.S.A. INC. and LeadDog Marketing Group, Inc. and their respective parent, subsidiary and affiliated entities, licensees, agents, employees and representatives (hereinafter collectively referred to as "Producers") from any and all liability and covenant not to sue Producers for any and all loss or damage on account of injury to your person or property, whether caused by negligence or otherwise; (iv) grant the right to Producers to utilize your image, likeness, actions, name, voice and statements in perpetuity in any live or recorded audio, video, or photographic display or any other transmission, exhibition, publication or reproduction made of, or at, this event without further authorization or compensation; (v) release and discharge Producers from any and all claims arising out of use of any images or footage taken at this event, including any claims for libel and invasion of privacy. Any unauthorized video recording is prohibited.

A sign displayed outside an event in a public park.

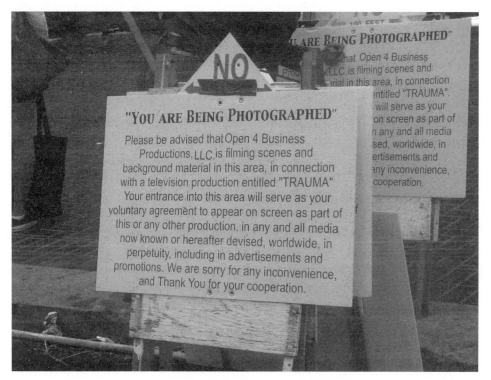

A placard addressed to passersby.

1.3 Can AT&T Change My Terms And Rates?
Print this section | Print this page

We may change any terms, conditions, rates, fees, expenses, or charges regarding your Services at any time. We will provide you with notice of material changes (other than changes to governmental fees, promotional charges for governmental mandates, roaming rates or administrative charges) either in your monthly bill or separately. You understand and agree that State and Federal Universal Service Fees and other governmentally imposed fees, whether or not assessed directly upon you, may be increased based upon the government's or our calculations.

IF WE INCREASE THE PRICE OF ANY OF THE SERVICES TO WHICH YOU SUBSCRIBE, BEYOND THE LIMITS SET FORTH IN YOUR CUSTOMER SERVICE SUMMARY, OR IF WE MATERIALLY DECREASE THE GEOGRAPHICAL AREA IN WHICH YOUR AIRTIME RATE APPLIES (OTHER THAN A TEMPORARY DECREASE FOR REPAIRS OR MAINTENANCE), WE'LL DISCLOSE THE CHANGE AT LEAST ONE BILLING CYCLE IN ADVANCE (EITHER THROUGH A NOTICE WITH YOUR BILL, A TEXT MESSAGE TO YOUR DEVICE, OR OTHERWISE), AND YOU MAY TERMINATE THIS AGREEMENT WITHOUT PAYING AN EARLY TERMINATION FEE OR RETURNING OR PAYING FOR ANY PROMOTIONAL ITEM, PROVIDED YOUR NOTICE OF TERMINATION IS DELIVERED TO US WITHIN THIRTY (30) DAYS AFTER THE FIRST BILL REFLECTING THE CHANGE.

If you lose your eligibility for a particular rate plan, we may change your rate plan to one for which you qualify.

An excerpt from a cellular telephone contract.

2.2 Arbitration Agreement
Print this section | Print this page

(1) AT&T and you agree to arbitrate **all disputes and claims** between us. This agreement to arbitrate is intended to be broadly interpreted. It includes, but is not limited to:

- claims arising out of or relating to any aspect of the relationship between us, whether based in contract, tort, statute, fraud, misrepresentation or any other legal theory;
- claims that arose before this or any prior Agreement (including, but not limited to, claims relating to advertising);
- claims that are currently the subject of purported class action litigation in which you are not a member of a certified class; and
- claims that may arise after the termination of this Agreement.

References to "AT&T," "you," and "us" include our respective subsidiaries, affiliates, agents, employees, predecessors in interest, successors, and assigns, as well as all authorized or unauthorized users or beneficiaries of services or Devices under this or prior Agreements between us. Notwithstanding the foregoing, either party may bring an individual action in small claims court. This arbitration agreement does not preclude you from bringing issues to the attention of federal, state, or local agencies, including, for example, the Federal Communications Commission. Suce agencies can, if the law allows, seek relief against us on your behalf. **You agree that, by entering into this Agreement, you and AT&T are each waiving the right to a trial by jury or to participate in a class action.** This agreement evidences a transaction in interstate commerce, and thus the Federal Arbitration Act governs the interpretation and enforcement of this provision. This arbitration provision shall survive termination of this Agreement.

The arbitration clause from the same cellular telephone contract.

CHARGES ARE FOR USE OF PARKING SPACE ONLY. WE ASSUME NO RESPONSIBILITY WHATSOEVER. FOR LOSS OR DAMAGE DUE TO FIRE, THEFT, COLLISION OR OTHERWISE TO THE VEHICLE OR ITS CONTENTS HOWEVER CAUSED.

THIS IS A LICENSE. NO BAILMENT CREATED. HOLDER MAY PARK ONE AUTOMOBILE IN THIS AREA AT HIS OWN RISK OF ANY FIRE, THEFT OR DAMAGE TO AUTO OR CONTENTS OF SAME.

DISCLAIMER

The vehicle for which this ticket is issued is accepted for parking purposes only, and under the following conditions to which the holder hereof assents by receiving this ticket. No responsibility is assumed by the operator of the lot for loss from fire, damage, or theft of the vehicle or any articles left in the vehicle or for any damages whatsoever. No employee has any authority to vary any of the above terms.

The ticket is subject to the days and rates specified on the front of said ticket.

Parking garage tickets.

ticket*fly*

KEEP IN A COOL PLACE
tickets can be damaged by
exposure to heat or sunlight

TF-6879112   TF-6879112

A concert ticket.

By breaking the seal of this software packet, you
accept the terms and conditions of the End-User
License Agreement and/or the GNU General Public
License included with this product.

An adhesive label on a software CD.

14. USER MATERIAL AND INFORMATION

...

You will have the option to create, post, stream or transmit content such as pictures, photographs, game related materials, or other information through PSN to share with others ("User Material"), provided no rights of others are violated. To the extent permitted by law, you authorize and license SNEI a royalty free and perpetual right to use, distribute, copy, modify, display, and publish your User Material for any reason without any restrictions or payments to you or any third parties. You further agree that SNEI may sublicense its rights to any third party, including its affiliates and subsidiaries. You hereby waive all claims, including any moral rights, against SNEI, its affiliates and subsidiaries for SNEI or any third party's use of User Material to the extent permitted by applicable law. By creating, posting, streaming, or transmitting any User Material, you represent and warrant that you have the appropriate rights to use, create, post, distribute, and transmit User Material and to grant SNEI the foregoing license. You further agree to cooperate with SNEI in resolving any dispute that may arise from your Information or User Material. SNEI reserves the right to remove any Information or User Material at its sole discretion.

...

19. WARRANTY DISCLAIMER AND LIMITATION OF LIABILITY

No warranty is given about the quality, functionality, availability or performance of SEN First Party Services, or any content or service offered on or through SEN First Party Services. All services and content are provided "AS IS" and "AS AVAILABLE" with all faults. SNEI does not warrant that the service and content will be uninterrupted, error-free or without delays. In addition to the limitations of liability in Sections 1, 2, 12 and 14 of this Agreement, SNEI expressly disclaims any implied warranty of merchantability, warranty of fitness for a particular purpose and warranty of non-infringement. SNEI assumes no liability for any inability to purchase, access, download or use any content, data or service. YOUR SOLE AND EXCLUSIVE RECOURSE IN THE EVENT OF ANY DISSATISFACTION WITH OR DAMAGE ARISING FROM SEN FIRST PARTY SERVICES OR IN CONNECTION WITH THIS AGREEMENT AND SNEI'S MAXIMUM LIABILITY UNDER THIS AGREEMENT OR WITH RESPECT TO YOUR USE OF OR ACCESS TO SEN FIRST PARTY SERVICES SHALL BE LIMITED TO YOUR DIRECT DAMAGES, NOT TO EXCEED THE UNUSED FUNDS IN YOUR WALLET AS OF THE DATE OF TERMINATION. EXCEPT AS STATED IN THE FOREGOING SENTENCE, SNEI EXCLUDES ALL LIABILITY FOR ANY LOSS OF DATA, DAMAGE CAUSED TO YOUR SOFTWARE OR HARDWARE, AND ANY OTHER LOSS OR DAMAGE SUFFERED BY YOU OR ANY THIRD PARTY, WHETHER DIRECT, INDIRECT, INCIDENTAL, SPECIAL, OR CONSEQUENTIAL AND HOWEVER ARISING, AS A RESULT OF ACCESSING OR DOWNLOADING ANY CONTENT TO YOUR PLAYSTATION®3 COMPUTER ENTERTAINMENT SYSTEM, THE PSP® (PLAYSTATION®PORTABLE) SYSTEM, PLAYSTATION®VITA SYSTEM, BRAVIA® TELEVISION, SONY BLU-RAY® DISC PLAYER OR ANY HARDWARE DEVICE, OR USING OR ACCESSING SEN FIRST PARTY SERVICES. UNLESS THIS PROVISION IS UNENFORCEABLE IN YOUR JURISDICTION, THE FOREGOING LIMITATIONS, EXCLUSIONS AND DISCLAIMERS SHALL APPLY TO THE MAXIMUM EXTENT PERMITTED BY APPLICABLE LAW, EVEN IF ANY REMEDY FAILS ITS ESSENTIAL PURPOSE.

Excerpts from an online services contract regarding user-generated content and a warranty disclaimer.

PART III

Boilerplate and Contract Remedies

CURRENT JUDICIAL OVERSIGHT AND POSSIBLE IMPROVEMENTS

. . . .

Evaluating Current Judicial Oversight

Traditional Judicial Oversight of Contract Law

Before considering what is to be done about boilerplate, we should take a look at what is now being done about it. In other words, we should consider the extent to which boilerplate is regulated as contract; that is, regulated by means of the normal, traditional legal doctrines of contract law that are supposed to function to allow enforcement of those (and only those) contracts that meet the requirements for contractual validity. These oversight doctrines embody the procedures and reasoning used by courts to invalidate or revise contracts—sometimes—when they are challenged.

What are the normal, traditional oversight doctrines for contracts? The main oversight doctrines can be grouped into three categories, corresponding to different types of acts and circumstances that vitiate contract: (1) coercion or duress; (2) fraud, deception, or misrepresentation; and (3) invalid contract formation. The category of coercion or duress by extension sometimes includes related doctrines such as economic duress or undue influence. The category of fraud, deception, or misrepresentation by extension sometimes includes related doctrines such as mistake and failure to disclose information that should have been given. This category should also include what I have called sheer ignorance, as well as the failure to disclose needed information that would enable appropriate choice. The category of invalid contract formation includes indefiniteness, lack of appropriate offer and acceptance, lack of consideration (referring to the bargained quid pro quo), and sometimes the notion that a valid contract requires a "meeting of the minds" of the two parties. (The notion of "meeting of the minds" is of ancient vintage and seems to be peripheral to standard contract doctrine today, but courts still rely on it sometimes, a pocket of subjectivity in a realm of objective interpretation.)

All of the areas I am calling extensions are (in their outer reaches) doctrinal grey areas, penumbras that are fought over by advocates, judges, and scholars. For example, the concept of economic duress, and to what extent, if any, it can invalidate a contract, is extremely contentious. The category of failure to disclose is also very contentious, because it involves finding that under certain circumstances contractual failure might attach merely to keeping silent. If firms that use boilerplate rights deletion schemes have a duty to ensure that recipients understand what their terms mean, by remaining silent they risk invalidation of their boilerplate schemes. Occasionally a judge in a particular case will rely on a finding of economic duress, or failure to disclose, or even no meeting of the minds, as a means of contract invalidation; but such occasions are both rare and unpredictable. Whether or not a contract will be declared invalid for indefiniteness is also unpredictable, because one judge's definite plain meaning is another judge's incomplete interpretive morass. Thus, these doctrines of invalid contract formation are each something of a wild card; they turn up rarely and are applied unpredictably.

Unconscionability

The doctrine of unconscionability is a particularly salient kind of wild card, because its main field of application is boilerplate (so-called contracts of adhesion). Courts have often defined unconscionability as "an absence of meaningful choice on the part of one of the parties together with contract terms which are unreasonably favorable to the other party."[1] Unconscionability is typically claimed by recipients attempting to invalidate sets of boilerplate terms, or specific clauses in boilerplate.[2]

In evaluating whether or not a contract looks unconscionable, courts in the US almost always look for both "procedural" and "substantive" unconscionability.* Procedural unconscionability refers to the notion that the way in which the contract came into being looks somehow improper. Conceptually this aspect falls into the penumbra of meaning of either coercion or deception. It refers to defects in bargaining—often described as "absence of meaningful choice"—not defects in the bargain.

By contrast, substantive unconscionability refers to defects in the bargain itself: the notion that some contracts may look so one-sided or unequal or oppressive that the court in good conscience simply should not tolerate enforcing them. Substantive unconscionability falls into the conceptual penumbra of the traditional doctrine of consideration (the quid pro quo of the bargain). Classical contract law did not permit courts to inquire into the adequacy of consideration, but when a modern court sees a transaction that looks too one-sided (like paying $1,000 for a product worth $100), the court will likely be willing to consider unconscionability, especially if duress or deception is suspected but cannot be proved.

Contemporary adherents to classical contract doctrine interpret unconscionability narrowly, focusing on the procedural aspect and discounting the substantive.[3] The gulf between this interpretation and the one endorsed by interpreters willing to admit substantive unconscionability is one reason why unconscionability remains so controversial and unpredictable. Procedural unconscionability can be interpreted as countenancing court intervention only within the standard traditional oversight realm of preventing subversion of a party's will by duress or deception (or their extensions). Substantive unconscionability, because it allows courts to look into the basis of a bargain, has always looked more questionable to most courts, because it seems like substituting a government decision for the will of a party. A judge who is sympathetic to the plaintiff's case, however, may reason from the substantive one-sidedness of the deal to an inference that the deal must have been procedurally improper.

---

* Here, I am referring to US law as it is applied in each state. (Contract law, as a common law heritage, is primarily state law in each of the fifty US states.)

Some courts say that the worse the deal looks the less strong the evidence needs to be for a finding of procedural shortfall.[4]

Unconscionability cases ask the judge to look, on a case-by-case basis, at the facts and circumstances that might relate to these two doctrinal aspects—the procedural and the substantive—and how they might be weighed. The need to evaluate each case individually on its own facts makes it difficult if not impossible to generate rules that might predict outcomes in future cases. Often courts try to evaluate whether the parties possessed unequal bargaining power; and/or they investigate the question of whether the contract was commercially unreasonable, or "so extreme as to appear unconscionable according to the mores and business practices of the time and place."[5] The Uniform Commercial Code (UCC),* taking up these threads in the evolving case law of the time (roughly the mid-twentieth century), promulgated a section on unconscionability that reads as follows:

Section 2-302:

1) If the court as a matter of law finds the contract or any clause of the contract to have been unconscionable at the time it was made the court may refuse to enforce the contract, or it may enforce the remainder of the contract without the unconscionable clause, or it may so limit the application of any unconscionable clause as to avoid any unconscionable result.

(2) When it is claimed or appears to the court that the contract or any clause thereof may be unconscionable the parties shall be afforded a reasonable opportunity to present evidence as to its commercial setting, purpose and effect to aid the court in making the determination.

This section gives the court a great deal of discretion in individual cases.

* The Uniform Commercial Code is a model law under the supervision of an NGO, the National Conference of Commissioners on Uniform State Laws (NCCUSL), organized for the purpose of promoting harmonization of formerly disparate state laws, along with

Unconscionability may depend on whether other sellers in the same geographical area are doing the same thing, in which case it becomes difficult for a court to find an industry-wide boilerplate scheme unconscionable. Yet this is exactly the kind of case where onerous boilerplate would be inescapable and most oppressive to recipients.

A ruling accepting or rejecting unconscionability may also depend on whether the judge thinks that the practice in question is economically rational. Judges might consider whether the product would have to be more expensive if the onerous clauses were not allowed. Some judges are sympathetic to the argument that sellers must be passing on to recipients the money they save as a result of the onerous clauses, and that consumers must be presumed to be consenting to them.[6]

Moreover, if the product in fact would be more expensive without the onerous clauses, then perhaps poor people would be priced out of the market, which might be a worse consequence than subjecting them to the onerous clauses.[7] This argument might move the court to rewrite the unconscionable clause to render it reasonable, instead of invalidating the contract; arguably a better result than a set of legal decisions that makes it appear to firms that poor people cannot enter into enforceable contracts. But there would be a problem in having courts rewrite contracts piecemeal; the firm would argue that its pricing is based on the set of terms as a whole.[8]

Depending upon their positions on issues such as these, the courts of different jurisdictions take different positions on unconscionability, even when, for sales of goods, they are interpreting the same provision, UCC 2-302. As I have mentioned, unconscionability is most often brought up in cases of "adhesion contracts" (that is, most often mass-market boilerplate schemes). How does the adhesion figure in concerns about oppression and bargaining power? If the term is buried in fine print, it can constitute "unfair surprise."

---

another NGO, the American Law Institute (ALI). The model provisions of the UCC have been widely enacted by state legislatures in the US. Article 2, in which the quoted section 2-302 appears, applies only to sales of goods. There is no analogous general model law for service transactions.

Terms can be found "oppressive" if the standardized form results in "no meaningful choice" for the recipient.

In jurisdictions where courts are inclined to enforce most adhesion contracts, they will tax the recipient with the burden of proving that the form was indeed a contract of adhesion, and will also tax her with the burden of proving that she indeed had no meaningful choice, such as the option of finding a different employer with a better contract to offer.[9] In jurisdictions where courts are more suspicious of adhesion contracts, the courts may come close to assuming, without demanding other evidence, that any form contract is an adhesion contract in the sense that would make it suspect under the doctrine of unconscionability.[10]

Void as against Public Policy

A related wild-card doctrine, though one currently less often invoked than the doctrine of unconscionability, makes it possible for courts to declare a contract void because it undermines public policy. Contracts contemplating performance of an illegal act are held void because they are against the public policy of the state, as are contracts that are considered injurious to the state or its citizens. Examples range from contracting for perjured testimony to exacting usurious interest rates to forcing someone to become a parent.[11] Common-law courts have broad power to find that certain kinds of contracts violate their state's public policy, but most courts today are conservative in using that power. A common position today is that in order for a court to find that a contract violates public policy, there must be a statute or some other kind of authoritative legal directive explicitly supporting that result.[12]

The Jurisprudential Problem with "Wild-Card" Doctrines

In an awkward jurisprudential terminology that became popular in the 1970s, the doctrine of unconscionability is the quintessential "standard" rather than "rule."[13] So is the doctrine of "voidness as against public policy," unless a court adopts the rule that nothing will be held to be void as against public policy unless there is already an authoritative legal directive disallowing it. I am not fond of this "rule" vs. "standard" terminology, because (1) what legal academics call a "rule" is what engineers would call a "standard" (as in standards for plugs and sockets, or standards for measurement, and so forth); and (2) the difference between the modes of decisionmaking is a continuum, not a dichotomy. The place on the continuum of any particular directive is based on how vague the words in the directive are. So, for example, "One must be mature to enter this bar" would be called a standard, but "One must be over twenty-one years old to enter this bar" would be called a rule. "One must be a grown-up" might fall somewhere in between. Most directives with a number in them will be considered rule-like. There are circumstances in which rules are procrustean—suppose, for example that a teenager wants to enter the bar to call an ambulance for someone who has collapsed outside—but rules are easier to apply consistently (or at least they look as if they would be). Most directives with the word "reasonable" in them will be considered standard-like; an example is the doctrine of "reasonable expectations." How this criterion might apply to specific cases is not easy to figure out.[14] Standards are valuable for giving the decisionmaker leeway to do justice in each individual case; but standards are inconsistent in application (or at least they look as if they would be).

The virtue of standard-like legal doctrines is that the decisionmaker can use discretion to tailor the decision to fit the individual case. Their vice is that discretionary decisionmaking is not consistent and predictable, but results in a patchwork that does not appear to treat like cases alike. It is because of the inconsistency and unpredictability of these oversight doctrines that I am calling them "wild-card" doctrines.

Application of the doctrine of unconscionability is a process of relentless case-by-case adjudication, with many discretionary judgment calls in each case. Perhaps with the exception of truly egregious cases, outcomes are extremely unpredictable. Moreover, the fact that the doctrine is formulated so as to address particulars of individual cases makes it difficult to apply to mass-market contracts in the aggregate. It is not, therefore, a judicial oversight method well suited to evaluating and limiting large-scale boilerplate rights deletion schemes. Although thousands, or even hundreds of thousands of people may be subject to such a boilerplate scheme, only a few will bring suit challenging it, and the results in different courts may be half for and half against the challengers. This kind of jurisprudence neither validates nor invalidates such a scheme for everyone else who is subject to it.

The Current Legal Situation: How Are Traditional Oversight Doctrines Faring with Regard to Boilerplate Rights Deletion Schemes?

Arbitration Clauses

Many people are familiar with arbitration only because of its use in sports. Arbitration is, however, a form of dispute resolution that is widely used as a substitute for adjudication (resolution by courts). Along with other nonjudicial modes of dispute resolution, arbitration is a form of "alternative dispute resolution" (abbreviated "ADR"). Arbitration is conducted under the rules of the American Arbitration Association, or a similar non-governmental organization. Many arbitrators are retired industry professionals. Some are attorneys or law professors. Arbitrators are not judges.

Arbitration clauses in boilerplate rights deletion schemes deprive large numbers of people both of their right to jury trial and their right to aggregative remedies (either class actions or classwide arbitration). Mandatory arbitration clauses are often challenged as unconscionable, and they are accordingly sometimes invalidated, though not predictably.[15] How did this situation come about?

Because arbitration is outside the normal common-law adjudication process, agreements to exclude legal remedies in favor of arbitration, thus making arbitration binding on the parties, were not routinely enforced in the US legal system in the nineteenth and early twentieth centuries.[16] Commercial firms in disputes with each other wished, however, to use arbitration by contractual choice, and pushed for legislation validating it. Eventually Congress enacted a law—the Federal Arbitration Act (FAA) of 1925—to make it easier for parties to oust common-law adjudication and commit, by agreement, to resolve any contract dispute by arbitration. The

FAA provides that "an agreement in writing to submit to arbitration a controversy" involving a contract "shall be valid, irrevocable, and enforceable, save upon such grounds as exist at law or in equity for the revocation of any contract."[17]

It seems indisputable that the FAA was intended to benefit commercial parties in federal cases. Starting in the 1960s, however, the US Supreme Court began systematically to expand the FAA's reach, both to noncommercial parties and to state cases. One scholarly article refers to this development as "[t]he hyperinflation of the FAA by the Supreme Court."[18] Contract law is state law, but the Supreme Court currently holds that the FAA widely preempts state law on arbitration agreements.[19]

Preemption means that federal law trumps state law.[20] The effect is that no state may single out arbitration clauses for special restrictions. Because state law must not treat arbitration clauses differently from its other contracts, a state legislature cannot outlaw arbitration clauses in consumer or employment agreements. A state consumer protection agency probably cannot require that an arbitration clause be printed in bold type. State courts can hold arbitration clauses to be unconscionable, but only in circumstances where any other clause would be held to be unconscionable; they cannot hold that arbitration clauses in adhesion contracts are prima facie unconscionable, unless they want to hold that all clauses in adhesion contracts are prima facie unconscionable.[21]

Lower federal courts have followed the US Supreme Court in holding that arbitration is strongly favored. In many jurisdictions it is at best an uphill battle for any plaintiff who has received an arbitration clause in a form contract to avoid getting her lawsuit dismissed from court and sent to arbitration.[22] As we saw in Tonya C.'s story in the prologue, five circuit courts of appeal hold that when a party agrees to arbitrate she gives up the right to jury trial, whether or not she has been informed that she is giving up that (constitutional) right. One circuit court said that once the claims are properly before an arbitral forum pursuant to an arbitration agreement, "the jury trial right vanishes."[23] The US Supreme Court held in 2001 that federal antidiscrimination law does not preclude forcing plaintiffs who are trying to vindi-cate civil rights into arbitration rather than jury trial in a federal court.[24] Various circuit courts of appeal have been hostile to civil rights plaintiffs trying to escape arbitration clauses in boilerplate schemes in order to get their case into federal court and thus be-fore a jury.[25]

Why do firms put mandatory arbitration clauses in their boiler-plate rights deletion schemes, making the recipient waive all other legal remedial procedures? The ostensible purpose for taking dis-putes to arbitration is that it is less expensive and time-consuming than going to court; and this is probably the primary policy reason behind the FAA. That is, this is probably the main reason why the commercial firms that lobbied for the FAA at the time of its enact-ment wished to have this option for dispute resolution.

Four other aims that firms hope to achieve through the arbitra-tion clauses in their boilerplate used with consumers or employees, however, are readily to be inferred.

One aim is to avoid collective remedies (class action lawsuits, or even classwide arbitration).[26] If a firm that provides a service takes a month to cancel its monthly automatic deduction of $15 after the customer discontinues the service, no one individual cus-tomer will find it worthwhile to sue the firm for $15. If the firm has a large number of cancellations every month, this means it will be taking in a considerable amount of money in breach of its contract, with little risk of a lawsuit.[27] Even if some disgruntled customer is will-ing to foot the legal bill to make a point, the firm still profits from all the other individuals who find that filing suit is not worthwhile. This is exactly the type of situation that motivates legislatures to provide for class actions.[28] When a legislature makes a class action remedy available, its action signifies a legislative judgment that it is unjust or inefficient for society to tolerate small recurring unre-dressable losses, which in the aggregate can add up to large-scale redistribution in favor of the firms causing the losses. Class action remedies are designed to prevent a certain kind of divestment of recipients' legal rights that lodges the ensuing advantage with a firm and leaves recipients no practical avenue for seeking redress.

Thus, firms insert arbitration clauses in order to prevent the aggregation of plaintiffs' claims via class actions. Led by California, a few state courts pushed back by instituting class-wide arbitration. In the *Discover Bank* case of 2005, California relied on its state policy of adequate redress for its citizens, which applies to all contracts in its state, in holding that the preclusion of class-wide arbitration may be unconscionable under state law in certain situations where no redress will be otherwise available. In 2011 the US Supreme Court drove the final nail into the coffin of aggregate legal remedies for consumers by overruling *Discover Bank* and holding that the Federal Arbitration Act preempts states from trying to protect their consumers as California had. In *ATT Mobility v. Concepcion*,[29] Justice Scalia for the majority held that "Requiring the availability of class-wide arbitration interferes with fundamental attributes of arbitration and thus creates a scheme inconsistent with the FAA."[30] An important feature of his reasoning about the "fundamental attributes of arbitration" was arbitration's informality:

> The switch from bilateral to class arbitration sacrifices the principal advantage of arbitration—its Informality—and makes the process slower, more costly, and more likely to generate procedural morass than final judgment.[31]

Justice Scalia took the opportunity to imply that profit-maximizing lawyers would be interested in bringing aggregative actions rather than those involving one individual against a firm. He also weighed favorably the financial advantage to defendant firms of disallowing aggregative procedure:

> Third, class arbitration greatly increases risks to defendants. Informal procedures do of course have a cost: The absence of multilayered review makes it more likely that errors will go uncorrected. Defendants are willing to accept the costs of these errors in arbitration, since their impact is limited to the size of individual disputes, and presumably outweighed by savings from avoiding the courts. But when damages allegedly owed to tens of thousands of potential claimants are

aggregated and decided at once, the risk of an error will often become unacceptable. Faced with even a small chance of a devastating loss, defendants will be pressured into settling questionable claims.[32]

Justice Scalia omitted mention of the risks to plaintiffs, who could be deprived of all remedy against a firm free to gouge them out of small amounts, an issue which the dissent did notice.[33]

A second reason firms include mandatory arbitration in their boilerplate may well be the fact that arbitration has no precedential value. It leaves no written public record. Once the arbitrator (or committee of arbitrators) renders a decision, that ends the matter. If a firm wins most of its cases but loses a few, those lost cases will not influence future cases. A third reason firms use arbitration, allied to this one, is secrecy. Arbitration is confidential; a firm that loses an arbitration because it has engaged in unfair or unethical business practices avoids having its reputation damaged by the publication of this fact.

The fourth reason firms include mandatory arbitration in their boilerplate is probably the fact that arbitrators are likely to be business people, often retired from the industry in question, or perhaps law professors or lawyers. They are not likely to be consumers or consumer advocates. Firms may well believe that arbitrators will be more sympathetic to their case than juries; and consumers may believe this as well.[34]

Although common-law case-by-case adjudication might not be the most efficient way to solve a problem, to force disputes out of the courts and into alternative dispute resolute could be worse. It might be unjustified, and also inefficient, for society as a whole to permit firms to impose mandatory arbitration on every party they deal with. Arbitrators and arbitration mechanisms vary in expertise and even-handedness. Their decisions, unlike decisions in the common-law system of precedent, are not made public and do not create a body of law that has any bearing on future cases, and are generally not subject to appellate review.

Indeed, to the extent that arbitration comes to occupy a large place in dispute resolution, the virtues of the common law are abrogated. Prominent among those virtues is the system of precedent that uses prior cases as law for subsequent cases. If enough cases come to be subject to binding, secret, ad hoc, nonprecedential arbitration, the common-law legal system of precedent would, at least as regards consumers, cease to exist in practice.

In spite of the view of Justice Scalia (and others) that arbitration is efficient because it is informal, the ad hoc aspect of arbitration may be inefficient, because efficiency is generally thought to be enhanced by transparency, clarity, and consistency. Information is widely thought to be a significant driver of efficient markets. Widespread unpublished ad hoc decisionmaking may interfere with market functioning. Over and above such efficiency concerns, widespread unpublished ad hoc decisionmaking may also be unjustified because it is incompatible with our legal system's commitment to the ideal of the rule of law. The replacement of the precedent system by a system of ad hoc, unreviewable, unreported decisions at the very least creates a tension with the commitment of the rule of law that the law should give people notice of what actions are required of them before they embark on a course of action.[35]

Choice of Forum Clauses

A choice of forum clause is a contractual clause in which parties agree to conduct litigation in a particular jurisdiction. (Such a clause often appears in tandem with a choice of law clause in which parties agree on whose law will govern any disputes between them.) Clauses of this kind may make sense for sophisticated commercial parties. When extended to boilerplate schemes used by firms with their customers, however, they are problematic, because requiring a consumer to litigate somewhere far away from home may in effect deprive the consumer of any reasonable opportunity to obtain a legal remedy (or as traditional language puts it, "to have her day in court").

A choice of forum clause most often becomes an issue in a lawsuit when the consumer recipient initiates a suit in her home state, and the defendant moves to dismiss the suit because it was not filed in the forum designated by the clause. In the 1991 *Carnival*

Cruise case discussed in chapter 1,[36] a woman from the state of Washington who wanted to sue for personal injury in Washington was limited to bringing suit in the state of Florida, by the operation of a purported contractual "choice." In reality the "choice" appeared in boilerplate that was printed on the last page of nonrefundable tickets bought by the woman and her husband. When this case reached the US Supreme Court, for some reason the case was treated as if the plaintiff and her husband had known about the existence of the clause prior to purchasing the tickets and had agreed to it, which most likely was not true. Moreover, even if recipients do actually give real (not hypothetical) consent to a remote forum, the operation of forum selection is at least theoretically limited by the US constitutional guarantee of due process of law.

The constitutional requirement of due process is usually stated in terms of a guarantee that those who invoke the law through courts will be treated in accordance with traditional notions of fair play and substantial justice.[37] In *Carnival Cruise*, because the court assumed that the recipients knew about the clause and had agreed to it, the question remaining for the Court to decide was whether, even if recipients had agreed to it, that is, actually chosen it, the clause nevertheless violated the constitutional standard of due process. The constitutional limitation is (or was) a viable question for the Court, even in the presence of actual choice.

But the Court, assuming the presence of actual choice, decided that the clause did not violate due process standards. A primary rationale was the argument—presented without empirical support—that allowing the company to compel all litigants to come to its home state to litigate would save money for the company which in turn would be passed on to recipients.

As we have seen, this argument has since been used (sometimes with more sophistication) by many defenders of boilerplate. The assumptions that underlie this rationale are both empirical and normative. There are two empirical assumptions: that the firm would pass on its savings rather than simply pocketing the money, and that claimants would trade their rights for that particular amount of money; and there is the normative assumption that trading such rights for money is permissible. A further normative assumption often part of this rationale is that even if recipients do not explicitly agree to such a trade-off they can be legally treated as if they did, because hypothetically they "would" so choose, or at least they would if they were economically "rational."[38] The Court in *Carnival Cruise* did not need this last normative assumption, because it assumed that the Shutes did actually choose and agree to this clause. Lower federal courts do need the second normative assumption, however, because they have enthusiastically followed *Carnival Cruise* by saying that that case held that such clauses are valid, conveniently submerging the fact that *Carnival Cruise* actually held only that such a clause is valid in the situation where recipients have actually agreed to it.[39] The compensation rationale overran the context in which the Court applied it.

Where, then, do matters stand with regard to the constitutional due process limitation on choice of forum clauses? If *Carnival Cruise* is held to validate all choice of forum clauses, even those that render litigation almost impossible for claimants and thus deprive them of any viable opportunity to have their day in court, the mere existence of boilerplate can have the effect of negating a constitutional limitation.[40] This constitutional limitation remains viable in other aspects of due process adjudication,[41] so it looks as if federal courts have allowed purported contractual agreements to trump a constitutional right of due process, the right to have a reasonable opportunity to pursue one's day in court. Perhaps we may hope that this is a situation that will not endure. As I have noted with respect to foreclosure of remedies for widespread small losses to consumers by the expedient of required arbitration, depriving a wide swath of the public of any viable remedy from the legal system undermines the rule of law.

Meanwhile, the doctrine of unconscionability has been invoked by some courts to invalidate onerous forum selection clauses in boilerplate schemes (where consent is problematic).[42] Some jurisdictions, especially California, look with more disfavor than others upon adhesion contracts, especially those that look like boilerplate rights deletion schemes; and some jurisdictions, again especially

California, have more solicitude than others with regard to preserving viable remedies for consumers in their state. The overall situation is thus quite favorable to the enforcement of choice of forum clauses, but it is also somewhat unpredictable, depending to some degree on the jurisdiction in which the litigation begins.

Exculpatory Clauses

It is not unusual for boilerplate to eliminate tort remedies, such as all damages for personal injury, by means of what are called "exculpatory clauses." For example, many contracts that you might sign at a fitness studio or at a summer camp to which you take your children provide that the establishment will not be liable for any injury it may cause to you or you children, no matter what the cause. (For a sample exculpatory clause, see page 114.) The question arises whether such a waiver can be valid.

Courts have tended to look at exculpatory clauses in contracts differently depending on the level of fault (in tort) of the injurer. Probably no court would enforce the aspect of a blanket exculpatory clause that would immunize the injurer from harm inflicted intentionally on a person, because that would allow a boilerplate contract to excuse a crime—the crime of assault. Nor would most courts enforce the aspect of a blanket exculpatory clause that would immunize the injurer from paying damages for harm caused by its own recklessness or gross negligence. Such contractual clauses would be declared violative of public policy.

In view of these judicial limits on enforcement, why do firms nonetheless use blanket exculpatory clauses that purport to immunize them against all injuries including death, and no matter how caused? (See the case of Michael J. whose story appears in the prologue to this book.) Perhaps the firm hopes (or even knows) that the clause will deter some people from even thinking about suing them. Most people, supposing that they read the clause, probably would be unaware that an over-reaching aspect of the clause would be held invalid in their jurisdiction. Some who consult an attorney may know that the question whether the clause would be held invalid as applied to their particular case is in doubt and would be expensive to adjudicate, because the validity of the clause would have to be litigated in addition to the particular events that caused injury.

Although courts would most likely uniformly invalidate as against public policy exculpatory clauses that immunize intentional harm or reckless or grossly negligent behavior causing harm (and thus many of the clauses in use today are unenforceable to the extent they cover harm *however caused*), some courts now do enforce exculpatory clauses insofar as they apply to merely negligent behavior. One often finds such clauses in boilerplate deployed by gyms, training facilities, summer camps, resorts, and tour companies. (See, for example, the story of Garrit S. in the prologue.) Anecdotal evidence suggests that firms are using these clauses because their insurance companies make it a condition of their coverage. (When checking in at a gym, for example a client is likely to see an exculpatory document beside the sign-in sheet. It is there most likely because it is required as a condition of the gym facility's being able to purchase insurance.)

Exculpatory clauses for merely negligent harm-causing behavior are upheld against public policy challenge in many states, but not uniformly.[43] Some courts now hold that they are generally enforceable;[44] others that they are enforceable unless they relate to essential services, or unless the parties have unequal bargaining power.[45] A few courts may still adhere to the older view that such clauses are generally unenforceable if they fall into the categories delineated in a California case from the early 1960s.[46]

It seems that the argument in favor of exculpation for harm caused by negligence (which would otherwise subject the firm to tort liability) is that it is efficient to force clients and customers to bear the risk of harm because it will incentivize them to bear the cost of insuring against it. Many would see this as a weak rationale for validating these clauses. For one thing, this practice seems to entail some risk of moral hazard. ("Moral hazard" refers to the risk that firms may not take the proper level of precaution against accidents causing harm to customers if no liability ensues for their negligence.) Also, to the extent that insurance companies require their insureds to impose these clauses on their clients or customers, insurance companies seem to be insuring firms against liability they will not have to cover, since as a condition of coverage the insurance company is requiring the firm to disclaim liability and shunt it to the client or customer.

If the real argument in support of allowing firms to exculpate themselves from tort liability for their own negligence is not this weak efficiency argument, but is simply an argument based on "freedom of contract," one would expect to find courts making a distinction between how they evaluate such a clause in a commercial contract between parties who have apparently engaged in cognizant risk allocation versus how they evaluate it in a boilerplate rights deletion scheme. Some courts will make this distinction, and some will not.

Limitation of Remedy

In the US, Article 2 of the Uniform Commercial Code governs contractual transactions involving the sale of goods, and provides for severe limitations of remedy in many cases. The UCC adopted a particular compromise in how it treats damages to buyers caused by breach of warranty (i.e., by defective products).[47] Section 2-715 provides in part:

> (2) Consequential damages resulting from the seller's breach include
>
> (a) any loss resulting from general or particular requirements and needs of which the seller at the time of contracting had reason to know and which could not reasonably be prevented . . . ; and
>
> (b) injury to person or property proximately resulting from any breach of warranty.

Section 2-719, entitled "Contractual Modification or Limitation of Remedy," allows firms to curtail the remedies otherwise available under Section 2-715. Section 2-719 provides in part:

(1) . . .

(a) the agreement may . . . limit or alter the measure of damages recoverable under this Article, as by limiting the buyer's remedies to return of the goods and repayment of the price or to repair and replacement of non-conforming goods or parts;

. . .

(2) Where circumstances cause an exclusive or limited remedy to fail of its essential purpose, remedy may be had as provided in this Act.

(3) Consequential damages may be limited or excluded unless the limitation or exclusion is unconscionable. Limitation of consequential damages for injury to the person in the case of consumer goods is prima facie unconscionable but limitation of damages where the loss is commercial is not.

Section 2-719(1)(a) provides that remedies may be severely limited, without providing that such limitations need to be communicated especially carefully or that separate consent must be obtained.[48] This invitation to shrink remedies is very widely used. The next time you receive boilerplate with a product, check to see whether your remedy is limited to return of the goods for a refund, or repair of the product. But also note that a recipient can try to claim, under § 2-719(2), that these limitations cause the remedy to *fail of its essential purpose* (whatever that means); or can try to claim, under § 2-719(3), that a limitation of consequential damages is unconscionable (and damages for personal injury in the case of consumer goods is prima facie unconscionable).[49] There is plenty to argue about here; and, as discussed above, case-by-case adjudication by courts may result in considerable variance in how the imposition of shrunken remedies is treated. (For an example of boilerplate that attempts to cancel the possibility of asserting "failure of essential purpose," see page 119.)

One simple conclusion to be drawn from the overview of how traditional judicial oversight doctrines are faring with boilerplate rights deletion schemes is that current doctrines are not formulated so as to address the mass-market nature of the issues raised by boilerplate, nor do they address the need for consistency in how these schemes are treated in the courts. In the next chapter, I will take up the question of whether these traditional modes of contract oversight can somehow be improved or better applied in order to deal adequately with the problems raised by boilerplate.

. . . .

Can Current Oversight Be Improved?

Are Boilerplate Rights Deletion Schemes "Sturdy Indefensibles"?

In Fowler's *Modern English Usage* and in Strunk & White's *Elements of Style*, there is a category declared to be "sturdy indefensibles."[1] Sturdy indefensibles are ungrammatical expressions that we nevertheless admit to English usage, such as "It's me" instead of "It's I." The notion of the sturdy indefensible also makes an appearance in Irma Rombauer's *Joy of Cooking*, to describe a cookie recipe that is not especially good but uses up the egg yolks that the cook has on hand after making angel food cake or meringues with the egg whites.[2] Shall we say that World B contracts, and in particular those that are in the category of rights deletion schemes, are another form of sturdy indefensible? They don't fit the "grammar" of the legal infrastructure of contract law, a foundational building block of the private ordering regime that justifies the state, at least in the narratives of political liberalism that still undergird our system. Nevertheless, they are thoroughly ensconced in practice. If all of them were declared invalid tomorrow, it is feared that there would be significant economic disruption.

In spite of this fear, I am reluctant to declare boilerplate rights deletion schemes a sturdy indefensible by fiat, without careful investigation of possible alternatives. English grammar is one thing, and recipes another, but divestment of entitlements and affront to the rule of law is another matter entirely. For anything that is really economically necessary there should, upon full consideration, exist some solution(s) that do not invite the use of the word "indefensible." If firms must have some ability to restructure the legal environment for themselves, there must exist legal solutions compatible with the underlying commitments of legal infrastructure and the rule of law. But it is possible that once we do accord full consideration, we might find that some of the "sturdy indefensible" practices may not actually be economically necessary.

What varieties of solutions can we consider?

Can Standard Oversight Measures Be Improved?

The question before us is whether the standard oversight measures of traditional contract law could be enhanced to alleviate the normative degradation caused by purported contracts where consent is absent or seriously problematic; and to alleviate the democratic degradation caused by firms' practice of using boilerplate schemes to delete the legal rights of the recipients.

Someone might simply assert that these oversight doctrines work fine as they are: "If it ain't broke, don't fix it." (In which case, see chapter 7; in my opinion, it's broke all right.) Otherwise, if the question really is whether these doctrines could be applied by courts in such a way as better to alleviate normative and/or democratic degradation, the answer is, "It looks as though that would be very difficult indeed." This is especially true with respect to the doctrines of unconscionability and voidness as against public policy, the main doctrines hitherto applied to evaluate boilerplate and oversee its limits.

There are two reasons why it would be very difficult to improve the ability of these doctrines to do a better job of alleviating normative and democratic degradation: (1) Unless compelled by a higher court, there is no way to get common-law courts to take up a particular interpretation or stance toward a doctrine (judges are independent, and that's a good thing); (2) Because these traditional doctrines are purely discretionary and case-by-case in their application, they would be extremely difficult to make more uniform; and their nonuniformity leads to different results in different jurisdictions.

Perhaps the courts could take it upon themselves individually to declare, in a more rule-like way, that certain specific clauses are per se or prima facie unconscionable, or per se or prima facie against public policy, in each court's particular jurisdiction. It seems that clauses eliminating or severely limiting the possibility of real redress of grievances would be good candidates for this treatment. Leaving aside mandatory arbitration clauses (because of how the Supreme Court has severely limited the power of state courts), that would include exculpatory clauses, perhaps some choice of forum clauses, and severe limitation of damages remedies that make it not worthwhile for an injured party to take action against a wrongdoer. (Of course, Congress could just outlaw mandatory arbitration clauses in consumer contracts by amending the Federal Arbitration Act to reverse the Supreme Court's over-expansive interpretations, in which case these clauses would be taken out of the realm of case-by-case evaluation.[3] Proposals to overcome the two difficulties with common-law adjudication by addressing legislation to particular aspects of the problem, or to particular kinds of clauses, will be considered in chapter 12.)

In cases dealing with sales of goods, courts are unlikely to declare that application of UCC 2-719 (allowing severe curtailment of remedies, without any particular warnings to the recipient) is per se or prima facie unconscionable. Courts would be likely to feel that alteration of this statute is a legislative prerogative. But they could perhaps limit its application in cases of mass-market boilerplate the purpose and result of which is to leave large numbers of people effectively without remedy.

Courts inclined to do so could certainly make more use of section 2-719(2) in such cases. As we have seen in chapter 7, that section provides that "[w]here circumstances cause an exclusive or limited remedy to fail of its essential purpose, remedy may be had as provided in this Act"[4]—that is, according to the UCC default rules, and also according to whatever background rules of law have not been abrogated by the UCC.[5] Unlike the severe limitations permitted by section 2-719, the UCC default rules do permit full damages remedies, including consequential damages for harm caused by defective goods. An example would be recovery of lost profit caused by the malfunction of the defective product. Moreover, courts could review more carefully the issues surrounding when a remedy fails of its essential purpose. (In such a review, as I will lay out in chapter 9, I hope the court would take into account the quality of recipients' consent, the nature of the right, and the extent of the mass-market dissemination of the clause restricting remedy.) And, of course, in many cases not dealing with sales of goods and therefore not governed by Article 2 of the UCC, judges often can apply common-law solutions, such as voidness as against public policy.

Courts could also be more willing to invalidate choice of law and choice of forum clauses in mass-market boilerplate deletion schemes, which in practice make it difficult or impossible for recipients to utilize whatever legal remedy would be available. Unfortunately, the *Carnival Cruise* case, decided by the US Supreme Court in 1990,[6] declared that a boilerplate clause limiting litigation to a very inconvenient forum did not violate constitutional standards of due process. Many courts are inclined to follow that case without looking too deeply into how its result might not apply to all circumstances of boilerplate deletion of legal process rights. Nevertheless, very occasionally a court will find reason to invalid a choice of law and/or choice of forum clause. For example, a California appellate court refused to enforce a clause that would have sent its consumers to Virginia to litigate against an online service provider who was overcharging them, because it found that California's public policy was to protect its consumers with its own consumer protection and procedural laws, which it considered superior to Virginia's.[7]

A particularly inauspicious situation exists for state courts that might want to void some arbitration clauses—which preclude jury trial and also preclude class actions—in cases where recipients are in effect denied remedy. As discussed in chapter 7, under the US Supreme Court's current interpretation of the Federal Arbitration Act, state courts must treat arbitration clauses in exactly the same way as they treat all other contracts. This means that a state court may not declare a mandatory arbitration clause per se unconscionable, and probably cannot even require special notice when an arbitration clause is present.[8] A state could not successfully hold that adhesion contracts containing a mandatory arbitration clause should be more closely scrutinized than adhesion contracts that do not contain such a clause; but the state could treat *all* adhesion contracts more rigorously under its state law. Some states already do this (compare California to Texas, for example[9]), but it is doubtful that those judges who do not treat adhesion contracts with careful scrutiny would be persuaded to do so just because of the normative degradation stemming from the dubiousness of consent. Nevertheless, perhaps a state court could create a special category for waivers of rights in mass-market boilerplate, and apply a separate and more rigorous standard. In my opinion, this would be helpful in attempting to alleviate democratic degradation.

Even if state courts were to begin to declare certain clauses per se unenforceable—for example those that shrink remedies beyond what seems necessary to preserve realistic opportunities for redress—that would only invalidate those clauses that came before a court. Probably very few of them do. Nevertheless, even a few high-profile court decisions might incentivize firms to adopt "best practices" that would phase out the most onerous of these clauses. If very few of their onerous clauses come before a court, however, firms might not have sufficient incentive to develop consumer-friendly "best practices" to eliminate them, but instead might allow them to be excised only in those few cases that reach adjudication. By leaving unenforceable terms in its boilerplate, the firm can hope to deter attempts to exercise legal rights when a recipient does read the terms but doesn't realize that they are unenforceable. It may be profitable for a firm to behave in this way, because punitive damages are not available in contract law to deter such behavior.

Would it be better instead if the legislature were to declare certain clauses invalid, and perhaps levy fines on firms that persist in using them? Or maybe an agency such as the Federal Trade Commission could do this? That would create a "public" regime, a form of governance that I will consider in chapter 12. It does seem appealing to have a legislature or an agency declare certain clauses to be prima facie an unfair trade practice. It also seems appealing to fine firms that knowingly persist in delivering unenforceable terms to recipients. But there are political reasons, not legal reasons, why such moves are difficult to accomplish in the US.

Other Traditional Oversight Methods

We can also consider possible improvements to other traditional methods of oversight. Is there a way to apply the doctrines of contract formation so as better to separate relatively benign from over-reaching boilerplate? In particular, is there a better way to rescue consent in practice, so as to alleviate normative degradation—rather than relying on reinterpretations of what is happening when a recipient clicks a box saying she has read the terms when it is extremely likely that she has not?

Robert Hillman has proposed some legal and practical strategies for making it possible for recipients to read and understand the significance of boilerplate terms *before* they become bound by them. One example, posting terms on a website so that anyone who wishes may view them in advance of entering into a transaction, seems easy enough to implement.[10] Firms may discover incentives to do this. Indeed, a firm might write terms that look reasonable and be happy to post them, hoping to enhance its reputation and also hoping that its terms will proliferate and become a widespread standard, thereby enhancing its effectiveness.

To the extent that this proposal depends on firms themselves implementing a policy of making their terms more readily available and perhaps more understandable, it would constitute a "private" initiative to improve the boilerplate status quo. (I will discuss "private" solutions in chapter 10.) To the extent, however, that this proposal suggests that courts should be more inclined to find that terms made available on a website are thereby to be deemed appropriately consented to by all recipients, it seems also a method of trying to simplify judicial contract oversight doctrines. And to the extent that the proposal suggests that website disclosure might be made mandatory in some way, it would tend to coalesce with "public" schemes of improvement, which I will discuss in chapter 12.

Hillman, in his role as chief reporter for the American Law Institute's project on *Principles of the Law of Software Contracts*,[11] does propose that judges follow the principle that a "transferee will be deemed to have adopted a standard form as a contract if . . . the standard form is reasonably accessible electronically prior to the initiation of the transfer at issue."[12] In the Principles' Summary Overview, Hillman says: "The preferred strategy of these Principles is to establish [vendor] best practices that promote reading of terms before a transferee commits to a transfer. . . . Increasing the opportunity to read supports autonomy reasons for enforcing software standard forms. . . ."[13]

In other words, Hillman hopes that courts will apply these Principles, thereby encouraging firms to comply with electronic disclosure as a best practice. He is in effect suggesting a "private" solution that is incentivized by a "public" change in legal decisions; that is, courts following the Principles would be creating a safe harbor for firms' boilerplate schemes. Hillman also predicts that giving recipients the opportunity to read terms before committing to a waiver of their rights would, at least in theory, result in an increased number of readers of boilerplate and shoppers for preferred terms.[14] But what the Principles actually say is that recipients will be "deemed to have adopted" boilerplate that has been made reasonably accessible. "Deeming" does not amount to reading and understanding. Perhaps Hillman believes that the mere opportunity to read is autonomy-enhancing; I don't think he believes that opportunity somehow substitutes for consent. Elsewhere, Hillman is perhaps even more cautious, but he believes, or at least hopes, that making terms more readily available will result in recipients reading them.[15]

Omri Ben-Shahar is certain that it will not. According to Ben-Shahar, people are wise not even to try to read boilerplate terms, because they would not understand them if they did try; and because he (like many other economic analysts) believes it is economically rational, usually, to accept onerous terms in exchange for a cheaper price for the product. He believes that "the most basic reason why it is irrational to read standard form terms is that it is too difficult to know which terms are desirable and which are not." Moreover, recipients don't necessarily want "the best" legal terms, but only those that are "worth the price"; and for most recipients that is the "economy class" not the "first class" terms.[16]

As I hope will be evident, Ben-Shahar is an adherent of the view that the decision not to read terms and not to care about them—and probably not even to know that they exist?—is itself a choice that satisfies the requirement of consent; whereas Hillman is an adherent of more traditional autonomy theory. I have argued that traditional autonomy theory should not be relinquished, because to relinquish it threatens the ideal of private ordering in the traditional narrative based on enhancing freedom, a foundation of our legal infrastructure. But Ben-Shahar is almost certainly right that the vast majority of recipients will not read these terms even if they are made available on websites, and almost certainly right as well that the vast majority would not understand them if they did read them.

That does not end the matter. The fact that people will not read boilerplate, and the fact that they may be rational not to do so, does not imply that therefore all boilerplate that is made available should accomplish valid transfers—except in case of the radically unexpected, or whatever the wild card may be. At least, it should not do so; not before we consider other methods of evaluating divestment of entitlements by means of boilerplate—methods that do not rely on gerrymandered notions of individual consent by recipients.

The Dilemma Posed by Disallowance of Rights Deletion

When considering the enhancement of traditional oversight measures, we must return, not for the last time, to the problem that arises if invalidating a boilerplate rights deletion scheme would throw poor people from the frying pan into the fire. (The *frying pan* is being deprived of rights without consent; the *fire* is being deemed unable to enter into enforceable contracts.) If we think that poor people, given this choice, would consent or even actually do consent to the loss of important rights, such as any realistic possibility of redress of grievances, does that amount to a valid choice?

Maybe not. Perhaps this situation could be understood as economic duress. Only a very few economists believe that "Your money or your life" actually poses the kind of alternatives for which choosing to yield up the money constitutes consent and not coercion. The question of what kinds of circumstances can amount to coercion or duress is not open-and-shut, something that can be read off easily, merely by observation. It is a subject of lively philosophical dispute.[17] The notion of economic duress is especially controversial. It is possible to say, at the least, that some parties to the philosophical dispute do believe that sufficiently exploitive terms, even if the addressee says yes to them, are coercive. Courts could try to explain better what sorts of terms those are, and in particular what specific terms can give rise to economic duress.

Courts could abandon the notion of *expectation* and take up the topic of *exploitation* more seriously. The difference between "expectation" and "exploitation" roughly tracks the distinction between "positive" and "normative"—"is" vs. "ought"—unless (as I suggested in chapter 5) we treat the term "expectation" as being ambiguous between "is" and "ought," between what I can empirically expect vs. what I have a right to expect if treated as my rights require. It may be that what "is" routine in practice is that firms use onerous boilerplate to cancel consumers' rights of redress; and if this is what "is," then this is what people will expect. (Again, unless we treat expectation as meaning a normative right to expect something that in practice is not available.) The more that something normatively inappropriate is happening to people, the more that society is deviating from what is justified. Thus, even if this becomes what is expected (empirically), it is nevertheless a form of exploitation, or a defeat of the normative aspect of expectation, the right to expect. Courts should take up exploitation forthrightly if only to avoid this badly obfuscatory ambiguity regarding the meaning of "expectation."

Asking courts to look more to exploitation does not answer, however, the argument that it might be worse for poor people if they are thought to be incapable of making valid contracts when those contracts contain onerous terms, because then, so the argument goes, firms will be reluctant to contract with them, and then poor people will become second-class citizens in the marketplace. Tolerating exploitation, the argument continues, could be a lesser evil than tolerating second-class citizenship. Of course, from the point of view of justice, it is hard to see such a choice as tolerable from any angle. It is simply intolerable that people of greater wealth should have more rights. That would make a mockery of the commitment to equality before the law.

Severe wealth disparity is at the root of this problem, as it is at the root of much that ails the US. And wealth disparity is not a problem that our legal infrastructure takes much cognizance of (for example, the US Constitution does not set forth, and is not interpreted to contain, welfare rights). Nor is wealth disparity a problem that can be much alleviated by tinkering with contract law.

Nevertheless, the argument that it is better to burden poor people with onerous clauses than to create a situation in which they cannot enter enforceable contracts—which could lead a court asked to consider severe clauses under UCC 2-302 to decide that they are not unconscionable—rests on empirical assumptions that should be investigated. To what extent are more severe rights deletion schemes found in areas where poor people live? To what extent is the presence of these clauses due to the fact that recipients are not able to shop elsewhere, so that firms are free to impose clauses favorable to themselves without the check of competitors? To what extent is it really more expensive to sell to poor people? And if it is, how much more expensive, and in which product sectors and methods of marketing?

Not just in this case, but in general, current oversight measures might be improved if there were less reliance on sweeping inferences based on assumptions, and more empirical data that courts would actually take into account. Yet it is not easy for courts to take empirical economic data into account. Judges are not economists, and it is expensive and time-consuming to try to base a legal decision on empirical data (consider antitrust litigation and the spectacle of conflicting economic experts). So what is at issue here is the institutional competence of courts, just as many law-and-economics writers such as Richard Craswell warn.[18] Nevertheless, in the case of a widespread boilerplate rights deletion scheme, perhaps it would be useful to have courts order a special master to oversee an investigation, similar to the type of investigation that must be undertaken in mass tort cases.[19]

My conclusion here remains. Although it seems possible to improve current oversight in certain circumscribed ways, to strengthen these measures so as to achieve real alleviation of the normative and democratic degradation caused by mass-market boilerplate constrictions of recipients' rights would be very difficult indeed.

· ·

Improving Evaluation of Boilerplate

A PROPOSED ANALYTICAL FRAMEWORK

Questions for Evaluating Rights Deletion Schemes

Rights of individuals are granted and/or maintained by the state.* As I discussed in chapter 3, the system of private ordering relies on the notion that individuals—and also entities such as firms[1]—exercise freedom of choice in trading their rights. The ideal of private ordering often assumes a universe of default rules that individuals are free to alter. Thus, one primary question for evaluating boilerplate rights deletion schemes can be framed this way: Are *all* of the rights granted and/or maintained by the state appropriately considered default rules? If not, then how does the analysis of whether or not an entitlement is a default rule figure in analysis of whether a particular boilerplate deletion scheme should be enforceable?

Another primary question for evaluating rights deletion schemes is: How does the presence or absence of real consent to waiver of individual rights affect the analysis? (If consent is problematic or unclear, how should this situation be evaluated?) And a third

---

* Depending on one's conception of what "law" is, one may believe that all rights of individuals originate in positive law enacted by the state's authorized entities such as legislatures; or (if one is committed to natural law or prepolitical rights or background rights) that no rights originate in positive law, but that they preexist positive law and that the role of positive law is to recognize them. Various strands of liberal theory have advanced different positions on legal positivism "versus" natural law. Most positions are mixed: some rights originate in positive law, some rights preexist positive law. Rights originating in positive law are both granted and maintained by the state; those preexisting positive law are maintained by the state.

question: To what extent does the extent of social dissemination of a particular rights deletion scheme affect the analysis? That is, might deleting the rights of tens or hundreds of thousands of consumers in some circumstances be properly analyzed differently from deleting the rights of just one?

The current wild-card contract doctrines of unconscionability and void as against public policy, as we have seen in chapter 7, function to single out situations where a waiver will be disallowed. The purpose of this chapter is to develop an analytical framework that can help illuminate in more detail how boilerplate waivers should be evaluated.

Elements of Analysis

Boilerplate rights deletion schemes cause waiver of rights by the recipients. ("Waiver" is the legal term for relinquishing a legal right.) As we have seen, some of the rights that are commonly waived are: the right to jury trial, the right to class-action litigation, the right to litigate (or arbitrate) in a convenient forum, the right to hold those who cause harm to persons or property liable for damages in tort. The first element of analysis is an evaluation of the nature of the right in question, to determine whether that right is alienable; that is, detachable from the holder[2]. Rights that cannot be sold are market-inalienable. (The term "market-inalienability" refers to a right that may not be relinquished in return for payment.[3]) The second element to evaluate is the quality of consent by a recipient. The third element to evaluate is the extent of social dissemination of the rights deletion, where we can deem that element to be relevant.

Then we will have to consider how these elements of analysis can be combined. There is a broad range of possibilities. There is a continuum ranging from the standard ideal inherent in the theory of World A to the frequent reality in practice with regard to certain onerous clauses in World B.

In the standard ideal inherent in the theory of World A, there is unquestionable (full) alienability of the right being relinquished, clear consent by the promisor to the relinquishment, and only one individual is relinquishing the right. The situation imagined in World A can be schematized in this way: .

Standard Ideal of World A

> Full alienability
> Clear Consent
> One individual

In certain situations in World B, there is clear market-inalienability, sheer ignorance (nonconsent) on the part of the recipient, and very large numbers of people are relinquishing the right. An example would be a widespread waiver of tort damages that is clearly void as against public policy—such as an exculpatory clause waiving rights to sue the firm for any harm it causes on purpose or recklessly—contained in a browsewrap that no one sees, and made applicable by the firm to a very wide swath of consumers.

Worst Case Situation in World B

Market-Inalienable Right
Nonconsent
Large Numbers Affected

It is important to realize that these schematics represent endpoints of three continua. Between clear market-inalienability and clear alienability of a right there can exist a grey area of partial market-inalienability ranging from not-quite market-inalienable to not-quite fully alienable; and between clear consent and clear nonconsent there can exist a grey area ranging from consent that is not quite clear to nonconsent that is not quite clear; and, likewise, there can exist a grey area of social dissemination in which multiple individuals are affected, but not necessarily a very large segment of the consuming public. One of the aims of this chapter is to make progress with respect to how these three continua should be analyzed.

The Range of Alienability

Legislatures have the power to treat certain rights as less than fully alienable, and so do courts. Courts usually do this by applying an adjudicatory technique known as "strict scrutiny," in which courts may require more evidence, clearer arguments, and/or that other specific legal prerequisites be met before approving alienation of a right. Strictness of scrutiny can vary with the nature of the case before the court. I will call this situation "partial market-inalienability," because it renders sale of a right more difficult. It could also be called by a more traditional term, "restraint on alienation," a term that reflects free-market assumptions, the ideal parameters of World A, in which alienation is theoretically unrestrained. Sometimes a court will face a situation in which a partial market-inalienability has already been determined by the legislature or by prior common law; and sometimes a court will feel called upon to create a partial market-inalienability on its own. Because "scrutiny" can vary in strictness, we can view the nature of the right with respect to alienability on a continuum ranging from market-inalienability to full alienability:

Nature of Recipient's Right Waived

Market-Inalienability	*Partial Market-inalienability*	*Full Alienability*
	ranging from not-quite market-inalienable to not-quite fully alienable	

The Range of Quality of Consent

Consent may seem to be an either-or issue: either someone consented, or she did not. Yet consent may be indeterminate if it depends in an indeterminate way on the person's possession of information. This issue is compounded when outsiders such as judges and juries are called upon to evaluate the probability that a relinquishment of a right was or was not consensual.

Thus, we can look at quality of consent as occupying a continuum from clear consent to clear nonconsent:

Quality of Consent to Waiver by Recipient

Clear Nonconsent	*Questionability of Consent*	*Clear Consent*
	ranging from not-quite-clear nonconsent to not-quite-clear consent	

The Range of Social Dissemination

As I will explain later in this chapter, social dissemination may not always be a significant factor in evaluating rights deletion schemes. In cases where I will argue that the social dissemination of a scheme should be taken into account, the sheer number of recipients, and/or the presence of industry-wide standardization that prevents consumers from obtaining goods or services without becoming subject to the boilerplate clause in question, may be relevant. Thus, we can schematize social dissemination as a continuum ranging from large numbers to only one individual:

Extent of Social Dissemination of Waiver

Large numbers lose the right	Varying characteristics of market affected (number of recipients; presence of industry-wide standardization)	Only one individual loses the right

For each of the three continua, I want to urge consideration of the grey area between the two poles, rather than assuming that a situation must belong to one pole or the other.

The Effect of Nonconsent or Market-Inalienability

Before focusing on the grey areas, however, we should begin by noticing that *either* nonconsent or market-inalienability will invalidate any purported contract, whether mass-market or not, whether boiler-plate or not. It is important to bear in mind that market-inalienability trumps all other parameters. Even with full consent, an individual cannot trade off a right that the legal system declares cannot be sold. It is also important to bear in mind that nonconsent like-wise trumps all other parameters. Even if an entitlement is fully alienable, an individual cannot relinquish it without her consent. Because market-inalienability and nonconsent are trump factors, debates will center around which rights are now market-inalienable or should be declared so; and around whether consent existed.

Market-Inalienability and Partial Market-Inalienability

Only a few libertarians would give an unqualified "Yes" to the question whether all entitlements granted and/or maintained by the state are appropriately considered fully alienable; i.e., merely de-fault rules. Most others believe that society must impose (or must interpret the existing legal infrastructure as containing) certain mandatory or immutable rules to modify the universe of default rules. For the most part, that is, the main arguments are about which baseline rights of persons are fully or partially market-inalienable. (As I mentioned above, by partial market-inalienability I refer to the situation where an entitlement may be alienable but only with difficulty or restrictions.)

The classic case of debate about inalienability involves selling oneself into slavery.[4] There are other rights of the person that are usually held to be fully inalienable (meaning that they cannot be divested at all, even by free choice of the holder) or at least market-inalienable (not to be divested by sale—contract—even by the free choice of the holder).[5]

There are not too many instances of boilerplate attempting to accomplish the waiver of a right that is fully inalienable, though occasionally we come across an attempt that can be viewed as con-travening full inalienability. One example is the purported waiver of tort damages for intentional bodily harm; one cannot waive one's right against being assaulted, with or without an exchange of money. The legal system has enacted certain other inalienabilities that may be operable whether or not money is exchanged, but certainly would be at least market-inalienabilities. These include: the right to habitability in rental housing; the right not to be charged usurious interest rates; the right not to be subject to discrimination on the basis of sex, race, religion, or national origin.[6]

The boilerplate rights deletion schemes of World B often raise a question of market-inalienability. The common argument put forward by firms using these boilerplate schemes, and also by those law-and-economics scholars who support them, is that recipients are compensated for loss of their legal rights by the lower prices charged by the firm, and that recipients "would" (or hypothetically "do") choose this trade-off. As I argue elsewhere in this book, there are compelling reasons why this argument should not be accepted wholesale in the form in which proponents present it.[7] Nevertheless, even if we accept the trade-off argument, it involves assuming that recipients are being paid in return for divesting themselves of legal rights. This assumption squarely invokes the question of market-inalienability. There are some rights that cannot be relinquished for pay, no matter what the other parameters of the transaction are. Rights that cannot be relinquished for pay cannot be "traded" either hypothetically or actually, no matter what level of consent exists.

Waivers of rights that might be considered market-inalienable occur in boilerplate rights deletion schemes with some frequency. If we were to hold that the right to jury trial is market-inalienable, for example, then attempts to waive the right to jury trial in exchange for compensation would be void. Therefore, an arbitration clause that automatically waives the right to jury trial, assuming that we accept the argument that the waiver was sold by the recipient to the firm in return for the firm's charging a lower price to the recipient, would be void.[8]

Later in this chapter, I will investigate what kinds of rights waived in boilerplate might be held market-inalienable, and under what circumstances. *Again, a conclusion that a right is market-inalienable means that it simply cannot be sold for money, and, consequently, that the attempted waiver of such a right in return for compensation would be invalid, no matter what the other parameters of the transaction.* For example, a prime candidate for market-inalienability is a situation in which boilerplate withdraws all avenues of legal redress, because a contract withdrawing legal recourse is essentially an attempt to opt out of the rule of law.

It is important to recognize that market-inalienability and the full alienability represented by default rules represent the two opposite ends of a continuum. Along the continuum between them are various situations where a right may be alienable, but only with some individualized investigation of the appropriateness of that alienation under the circumstances. Near the market-inalienability end of the continuum are rights that can be alienated only with great difficulty, such as those that are prima facie inalienable. For example, the waiver of a consumer's right to consequential damages for personal injury caused by a product is, under the UCC, prima facie unconscionable.[9]

Partial market-inalienability, in between the two ends of the continuum, characterizes the situation in which trades of a right are permissible, but only upon review or oversight by public institutions, such as courts or administrative agencies. The level of review required (how serious or stringent it is) defines the appropriate place of the right in question on the continuum between market-inalienability and easily waivable default rules. In conjunction with this understanding, it is also important to recognize that courts as well as legislatures have the power to decide what is market-inalienable, as well as what is partially market-inalienable and where on the continuum of stringency of review or oversight such partially inalienable rights should fall.

The Quality of Consent

Consent by a party to a purported contract may be unquestionably present (clear consent) or unquestionably absent (clear nonconsent). I will sometimes refer to the situation where consent is unquestionably present as "full consent," and the situation where consent is unquestionably absent as "nonconsent." Although in the abstract there may be no conceptual space between these two situations, in practice, because consent must be judged by whatever evidence of behavior (words and action) we have, plus whatever we can make of the context(s) in which the behavior occurred, there is a large grey area in between these poles. In that grey area, consent varies from only slightly doubtful to not quite clearly absent. Consent, in other words, is going to be problematic to varying degrees in the many contexts that arise in real life where we need to ask the question whether consent existed. In those cases we are actually asking to what extent we lean toward believing it did or did not exist.

Nonconsent and Situations in which Consent is Problematic

If an exchange or waiver of rights is sought, but consent is unquestionably absent, then, whatever else has taken place, a contract has not come into being. Nonconsent trumps other parameters in evaluating the appropriateness of enforcement as a contract. In the situation that I have called sheer ignorance, in which those who are receiving boilerplate purporting that recipients are waiving their rights do not know that anything is happening, much less that they have "agreed" to cancel rights, a contract does not come into existence. (Examples of sheer ignorance may be found in the purported contracts of the form that are called "browsewrap.") At least, a contract does not come into existence *unless* those who wish to defend such a deletion of rights as contractual can succeed in arguing that hypothetical consent (by which the unknowing recipient "would" have consented to loss of her rights had she known about the offer to trade them for a cheaper price) should be treated as if it were actual consent. Or *unless* those who wish to defend such a deletion of rights as contractual can succeed in arguing that anyone who had enough opportunity to see terms deleting his rights (whatever level of opportunity a judge may decide is "enough") should be treated *as if* he consented to the deletion.[10] My view is that hypothetical consent is not consent, and neither is as-if consent.[11] (Of course, even if the argument succeeded that a contract came into being in a case of sheer ignorance, the contract would still be unenforceable if the right purportedly being deleted is fully inalienable or market-inalienable.)

What shall we make of situations in which it is claimed that recipients have consented to boilerplate loss of legal rights, but consent looks problematic? Here we should consider situations in which the recipient does know that boilerplate exists and contains terms, but does not read it or take any action to understand what it means. Many recipients just sign papers that are put in front of them, or just click "I agree" when the box appears online. (Perhaps they are thinking, "I don't understand this legalese, anyway," but it is even more likely that they aren't thinking anything, other than maybe, "Let's get on with this transaction.") One way to interpret this behavior is to conclude that it amounts to consent. The person has signed a document containing unknown terms, but should be held to know (at least if socialized in this culture) that signing something signals acceptance and commitment, so the behavior in this context should be interpreted to mean, "I consent." Or the person has clicked "I agree" to unknown terms, knowing what the word "agree" means (at least if socialized in this culture), so the behavior in this context too should be interpreted to mean "I consent."

This is roughly the interpretation adopted by Randy Barnett and others who agree with him,[12] and often it has seemed that American judges take this view.[13] Yet the position is not hard and fast, because those who espouse it use the trope of "reasonable expectation" to mark an outer limit to what boilerplate may accomplish. One could interpret this trope as encapsulating some admixture of concern for the nature of the divested rights, even though its usual use is directed toward the issue of consent. (I think the reasoning would go like this: "No one would consent to forfeiting his entire account, so if that's in the fine print, let's say the recipient did not consent because he did not reasonably expect this clause.") A better reasoning process would avoid the confusion of the "expectation" trope by explicitly inquiring separately into the quality of consent and the nature of the right being relinquished, before attempting to combine them.[14]

We must also keep in mind the extent to which information asymmetry and prevalent heuristic biases undercut any simple interpretation of the behaviors of signing or clicking. Heuristic biases tend to render consent problematic. Contrary to the argument espoused by many law-and-economics practitioners, we should not assume that in each market there will be at least a substantial subset of people who understand the risk properly and price the product accordingly for themselves and for everyone else in that market.[15] Even if people do mean to assume the risks posed by boilerplate clauses, we should understand that they are likely to be mistaken about the level of risk that they face, because people tend to feel that serious risks result primarily in harm to others, not to themselves.

Situations of problematic consent to boilerplate often coincide with waivers of rights that have been or should be declared to be at least partially market-inalienable, in the sense that more investigation should be undertaken and more justification offered for relinquishment of the right than the mere (purported) fact that the relinquishment was contractual. We can represent this situation schematically in various ways, depending upon how likely is nonconsent (that is, how poor the quality of consent is judged to be) and upon what level of market-inalienability is appropriate for the right in question. One situation might be represented this way:

Problematic Consent and Market-Inalienability

Strong case for less than full alienability
Nonconsent likely

Other permutations of this diagram would involve different degrees of likelihood of nonconsent; and different strengths of the case for less than full alienability, giving rise to different levels of partial market-inalienability.

The concurrence of a questionable quality of consent with the waiver of a right that is less than fully alienable can be treated as synergistic in situations where the level of partial market-inalienability has not previously been firmly entrenched in the legal system. That is, where consent appears problematic, that uncertainty could influence a court to implement partial market-inalienability (stricter scrutiny); and where the right appears to be one that is or should be held waivable only after serious evaluation of the circumstances, that observation could influence a court to decide that consent is too problematic to uphold the waiver.

The Nature of a Divested Right or Interest

Earlier in this book I have looked at issues of consent, and what circumstances render consent problematic. Now I will look more closely at the nature of the rights that are commonly divested by means of boilerplate rights deletion schemes, with a view toward judging what kinds of rights are or should be subject to market-inalienability or partial market-inalienability in the presence of problematic consent. At the same time, I will consider the extent to which imposing the boilerplate rights deletion scheme on a large number of recipients might alter the analysis. This class of situations can be rendered schematically this way:

Mass-Market Delivery of Boilerplate

Varying strength of case for
partial market-inalienability
Varying levels of problematic
consent

Large numbers
affected

The ultimate question I will reach is to what extent delivery of mass-market boilerplate in cases of less-than-clear consent and less-than-clear alienability presents a stronger case for nonenforcement of a clause in a mass-market rights deletion scheme than do situations in which the large numbers affected are not included in the analytical framework. To begin this discussion, I will divide rights and interests into political rights and interests and basic human rights and interests. I will consider the general maintenance of legal and democratic structures and processes to be political rights and interests, and I will consider cultural and individual background commitments to be human rights and interests. Therefore, I will include the following among political rights and interests: the redress of grievances, avoidance of democratic degradation, and the protection of rights and interests that are politically vulnerable. And I will consider the following to be human rights and interests: freedom of speech, individual autonomy, and individual privacy.[16]

Political Rights and Interests

Political rights and interests relate to maintaining the rule of law and avoiding democratic degradation. Of crucial importance for the rule of law is overseeing proper functioning of the legal system, and therefore the right of redress of grievances is paramount. If a contract were to provide that a party would forfeit all rights to legal action or remedy under any circumstances, that would take the transaction completely outside the legal system, outside the rule of law, and back to the situation (traditionally called the state of nature) where one must depend on self-help or the help of one's friends and relatives to enforce promises or maintain possession of one's resources. There would be no reason to call this transaction a contract and no reason to implicate the state (the courts) in enforcing it.

If a boilerplate form were to contain a clause divesting the recipient of all legal remedies, what should a court do if the recipient nevertheless files suit against the firm that imposed it? The court could declare that no contract exists, but more likely the court would just throw out the no-remedies clause and allow the recipient to proceed with the suit. In most cases involving boilerplate, that would be the right result, because the parties did intend a contract (sale and purchase of a product or service). This result is in effect a legal declaration of market-inalienability of the right to redress of grievances; the right is nonwaivable. It would be nonwaivable even if a party fully consented to it, not just if consent were problematic.[17]

In the US we are faced with a situation in which our courts have rendered redress of grievances all but impossible in practice for large numbers of consumers. Especially in situations of recurring

small harms (such as that inflicted by a bank that charges customers a $29 late fee on their credit cards at midday on the day that
the payment was due instead of at the end of the day)[18], consumers
in practice have no legal redress available, because of the operation
of arbitration clauses, waivers of class action and class-wide arbitration, and choice of forum clauses. Firms that impose arbitration
clauses argue, of course, that arbitration is a well-respected procedure for the redress of grievances and one for which parties may
freely contract. That is no doubt largely true in the commercial
arena in which arbitration by agreement was first validated. It is
almost certainly not true in the arena of consumer transactions involving boilerplate rights deletion schemes, as shown by the small
number of cases that ever do go to arbitration, and the small number that are won by consumers.[19]

Any time even one individual is explicitly deprived of *all* redress of grievances, that is a situation that courts should (and I
am relatively sure would) disallow, because the right to redress of
grievances (in its entirety) should be treated as market-inalienable.
But how should we evaluate the situation where large swaths of
consumers are not specifically deprived of all rights of redress (because in theory arbitration or perhaps litigation in a remote forum
is open to them), but in practice it becomes almost impossible for
them to exercise these rights? It is a difficult question to what extent redress is foreclosed when it remains theoretically open but is
almost completely closed in practice. My view, to which I return
later in this chapter, is that this is a case in which the large number
of recipients affected should matter. When a large swath of the
public has no access to redress of grievances in practice, that is a
democratic degradation and a serious flaw in the implementation
of the rule of law.

Politically Weak Rights and Interests

It is important to take note of another aspect of democratic degradation: the role of rights and interests that can be considered
politically weak or vulnerable. These are rights and interests that

are attacked by lobbying campaigns and other forms of pressure by motivated minorities. The majority may not be willing and able to organize to protect its interest against the well-organized and motivated minority. Such politically weak rights and interests must rely especially on courts to protect them, because political processes do not do so effectively.

A politically weak right is characterized by these conditions: strong interest groups have an incentive to undermine the right, as well as the resources to do so; and the right under attack does not have a politically strong interest group of its own with the resources to defend it.

Example: Federal Intellectual Property Regimes and User Rights

Owners of intellectual property (IP) rights have the incentive and possibly the power to undermine user rights, such as fair use of copyrighted materials,[20] whereas users are often not able to push back against them. I suggest that deployment of boilerplate to achieve widespread cancellation of user rights contributes to democratic degradation, and that those rights should not be treated as fully alienable. To examine this assertion, I will briefly outline the situation with regard to boilerplate and user rights.

The "public" entitlement regimes that impact in contracts in the digital environment in the US are most often those of intellectual property; primarily the three federal regimes of patent, copyright, and trademark. These intellectual property regimes are comprehensive schemes of positive law enacted by Congress. They grant certain entitlements to holders and withhold others. For example: Patents are not to be granted on inventions that are obvious in light of the prior art (that is, prior knowledge related to the field of the claimed invention). Copyright does not give exclusive rights to ideas (but only to the expression of ideas), and there is a savings clause for otherwise infringing uses that are determined to be fair use. Trademark cannot extend to ownership of marks that are (or become) generic descriptors of products. Because of the rights *not* granted to IP owners, the federal regimes of information propertization have left some uses free of ownership and therefore have created user rights (entitlements of the user). Anyone may make, use, and sell someone else's obvious product, because a patent on such a product would be invalid; anyone may copy and publish ideas (rather than expressions of ideas); anyone may use a trademark (such as "aspirin") that has become a generic descriptor.

Such user rights are among the rights that firms seek to cancel by means of mass-market boilerplate deletion schemes. For example, many of us are governed by the Microsoft EULA ("End User License Agreement") and not by the Congressional law of copyright. EULAs greatly expand the rights granted to copyright holders by Congress, and greatly diminish the rights of users. To put it bluntly, EULAs (in practice and taken in the aggregate) look like a devolution into the hands of firms of power that in my view properly should belong to the realm of the state. In other words, we seem to be looking at a core case of democratic degradation as described in chapter 3.

The large numbers of people affected seem to matter in this case. Altering user rights by voluntary agreement between one individual and another would represent the ideal of World A, or something akin to it, unless the rights were held to be market-inalienable. But boilerplate rights deletion schemes are not like the imagined voluntary agreements between individuals, but rather an ordering scheme deployed by a firm and received by its customers and users. Those who need to use Windows cannot reject or bargain over its terms. Thus, the Windows EULA can override, for a large number of people, what the federal intellectual property regimes enacted as appropriate user rights. (For an example of a EULA altering user rights, see page 119.)

To be sure, in the analytical framework I propose, the influence of the number of people affected would be different if users routinely had a choice to purchase or use whatever goods are covered by these mass-market boilerplate schemes under other more user-friendly terms; that is, if monopolization or industry-wide standardization were not present.[21] It seems that the rights granted by patent and copyright are with few exceptions alienable; that is, they are default rules.[22] Even though the rights granted by patent and copyright are with few exceptions alienable, it is threatening for the ideal of private ordering that the "public" schemes governing information propertization are being undermined by these "private" mass-market replacement schemes. Such schemes are, in effect, a form of private preemption. The fact that the rights waived are (or at least are usually thought to be) by and large alienable does not fully alleviate the problem of democratic degradation.

"Defection" from Legislative "Bargain"

I do not espouse public choice theory, the political economy explanation of how democracy works (which I discussed in chapter 3), at least not in a general or total way. But it cannot be denied that sometimes firms lobby for and obtain legislation to further their own private interest (profit) rather than the public interest, a process economists call rent-seeking. So, giving political economy credence for a moment, it is possible to argue that democratic degradation is a threat even under political economy's version of democracy, because when a firm deploys a boilerplate rights deletion scheme it is defecting from a legislative bargain. One could view the copyright regime, for example, as a legislative compromise embodying acceptance of firms' second-best choices for restraining themselves provided everyone else does. In that case, when a firm deploys a boilerplate scheme deleting user rights arrived at in the compromise, it is defecting from its commitment to the compromise.

This possibility can be seen as a standard coordination problem of the kind usually labeled a "prisoner's dilemma." Suppose a situation in which each firm would prefer to keep all of the information it discloses from being used by others, but at the same time would prefer to have access to the information disclosed by others. In other words, the firm would prefer strict copyright law for itself, but expansive fair use as regards others. This situation could very likely occur when a firm needs access to others' information as inputs to further innovation and information asset creation, but at the same time wishes to lock up the information assets it already has.

It would be impossible to implement for all firms their first-best solution (in which everyone says, "Free access for me to your stuff, no access for you to my stuff"). Suppose further, then, that the second preferred option is that everyone be allowed access to a certain portion of information disclosed by others. Here we suppose that as a fallback option, a firm would be willing to allow other firms access to some portion of its information in return for free access to some portion of the information of all other firms. This second preferred solution could be achieved through coordination.

Spontaneous coordination is unlikely, however, and also unstable if it does occur, since each individual firm is tempted to defect by trying to lock up its own information while still having access to the information of others. The classic prescription for securing the second preferred solution is precommitment through legislation. Firms agree in advance to have the state require them to cooperate in this rational manner, and the state's threat of enforcement deters defection after the deal is imposed.

Parts of the copyright regime, including the exclusion of ideas and facts from ownership, as well as the notion of fair use, can be interpreted as a solution to the coordination problem. To the extent that this is true, the copyright regime should be seen as setting out some rules for when information developed by one entity is to be available for use by others, rules that all entities have an interest in supporting. Firms have a rational incentive to organize and get copyright legislation enacted that will allow each firm to have access to some portion of the information held by others, on a reciprocal basis. In the case of copyright law, this seems in fact to be what firms actually did.[23] To the extent that copyright protection has holes—rules that establish categories of information that are not propertized (for example, facts, functional items, ideas, merged ideas, and expression), or rules that describe situations in which propertization can be overridden (for example, fair use)—copyright may represent an efficient solution to a coordination problem.

If the law treats such rules merely as default rules, however, then an individual firm will be able to contract around these access rules. That is, the copyright holder can market its works with a clause cancelling fair use and other user rights. This capability destroys, or at least destabilizes, the commitment enacted in legislation that is meant to secure a solution to the original problem. Using mass-market boilerplate to eliminate the holes in copyright coverage may amount to defection from the coordination bargain.[24] Thus, widespread boilerplate schemes that obviate the legislated nonpropertization should perhaps be disallowed, or at least be scrutinized carefully rather than assumed to be efficient.

In other words, user rights should be treated as at least partially market-inalienable. User rights in a scheme of information propertization are not just any old default rules, even in an interpretation based upon economic reasoning.[25] Because those user rights may have resulted (particularly in the case of copyright) from a process in which firms collaborated to obtain protection for themselves while leaving open avenues for reuse and repurposing of information developed by others, it may be that firms as a group would—and (at least ab initio) did and (at least hypothetically) should—approve of a stricter analysis, a partial market-inalienability rather than a mere default rule. (If economic analysts insist that recipients can be held to hypothetical consent on the basis of economic "rationality," the same reasoning should apply to firms, where indeed it seems to have more justification.)

No doubt firms would like to have easy waiver of user rights by boilerplate rights deletion schemes against their customers and the browsing public, while themselves retaining user rights for information developed by competitors and others. But copyright law is written generally and does not (yet) embrace such a double standard. Double standards look bad for the ideal of the rule of law, unless they can be justified. But by what means could such a double standard be justified? Firms might argue economic efficiency, alleging that user rights are more valuable to firms competing against other firms than to recipients of information on the Internet; and suggesting that user rights for recipients on the Internet are more expensive to maintain than user rights against other firms, primarily because of the difficulties involved in distinguishing between user rights that copyright law does not grant versus those that it does. This argument would surely be disputed by Internet user groups, who say it is precisely the openness of information to all that makes for interesting innovation and astonishing creativity, to the benefit of society as a whole.

Example: Redress of Grievances

Now let's return to the issue of the redress of grievances. Redress is of primary importance among the rights I am here treating as political. It is even more disruptive of the liberal ideals of private ordering under the public governance of the rule of law if "public" regimes affording rights that are less readily alienable than those of intellectual property are reshaped by these "private" rights deletion schemes. Those entitlements that are inalienable, or at least less readily alienable, are components of "public" regimes underwritten by the polity for the sake of the structure of the polity itself. The idea of redress of grievances through law is primary among them. The narrative of traditional liberalism has it that individuals cannot be divested of their rights to redress of grievances without undermining the very structure of rights that the state is charged with maintaining in order to foster individual freedom. For example, if the remedies for breach of contract or for exchanges obtained through coercion or deception are nonexistent or inadequate, then the liberal ideal of private ordering cannot be implemented. If we were to reach a situation in practice in which the ability of a party to claim coercion or deception was routinely waived, we would not have a regime of contract or of private ordering compatible with our received ideals of freedom of contract and the enforcement of those and only those contracts that accord with it.

When mass-market purported contracts exclude litigation and thereby exclude class actions, and when they can easily exclude even class-wide arbitration, they are using "private" tools to do away with a "public" avenue of redress. In addition to imposing mandatory arbitration, many mass-market boilerplate schemes limit remedies to the amount paid for the product, thereby attempting to exclude any kind of consequential damages. In the presence of such limitations, combined with a ban on class actions, it is not worthwhile for an individual to bring suit or initiate arbitration against a firm.

Boilerplate schemes limiting or eliminating redress of grievances pose troubling questions for the ideals of contract, individual entitlements, and private ordering, and for the state's role as overseer administering the rule of law. To what extent can a "private" regime (contract) be allowed to undermine "public" remedies for abusive use of that very private regime? If all firms can individually disclaim the "public" rules of the road—i.e., the legal infrastructure of contract, including redress of grievances—then we would not be living under a rule of law that makes possible a realm of private ordering. The fact that such an outcome is possible highlights the threat posed for democratic ordering.

Human Rights and Interests

In the category of human rights and interests, it is useful to consider individual autonomy, freedom of speech, and individual privacy. Individual autonomy is harmed any time an individual is legally treated as if he had consented to a transaction when in reality—could we but know reality—he did not consent. So, individual autonomy is at risk in situations where consent is problematic. That is the root of the normative degradation underway in the system in which we find ourselves, given that consent appears problematic in a very large number of situations where individuals are divested of legal rights. It then becomes important to try to evaluate the level of importance of those rights (and consider that level of importance together with the level of doubt about consent).

Freedom of Speech

Freedom of speech is part of the US Constitutional Bill of Rights, of course, but it also permeates much of the common law as received from England and elaborated in the US. Relinquishing freedom of speech may give us concern because of its importance as a fundamental human right in our legal and political system—even though freedom of speech as an official Constitutional right requires a court to find "state action"—that is, government action—in order to find a First Amendment violation.[26] Questions of freedom of expression are raised when firms want to make available content that another country may disallow, as happens with some frequency, for example, in situations where "hate speech" which would be allowed in the US is disallowed in another country.[27] Questions of freedom of speech also have bearing on the circumstance when one person or firm wants to show its competitor or its competitor's product in a disparaging light in a way that is not misleading, even if courts do not always recognize this concern.[28] A provision that the user agrees not to publish a critical review of a software program has been seen more than once in mass-market boilerplate contracts.[29]

A person—even if consent is not in question—cannot validly exchange all of his freedom of speech for a payment, just as he cannot give up all of his right to a legal remedy in exchange for a payment. Freedom of speech (in its entirety) is market-inalienable. As with legal remedies, however, the question arises, as long as not all freedom of speech is precluded, to what extent *can* a person limit his own freedom of speech by contract? Confidentiality agreements limit freedom of speech and are valid, providing of course that the contract is valid. Trade secret law precludes some kinds of freedom of speech, as does fiduciary duty. Difficult questions arise in situations where this significant human right is waived in part, under circumstances of problematic consent. Especially troubling are situations where there is extensive social dissemination of the scheme curtailing freedom of speech, because in such a case the effect is not only to limit individual autonomy but also to shrink the realm of political and social dialogue.

Copyright law limits freedom of expression, because once an author (or, most often, a firm to which the author has transferred her copyright) owns a copyright, she owns the right to "silence" those who repeat the material she owns in a manner that the Copyright

Act prohibits.[30] But we should note again that the federal regimes of information propertization have left some uses free of ownership and thereby have created user rights.

When a EULA declares that the user "agrees" not to copy or distribute anything on a website, that "agreement" supersedes the law of copyright. The law of copyright would have allowed free copying and distribution of anything that is a fact rather than expression, of anything with an expired copyright, of anything that is an idea rather than an expression of an idea, of anything that is as short as a title, of anything that would be construed as fair use, and of anything that would fall under other doctrines related to the language needs of other creators, such as merger and scènes-à-faire.

These user rights have freedom of speech implications. Fair use in particular might even be considered to be constitutionally required—an aspect of political dialogue, criticism, and knowledge acquisition. Some US courts and legal scholars used to think so, but in modern law they tend to bypass Constitutional issues and proceed directly to economic analysis.[31] Nevertheless, the movement to reestablish the importance of a public domain can be seen in this light; that is, as expressing the idea that certain uses of information are important for individuals, for culture, and for the polity.[32] This should especially be taken into account in situations where consent is problematic and where the boilerplate scheme is widespread enough so that there are implications for the legal structure as a whole. In those circumstances, courts should consider at least heightened scrutiny for purported waivers of these user rights.

Privacy

Individual privacy seems to protect—or reflect our aspirations to protect—one subset of the many aspects of information and knowledge important to personal identity,[33] a subset concerning nondisclosure. It is unclear what kind of human right individual privacy is.[34] Perhaps it should not be considered a right that is fully inalienable, or even market-inalienable under many circumstances. Waiver of individual privacy rights causes most concern in situations where consent is lacking or problematic.[35] The regulations enacted to protect the privacy of medical records from waiver by an individual provide an example of regulatory efforts to make waiver more difficult and to insure actual consent.[36]

Individual privacy rights and interests are especially sensitive to heuristic biases. People probably do not know their own true valuation of these kinds of rights, or the extent to which they might later regret waiving them. Consider, for example, a bank that offers accounts free of service charge if the individual will agree to allow information about him that is useful to marketers to be freely sold to firms and used to direct solicitations and advertisements to him. What appears to be at one time a surplus information resource may appear quite differently once control has been surrendered. And, control of information, once surrendered, generally cannot be recovered. Perhaps even unproblematic consent should not give rise to the easy waiver we assume with default rules.

Privacy waivers pose broader concerns in situations where the waiver scheme is socially widespread. Even if we assume for the sake of argument that the majority has made informed consent, the effects of this consent on the recipient group as a whole might be unwanted. In order to preserve a widely valued aspect of social affairs, a society as a whole might not agree that waiver of privacy rights should be entirely determined by individuals. When enough individuals waive their rights, the character of society might be seriously altered for those who do not waive their rights. The minority who do not want to see control transferred may have no recourse once the majority has consented.

Suppose, for example, that it became common to waive privacy rights in intimate communications and pictures, and allow them (perhaps for a small fee) to be used in advertising e-mails to all customers who have previously done business with a firm. (US law permits e-mail marketing to any previous customer unless she performs an opt-out procedure. That's why you start getting e-mails from an online seller as soon as you buy something.[37]) A substantial minority of those receiving e-mail containing other people's intimate communications and pictures might be seriously disturbed by it, and feel that it has altered the character of their daily lives and society in general. The market won't fix the problem if the practice is so profitable for the firms that it maximizes profit for them on balance even if the minority refuses to do business with them. The option to perform op-out procedures is small comfort to these people.

The Extent of Social Dissemination of Boilerplate

To recapitulate some points made earlier in this chapter: If a right is clearly market-inalienable, then it cannot be sold even by one individual. If a trade is clearly not consented-to, then it cannot be enforced even against one individual. Moreover, inquiries about alienability and about consent can be synergistic: the more consent looks problematic, the more a court or a legislature might implement at least partial market-inalienability; the more a right looks to be at least partially market-inalienable, the more a court or a legislature might seriously examine the consent and tolerate less uncertainty about it.

In addition, as I have been saying in the preceding pages, an evaluation of waivers in mass-market boilerplate rights deletion schemes should often also take into account a third factor: the extent of social dissemination of the waiver(s). That is, how large a portion of the polity is affected? Consent that is problematic or nonexistent becomes socially and democratically more troubling as it becomes more widespread. Any instance of lack of consent resulting in the loss of a right is normatively troubling from a philosophical point of view, because any such loss of a right is wrong; but a society that allows this to happen routinely and on a large scale has a legal system that is normatively degraded.

Yet, in spite of the importance of normative degradation, an assessment of the social prevalence of a waiver in a rights deletion scheme is needed primarily because the democratic degradation that replaces the law of the state with the "law" of the firm becomes more and more salient as the number of people who are subjected to the firm's alternative legal universe increases. The extent to which the alternative scheme prevails depends both on how many people are recipients of a boilerplate scheme containing the waiver in question, and the extent to which those recipients could perhaps escape from the alternative scheme by buying the product or service they seek from a different firm or by doing without the product or service.

Market Factors

Various market conditions are empirically relevant to the question whether recipients can escape from a boilerplate scheme by buying the product or service from a different firm or by doing without.[38] Necessities of life cannot be done without; other things can, with various degrees of difficulty. (In economic parlance, this issue relates to the elasticity of demand.) If there is a single seller of the product, then the recipient who buys the product is stuck with its clauses. If there are multiple sellers but they all use the same clauses, the result is the same. But the situation is different if the product is available with different terms from different sellers. (In economic parlance, this issue relates to market structure, whether or not it is competitive, and whether or not the product together with terms is fully standardized.)

Another important factor in any consumer market is the prevalence of various heuristic biases, and information asymmetry. Although heuristic biases seem to relate mainly to the issue of consent, the more that people cannot (or cannot be expected to) escape the boilerplate scheme, the more that democratic degradation becomes a salient issue.

The Number of Recipients

It is safe to say that there are tens of millions of people subject to the Microsoft EULA, though it might, for various reasons, be difficult to say precisely how many.[39] The Mac EULA has a large number of recipients, too, as do many other software products, from games to accounting programs. Consider the mobile phone contracts offered by the big phone companies, which are so complex that intermediaries offer themselves as a way of helping you understand what the phone contract is doing.[40] On a more mundane note, almost everyone who has ever parked a car has come under the (purported) sway of a parking lot ticket contract. Many boilerplate schemes do purport to bind millions of people. So how many people would such a scheme have to bind in order for it to count as a rights deletion scheme that is likely to create salient democratic degradation?

It is not going to be possible to answer this question with a number, at least not using abstract reasoning. The question whether people can escape the imposed clauses must interact at some level with the number of people affected. A legislature or agency could place a number on the problem, however, because it has the power to use estimates that it decides are in the public interest. It could decide, for example, to consider a boilerplate scheme to be a troublesome rights deletion scheme when there are likely 100,000 people (or whatever number the legislature deems appropriate) covered by the scheme, and when there is evidence of market structure or other market factors that make it impossible or very difficult for recipients to be able to escape the scheme. Legislatures or agencies could do this on a general basis or industry-by-industry, depending upon whether the issues seem generalizable in context.

A court could also come to a decision in a particular case on this pragmatic basis. It would not necessarily hold that any scheme dropped onto (let's say) 100,000 or more people was suspect, while any scheme dropped onto fewer than 100,000 was safe; courts do not draw lines by applying numbers the way legislatures do. But courts could be attentive to the problem of democratic degradation as well as the problem of normative degradation, and they could develop procedures for understanding and dealing with these questions. These procedures would need to take into account the market factors I have mentioned in this section, and therefore would have to develop procedures for doing so.[41]

Applying the Analytical Framework

It should be evident by now that an evaluative framework is needed when a court—or a legislature or agency—must rule on a waiver of a background legal right. In this chapter I have suggested that three main parameters of such a framework should be: (1) the nature of the divested right; (2) the quality of consent by recipients; and (3) the extent of social dissemination of a scheme that supersedes recipients' background rights. Moreover, I have tried to show how these factors of analysis interact with each other in specific kinds of cases.

The appropriate response to the question whether a waiver is valid or invalid will often depend upon a reasoning process that takes into account all of these parameters. In general this evaluation cannot be an exclusively rule-driven endeavor, but rather must be a process of pragmatic judgment. Nevertheless, under some circumstances there are conclusions that rely in large part on rules. If consent is totally lacking (and we do not accept hypothetical consent or gerrymandered procedures such as I discussed in chapters 2 and 5), then whatever else is happening, there is not an enforceable contract. Sheer ignorance, if we reject the idea that a judicial finding of opportunity to find and read the terms assimilates to consent, is an example of this. If the nature of the right is such that it must be recognized as fully inalienable or market-inalienable, then again, whatever else is happening, there is not an enforceable contract. Examples of the latter include the purported relinquishment of one's right not to be discriminated against on the basis of race, sex, religion, or national origin, and the portion of a blanket exculpatory clause that purports to delete one's right to tort damages for the intentional or reckless infliction of harm. In such cases, social dissemination need not be taken into account in order to invalidate a purported contract. (But, of course, democratic degradation is worse if such clauses are allowed to govern a wide swath of recipients.) There may also be situations in which questionable alienability interacts with questionable consent to render a specific contract unenforceable, without regard to the number of people affected.

Most cases that come before courts will be less than clear-cut and require a pragmatic judgment: perhaps consent is problematic, but not totally absent; perhaps the right being purportedly waived is an important political or legal right, but not one that is per se inalienable. For such cases, the idea of partial market-inalienability (or some restraint on alienation) should be helpful. The legislature can declare a partial market-inalienability. It could say, for example, as the UCC does,[42] that waiver of consequential damages for personal injury caused by a product is prima facie unconscionable, thereby placing a difficult burden of proof on the firm deploying the waiver to justify it. Or it could say, as the UCC also does, that waiver of warranty protection (the implied warranty of merchantability) must be in writing and use certain words,[43] thereby placing a much less stringent burden of proof on the firm deploying the waiver. My term, "partial market-inalienability," as exemplified by these UCC provisions, is meant to direct decision makers' attention to the continuum of levels of scrutiny or requirements of justification that is open to them. Courts can vary burdens of proof; they can adopt appropriate rebuttable presumptions. Courts can also use the tool of partial market-inalienability. They should become more aware of the wide range of possibilities between market-inalienability and full alienability.

Often it will be necessary to consider the extent of social dissemination in making a judgment about the permissibility of a particular boilerplate rights deletion scheme. Judging the extent of social dissemination of a waiver scheme and its effect on the enforceability of that scheme will in some instances lead to decisions that are not as rule-driven as decisions based on lack of consent or market-inalienability might be. Instead, the extent of social dissemination must be taken into account in making a judgment call in cases that are not rule-like, such as those in which consent is uncertain and/or the alienability of the right relinquished is in doubt. Unless the waiver scheme is challenged in a class action, courts in contracts cases do not have a procedure for addressing the social effect of the scheme by declaring it invalid with regard to everyone who has become subject to it; nevertheless, a ruling in an individual case can serve as precedent for others.

Conclusion: Reconsidering Redress

The wrong of depriving individuals of their right to meaningful legal redress of grievances is especially apt to grow in severity as the number of affected individuals increases. That is because if large numbers of people have no realistic recourse when harmed in a transaction, the rule of law is undercut and democratic degradation is full-blown. Clauses that call into question the background right of redress of grievances include, first and foremost, mandatory arbitration clauses and severe remedy limitations. In many circumstances, choice of forum clauses also effectively negate this right, as do, in some circumstances, warranty disclaimers. Mandatory arbitration clauses erase the right to a jury trial, and, when they preclude collective (classwide) relief, they thereby preclude (in practice, most of the time) any legal remedy at all.

The analytical framework I have proposed suggests that mandatory arbitration clauses should be disallowed in mass-market deletion schemes (schemes that satisfy a criterion of widespread social dissemination), where their practical effect is to deny any remedy; such as a case where only a class action would be effective (small losses for many people). A fortiori, mass-market arbitration clauses at least should be disallowed where such clauses are deployed to prevent employees from trying to enforce other rights that are market-inalienable, such as in particular the right not to be discriminated against on the basis of race, sex, or another invidious category, and where some form of aggregative relief seems necessary to accomplish this goal. Of course, the US Supreme Court does not agree with my view. Rather, it has (in my view) underwritten democratic degradation by making redress impossible, in practice if not in theory, for large numbers of people. Perhaps the Court will change its collective mind, or perhaps Congress can overrule or chip away at what it has done and cabin the Federal Arbitration Act to its original intent.[44]

In a related vein, severe remedy limitations, such as those now permitted by the UCC for sales of products, should not be as easy to accomplish as they are in the UCC's current version. The UCC does not permit a merchant seller to disclaim a warranty without specific kinds of disclosure; but it does not require any disclosure in order to limit the remedy to the price paid for the product or the cost of repair, even in situations where this could cause large losses, excepting only personal injury or "failure of essential purpose."[45] Firms do take advantage of this kind of remedy slashing. (For example, see one firm's warranty limitations, excerpt on page 112; another firm's attempt to cancel the court's discretion with regard to specific performance, excerpt on page 112; and another firm's attempt to cancel the exception for failure of essential purpose, excerpt on page 119.) As I mentioned in chapter 8, courts could certainly put some teeth into the UCC's notion of failure of essential purpose. Such heightened scrutiny would be especially appropriate if the minimalist remedy is imposed on a large number of people who cannot choose otherwise, perhaps because the clause is attached to their purchases of essential products or services, and/or because there are identical clauses industry-wide.

Exculpatory clauses for negligence—those that immunize a firm from having to answer legally to someone it injures through its own fault—deny redress for harm caused by incursions on personal safety that would have been avoided had the firm used ordinary due care. This kind of waiver, if enforced, is an incursion on an important personal right, and also on the redress of grievances provided by law. Elimination of a whole field of remedy when a personal right is at stake should not be treated as if the entitlement in question is held under a fully alienable default rule. As mentioned above, the UCC has a stringent rule of partial market-inalienability for consequential damages for personal injury caused by a product: a contract that purports to waive this remedy is prima facie unconscionable. Courts are free to hold, and in some cases they should hold, that service providers as well as product providers cannot easily and as a matter of course exculpate themselves for causing personal injury. This should follow a fortiori in cases of industry-wide disclaimers of liability that change the whole structure of personal injury law as it relates to recipients.

Warranty disclaimers are a different matter. Not all warranty disclaimers erase a significant right of recipients, though some do; and not all warranty disclaimers have serious issues surrounding consent. Most customers know what "as is" means, and if they do, this is one situation where the waiver may in fact be reflected in the price. The UCC has legislated specific solutions for product warranties, and it has already made disclaimer less than a completely cursory procedure. It is permissible to sell a product "as is," for example, but that must be plainly stated. Moreover, the Magnuson-Moss Federal Warranty Act, one of the few Congressional interventions into contract law, has preempted the UCC provisions in part by providing that certain warranties in consumer transactions are market-inalienable (may not be disclaimed).[46]

My suggestions here for how the proposed analytical framework may be applied are merely pointers for how a decisionmaker might evaluate a specific situation. This is one field where the devil really is in the details. Nevertheless, I think use of this analytical framework will result in a substantial improvement over the notion of "reasonable expectation," with its normative/positive ambiguity; and also a substantial improvement over the tendency to look at clauses as if only one individual were involved, thereby excluding from consideration the danger of democratic degradation that can be caused by the large-scale use of boilerplate rights deletion schemes.

As readers in the law world will know, some of the existing law on this subject might be fitted into the categories I suggest. For example, the UCC provides that a court may take commercial setting into account in deciding whether a contract is unconscionable.[47] The idea here was that courts should be able to figure out in some cases whether recipients really are trading off rights for a lower price; I would add that courts should further try to figure out whether the rights that recipients are really trading off are really tradable in nature. They should not let this duty decay into a mere assumption. The UCC drafters probably intended the widespread commercial use of a clause to be a defense for the firm using it; whereas I think the opposite is more likely—that is, that widespread use of a clause may be a greater wrong than using it against only one or a few individuals. The widespread commercial use of a clause might well be grounds for disallowing it, because by now we should be aware that industry-wide standardization by no means indicates that a clause is either efficient or what consumers "would have chosen."[48]

I think the three categories of inquiries suggested here will be clarifying. They should replace categories such as "procedural" vs. "substantive" unconscionability or "reasonable expectation" that are not very workable, at least when it comes to evaluating boilerplate rights deletion schemes. The category that current law is missing—the extent of social dissemination of a rights deletion scheme, considered in context with the nature of the right and the quality of consent—is one that ought to become part of the analytical framework, because it is the category that directs us to recognize democratic degradation and the undermining of the rule of law.

· ·

PART IV

Escaping Contract

OTHER REMEDIAL POSSIBILITIES

. . . .

"Private" Reform Ideas

POSSIBLE MARKET SOLUTIONS

I F THE MARKET WERE to find its own solutions for boilerplate issues, that would be a development welcomed by many scholars
and business people in the US. Market solutions would appeal
not only to those who favor market solutions in general for most
everything, as a matter of political principle, but also to those companies or entrepreneurs positioned to profit from such markets. As
we shall see, however, market solutions tend to raise issues of their
own that must be addressed.[1]

What forms might market solutions take? Here are some ideas I
will sketch in this chapter. Advocacy groups such as the Electronic
Frontier Foundation or the Electronic Privacy Information Center
sometimes monitor firms' terms of service, and can highlight those
terms that firms should be either proud of or ashamed of. In this
sense they can be watchdog groups. Firms may of course develop
as a best practice of their own the use of terms that recipients
would find reasonable. Seals of approval, supplied perhaps by firms
such as Consumer Reports, might be developed to alert purchasers, either online or offline, that the firms' terms are user-friendly.
Internet users themselves might alert each other to threatening
terms or changes in terms and thus push back against the firm
deploying them. Rating agencies might be organized for the purpose of reviewing and rating the terms offered by various firms.
Technological filtering approaches or machine bargaining developments could help recipients avoid terms they don't want and select
those they prefer.

Reputation and Consumer Pushback

All of the approaches just mentioned are "private" or market suggestions for improving the normative and democratic acceptability
of boilerplate terms. One potentially important "private" incentive
is reputation. If watchdog groups were to monitor firms' terms of
service and develop lists of onerous terms that users may wish to
avoid, firms might take measures to avoid being on such a list in
order to preserve their reputations with their customers.[2] Similarly,
firms might decide to develop best practices, including the use of
terms that recipients would consider reasonable, and then publicize that fact. Perhaps firms could be encouraged to develop such
best practices by legal "safe harbors," such as the one proposed
by the American Law Institute's *Principles of the Law of Software
Contracts* for terms that are made available electronically.[3]

Some firms (in specific kinds of markets) are likely to be especially cognizant of the need to maintain good relationships with
their users, and therefore responsive to the threat of reputational
harm. This is most likely to be true for firms that possess three
characteristics: (1) a business model that requires the presence of
users who participate continually; (2) users who are reasonably
savvy about issues of user rights, such as data privacy or information copying; and (3) the need to survive in a market structure that
is reasonably competitive.

Firms that require the presence of users who participate continually are primarily online sites that derive revenues from delivering
advertising to the "eyeballs" of their users. Firms whose users are
reasonably savvy about user rights are likely to be firms with purely
online business models, whether or not they depend on "eyeballs,"
because users of such firms' services are likely to be experienced
computer and software users and likely have some awareness of
user rights issues involving intellectual property, data privacy, and
perhaps remedies. Savvy users may exercise "voice" against such
a firm, pushing back against the imposition of terms they dislike.
They may also "exit" if their desires are ignored—something a
firm in this position particularly wishes to avoid. These conditions

conducive to consumer pushback will also be more likely to influence a firm significantly if its market is reasonably competitive, because the incentive to avoid reputational harm is likely to be muted in noncompetitive markets.

These three conditions suggest that social networking sites are particularly likely to experience user pushback and to be responsive to it. Indeed, this is exactly what happened to Facebook when it tried to impose new rules about privacy.[4] Other sites with social networking components, such as LinkedIn, Yahoo!, Google, and perhaps eBay, may also be likely to receive user pushback and to be responsive to it.

On the other hand, major cell phone service providers have apparently been less responsive to widespread consumer unhappiness with their contracts. (Often when I tell people I'm writing a book about boilerplate, they tell me, sometimes in awesome detail, how terrible their cell phone contract is. Not because they read it before clicking "I agree," of course, but because they were later burned by it, sometimes repeatedly.)

Cell phone companies do want to keep their customers, of course. Indeed, most of them impose boilerplate that locks customers in, such as large fees for failing to stick with the service provider for two years. But cell phone service providers probably are not subject to the other conditions that make for successful consumer pushback: their customers by and large are not savvy about the system and its parameters to the degree that users of social network sites are. It seems, also, that their market is not competitive in the way that would be needed in order for consumer preferences to motivate a change in practice. Nor, apparently, has the bad reputation of cell phone service providers harmed them enough—relative to the amounts they can save by imposing onerous fees and incomprehensible terms with regard to data transmission, etc.—to incentivize better practices. In addition to telephone service providers, other providers generally known to have onerous terms are Internet service providers, banks, and other financial firms.[5] When it comes to these kinds of firms, private watchdog groups or user pushback are less likely to be efficacious.

If and when user pushback stimulates competition among firms, it is likely to be centered on terms that recipients experience immediately as annoying or harmful, such as (in the case of social networking sites) lax user privacy or commercial use of recipients' information, or (in the case of cell phone providers), two-year lock-in provisions. Pushback is less likely to occur in response to the kind of terms that, because of heuristic bias, are not immediately salient. Even savvy customers are less likely to push back against terms such as those that deprive recipients of remedies against the firm, because people do not expect that they will experience the need to bring suit or become part of a class action.[6]

Rating Agencies, Seals of Approval, Certifications

Another "private" or market approach that might be considered involves rating agencies or stamps of approval by third parties. The idea here is that a disinterested third party would evaluate the terms offered by firms and make it easy for recipients to decide whether the terms that come with a product are or are not acceptable to them, at least in general. Firms' boilerplate terms could be rated in the manner of bonds, for example, from AAA to CCC or D, and those that are highly rated might be encouraged to advertise that fact. Recipients would know without the need to read the boilerplate that they were unlikely to find nasty surprises in an AAA rated scheme.

Firms' boilerplate terms could be evaluated and monitored in the same way that security structures and precautions are monitored and certified by independent third-party entities.[7] Most firms that employ independent security certification entities, however, are online businesses that need security certification in order to attract customers. Customers want to be sure that there are no weaknesses or secret backdoor entries in either the physical deployment of services or in the digital systems themselves. There may be less incentive for firms marketing other products or services with attached boilerplate terms to employ independent certification authorities, because in most cases recipients of boilerplate are not (or not yet) demanding that the boilerplate they receive be certified as safe, or user-friendly, or free of nasty surprises. Nevertheless, some firms might well get reputational mileage out of doing this and advertising it. And if that were to happen, others might need to follow in order to compete effectively; the practice could snowball.

Unfortunately, private rating agencies or security certifiers cannot always be trusted to be unbiased. Those who use them will have to be wary of capture (for example, if a third-party certification agency has a stake in a security product and tends to boost the rating it applies to those who purchase that product). Those who use such rating agencies will also have to be wary of ideological bias: an independently organized rating group may have as its goal the eradication of the doctrine of unconscionability, for example.[8]

Automated Filtering or Choice Systems

Automated contracting—"machine bargaining"—could have the effect of enabling parties who have the capability of using such an automated system to obtain the terms they want. They could program computers with sets of terms acceptable to them, and have the machines communicate with each other to create transactions. Such a protocol would cut the cost of many routine transactions. That is the reason why automated supply-chain management is an important topic in contemporary operations management engineering. This kind of automated procedure holds out the hope that parties might come to actual agreement via private market methods rather than being stuck with possibly conflicting boilerplate, in which the parties exchange forms (such as orders, invoices, etc.), each of which contains boilerplate favorable to the sender. (Conflicting boilerplate, know to contracts students as "the battle of the forms," causes conflict if a problem comes up later and each side believes its boilerplate has made the other side assume that risk.[9]) But machine bargaining seems to be more readily adaptable to firms doing repetitive transactions that can be automated and less likely to be available to boilerplate recipients who are consumers. Consumers usually do not engage in repetitive transactions of a sufficiently large scale, and therefore normally do not have computer systems that automate transactions beyond the fact that their personal computers show them boxes to click to signal agreement to terms that they have not read. Would it be possible to use automation in a manner similar to that used by industrial systems, so that consumers too could get the terms they actually would prefer?

Here are a few possibilities: Filtering systems could be implemented for personal computers. Such a system might alert the user if an arbitration clause (for example) is included in the boilerplate attached to the product she is thinking of purchasing from an online retailer. Or, the system could just screen out suppliers whose boilerplate was unacceptable to the shopper. Or, the recipient's computer could filter out products offered for sale with sets of terms that are not the set (or sets) that the user has previously programmed the system to accept. Or, online systems could be developed that would enable users to customize their own terms.

Filtering systems on personal computers would be market solutions, because computer users would be free to use them or not, depending on their willingness to pay for the system. Computer firms' trade associations might develop an engineering standard available for industry-wide use, and firms might supply an implementation bundled with personal computers and/or standard software packages,[10] in which case it would be easier for users to decide to turn them on than if the software were offered for purchase separately. One kind of filtering system might be analogous to systems proposed for protecting online privacy or for preventing children from viewing pornography.[11] In an implementation that was marketed some years ago, teams of students had summer jobs judging whether certain websites contained pornography or not.[12] In an analogous variety of filter, the user could set her computer to flag arbitration clauses, or no-copying clauses, or whatever clauses she wanted to avoid. A slightly different variety of filter would screen out products offered by firms whose complete set of terms contained one or more clauses previously determined to be unacceptable. If many recipients implemented such a filter, it would amount to a boycott of firms offering boilerplate unacceptable to a significant number of users. (There might, however, be a drawback to this particular system, in that the incentive for entrepreneurs to design and manufacture it might be offset by the fear that the designer or manufacturer of a boycott-machine might itself be boycotted by other firms.)

Increased customization of transactions can also be considered. When buying a product online, the customer might at some time during the checkout process be offered the option of checking a box to pay an extra (say) $2.19 to extend the warranty from one year to two, or an extra $0.52 to have dispute resolution by litigation rather than arbitration. The determination of what the consumer should pay for each clause, and what should be the total charged for the transaction with the selected clauses, could be outsourced in real time to an actuarial intermediary, and the customized terms could be presented to the recipient in printable form very quickly. There is an analogous market offline for extended warranties and service on items such as cars, electronic devices, and washing machines. The online market would be able to accomplish the customization with much more granularity; that is, for smaller items and smaller changes in price.[13]

Why are automated systems such as these not in use? Perhaps they are more difficult to develop than I realize. (Needless to say, I am not a software engineer.) Perhaps there isn't a market for these systems—or even for other systems that are better than the ones I can think of—or perhaps it is *believed* that there is no market for them. Perhaps, that is, recipients really *don't* care what terms are inside boilerplate; or at least firms *believe* that they don't.

It may be true that almost all recipients really don't care at all about what terms are inside the boilerplate at the outset.* But it's also true that recipients do care when they find out later that although they suffered damages caused by a product, they can't sue for consequential damages, can't bring their case before a jury, have waived their information privacy rights, or are subject to being cut off as a user for exercising rights that copyright law grants to

---

* Almost all. I recently saw an ad in an airline magazine directed at customers who hire private jets. The ad said, "Surprises are best meant for family (not contracts)." The airline obviously thought that advertising its contract as without surprises would be attractive to this clientele.

users. In other words, the apparent lack of demand for these systems could be a classic case of heuristic bias or bounded rationality. Practically nobody thinks that an unexpected loss will befall her, or that she will have to sue someone. This is a condition that seems not to be amendable to market solutions.

Should the legal system try to correct for this type of bias? Maybe yes, at least sometimes. The question whether the legal system should try to correct for prevalent heuristic biases does not have a consensus answer.[14] Nevertheless, this concern moves us toward considering the role of "public" regulation in overseeing and structuring these "private" market solutions. The issue of hybrid regimes—that is situations in which possible market solutions would need to be shored up by government regulation of some kind—will be taken up in chapter 12.

Reconceptualizing (Some) Boilerplate under Tort Law

Introduction: From Contract to Tort

Receipt of boilerplate is often more like an accident than a bargain. What follows from this fact for legal oversight of boilerplate? Bargains come under contract law; accidents come under tort law. Contract is basically focused on situations where two parties enter into consensual transactions of exchange, whereas tort is focused on actions (and sometimes non-actions) that injure someone in a way that is not part of a consensual undertaking. As a general matter, tort law comes into play in interactions between strangers, whereas contract law is premised on the idea that there are two parties who have bargained with each other.[1]

As soon as we realize that many recipients of boilerplate have had rights divested without a consensual undertaking, the possibility arises of regulating such boilerplate rights deletions under tort law rather than contract law. Most boilerplate rights deletions are not readily understandable as the result of two parties bargaining with each other, and they are forced into that paradigm only with great difficulty and with a concomitant gerrymandering of the notion of consent. These schemes are, in fact, more like something that happens between strangers, or at least to someone in less contact with the instigator of the happening than the conceptions underlying contract allow. In other words, many of these schemes are more like the relationship between the manufacturer of a product and the end-user who might wish to claim that the product is defective and has caused him injury, than they are to bargains, exchanges, or voluntary transfers.

There is precedent for the creation of new torts by common-law courts when the need arises to recognize a category of injury. The most prominent example is the development of torts involving invasion of privacy. These torts, such as the tort of unauthorized use of one's name and likeness, were developed after an 1890 law review article by Samuel Warren and Louis Brandeis suggested the existence of a right of privacy.[2] In this chapter, I will propose that abusive boilerplate could either be treated as a defective product, or else regulated under a new tort of intentional deprivation of basic legal rights.

. There would be advantages to regulating at least some boilerplate rights deletion schemes under tort law. For one thing, we would be spared the efforts of boilerplate apologists to shoehorn these transactions into a core legal category based upon consent, and the law would be spared the misshapen version of contractual ordering that results when courts adopt the apologists' theories. There would be perhaps a more significant advantage as well. Tort law has developed a legal infrastructure for dealing with mass torts, whereas contract law has not developed an infrastructure for dealing with mass contracts.[3] Indeed, the difficulty caused by the fact that contract law has no infrastructure for dealing with mass contracts is one way we might understand the basis of the contract-as-product theorists' complaint that I discussed in chapter 6.[4] Although I differ with these theorists in important respects, this is an understanding of their complaint that I endorse.

If we accept the contract-as-product view, the reconceptualization of boilerplate as part of a composite product brings us at least half way to a tort theory of boilerplate rights deletion schemes. Perhaps we should go all the way. Seen as products, boilerplate schemes, just like any other products, can be defective, unsafe, or otherwise likely to cause injury. We should stop considering these boilerplate schemes one at a time as a contract between two individuals. Instead, I want to suggest that we should take Douglas Baird and his colleagues in the law-and-economics world to the logical conclusion of their view. We should go all the way and put these "products" into the legal category—tort law—in which we can actually consider them as products.

If some boilerplate schemes are reinterpreted or reconceptualized under tort law, it will be possible to apply the same body of law to technological protection measures (TPMs), which in the digital world are often a substitute for a boilerplate scheme.[5] In the case of a TPM, the curtailing of user rights is much more literally a part of a digital product than is a set of boilerplate terms that comes with a physical product or a service. If TPMs, or some of them, are more like machines controlling users' range of activities than they are like contracts, then it is not a strain on language and tradition to consider them under the rubric of products that are potentially defective or likely to cause injury to the user. Right now TPMs appear to be largely unregulated. Whereas the user is legally prevented from disabling a TPM,[6] TPMs are not legally prevented from disabling a user. TPMs could be brought within the rule of law by court decisions in the realm of tort law, because courts could distinguish TPMs that represent excessive self-help from those that represent acceptable product functionalities in a well-ordered private sphere.

It would by no means be contrary to the normal development of law and its categories to look to tort law to regulate not only TPMs, but also some types of boilerplate. Indeed, a tort regime rather than a contract regime has already been outlined when the boilerplate product is an insurance policy.[7] As I mentioned above, common-law courts can create a new tort when the need arises for it. The distinction (what I will call the "doctrinal borderline") between contracts and torts has always been malleable, because the legal categories overlap, and their contours have evolved as the need for them shifted over time. I will review next some of the history, of theory and of practice, that demonstrates the lack of a clear-cut boundary between contracts and torts. Then I will come back to the main project of this chapter, which is to consider how a tort regime for dealing with boilerplate rights deletion schemes might be structured, and to examine a few of the problems that might arise in structuring and implementing such a regime.

The Shifting, Malleable, Fuzzy "Line" between Contracts and Torts

In a book entitled *The Death of Contract*, which originated as a set of lectures in 1970 and was published in 1974, Grant Gilmore argued that the self-contained, formal, logical system that was contract law according to the theory of the late nineteenth and early twentieth centuries was dead.[8] This self-contained and logical view of contract law is known as the "classical theory of contracts." Gilmore declared classical contract law "dead" because of the breakdown of any pretense that contract law could be scientific and unified. He called his diatribe "a study in . . . the process of doctrinal disintegration."[9] One of his main pieces of evidence for the breakdown of classical unity was the fact that the first Restatement of Contracts, published by the American Law Institute in the 1920s, was "schizophrenic."[10] (He might have said "eclectic," or "inconsistent," but "schizophrenic" is an arresting word.)

A primary basis for Gilmore's dubbing the Restatement "schizophrenic" was the difference between its first sections and section 90. In its first sections it adhered to doctrines of classical contract law, such as "offer" and "acceptance" and "consideration," all of which rely on either a two-sided, bargained exchange of a promise for a promise, or a two-sided bargained exchange of a promise for a performance. But then, in section 90, the Restatement introduced the idea of finding obligation based on a one-sided promise that the other party had relied on. In other words, what signaled schizophrenia, and the death of contract in its classical sense, was the onset of enforcing one-sided promises in the presence of reliance.[11] Enforcing promises based on reliance had begun to make inroads into the court decisions of the early twentieth century. That is how the concept found its way into the Restatement, but the Restatement pushed this trend further. And in 1981 the second Restatement went further still.[12]

Enforcement of a one-sided promise if the other side has relied on it (in a manner and to the extent deemed appropriate by the doctrine and by the interpretation of particular courts) has remained a part of contract law, even if sometimes uneasily.[13] Classical contract law is indeed dead in one sense that Gilmore intended, because very few suppose that contract doctrines can be gathered up into a deductive and logical unified system. But classical contract law is also alive and well in the sense that new formalists have arisen, and formalist principles are still adhered to in some doctrines, by some judges, and by some academics.[14]

The borderlines between various legal doctrines are not so hard and fast as we lead law students to believe by requiring them to take separate courses called "Contracts," "Torts," "Criminal Law," and so on. Gilmore thought that the underlying schema suggested by section 90 of the Restatement, or portions of it, would fit better into the category of tort law than the category of contract law. In fact he thought that we were "fast approaching the point" at which "there is really no longer any viable distinction between liability in contract and liability in tort."[15]

Gilmore may have been the first, but he is not the only contracts scholar to suggest that at least some cases that currently come under contract law would be better conceptualized under tort law.[16] Meanwhile, as legal historians know, the category of "tort" was itself a synthetic concept, a unifying conception bringing together separate legal categories that gradually coalesced in the late nineteenth century. Legal doctrines evolve.

Overlapping or Interlocking Doctrines: Blended Tort and Contracts Principles

The simplistic distinction between tort and contract—according to which contract relates to injuries occurring as part of a bargaining relationship, while tort relates to harm caused in a way that is not part of a consensual relationship—must be modified when we take into consideration situations in which both contract and tort are (or may be) implicated. We can think of these as doctrinal border areas, in which doctrines overlap or are interlocking.

One example of a doctrinal border area is fraud or misrepresentation. It is actionable under tort principles for one to induce action by someone else by means of lying or deceiving, under conditions where the misrepresentation is important to the other party and the deceiver knows or at least ought to know that the deceived party is relying on the deception in changing his position. The tort of fraud or misrepresentation is adjudicated under principles taking into account what constitutes the elements of the case, what defenses are possible, and what remedies are available. Another example of a doctrinal border area is malpractice—whether medical, legal, accounting, or of some other kind. If a medical professional treats someone incompetently, that can constitute the tort of malpractice; indeed, operating on someone without her knowledge or consent can constitute the tort of battery.

Both fraud and malpractice are doctrinal border areas because contract is often involved as well in situations where they arise. Fraud and misrepresentation are contract doctrines as well as tort doctrines, which will operate to invalidate (or render voidable) a contract because of lack of consent. Mistake is considered a contract doctrine and not within the usual notions of tort doctrine; yet mistake in contract law often looks to the fault of one party, or to an assumption of risk by one party, and these are ideas that are imported from tort. Malpractice is a border area because a contract is often involved, and the quality of consent to the contract often becomes an issue. The contract employing the doctor or the attorney can also become an issue because a poor result can be judged either as failure to do what was promised, which would refer to contract doctrine, or negligent performance of the duty, which would refer to tort doctrine.[17]

Another border area is bad faith breach of contract. Contract doctrine says that all contracts contain an implied obligation of good faith and fair dealing that cannot be waived.[18] The right of each party to be treated in good faith is inalienable. In other words, even if two fully cognizant parties were to state in writing that they were allowed to treat each other in bad faith, such a provision would be null and void. Bad faith could amount to the tort of fraud, but it need not. For example, under certain circumstances a firm could be in bad faith if it fails to inform the other party of a risk it is running, when it could easily do so; or (in cases of employment contracts) certain types of wrongful termination claims might come under bad faith and be remediable as breach of contract.[19]

In short, the boundary between contracts and torts is both fuzzy and shifting. There is nothing especially odd or radical about the proposal I will offer, to evaluate (some) boilerplate under tort law instead of contract law.

Warranty

Probably the main example of the overlapping of concepts, and the evolutionary process at the contract/torts boundary, is the history of warranty. The idea of warranty began as a contract doctrine: the seller promises to the buyer, the person actually party to the contract of sale, that the product will function as promised (or as impliedly promised; that is, as it is supposed to). Warranty migrated into an area more like tort when warranty became applicable to parties remote from the original seller, such as, on the seller's side, the manufacturer, and on the buyer's side, a person who receives the product from the original buyer or from someone further down a chain of distribution; or (most tort-like) a person who finds the product in the street (where, for example, it blows up and injures him). The reason that warranty can be seen as migrating toward tort is because contract is supposed to be about deals between two parties (a situation called "privity"); whereas tort is supposed to cover other situations of injury.

Exactly how far producers and sellers of products can be liable to anyone other than the immediate buyer is still a matter of considerable dispute. Much of the dispute is now located in the tort category of liability for defective products.[20] Nevertheless, the overlapping contract category of breach of warranty still exists as well. When a nonfunctional product meets the legal criteria for being defective and causes personal injury, that is most likely to be seen as a tort cause of action; whereas when a nonfunctional product causes economic loss, that is more likely to seen as a warranty problem in the realm of contract. Warranty has been extended by the legal system in some respects to apply to those who are not parties to the original deal but located somewhere else in the chain of distribution.[21] But tort remedies for economic damages are limited in some cases,[22] so, where breach of warranty is involved, a plaintiff who has suffered only economic damages may fare better under contract law, even if he is not a party to the contract.

In short, the development of the tort doctrine of liability for defective products arose when the contractual notion of warranty expanded beyond the parties to the original transaction. Not only the immediate seller can be held liable, but also the manufacturer and perhaps other intermediaries in the supply chain. Likewise, not only the immediate purchaser can be the beneficiary of the protection, but also those further down the distribution chain, or indeed those unrelated to either the supply chain or the distribution chain (e.g., someone who finds the product in the street). The expansion of liability to those who are not part of the original transaction, and indeed to those who are strangers to it, makes the notion of warranty a hybrid between contract principles and tort principles.

This is especially true when the warranty is implied (that is, imposed) by law rather than agreed to by the parties. Such is the implied warranty of merchantability provided for sales of goods by the Uniform Commercial Code.[23] In this case, the law simply says that sellers who meet the criteria of being merchants are liable to buyers for certain kinds of product defects. Proposed (but not enacted) revisions to the implied warranty provisions of the UCC would have made clear that liability is intended to extend to those earlier in the supply chain and later in the distribution chain than the contracting parties (immediate seller and buyer). The question would then become whether the implied warranty is a mere default rule that sellers can escape by means of contract, especially by means of boilerplate schemes. As I discussed in chapter 7, the UCC is rather lenient in this regard.

Case Study: Implied Warranty of Habitability in Residential Leases

Leases are normally considered contracts. It used to be true that the lessee (tenant) was liable to pay rent whether or not the leased residence was in habitable condition. Then, starting in the late nineteenth century, city housing codes imposed standards of safety and fitness on landlords renting premises for human habitation. Eventually, courts began to read into the lease an implied warranty of habitability based on the provisions of the housing code.[24] This meant that the tenant's obligation to pay rent could be diminished or suspended if the premises were not in habitable condition. (In legalese, the promise to pay rent became dependent on an implied promise by the landlord to deliver habitable premises, rather than being an independent obligation of the tenant.)

Courts developed standards of habitability that did not need to track housing codes in detail, and, following this common-law development, many states enacted an implied warranty of habitability by statute.[25] Such statutes declare that the implied warranty of habitability cannot be waived by contract between a landlord and tenant. Otherwise, the legislators realized, landlords would just use boilerplate leases that waived the implied warranty. Had this happened, we would have had a core case of democratic degradation. The action of state legislatures in making the implied warranty nonwaivable (inalienable) shows that legislatures have at least this remedy available against the threat that firms deploying boilerplate will simply bypass their enactments.

As courts developed standards of habitability, they developed standards of relief for tenants claiming breach of the implied warranty. Many courts held that if the shortfall in habitability caused by the defects of the premises—such as broken windows, nonfunctional plumbing, etc.—was (say) 25 percent, then the rent should be reduced by 25 percent. The Restatement 2d of Property adopted this formula.[26] If the market for substandard apartments is competitive, as it might be in some neighborhoods in which rental housing is dilapidated but cheap, then the rent laid down in the lease could well be the going market price for an apartment in poor condition. In that case, tenants and landlords are contracting at the market price. When a court reduces the price by its estimate of the percentage lack of habitability, it is reducing the market price. Courts often speak of this as a contractual remedy, but it is actually a hybrid between contract and tort, with emphasis on the tort side. That is, the transaction can more readily be understood in tort terms than in contract terms. It does not look as though courts are enforcing a contract between a landlord and a tenant in such cases, but rather as if the court is declaring that the landlord has "wronged" a tenant by putting a substandard unit on the market. The reduction in rent to below the market price is more like compensation to the tenant for that "wrong" than it is like enforcement of a contract.

Tort and Contract Remedies: Comparison and Interaction

When a person wants to bring a claim against a company for a product that has malfunctioned and caused him some loss—let's suppose it's a software product that crashed and took all of the user's data with it—he doesn't tell his lawyer whether he has a contracts case or a tort case. Nevertheless, there is a reason that plaintiffs (and their lawyers) might prefer to bring cases in tort if they can,[27] because tort remedies cover certain things that contract remedies do not. Most important for our purposes, tort remedies can extend to mass-market harms. Also, punitive damages are available in tort cases but not in contract. Nor is there a remedy for emotional distress or pain and suffering in contract, as there is in tort. Tort applies to everyone who causes harm, whereas contract very rarely applies to third parties to the contract involved. As I mentioned, breach of warranty is an exception, and a plaintiff who has suffered economic loss but no damage to property or personal injury might be better off with contract in certain circumstances, but most often the other more generous damage availability in tort would make plaintiffs (and their lawyers) hope for a tort recovery.

Tort remedies in general are limited by a doctrine known as "proximate cause," which cuts off damages if they are considered too remote in the causal chain from the defendant's act.[28] Contract remedies are, limited in general by a doctrine known as the "rule in *Hadley* v. *Baxendale*," which limits damages to those that are foreseeable at the time of contracting.[29] The contract rule is considered to be generally stricter than the tort rule. For this reason as well, tort is superior to contract for plaintiffs in situations where plaintiffs can obtain a tort remedy in a case that also involves a contract.

But under current practice, contract trumps tort in many areas, because the purported contracts of World B, when they are enforced, tend to curtail recipients' entitlements to remedies in tort as well as in contract. As we saw in the prologue and in chapter 7, boilerplate rights deletion schemes often contain blanket exculpatory clauses purporting to exclude all tort liability for the firm.

Contract conceptions of remedy are routinely intermingled with tort conceptions of remedy. As we also saw in chapter 7, the Uniform Commercial Code adopted a particular compromise between contract and tort in its provision for buyers' remedies caused by defective products (breach of warranty). The UCC appears to adopt the tort category of proximate cause of harm, rather than the contract category of reasonable foreseeability at the time of contracting. But it also provides that remedies can be very severely limited by contract, unless the limitation causes the remedy to fail of its essential purpose, adding that a limitation on consequential damages for personal injury to a consumer is prima facie unconscionable.

One more area of contract/tort overlap—or at least of conceptual intermingling—seems to be the doctrine of "reasonable expectations." Courts apply this doctrine primarily to insurance policy contracts. But, as we have seen in chapter 5, contracts scholars have suggested that the "reasonable expectations" of the recipient of boilerplate should determine whether or not boilerplate terms are enforceable, and the idea that only terms that are "radically unexpected" should be unenforceable seems conceptually similar. In that latter strategy, the consent of the recipient is attenuated to mean that the recipient who does not read the boilerplate intends to take the risk of whatever divestment of entitlement is inside that boilerplate, provided only that what is inside is "not radically unexpected." As we saw, in this strategy "radically unexpected" seems to mean objectively, to a "reasonable person" in the recipient's position, and not subjectively, to the recipient in actual fact in his own mind. The notion of "reasonableness in the circumstances," or what a reasonable person would do in a certain situation, is a standard conceptual schema of tort law.

It must be added that the idea of assumption of risk, another standard conceptual schema in tort law, is deployed in an attenuated way by theorists defending boilerplate. In order for a tort defendant to prevail against someone its actions have harmed by claiming that the plaintiff assumed the risk, a lot more argument and attention to specifics is required than the blanket assent-to-risk strategy employed by these contracts scholars. That is, in a tort framework, once we understand "reasonable expectations" together with assumption of risk, then arguments about these matters must include much more attention to specific context. In tort cases, courts are still strict in evaluating this defense,[30] rather than just by-passing the issue as is often done in contracts cases—and in contract theorizing. Some theorists, and some judges, just take it as given that recipients "assume the risk" of waivers in boilerplate whose risk the recipient does not understand, so that boilerplate can be contractual, an instance of freedom of contract, of free choice. In contrast, theorists and judges are much less likely to say that a consumer who does not know when he chooses to purchase a package of meat that it contains *E. coli* assumes the risk of getting sick, or that a passenger who chooses to travel on a jet plane without knowing that the engines have not been properly maintained assumes the risk of the engine falling off. It seems that the problem of information availability as it relates to choice is much better understood in tort than in contract. A contract theorist might say that recipients know that boilerplate can contain terms that are onerous; therefore a recipient has assumed the risk that an exculpatory clause will exclude liability of an injurer for negligently causing the death of her sister. A torts theorist would not say that people know that meat can be contaminated, therefore a meat purchaser has assumed the risk that her child will die of *E. coli* infection.

Insofar as "reasonable expectations" or "reasonable person" theories about contracts do not ask what an actual person was doing in a particular situation but rather what a generalized hypothetical reasonable person would have done in that situation, they are at least straddling the theoretical border between contract and tort.[31] That is part of the reason why Grant Gilmore thought contract was close to its "death"; it was being swallowed up by tort.[32]

Considering a New Tort

In some situations in which firms deploy mass-market boilerplate, consent is clearly absent and significant rights are deleted. At least in such cases, a tort conception covers the situation much more readily than a contract conception. There are legal obstacles to overcome, however, which stand in the way of judicial review of boilerplate under tort law. Some US courts hold that the presence of a contract between two parties excludes application of tort law with respect to claims of one of the parties. Tort law, the reasoning goes, basically covers injuries incurred in interactions between "strangers" and is inapplicable to nonstrangers; i.e., those who are in a contractual relationship.

Even if this principle is deemed appropriate, as I believe it should not be, it could not include all fields of tort. If it were interpreted to include the tort of fraud or misrepresentation,[33] it is too broad no matter what the relationship of the parties, at least when the fraud relates to how one party induced the other to enter the contract. That is because contracts obtained by fraud or duress are outside the basic premise of voluntary agreement underlying the enforceability of contracts. Such a purported contract is actually a noncontract.[34] Malpractice is also a large area of exception to the claim that the presence of contract excludes tort. Malpracticing accountants, physicians, and attorneys are frequently held liable in tort to clients with whom they have contracts.

Even if a principle of excluding tort law where a contract is involved is understood more narrowly, so as not to include the tort of fraud of misrepresentation, or the tort of malpractice, nonetheless it should not apply to the purported contracts of World B. The principle in question, according to the courts that developed it, is one of protecting the ideal of freedom of contract. It is designed for the situation pictured in World A. World B contracts are prob-lematic from the outset on the issue of voluntary interaction. This is the problem of normative degradation. Moreover, and equally if not more important, World B contracts which amount to rights deletion schemes do not usually signify a nonstranger relationship between two parties.[35] Being the recipient of boilerplate, especially in the situation I have called sheer ignorance, is often more like being hit by a one of thousands of dumped projectiles than it is like entering into a relationship with the entity that dumped them.

Courts should not extend to World B this and other traditions developed for World A in order to protect the scope of contract law from being taken over by tort law.[36] In fact, a tort takeover of World B—at least in its mass-market manifestation of boilerplate rights deletion schemes—seems appropriate. As long as the justi-fication for contract enforcement remains the voluntariness of a transaction between two parties, then protection of the domain of contract—if indeed it needs any— should be limited to those con-tracts that belong to World A.

World A can include adhesion contracts to some extent, as well as some standardized sets of terms that do not purport to rear-range one party's background legal entitlements in favor of the other (such as purchasing a product at the grocery store; many insurance policies; purchases of stocks and bonds, and much else). World A should *not* include purported contracts whose aim is to transport recipients to a different legal universe where many of their background rights are deleted. As I discussed in chapter 3, the background rights that should not be subject to wholesale deletion are those whose "public" character supports the commitment of the polity to appropriate oversight of a democratic order and of private ordering.

The difficulties involved in stretching contract justificatory ra-tionales to include much of World B may indicate that it is time to give up this attempt, that it is time to use another legal domain to evaluate the boilerplate schemes of World B. Indeed, the migration of World B purported contracts to tort would be reminiscent of the migration of defective-product liability to tort, where a primary motivation was the difficulty caused by the doctrine of privity in the realm of contract law.[37] Analogously, trying to fit boilerplate rights deletion schemes into the categories of contract law— bargaining, agreement, promising, consent—has proved procrustean. Especially if one accepts the prevalent economic view that boilerplate is part of the product that a recipient is purchasing,[38] it seems to make sense to regulate boilerplate by the same law that regulates products. Legal argument would be relieved of the need for gerrymandered definitions, which in itself is no small benefit.

What would we call the tort of imposing on recipients a rights deletion scheme that is beyond the bounds of appropriate "lawmaking" by firms? Perhaps we could assimilate this to the tort analysis of liability for marketing defective products.[39] A "browsewrap" purporting to exculpate for all harms, or a "money-now-terms-later" boilerplate that announces severe remedy deletions such that all practical avenues of redress are negated could well render the combination of the functional modality together with the boilerplate a composite product that is defective.

Intentional Deprivation of Basic Legal Rights

Nevertheless, I think we might well consider a new tort category such as "intentional deprivation of basic legal rights."[40] A firm that imposes severe remedy deletions of rights that are at least partially market-inalienable, under circumstances of nonconsent and mass-market distribution, could be liable in tort for intentional deprivation of basic legal rights.

How would courts determine when a firm is liable for this tort? And when a firm is found liable, what would be the remedy?

With respect to determination of liability, I propose that the courts use the categories that I have laid out earlier (in chapter 9), with particular attention to political rights, such as redress of grievances, and human rights, such as freedom of speech and privacy, all of which should be understood as at least partially (and sometimes fully) market-inalienable. Courts should consider the extent of democratic degradation when an entire legislative scheme is in danger of being erased for many people by the simple expedient of deploying boilerplate. At the least, when evaluating the extent of democratic degradation, courts should consider what kind of legislative scheme it is that boilerplate is deleting; whether it is one that is properly "public" (placed in the care of the polity, for the benefit of the polity as a whole). Courts must also weigh the quality of recipients' consent.

The most likely case for finding a violation in tort by a firm deploying boilerplate is the situation in which a basic right is cancelled by a mass-market boilerplate clause under conditions of sheer ignorance or of apparent severe information asymmetry. Basic rights that should be market-inalienable, such as the right of a realistic avenue of redress of grievances, coupled with severely problematic consent (especially sheer ignorance) and large-scale distribution would be good candidates for a finding of liability under the tort of intentional deprivation of basic legal rights. (See "Worst Case Scenario" in chapter 9.)

A root problem of rights deletion schemes is precisely their mass-market character, so it would be a mistake to revert to a strict paradigm of considering only the individuals before the court. Of course, courts would have to determine when a clause or a complex of clauses—such as an arbitration clause, a remote choice of forum clause, and clauses limiting consequential damages to the cost of repairs or the price of the product—does actually amount (for example) to a denial of redress of grievances. But in making this determination, as I have argued in chapter 9, the court should take into account the widespread nature of the denial, such that the legal infrastructure of redress is altered for a large number of people.

Remedies

With respect to remedy for intentional deprivation of basic legal rights, it would be important to address the mass-market aspect of a situation. That is, a remedy should apply to everyone who was a recipient of a particular offending set of boilerplate. A damage remedy may not be the best solution, because there may not be strong reasons to favor those who bring suit over everyone else subject to the same set of boilerplate. Yet there could be some reason to favor those who bring suit, by analogy with the idea of "private attorneys general," which is used to argue for rewards to plaintiffs who bring class actions.[41] And, of course, there will have to be a means of paying attorneys representing recipients. It would be helpful to have a law granting statutory damages and attorney fees to successful plaintiffs.

Meanwhile, my preliminary suggestion is that a purported contract containing offending boilerplate should be declared invalid in toto, and recipients should instead be governed by the background legal default rules.[42] I am proposing invalidation in toto and recurrence to existing default rules, because it is much harder for courts to sever and excise only certain clauses; but this will be a matter for working out in practice. For example, if I were to buy a computer online and the firm charged my credit card, and then when the computer arrived a list of boilerplate fell out of the box, a contract for sale would already exist because the payment and delivery had already been made; but the rest of the contract's terms would be the default terms contained in background law, and *not* the later-arriving boilerplate, which this remedy would disallow. Those default provisions may be more expensive for the firm, as they might include warranties and liability for consequential damages and might protect the recipient's right to sue in court and be part of a class action. That increased cost could be the reason the firm imposed the boilerplate scheme to supersede the legal default provisions. (At least, that is the justification firms generally offer for their boilerplate, while assuring us that they pass on the resultant savings rather than pocketing them.) Just as in the case of the implied warranty of habitability in residential leases, the fact that abiding by legal background regimes entails a cost to the firm should not be a compelling reason against implementing the remedy, because the loss to the firm can be interpreted as what is deserved by recipients who have the right, for example, to a meaningful legal remedy. If a firm says it cannot stay in business without depriving its customers of legal remedy, what does that say about its products?

Inapplicability of US Common-Law Economic Loss Doctrine

One more possible obstacle in current US law to adjudication of claims regarding deprivation of legal rights by boilerplate is a tort doctrine called the "economic loss" rule that operates to limit tort remedies in negligence actions. The doctrine precludes relief in such actions for consequential losses that are merely economic. The primary rationale for this doctrine appears to be that allowance of recovery of economic losses would result in unlimited liability to an indeterminate class (a sort of consequential domino effect). In some cases preclusion of remedy may be on the ground that professional service providers do not owe obligations to third parties; and in some cases on the ground that the domain of contract law should be protected.[43] As I have argued above, the notion that the domain of contract law should be protected, whatever its relevance to World A, should not be applied to World B.

With respect to other rationales for the economic loss doctrine, the question might be raised whether remedies available in tort for the imposition of offending boilerplate (however its offensiveness is to be determined) would be limited by this doctrine. One should note that if we were to follow the contract-as-product theory to a logical conclusion and construe tort liability for harmful boilerplate as a variety of liability for defective products, the economic loss doctrine would bar recovery of monetary damages for the malfunctioning or damage or destruction of the product itself. Yet the harms inflicted by boilerplate (if found offending) often are not harms to the (composite) product itself—the functional item plus the boilerplate. The functional item still functions. What we previously thought of as the product is not the cause of the harm, but the composite product is defective because the boilerplate is defective in the sense that it should be unenforceable under the circumstances. Perhaps the contract-as-product amalgam breaks down here. (If so, the tort of intentional deprivation of legal rights might be a better alternative.)

Nevertheless, where the functional part of the contract-as-product does malfunction, should an economic loss rule be available to limit damages for the seller? Suppose that the functional portion of the product is software and the boilerplate says that liability for any sort of defect shall be limited to return of the (functional part of the) product and a refund of the price paid for it. Suppose that the functional part of the product is defective and destroys the user's data, thereby destroying her business. Should compensation (consequential damages) be available for that loss? Under the existing law of product liability, which considers only the functional part of the amalgamated "product," application of the economic loss rule might well preclude recovery, especially if the product is widely distributed. Yet it would be more sensible to hold that it is bad policy for the very fact of mass-market distribution (the fact that many users may be injured) to serve as a reason for denying liability.[44] When we are considering the product not to be the software, but the software-cum-boilerplate, we probably should not use the rule developed for functional products standing alone.

Moreover, the proposed tort for deployment of offending boilerplate should be distinguished to some extent from previous applications of defective-product liability. The harm here is to the recipient's rights, whereas products liability has been primarily aimed at physical injury to persons or property. Although products liability is a strict liability regime, it is not an intentional tort, whereas I think that deployment of boilerplate—in cases where it is found to offend whatever standards are developed for it—should be an intentional tort. Those who draw up and deploy boilerplate know exactly what they are doing and are fully aware of its effects, *and indeed intend those effects.*

That is why I advocate, at least preliminarily, that recognition of a new tort, intentional deprivation of basic legal rights, would be of better service than products liability. The type of injury contemplated here is more analogous to nonphysical types of personal injury, such as defamation, deprivation of privacy, intentional interference with contractual relations, or intentional infliction of emotional distress than it is to harm caused by a product such as a toaster. None of the torts relating to non-physical injury is subject to the economic loss rule.[45]

In sum, I think the common-law economic loss rule should not be extended to deployment of harmful boilerplate, and this for several reasons: (1) the doctrine applies to negligence torts, and to products liability, but not to intentional torts, whereas the deployment of boilerplate is intentional; so, if deployment of boilerplate were tortious under given circumstances, it would be an intentional tort; (2) the loss to the recipient is not merely an economic loss but rather a loss of basic rights granted by the polity, such as the right to redress of grievances.[46] Moreover, the economic loss rule is a common-law rule, so (3) to the extent that the cause of action might be based on statute, the rule would be inapplicable.

Conclusion

I have offered the proposal in this chapter as a way to launch thinking about using tort law to evaluate and, where appropriate, impose liability for abusive boilerplate schemes. A well-designed tort regime need not entirely displace evaluation of boilerplate under contract law, but it would offer many advantages over the procrustean application of contract law to the large-scale schemes of rights deletion that now are proliferating in practice. Such a tort regime would (I hope) help to deter the worst instances of boilerplate overreaching, and in doing so would alleviate the democratic degradation and affronts to the rule of law caused by boilerplate rights deletion schemes.

. . . .

"Public" and Hybrid Regulatory Solutions

AS I DISCUSSED IN CHAPTER 3, the notion of a realm of private ordering cannot now be interpreted conceptually (if indeed it ever could), but perhaps the role of private ordering can be interpreted pragmatically. Pragmatically speaking, certain projects belong to the state and to the democratic processes of the state, and certain other projects belong to individuals and firms and to their voluntary dealings with each other. There can be borderline cases, of course, as with any pragmatic interpretation of a dichotomy. But when we see large portions of projects thought to belong to the state and democratic processes being captured under the rubric of private ordering, as we do with boilerplate rights deletion schemes, the pragmatic interpretation of the dichotomy is undermined. We are seeing contracts metamorphose into boilerplate schemes, and those schemes metamorphose into machine rule through TPMs. This dynamic prompts the question whether some boilerplate clauses, and some combinations of them, should be brought under regulatory control. In this chapter I will consider the case for substantive regulation of boilerplate.

The realm of private ordering is, as we have seen, usurping the realm of the state and the governing power of the state over individuals. The case for restructuring the legal infrastructure through substantive regulation is strongest when it is the state's responsibility to protect rights that individuals cannot protect themselves. There is no reason that substantive regulation of the permissible content of boilerplate schemes should be called regulation of contracts, and a good reason why it should not. If boilerplate does not meet the standards of being contractual, then regulation of it is not regulation of contract. Rather, it should be seen as akin to product safety regulation, or as a sui generis regime for curtailing boilerplate excesses.

US political discourse has an entrenched preference for "private," "market" solutions for issues that arise with regard to boilerplate (and much else). Yet markets cannot exist without rules of the road, separating legal trades from illegal ones.[1] So, in one sense, markets cannot be purely "private," and our legal infrastructure of property and contract cannot be purely "private" either. This is a basic insight that the legal realists arrived at almost a century ago. There is nothing about the sanctity of private ordering that prevents democratic processes from making changes to the legal infrastructure that affect contracts or indeed boilerplate, as long as those changes are appropriate under the rule of law and better foster—or at least do not contravene (too much)—the received ideals that we still rely on for justification of the state. (Or whatever new and better ones we can come up with.)

As many readers will perhaps know, the European Union has a comprehensive regulatory regime applicable to contracts between businesses and consumers. Later in this chapter I will review the EU regime. I recognize that it would be exceedingly difficult to enact something resembling it in the US. Yet, it will be worthwhile to consider what might be done about international harmonization, especially since the number of cross-border transactions will continue to increase. Before considering general substantive regulation, however this chapter will look at some regulatory initiatives that are more limited.

US Patchwork Legal Infrastructure

The US preference for private, market solutions tends to result in a patchwork legal infrastructure. That is, when a problem arises in one sector or industry, legislation may be enacted to address only that particular problem, or the common law may evolve to address that particular problem.

A prime example is the US legal treatment of information privacy. Various federal statutes are relevant (this is not an exhaustive list): HIPAA (medical information);[2] TILA (loan terms);[3] FERPA (educational information);[4] COPPA (children's information on the Internet);[5] and the Gramm-Leach-Bliley Act (financial information).[6] There are state statutes as well, that regulate, for example, aspects of Internet privacy[7] or employee privacy.[8] There are common-law developments (judge-made law): the invasion of privacy torts (relating to damaging or embarrassing information about an individual and the unauthorized use of a name or likeness).[9] Privacy is written into some state constitutions.[10] It is read into the federal Constitution in the case of family and reproductive decisionmaking,[11] but also implicated in portions of the Bill of Rights, especially the Fourth and Fifth Amendments.[12]

Preference for Disclosure Regimes

Even when the need for regulation (revision of the legal infrastructure) is democratically recognized, the US preference for private, market solutions leads to a tendency to provide for disclosure rather than substantive regulation, so that individuals may make up their own minds about what to do. In privacy regulation this preference can lead to opt-out regimes, in which, for example, the firm discloses that the individual's information will be given—or more likely sold—to advertisers, unless the individual decides to opt out by sending in a form. In many kinds of marketing, the firm discloses to the customer that a subscriber fee will be deducted once a month, forever, unless the customer notifies the firm that she wants to terminate the service. As has been forcefully pointed out by Omri Ben-Shahar and Carl Schneider, the propensity to use disclosure as the solution tends to overwhelm recipients with disclosures and firms with paperwork (or its electronic equivalent) without accomplishing much.[13] At least, this is true in a patchwork legal infrastructure such as that of the US.

An analogous patchwork situation prevails in the legal infrastructure of contracts. There are disclosure regimes in US contract law that don't work, or don't work well, to protect those recipients whose protection is in fact the rationale for enacting and maintaining the regimes. Contract law is normally state law, but at times federal law can intervene. For example, the Federal Trade Commission has imposed a Used Car Rule that mandates certain disclosures by dealers who offer used cars for sale.[14] It may or may not prevent people from purchasing "lemons" from persuasive salespeople.

The legal treatment of warranties does not appear to work all that well either. An important federal intervention into contract law is the Magnuson-Moss Warranty Act, which requires that a warranty disclaimer be conspicuously disclosed in simple and readily understood language.[15] State law also requires that warranty disclaimers be disclosed in specific ways, that important clauses be printed in boldface type or capital letters, for example. But these measures don't work very well if the recipient doesn't read the contract; and they certainly cannot work when the contract arrives after the purchase, or when the contract is hidden on a website such that the recipient doesn't see it or know that it exists. As mentioned in chapter 8, the American Law Institute's *Principles of the Law of Software Contracts* proposes that common-law judges create a safe harbor for firms deploying boilerplate by making the terms available electronically, that is, on a website, so that recipients would be able to read them before purchasing the product. Opinion is mixed on whether this expedient would cause any more people to read them than do now.

Beyond Disclosure

State legislation and judge-made law also goes beyond disclosure to create substantive regulations of contract law in particular areas. For example, the content and enforcement of residential landlord-tenant contracts are regulated by state law, differently in each state.[16] Nevertheless, landlords may still put illegal clauses in leases, and tenants who actually read them may think they are binding.[17] The practice of door-to-door selling is regulated by some states. There are currently calls for federal regulation of the payday lending industry, and for federal revision of the US Supreme Court's expansive interpretation of the Federal Arbitration Act.

Federal legislation in 2010 created a Bureau of Consumer Financial Protection, which may call for regulation of consumer contracts with financial firms.

The legal infrastructure contains, in addition to such industry-specific or recipient-specific rules, some more general limits on contracts. For example, the general common law of contracts disallows punitive damages, even if the parties agree to them; the law disallows parties from enforcing a liquidated damages clause if the court finds the clause to be a penalty. Nevertheless, the US preference for piecemeal regulatory interventions intended to support private, market decisionmaking causes some internal conflict in contract law between general rules that hold for all contracts and specific rules that hold for one industry or one class of recipient only.[18] The Uniform Commercial Code quite deliberately adopted a theory under which contracts would be interpreted differently depending upon the industry the parties belonged to. Under the UCC, the presence of a "usage of trade" in a particular industry or market causes contracts in that industry or market to be interpreted in the way that members of the trade would customarily understand them, and differently from how they might be interpreted if the judge were only to look at the written contract terms themselves.[19] Is there a problem with piecemeal regulations such as these? In particular, is there a problem with the piecemeal regulations that now exist affecting boilerplate, or with new ones that might be considered to improve specific features of boilerplate schemes?

Problems of Industry-Specific Regulation

One issue with industry-specific regulation is simply the practical problem that many firms are vertically integrated, or conglomerates, or active in many different sectors, with the result that the different departments or subsidiaries of these firms might be subject to different regulations; which would increase transaction costs (more work for the legal department). (At national and multinational firms the legal departments already have enough work keeping up with the different laws applicable in different jurisdictions.) Such threshold characterization issues might be even harder for a recipient's lawyer to respond to, and even more expensive for recipients who want to sue a firm for imposing boilerplate on them.

Another practical problem has to do more with litigation strategy: firms might get into preliminary arguments about which industry's rules apply to them, adding a further layer of inquiry (and more transaction costs) to litigation. In cases involving a sale of goods, decided under the provisions of the Uniform Commercial Code, litigants get into elaborate (and expensive) arguments about which usage of trade may or may not govern their case.

It may appear prima facie that industry-specific rules are more efficient, because they can be more accurately targeted at the specific problems of a specific industry. And it is true, of course, that economists most often study firm behavior by industry or sector, and not globally. Nevertheless, once the costs of implementing industry-specific rules are factored in, it does not appear at all obvious that accumulating piecemeal rules to govern boilerplate would be more efficient than a more general regime.

Another concern, less practical and more jurisprudential, stems from the general applicability of law and the place of generality in the ideal of the rule of law. The underlying ideal is to treat like cases alike. Contracts are supposed to be contracts wherever they occur. That is one reason why scholars and judges try so hard to force boilerplate into the consensual bargaining template that is supposed to characterize contracts generally, by characterizing boilerplate schemes as "adhesion contracts." That is also one reason why it seems attractive to stop calling boilerplate terms "contracts," and to characterize them instead as a part of a product or as some other kind of legal animal. I refer to such moves as "reconceptualizations" of the status quo. "Reconceptualization" may or may not be associated with "change" in the status quo. The economic writers endorsing the "contract-as-product" idea are reconceiving adhesion contracts for the purpose of keeping things as they are. Whereas I am suggesting, among other things, that some mass-market boilerplate deletion schemes which impinge on regimes that are properly "public" should be evaluated under tort law rather than contract law, a reconceptualization that I hope would result in some change in the status quo. Alternatively, or in addition, I am suggesting that mass-market boilerplate deletion schemes should be regulated under a product safety rubric, or indeed as sui generis.

The contracts made by firms in a certain industry, or adhesion forms deployed by a certain industry, might seem more troublesome than others regarding recipients' reliance or lack of consent. The treatment of consumers by financial industry giants is often singled out for criticism. Nevertheless, industry-specific legal regulations cause uneasiness about the underlying ideal of the general applicability of law. Moreover, it is widely thought that strongly motivated interest groups are more likely to achieve legal regulation in their favor than broader coalitions or the public at large, and it may also be suspected that in some instances industry-specific rules are tainted by capture. (That is, they end up favoring firms, even if that was not the impetus that launched them.[20])

Proposals to "fix" the current regime in certain specific ways, so as the render "adhesion contracts" less normatively degraded, and perhaps also less democratically degraded, would make the contract landscape more of a patchwork than it is now. Possible progress in reversing the two kinds of degradation would have to be weighed against losses to legal generality. And whereas losses to legal generality due to piecemeal regulation aimed at particular problems ideally are supposed to result in gains in fairness and transparency, they may instead result in losses to fairness and transparency, because of the difficulties involved in figuring out which legal rule may be applicable in borderline cases (of which there may be many, multiplying as the number of categories multiplies); and because it is hard to figure out whether different treatment is nevertheless equal treatment in light of the differences of each industry's or sector's or group's situation; and, of course, because it is not realistic to assume away interest-group lobbying and other forms of capture.

Piecemeal "Fixes"

Would the expected improvement to the two degradations outweigh the risks associated with piecemeal "fixes"? One kind of piecemeal fix would be simply to outlaw the use of a certain clause.

This kind of fix would not necessarily lead to the negative effects of losses to legal generality caused by industry-specific regulation. Candidates for this kind of particular fix certainly include clauses that tend in practice to eliminate all avenues of remedy, and are in fact intended to do so: arbitration clauses, and some kinds of exculpatory clauses and choice of forum/choice of law clauses. The deployment of these clauses in combination might be especially proscribed.

What kinds of fixes might disallow these types of clauses? There have been various proposals to change the over-use of arbitration clauses, but because the US Supreme Court has interpreted a federal statute, the Federal Arbitration Act, to preempt states from adjudicating or legislating limits on arbitration, the fix would have to be accomplished by Congress.[21] Another piecemeal fix would be the preclusion of over-reaching exculpatory clauses, especially those that purport to exculpate a firm from all harms it inflicts on recipients, however caused. This fix could be enacted by legislation at the state level, or by judicial decisions, or by agency regulation. Legislation could likewise override the UCC rule making it prima facie unconscionable to limit damages for personal injury against a consumer, and simply outlaw doing so at all. Legislation also could override the UCC's permissive stance toward minimizing economic remedies, which undermines incentives to seek redress for the money lost from nonfunctional products or services, or from nondelivery of those products and services. Indeed, the UCC's stance, which allows firms to limit remedies to the return of the product for a refund or the repair of the product, is practically preclusive of firms' ever being sued, especially under the current regime where such a limitation of remedies clause likely occurs together with a mandatory arbitration clause that precludes classwide suits or class-wide arbitration.[22] Because the UCC says, vaguely, that these limits would not apply if the remedy "fails of its essential purpose," the overriding legislation might clarify for courts what might constitute failure of essential purpose of a remedy. (Meanwhile, it is not unheard of for a firm to use boilerplate to delete even this vestigial right to a remedy; see example on page 119.) Even absent such legislation, courts might be more proactive in recognizing that certain clauses do override the essential purpose of remedies. The legislature could make the revision of the permissive UCC rule even narrower by making it apply only if the firm is also using a mandatory arbitration clause and prohibiting class-wide relief. Or the legislation could be narrower still and more discretionary by making such drastically limited remedies prima facie fail of their essential purpose, leaving it up to courts whether or not the available remedy fails in a given case.

Hybrid Regimes

So far I have been considering piecemeal fixes to current law that may be enacted through legislation, imposed by agency rule-making,[23] or developed by judge-made law. (In chapter 11, I considered how judges could adjudicate certain species of boilerplate schemes under tort law.) Consonant with the US preference for private, market solutions, one might also consider hybrid regimes in which private initiatives would be supported or protected by legislation or judge-made law. The suggestion of the ALI *Principles of the Law of Software Contracts* that courts should create a safe harbor for firms that post their boilerplate on a website accessible to potential recipients, would, if implemented, constitute a hybrid regime; that is, a use of law to encourage firms to adopt, as a best practice, making boilerplate publicly available before the purchaser finds herself stuck with it.[24]

Other possible hybrid regimes might provide a legal infrastructure to support market initiatives employing rating agencies for boilerplate, or employing filtering systems or searchable tags. "Public" (governmental) support could be via legislation, administrative regulation, or judge-made law. In the case of rating agencies some caveats are in order: privately organized rating agencies are not transparent about the agendas of their sponsors; nor are they transparent about their relationships with those they are rating. Legislation could require disclosure of these matters; but since disclosure has not tended to work very well, legislation could go further and certify rating agencies that satisfy certain criteria thought to be less conducive to bias or capture. A hybrid regime might encourage technological filtering systems, because at present the market does not seem to be demanding them; perhaps the problem is that that those who might build and market them think that it will not. Governmental agencies might consider aiding development of prototypes and testing them. Some market research would be helpful, if it informs people about what these rights deletion schemes are doing and then gauges their desire to have products that could steer them away from particularly undesirable examples of such schemes.

A hybrid regime that comes closer to more generalized regulation would propose that allowable boilerplate be limited to certain specific sets of terms. It seems unlikely that an unregulated market could arrive at such a limitation on allowable boilerplate. But firms might develop boilerplate terms that they would like to use, perhaps working together in an industry association or in consultation with a government agency, which would have the final say in deciding which terms to allow. If this system provided for website availability of all the boilerplate terms that firms are allowed to offer, for example, plus easy identification of the boilerplate terms a given firm is using, it might lead to better terms (whether we call those terms "contracts," "products," or something else) being offered to recipients.[25]

If hybrid regimes resulted in better terms being offered to recipients, and/or more opportunity for recipients to understand and choose the terms offered to them—again whether conceived of as contracts, products, or something else—that might alleviate some of the concerns raised by boilerplate schemes. But it would not alleviate all of the concerns. It would probably not end concern raised by systematic and persistent heuristic biases in people's choices. Nor would such hybrid regimes change the fact that there are some entitlements that individuals are not, or should not be, allowed to waive at all. To put this another way, there are some products that simply should not be on the market. Unsafe cars and contaminated food should not be on the market. Neither should, to take one example, blanket exculpatory clauses for causing death or personal injury to recipients.

Black Lists, White Lists, and Grey Lists

Regulation may take the form of black lists or (by contrast) white lists, with a possible grey list somewhere in the middle of the continuum, between the black and white poles. A legal directive in the form of a black list would make certain specific clauses illegal to include in certain boilerplate schemes. The legal directive could black-list a clause for all contracts, as has been done for clauses waiving the implied warranty of habitability in residential housing. Or it could black-list a clause only for boilerplate schemes, because in such schemes the consent of the recipient is at best problematic and sometimes clearly nonexistent. Or it could black-list the clause only for boilerplate schemes imposed on a large enough number of recipients that the scheme is appropriately judged to contribute to democratic as well as normative degradation.

A legal directive in the form of a white list would inform firms that certain clauses, or indeed whole sets of them, are approved by a regulatory body. The white list would not declare other clauses illegal, but it would make the clauses or sets of clauses on the white list much easier for firms to adopt. The fact that the set of clauses were prevalidated would save legal expenses and would increase transparency to recipients, thereby perhaps making customers more confident about the firm.

White Lists

Clayton P. Gillette, in an important article taking the US perspective—that is, that private, market approaches are often likely to be superior to substantive regulation—surveys the possible pros and cons of a hybrid approach using a federal administrative agency. The agency would review proposed sets of terms submitted by firms and either reject or approve the terms. If the terms were approved, the result would be a white list, a safe harbor of boilerplate terms for the firm.[26] (Although Gillette is speaking of "contracts," we should read "set of terms" for "contract," because it will be better both for the clarity of contract law and for our understanding of boilerplate if we do not call these things "contracts." The basis of contract is the picture of World A, bargained-for voluntary exchange agreed to between individuals. In World B, as we have seen throughout this book, the picture is not one of voluntary bargains and agreements.)

Gillette reviews the possible advantages of his hypothesized white-list approach. Among them: a firm with an approved set of terms could advertise to recipients that the set of terms was agency-approved; an agency with a staff of lawyers and economists, able to consider public comments, might be better equipped than a court to decide whether a set of terms or a clause was unfair or unreasonable. Gillette also catalogues a number of problems that might arise: a firm that submits a set of terms and gains approval after going through an agency proceeding might find competitor firms free-riding on its effort by using the same set of terms; agency approval might lock in certain terms or sets of terms so that they continued in use even after conditions had changed and new terms would work better; use of a safe harbor to cover a wide variety of situations might not fit those situations well unless a lot of conditions are attached to it (and parties would litigate about those); agencies might not be institutionally competent to decide such issues as the difference between considering only one clause in a set of terms or considering the set as a whole (to evaluate whether a clause that looks onerous is balanced out by more generous ones, in light of the price of the product); agencies are subject to capture, either by trade associations or by consumer groups. Gillette concludes:

> A pre-approval process is unlikely to prove a panacea to the issue of standard-form contracts for consumer goods. Sellers will not necessarily take advantage of the process, contracts with terms that disadvantage consumers may be approved, and contracts that, on balance, fairly allocate risks will be disapproved. It remains unclear, however, whether such a process provides marginal advantages over the current market approach combined with litigation to root out oppressive clauses. . . . The relevant, and I fear still unanswered, question

is whether a pre-approval process will improve the desired match between contract terms found in the marketplace and those preferred by informed buyers.[27]

Gillette agrees with me that wild-card doctrines such as (primarily) unconscionability and voidness as against public policy are largely unsatisfactory, decided by courts after the fact (assuming that any recipients are able to bring an action), unpredictable, and not based upon empirical evidence. Because he subscribes to the contract-as-product view I described in chapter 6, however, and also believes that recipients are often being charged an amount appropriate to compensate them for entitlement waivers, he is not, all things considered, very troubled by the normative degradation caused by lack of consent. (He does not advert to the issue of firms turning recipients' property-rule entitlements into liability-rule entitlements.[28]) Gillette also subscribes to the view, expressed by a number of other law-and-economics writers as well, that firms may vary their boilerplate in individual cases in order to favor or disfavor certain recipients depending on the firms' interests in doing so. This is a practice that I think can hide discriminatory or anticompetitive behavior,[29] and one that helps create democratic degradation.

I am sure that Gillette is right that the hybrid agency-review process he analyzes, or indeed any other regulatory intervention, is not a panacea—just as doing nothing about the current situation is not a panacea either. Gillette did not advert to the issue I am calling democratic degradation (discussed in chapter 3), so perhaps he did not see it as a problem. When one does add concern about democratic degradation, then perhaps the balance tips in favor of recommending something like his hypothetical scheme.

Black Lists

In contrast to white lists, black lists are rarely utilized or even proposed in the US, no doubt because of the US preference for market mechanisms. There are nevertheless some terms that, in keeping with the limits of contract law, may not appear in any contract:

parties may not include a penalty clause because contract law does not allow for punitive damages; parties may not include clauses that permit parties to act in bad faith, because contract law contains a nonwaivable obligation of good faith; parties may not contract to perform illegal activities, because contract law does not immunize people from punishment for activities that are socially proscribed, nor does it encourage people to engage in those activities; and of course, a purported contract that permitted a party to act coercively or deceptively in obtaining agreement would not be a contract at all. Neither, I think, would a purported contract that excluded all recourse to legal remedy be a contract, because the concept of contract implies legal enforceability; that is what distinguishes contract from mere extralegal promising. Outside these excluded terms that are related to the limits of contract law, US law has few particular terms that are black-listed. One such disallowed term is a term allowing a usurious interest rate.[30] Another, which we have already noted, is a term in a residential lease waiving the implied warranty of habitability.[31]

Additional candidates for black-listing that I have previously mentioned are: a waiver of the right to sue for consequential damages for personal injury; exculpatory clauses purporting to cover not only negligence but all causes of injury (thereby including intentional and reckless harm-causing behavior); a limitation of remedy to the price of the product; and waivers of the right to bring a class action, as well as mandatory arbitration clauses coupled with preclusion of (or unavailability of) class-wide arbitration. Because of the nature of the rights deleted, these clauses might be candidates for black-listing even if not part of a mass-market scheme of rights deletion; that is because some of the rights might be held to be market-inalienable, or close to that end of the continuum of alienability)[32]. Others, such as terms limiting recipients' information privacy, as well of some types of terms limiting recipients' user rights in information made available by the firm, would be more dependent on the extent of social dissemination of the clauses. (Again, nothing says we must keep calling such terms "contractual," and there is a lot to be said for not doing so, because they do not fulfill the requirements of the underlying structure of contract law.)

Grey Lists

Instead of black-listing, at one end of the continuum, or white-listing, on the other, a regulatory procedure in the middle of the continuum would be one in which the legislature or an administrative agency directs courts to treat certain clauses with suspicion. (In legalese, this would be called "heightened scrutiny." We'll call it "grey-listing.") Before deciding to treat a clause with suspicion it would be necessary to look at evidence about its use in particular situations.[33] Such evidence would include investigating whether a claim that the clause economically benefits recipients was empirically believable; and, even if so, whether it was justifiable to benefit most recipients while a few were singled out for serious harm (when, for example, they were harmed by a product but had no viable remedy). Treating a clause with suspicion also includes the idea of a prima facie presumption against validity, so that it is up to the firm deploying it to prove that its clause is valid. An example is the Uniform Commercial Code's treatment of a clause excluding liability for personal injury caused by a product; such a term, if it appears in a contract with a consumer, is prima facie unconscionable.* If a firm wants to include this term, it must be prepared to prove that it is *not* unconscionable.

Terms that create an opt-out scheme for recipient privacy waivers are good candidates for treating with suspicion, as are those that limit or exclude user rights in information made available to the user—to the extent that they are not candidates for black-listing. So are choice of law and choice of forum clauses, especially if they are part of a full-blown rights deletion scheme, because they tend to foreclose the possibility of remedies for recipients. As I suggested in chapter 9, we can think of such "treatment with suspicion" as a partial market-inalienability.

---

* In my opinion, such a term is a good candidate for per se invalidity (see page 224).

Piecemeal grey-listing tends to have the unpredictability and wild-card drawback of referring cases to judges to decide on a discretionary basis. Courts are often thought—especially by people who believe such clauses are efficient, or at least not-so-bad-as-all-that—to be institutionally incompetent to deal with such matters.[34]

There is something to this claim, even if you disagree, as I do, with those who think that these clauses must be efficient, and that there is not much reason to worry about them. I think there is plenty to worry about. Nevertheless, institutional competence does not necessarily refer to the judge's intellectual competence, but rather to the fact that trying to get economic evidence and evidence about fairness, whatever that means, in a particular market, may involve great time and expense, and trying to evaluate such evidence involves judges in areas that are not within their expertise. Economic evidence is thought to be worthwhile in antitrust cases, and what results is an expensive battle of experts. It is hard to imagine that such a drawn-out battle would be an effective way to replace the current tendency toward armchair guesswork with actual empirical evaluation of boilerplate clauses by courts.

"Rules" vs. "Standards" and the Problem of Piecemeal Adjudication

As many readers probably know (and as I mentioned in chapter 7), when a decisionmaker has broad discretion about how to decide individual cases, that situation is known as a "standard" in one school of thought about jurisprudence. When a decisionmaker has no discretion because a higher authority has directed the decisionmaker to make the decision a certain way, that is known as a "rule."[35] A troublesome problem with the common-law evaluation of World B (purported) contracts—applying the contract doctrines of unconscionability, voidness as against public policy, and some others, such as "indefiniteness"—is that the doctrines are unhappily standard-like.[36] Also troublesome is the procedure of case-by-case adjudication, a procedure that seems to cohere tightly with these standard-like doctrines because of the commitment to individual discretionary judgment. These doctrines seem to operate very much as wild cards, occurring rarely and not predictably. Those who criticize this system might suggest that we adopt rule-like directives to cover the situations most in need of attention; or they might propose that we adopt the opposite rule; that is, do nothing, let this system alone. The idea is that the system will make some mistakes, but that tinkering with it by adding more "standards" would be worse.

As I mentioned earlier, I think that the existence of mass-market rights deletion schemes, which cause democratic degradation especially when divesting recipients of entitlements that are basic to our polity, should drive the search for something more rule-like in the direction of black-listing some terms, rather than toward the conclusion that (almost) everything a firm deploys is valid simply because courts are not institutionally competent to look into the matter. (Once again, when we black list some terms or sets of terms we should consider this to be sui generis regulation or perhaps a form of product safety regulation. There is no reason to call what we are doing "contractual regulation" in light of the mass-market use of these schemes, and the widespread lack of consent to them.)

Such a rule could look first for a mass-market rights deletion scheme, that is, consider the social dissemination parameter of the firm's boilerplate as of primary importance. The rule could be that a certain clause is invalid, if it appears in a mass-market rights deletion scheme. This would render the rule more standard-like, because firms could argue that their boilerplate does not constitute such a scheme. Or the rule could look only for the existence of a boilerplate scheme. Although perhaps over-inclusive in sweeping into its purview some boilerplate that does not amount to private (firm) preemption of rights that should be in the "public" realm, such a rule would be easier to apply, and therefore more predictable and consistent. But not trouble-free. Judges who dislike a rule can find ways to put up threshold barriers to its application.[37]

Comprehensive Regulation

A legal system may utilize comprehensive regulation instead of the piecemeal US approach. The primary example is the European Union. The European Community Commission (EC) issues comprehensive directives to member states to implement certain uniform regulatory legal regimes. For example, in contrast to the US piece-meal system of privacy regulation, the EU has issued a comprehensive privacy directive.[38] And in contrast to the US piecemeal system of contract oversight, the EU has issued a comprehensive directive on unfair terms in consumer contracts.[39]

This method of dealing with the problems of unfair terms in contracts with consumers comes from a political and legal culture that differs from that of the US. EU member states' legal systems are not faced, as US states are, with a one-size-fits-all legal infra-structure called "Contracts," because on the continent commercial contracts and consumer contracts traditionally inhabit two different bodies of law. Instead the EU member states are faced with having to adjudicate the distinction between consumer and commercial contracts, which is difficult in practice. At this point, the EU has taken some steps toward harmonization of consumer law and commercial law.[40]

The law of EU member states, except for the United Kingdom, comes from the tradition of civil law, rather than from the common-law tradition that grounds US law. Culturally, EU scholars and businesspeople and politicians do not tend to mistrust the government, or comprehensive regulation, or "top-down" ordering, the way scholars and businesspeople and politicians in the US do. Although it is feared in the US that this type of regulation would make an economy grind to a halt, that has not happened in the EU—at least not because of the implementation of a directive structuring permissible consumer contracts. Nor has eschewing this kind of regulation in the US saved the US economy from serious economic difficulty.[41]

EU Regulation of Consumer Contract Terms

The EC Directive of 1993 on Unfair Terms in Consumer Contracts provides (in part):

Article 3

1. A contractual term which has not been individually negotiated shall be regarded as unfair if, contrary to the require-

ment of good faith, it causes a significant imbalance in the parties' rights and obligations arising under the contract, to the detriment of the consumer.

2. A term shall always be regarded as not individually negotiated where it has been drafted in advance and the consumer has therefore not been able to influence the substance of the term, particularly in the context of a pre-formulated standard contract.

The fact that certain aspects of a term or one specific term have been individually negotiated shall not exclude the application of this Article to the rest of a contract if an overall assessment of the contract indicates that it is nevertheless a pre-formulated standard contract.

Where any seller or supplier claims that a standard term has been individually negotiated, the burden of proof in this respect shall be incumbent on him.

3. The Annex shall contain an indicative and non-exhaustive list of the terms which may be regarded as unfair.

Seventeen such terms are included in the Annex. Here (in part) is the list:[42]

ANNEX

TERMS REFERRED TO IN ARTICLE 3 (3) 1. Terms which have the object or effect of:

(a) excluding or limiting the legal liability of a seller or supplier in the event of the death of a consumer or personal injury to the latter resulting from an act or omission of that seller or supplier;

. . .

(e) requiring any consumer who fails to fulfill his obligation to pay a disproportionately high sum in compensation;

. . .

(g) enabling the seller or supplier to terminate a contract of indeterminate duration without reasonable notice except where there are serious grounds for doing so;

(h) automatically extending a contract of fixed duration where the consumer does not indicate otherwise, when the deadline fixed for the consumer to express this desire not to extend the contract is unreasonably early;

(i) irrevocably binding the consumer to terms with which he had no real opportunity of becoming acquainted before the conclusion of the contract;

(j) enabling the seller or supplier to alter the terms of the contract unilaterally without a valid reason which is specified in the contract;

(k) enabling the seller or supplier to alter unilaterally without a valid reason any characteristics of the product or service to be provided;

. . .

(n) limiting the seller's or supplier's obligation to respect commitments undertaken by his agents or making his commitments subject to compliance with a particular formality;

. . .

(q) excluding or hindering the consumer's right to take legal action or exercise any other legal remedy, particularly by requiring the consumer to take disputes exclusively to arbitration not covered by legal provisions, unduly restricting the evidence available to him or imposing on him a burden of proof which, according to the applicable law, should lie with another party to the contract.

The reader may observe from this "indicative and nonexhaustive" list that the EU in 1993 directed its member states to consider certain clauses that are routinely approved in the US to be of dubious validity in the EU when used against a consumer.[43] Among the questionable terms are mandatory arbitration clauses, the exclusion of liability for personal injury or death, binding consumers to terms that come after the product has been paid for, binding consumers to terms that can change over time at the firms' discretion, and refusing to respect promises that are not in the boilerplate but were made by the firms' employees. The preamble to the directive (consisting of many "whereas" recitals) makes clear that the questionability of the items on the list applies only to contracts or terms not individually negotiated (whether oral or written), and also that that the Annex is to be taken as "indicative" only.[44]

Member states had difficulty implementing this directive. Some states black-listed various terms, other states grey-listed them (meaning that they were viewed as presumptively unfair but not absolutely proscribed). Moreover, as reported by Hugh Collins, jurists and legislators in each member state faced the issue of how the new rules would fit into existing law. Many European countries decided not to amend their civil law but rather to enact a regulation implementing the directive. This worked well on an interim basis but left member states with two overlapping legal systems, one based on their legal code and one based on the regulation implementing the directive. As Collins says, "The resulting shambles in the national legal regimes has, ever since, been causing confusion to law students and has supplied a ripe topic for scholarly discussion."[45]

The EC commissioned a Consumer Law Compendium, published in 2007, which exhaustively analyzed the 1993 directive, cataloguing the levels of confusion and the various differences between member states' implementation in substance and procedure.[46] These variances depend to some extent on each member's existing legal tradition. For example, some member states already had black-listed terms in their national legislation. According to this report, member states' adoption of the list in the Annex ranges from a black-list outright prohibition through various shades of grey. Implementation varies as well with regard to whether all contracts are covered, or only those that are nonnegotiated, as the directive seems to intend; and whether business-to-business contracts are covered or only contracts involving consumers (as the directive seems to intend); and on a great many other parameters as well. No doubt these variances in implementation served as some impetus for the Commission to launch an initiative looking toward harmonization of contract law throughout the EU.

The Draft Common Frame of Reference [DCFR], published in 2009 after some years of work by teams of European jurists, catalogues the implementation differences of member states, and takes up the challenge of harmonization within the EU.[47] At the same time, other projects were also in progress, in particular the European Commission's Proposal for a Consumer Rights Directive, published in 2008, which proposed replacing four current directives, including the Directive on Unfair Contract Terms, with a new, overarching legislative regime in order to achieve greater harmonization of consumer rights law among all member states of the EU.[48]

The DCFR defines the meaning of "unfair" in a contract between a business and a consumer this way:

> In a contract between a business and a consumer, a term [which has not been individually negotiated] is unfair for the purposes of this Section if it is supplied by the business and if it significantly disadvantages the consumer contrary to good faith and fair dealing.[49]

Regarding the language in brackets, the DCFR notes that "not individually negotiated" is broadly defined, and also that the burden of proving that a term has been individually negotiated is on the business.[50]

The DCFR makes the substantive recommendation that choice of forum clauses restricting a consumer to the home jurisdiction of the business should be black-listed as "unfair."[51] The other items that were on the list included in the 1993 Directive on Unfair Contract Terms are deemed by the DCFR not just "indicative" of unfairness, as they were in the 1993 Directive, but instead presumptively unfair (grey-listed).[52] In particular, in a contract between a business and a consumer, all of the following are to be presumptively disallowed: clauses exculpating a firm for causing death or personal injury, clauses enabling a business to alter the terms of the contract without a valid reason specified in the contract (with limited exceptions for financial firms and for contracts of unlimited duration), clauses limiting the obligation of a business to respect obligations undertaken by its agents, and clauses excluding or restricting a consumer's right to take legal action or to exercise any other remedy, in particular by referring the consumer to arbitration proceedings.[53]

The European Commission's Draft Proposal for a new overarching Directive on Consumer Rights goes still farther than the DCFR in proposing that a number of terms be black-listed (deemed unfair in all circumstances) and like the DCFR proposes that others be grey-listed (deemed presumptively unfair). Five types of clauses are black-listed, including these three: exculpation for death or personal injury; limiting the obligation of a business to respect commitments made by its agents; and excluding or limiting a consumer's right to remedy, particularly through the use of mandatory arbitration clauses. The grey-listed terms correspond with the DCFR list and are stronger versions of the terms in the 1993 Directive.[54]

Both the DCFR and the European Commission proposal for an overarching Consumer Rights Directive are attempts to harmonize EU law among member states, in light of the different ways member states have implemented earlier directives, including the 1993 directive. Regarding harmonization within the EU, the proposed Consumer Rights Directive provides for strict uniformity: "Member States may not maintain or introduce, in their national law, provisions diverging from those laid down in this Directive, including more or less stringent provisions to ensure a different level of consumer protection."[55]

International Harmonization?

It would be foolish to imagine that the US will anytime soon adopt a comprehensive regulatory solution such as the one that the EU is in the process of reworking. Indeed, the EU's disapproval of onerous clauses seems on the rise as it is moving the list of suspect clauses from the "indicative" list to the grey list, and to the black list, while at the same time the US is allowing more and more exculpatory clauses and restrictions of remedy to be enforced. In this regard, the US and EU seem to be moving farther apart rather than closer together. Yet US legislatures or administrative bodies could at least consider disallowing certain clauses when used against consumers, such as overreaching exculpatory clauses, choice of forum clauses, and limitation of remedy clauses. Perhaps agencies and states within the US will take some steps in that direction, although limitation of the use of mandatory arbitration clauses will have to be accomplished by Congress unless the Supreme Court changes its stance.[56]

The US and EU are powerful trading partners, and it cannot be denied that the large differences between EU-style and US-style regulation cause difficulties for trade, especially for online commerce and other types of trading that move easily across borders. For example, conflict arose over the EU's comprehensive approach to data privacy when it appeared that data flowing through the US was not adequately protected.[57] Uncertainty exists over how EU rules concerning jurisdiction and choice of law will apply to US firms doing cross-border business, which is happening more frequently as online commerce progresses.

As I hope this discussion has made clear, US law and EU law are currently in almost polar opposite positions with respect to the acceptability of onerous clauses in consumer contracts. Given this situation, the question arises, How are US multinational firms and cross-border traders currently dealing with the EU regulation of contracts with consumers? The answer is, With difficulty.[58] How are they going to deal with it in the future? Insisting on a firm's own terms, even if they are (usually) found legal in the US may result in damage to the firm's international reputation—and loss of market share—when they are judged illegal abroad.[59] Advising or encouraging US firms to write different (and more consumer-friendly) contracts for use in the EU than for use at home seems like a bad idea; to say the least, such second-class treatment of US customers would probably damage a firm's reputation if it became widely known. Dealing with differing legal regimes is expensive for firms, though it provides time-consuming employment for lawyers. These issues surely create incentives for international harmonization.

Because lack of harmonization is costly to traders, the harmonization of contract law, both nationally and internationally, has been an important goal in the past. In the US a prolonged effort to harmonize sales law among the states resulted in the development of the Uniform Commercial Code (UCC). The UCC was the project of two NGOs, the National Conference of Commissioners on Uniform State Laws and the American Law Institute. It eventually achieved widespread enactment and replaced a diverse and confusing patchwork of individual state law. The Convention on the International Sale of Goods (CISG), a treaty signed in Vienna in 1980, was a project of the United Nations Commission on International Trade Law. As of August 2011, seventy-six countries had ratified the treaty, including all major trading countries except Brazil, India, South Africa, and the United Kingdom.[60] The CISG is still in the process of becoming the law preferred by international traders.

Perhaps the US could participate, if only informally, in the EU's ongoing conversation about harmonization of the law relating to contracts between firms and consumers. Certainly informal discussions on this topic go on already among legal scholars and among lawyers who advise US firms doing business in the EU. Such discussions at the least might be facilitated by the ongoing efforts to harmonize within the EU, and by the experience gained from past efforts at harmonization within the US and internationally. It seems unlikely that a US agency such as the Federal Trade Commission would issue a list of numerous terms that must be disallowed or presumptively disallowed (such as the list the EU is working on), but it might be easier eventually to agree on a white list. A US-EU white list would allow firms to use terms with assurance of their enforceability. Moreover, a firm could enhance its reputation for being consumer-friendly by using such validated terms, and this might well improve its bottom line, perhaps even more than continually enforcing onerous boilerplate against consumers; not to mention the savings in the various transaction costs caused by lack of harmonization.

As one step toward achieving more coherence in regulation of terms, I make the small suggestion that it would be better to stop referring to boilerplate as contractual, because of its lack of fit with contract theory and with the basic principles of the legal system regarding what a contract is and what a contract is for. Instead, it would be better to escape from the contracts template and develop a regulatory regime that is modeled on regulatory regimes for product safety; or indeed to develop a sui generis regime. Such a sui generis regime should not be characterized as regulatory interference with "freedom of contract," since boilerplate schemes deployed against consumers cannot be realistically said to exemplify freedom of contract.

As we have seen, the EU has a strong system of regulation of consumer contracts; but, for the reasons I have mentioned, such a system is better thought of as sui generis. If the US and the EU in the future become able to negotiate toward a harmonized system of boilerplate regulation, it would be better not to call it contractual. We should limit the purview of the law of contracts to behavior of the type that contract is supposed to govern. We should strengthen the ideal of "freedom of contract" by ceasing to assimilate contract to nonnegotiated mass-market transactions. Such boilerplate rights deletion schemes cause normative and democratic degradation for the ideal of freedom of contract, and for the rule of law in general.

THIS BOOK HAS GATHERED together many strands of thought about boilerplate. Now that these strands have been woven together, it is my hope that we can see opportunities for improvement in how we deal with boilerplate. I hope that pursuing such opportunities might enhance the rule of law, protect consumers from loss of equality before the law, foster economic activity, and protect the basis of contract law. In this endeavor there will be important roles for private sector actors—NGOs, firms that design and market software and hardware, and indeed firms that hitherto have been in the habit of deploying onerous boilerplate. There will also be roles for regulatory agencies, legislatures, courts, and lawyers and legal scholars. I hope this brief catalogue of suggestions might interest some readers, and that you—some of you—will come up with more and better ideas. (I have made some other suggestions in chapters 8 and 12.)

NGOs

NGOs can organize publicity campaigns to make known to the public what some of the onerous terms in the fine print actually mean. They can take the lead in organizing a rating site that will advise consumers which firms are using reasonable terms and which are not, and in general making consumers more aware of which terms to try to avoid. NGOs could help consumers make choices to patronize firms that use reasonable terms, which (in a competitive market) could avoid any "lemons equilibrium" and result in better terms industry-wide. NGOs could organize multi-faceted studies of what might constitute fair and reasonable terms. They could draw up and disseminate model sets of terms.

NGOs can work with state attorneys general to educate consumers and develop and advocate model legislation to deter the use of abusive boilerplate. One possibility would be a statutory damages remedy or fine assessed against firms that deploy boilerplate found to be abusive, under criteria to be developed; one suggestion would be a $500 fine for each use of the offending boilerplate, by analogy with the junk fax law (the Telephone Consumer Protection Act of 1991). NGOs can (and indeed already do) work together with regulators such as state consumer protection agencies and insurance commissioners.

The American Law Institute, a very prominent NGO in legal affairs, could advance the state of the legal system with regard to boilerplate by commissioning a project on boilerplate similar to the project on *Principles of the Law of Software Contracts* completed in 2009 (see chapter 8). ALI principles, once developed, would assist courts faced with challenges to boilerplate.

Software and Hardware Design and Marketing

Firms that are in the business of designing and marketing software, or start-ups that might enter this field, can consider developing recognition and filtering systems to enable online shoppers to know what is actually in the boilerplate they receive (see chapter 10). Such systems would amount to consumer technological protection measures. Market research could be conducted to see whether such products would be viable in the marketplace. Such research would have to be designed so as to explain exactly what the clauses flagged by such filtering products propose to accomplish by subjecting users to them, and would have to take into account various heuristic biases on the part of consumers. Users could themselves organize in order to rate websites and sellers who do online business transactions, perhaps forming a user consortium to develop (for example) a labeling mechanism that would tell a browsing customer what is inside the "browsewrap" of the websites she visits.

Firms Currently Imposing Boilerplate

Many firms do without boilerplate and allow the legal background rules to govern claims that may be made by their customers. (See the example on page 113, a firm marketing a product that would be very likely to cause serious harm or death if defective, yet not using an exculpatory clause or rights deletion of any kind.) Firms that do impose onerous boilerplate should reconsider whether they really are saving through its use, given the possible harm to their reputations, (especially if consumer awareness grows of the ways in which boilerplate functions to delete legal background rights), and given the transaction costs of litigating to enforce it. Firms that now deploy onerous boilerplate could enhance their reputations, and hopefully their market share, by instead deploying benign boilerplate (merely telling consumers how to make a warranty claim, for example, rather than disclaiming warranty), or indeed foregoing the use of boilerplate altogether. Especially for firms dealing internationally, substantial savings on transaction costs appear possible through developing and using a white list that could be valid in many different countries (see chapter 12).

Regulatory Agencies

Agencies, whether at the state or federal level, should evaluate the possibility of black-listing at least the clauses that are most likely to operate to deny recipients their day in court: choice of forum/ choice of law clauses and exculpatory clauses, especially when they are illegally overbroad (purporting to exculpate for harms caused through gross negligence or recklessness, or even caused intentionally). State consumer protection agencies may choose to consider the clauses that are indicative of unfairness when used against consumers under the EU's 1993 directive on unfair contract terms. Agencies can consider instead publishing a white list (or safe harbor): a list of clauses that are presumptively fair and will not normally be challenged, along with a method whereby firms could advertise that their terms meet those standards. Insurance commissioners can try to see that insurers are not forcing their policyholders to deploy exculpatory clauses against their own clients.

Legislatures

US Supreme Court decisions expanding the scope of the Federal Arbitration Act (FAA) have enabled firms to preclude aggregative relief for consumers. Congress could amend the FAA in order to reestablish consumer remedies in situations of recurrent small harms, which call for aggregative relief if any relief is to be had. In the Dodd-Frank Wall Street Reform and Consumer Protection Act of 2010, Congress has already prohibited mandatory arbitration in mortgage and home equity loans, and has given the Bureau of Consumer Financial Protection created by that Act authority to prohibit mandatory arbitration in consumer financial services more generally should that be found to be in the public interest after study. Congress could go further and ensure that federal civil rights claims will be heard by a jury in federal court, so that job applicants would not have to relinquish an important component of their civil rights in order to secure employment.

State legislatures could consider disallowing exculpatory clauses of various kinds, especially those that purport to excuse harmful behavior that is worse than merely negligent. State legislatures should consider including in their consumer protection legislation explicit disallowance of waiver of important recipient rights, as legislatures have done in provisions regarding residential leases.

Courts

Courts could reconsider the role of rights enumerated in the federal Constitution and in state constitutions, and they could, in response to such reconsideration, subject to stricter scrutiny waivers of due process rights (in onerous choice of law/choice of forum clauses) and of jury trial rights (in arbitration clauses).

Judges could take note of the category of sheer ignorance on the part of recipients, such as happens with "browsewrap." Judges could review under tort law (see chapter 11) rather than under contract law any clauses that firms attempt to impose under conditions of recipients' sheer ignorance, and they could make use of the analytical framework offered in chapter 9 to conduct such a review.

Judges could also conduct stricter scrutiny of "rolling contracts," or treat them as involving sheer ignorance. This would alleviate serious analytical difficulties for the law of contracts, not only because of lack of consent, but also because of the problem of late formation created by "rolling contracts." (If a contract is supposedly not even formed until the recipient has opened the box, seen the terms, and failed to return the product within (say) 30 days, who is the owner of the product during those 30 days?)

In cases involving recipients' clicking "I agree," judges could evaluate challenges to terms based not on the problematic idea of "expectation" (which is ambiguous between an empirical and a normative understanding, see chapter 8), but rather on the importance of the rights purportedly deleted by the clauses, together with the quality of consent, in light of the circumstances.

Because of the prevalence of information asymmetry (see chapters 2 and 6) in markets where boilerplate is widespread, and because of the well-recognized stubborn nature of heuristic biases, judges could subject the quality of consent to more than minimal scrutiny even when recipients have clicked "I agree." Judges could in appropriate cases consider problematic consent under tort law rather than contract law, unless they find it possible to develop procdures for adjudicating mass-market harms under contract law. Without procedures to deal effectively with mass-market harm, recurrent lawsuits might cause transaction costs for both courts and firms, while at the same time leaving many recipients without remedy.

The availability of redress of grievances is an important part of the infrastructure of legality that supports the rule of law. Overreaching exculpatory clauses that relieve a firm of any responsibility for harm it causes are damaging to this infrastructure of legality (see chapter 7). Judges can invalidate such clauses using traditional contract oversight measures, or indeed declare them tortious in themselves when they purport to exculpate for gross negligence, recklessness, or intentional harm, especially in situations where recipients might be deterred from seeking justice. Courts could be sensitive to deletion of remedial rights in general.

Where appropriate, courts could interpret statutory grants of important rights to include the idea that these legislative regimes are not freely waivable by the expedient of mass-market boilerplate. For example, it may be a good idea to read the Copyright Act to disallow blanket waiver of user rights by means of a mass-market EULA, because user rights are a central feature of a federal regime that was hammered out by extensive legislative processes; and user rights may be central to the purpose of the Copyright Act in promoting innovation. Even when statutes are not explicit on the subject of waivability, judges could read legislative provisions to be inalienable (nonwaivable), or partially inalienable (waivable only with difficulty), by looking to the nature of the rights granted, or to the purpose of the legislation and considering whether that purpose would be vitiated by treating a particular rule as a default rule waivable by mass-market boilerplate.

Lawyers and Legal Scholars

We—the legal community—should stop trying to shoehorn all varieties of boilerplate into the categories of contract law. We must find other ways to characterize the phenomenon and to analyze various instances of its occurrence in order to separate what is justified from what is not. Considering boilerplate a product is one way to do this. Bonds and commercial insurance policies whose fine print is understood, well settled, and relied upon are treated as products that can be the basis for negotiations between commercial parties; but with respect to the fine print that accompanies consumer products and services, the contract-as-product theory leads to reconceptualizing (some) boilerplate under tort law.

We should also consider starting over with the idea that boilerplate is sui generis, requiring its own legal categories.

We—the legal community—should not allow purported contracts to "take private" the legal infrastructure that makes justifiable exchange possible.

. . . .

Prologue

1. The court in the case from which I derived this story said that the arbitration clause was not against public policy because it merely traded the "procedures and opportunity for review" of the courtroom—including, of course, the right to jury trial as well as the right to appeal—for expediency. *Global Travel Mktg. v. Shea*, 908 So. 2d 392, 403 (Fla. 2005) ("An arbitration agreement constitutes a prospective choice of forum which trades the procedures and opportunity for review of the courtroom for the simplicity, informality, and expedition of arbitration.").

2. *See Cooper v. MRM Inv. Co.*, 367 F.3d 493, 506 (6th Cir. 2004), citing cases from the 5th and 7th circuits.

3. In two other suits against the same service provider, on the other hand, claimants in state courts in California and Washington were successful in getting courts to disallow the clause based on their states' public policy of providing remedies for aggrieved customers in their state. *Am. Online, Inc. v. Super. Ct.*, 108 Cal. Rptr. 2d 699 (Ct. App. 2001); *Dix v. ICT Grp., Inc.*, 161 P.3d 1016 (Wash. 2007).

Choice of forum clauses are unpredictable in outcome, sometimes, but this makes it worthwhile for companies to put these clauses into their boilerplate and send their lawyers around the country trying to dismiss lawsuits, because they will often be successful, especially if they can get heard in federal courts rather than state courts.

4. *Jordan v. Diamond Equip. & Supply Co.*, 207 S.W.3d 525, 535 (Ark. 2005).

5. Michael's story is based on a case from Arkansas. *See* John G. Shram, *The Collision of Tort and Contract Law: The Validity and Enforceability of Exculpatory Clauses in Arkansas: Jordan v. Diamond Equipment*, 28 U. Ark. Little Rock L. Rev. 279 (2006).

Chapter One

1. Indeed, in the case on which I based Tonya's story, the appellate court thought that arbitration would impose a one-sided expenditure on Tonya, which it found objectionable, and her right to sue in court was salvaged under the contract doctrine of unconscionability, which is one of the "wild-card" doctrines I will talk about in chapter 7. *Cooper v. MRM Inv. Co.*, 367 F.3d 493, 509–13 (6th Cir. 2004). The next claimant after Tonya probably would not be so lucky, because a firm could readily fix the problem to make its form enforceable.

2. *See Wong v. Partygaming Ltd.*, 589 F.3d 821, 825 (6th Cir. 2009), in which claimants tried to sue in Ohio, but a choice of forum clause upheld by the appellate court limited their available forum to Gibraltar (under Gibraltar law, because the choice of forum clause was coupled with a choice of law clause).

3. *Carnival Cruise Lines, Inc. v. Shute*, 499 U.S. 585 (1991).

4. *See* chapter 7. At present, for example, courts tend to hold invalid most exculpatory clauses excusing medical service providers when a patient has been injured because of their negligence. That could change, since some prominent policy commentators argue that even here, "freedom of contract" should prevail. *See,* e.g., Richard H. Thaler and Cass R. Sunstein, NUDGE: IMPROVING DECISIONS ABOUT HEALTH, WEALTH, AND HAPPINESS 212–14 (2008).

5. In a law review article published in 1943, Friedrich Kessler attributes the first use of "contract of adhesion" to Edwin Patterson in 1919. Friedrich Kessler, *Contracts of Adhesion—Some Thoughts about Freedom of Contract*, 43 COLUM. L. REV. 629, 632 n. 11 (1943).

6. I don't claim originality for the idea of dividing contracts observed in practice into two subsets, one that is more readily justifiable under a standard theoretical paradigm, and one that would cause more shoehorning. *See,* e.g., Friedrich Kessler, *supra* note 5, at 631; Alan Schwartz and Robert E. Scott, *Contract Theory and the Limits of Contract Law*, 113 YALE L. J. 541, 549 (2003); *See also* Samuel Issacharoff, *Disclosure, Agents and Consumer Protection*, 167 J. INSTITUTIONAL & THEORETICAL ECON. 56 (2011).

One could also argue that the contracts of World A, too, if they are between firms rather than individuals, do not conform very well to the liberal ideal of freedom of contract. Firms do not necessarily operate like the imaginary free individuals who inhabit the ideal of contract theory. Instead, they have internal conflicts of interest and other organizational difficulties. Many economic writers have taken up the argument about the internal transaction costs that plague business organizations. Nevertheless, as writers such as Schwartz and Scott recognize, contracts between business entities are more likely to instantiate freedom of contract than those involving consumers. Arguments about the extent to which contracts between firms do or do not conform to an ideal of freedom of contract are interesting, but I do not take up the subject in this book.

7. Even Judge Richard A. Posner, Chief Judge of the Seventh Circuit Court of Appeals, someone who has opportunities to judge cases involving boilerplate, told a conference audience that he doesn't read the forms he signs. David Lat, *Do Lawyers Actually Read Boilerplate Contracts? Richard Posner and Evan Chesler Don't, Do You?* ABOVETHELAW.COM, http://abovethelaw.com/2010/06/do-lawyers-actaully-read-boilerplate-contracts-judge-richard-posner-doesnt-do-you/ (June 22, 2010, 2:42 PM). *See also* Alexia Tsotsis, *South Park Scares You into Reading Apple's Terms and Conditions*, TECHCRUNCH (April 28, 2011), http://techcrunch .com/2011/04/28/south-park-scares-you-into-reading-apples-terms-and-conditions/ ("[In an episode of the popular animated series, *South Park*], Kyle, who apparently is one of the only people in South Park who didn't read the iTunes TOS [Terms of Service], inadvertently agrees to become the middle part of a Human CentiPad or a 'part human, part centipede, part web browser and part emailing device.'").

8. Scholars of contract debate whether contract is based on (reciprocal) promises, or on agreement, or on consent. The common-law legal regime tends to speak of promising, and the civil-law legal regime tends to speak of agreement. I will discuss theories of contract, theories of World A, in chapter 4. Meanwhile, nothing I am saying turns on these distinctions.

9. The relationship of contract law to underlying moral premises is more complicated than this. I will allude to it in chapter 4 on voluntariness and the philosophy of contract. *See*, e.g., Seana Valentine Shiffrin, *The Divergence of Contract and Promise*, 120 HARV. L. REV. 708, 722 (2007) (discussing how "U.S. contract law diverges from the morality of promises.").

Chapter Two

1. Illegal contracts are unenforceable, as are contracts without a bargained quid pro quo (known in contract law as "consideration"), as well

as contracts that are too indefinite, and those that are based on fraud or certain kinds of mistakes, and so on.

2. A fuller treatment will be found in chapter 5. As I noted earlier, philosophy of contracts tends to talk about promising or about agreement rather than about consent, but that is a matter that can wait until chapter 4.

3. More detail about unconscionability is provided in chapter 7, where I will consider whether the doctrine of unconscionability is currently doing a good job of overseeing boilerplate rights deletion schemes, and also in chapter 8, where I will consider whether it can be improved.

4. In the US all contracts have an implied obligation of good faith and fair dealing; *see* RESTATEMENT (SECOND) OF CONTRACTS § 205 (1981). (The Restatement is a set of principles compiled by the American Law Institute. The American Law Institute is an NGO, consisting primarily of senior lawyers and judges, making recommendations for guidance in what the law is, and sometimes in what it ought to be. Starting in the 1930s, the ALI began a series of "restatements" of the law intended to gather together the common law and boil it down into a set of principles. The Restatements of contract law have been very influential in subsequent development of contract common law.) In the US, the obligation of good faith and fair dealing only exists after the contract has been formed. (Bad faith in negotiation before formation has to be dealt with under other doctrines, or just tolerated.) In civil-law countries, the obligation of good faith extends to the negotiation process. *See* Christian von Bar and Eric Clive, DRAFT COMMON FRAME OF REFERENCE [DCFR], vol. 1 (2010).

5. *See,* e.g., ROBERT NOZICK, ANARCHY, STATE AND UTOPIA (1974). Libertarians have the problem of trying to keep the state minimal while setting up and maintaining a well-defined system of property rights that can be traded and a well-defined system of contract rules to separate allowed exchanges from disallowed ones. Neither setting up and interpreting the boundaries of property rules nor the application of contract rules, including preventing coercion and fraud, are as simple as minimalists would like.

6. *Moore v. Regents of Univ. of Cal.,* 793 P.2d 479 (Cal. 1990). Did the doctors have to turn over their profit to Mr. Moore, or at least share it with him? No. The California Supreme Court held that Moore did not have a property right in his cell line; but the court implied that he could have sued in tort for fraud for failure to meet the requirements of

fiduciary duty and informed consent. There are other disturbing examples from the medical world, such as women who were sterilized after childbirth without knowing that this was happening. *See* Myla Vicenti Carpio, *The Lost Generation: American Indian Women and Sterilization Abuse,* 31 SOCIAL JUSTICE 40 (2004).

7. The notion of informed consent is not as prevalent in contract law as it is in matters involving (for example) consent to sexual activity or to medical treatment. For further discussion, see chapter 5.

8. Others, who do know they are receiving boilerplate, don't know what is in the boilerplate or understand its significance for them. Whether it could be considered consent when a person who does not understand anything about the boilerplate nevertheless clicks "I agree" will be considered in chapter 5.

9. *See* RESTATEMENT (SECOND) OF CONTRACTS § 69 (1981). As mentioned earlier, *supra* note 4, the American Law Institute is an NGO, consisting primarily of senior lawyers and judges whose Restatements of contract law have been very influential in the subsequent development of contract common law.

10. See chapter 11, in which I consider moving legal analysis and oversight of certain species of boilerplate out of contract law and into tort law.

11. Tort law is complex, and it does come into play in other situations, such as malpractice or invasion of privacy or interference with contractual relations. I would only suggest that a core tort paradigm fits certain types of boilerplate deployment better than a contracts paradigm.

12. For an introduction to the psychological literature and its various applications to law, *see* BEHAVIORAL LAW AND ECONOMICS (Cass R. Sunstein, ed., 2000). For an explanation of these phenomena that is written for laypeople, *see* Richard H. Thaler and Cass R. Sunstein, NUDGE: IMPROVING DECISIONS ABOUT HEALTH, WEALTH, AND HAPPINESS, 22–37 (2008). Daniel Kahneman, THINKING, FAST AND SLOW (2011) is a masterful and delightful exposition of the psychological phenomena, as well as a recounting of the work with Amos Tversky for which Kahneman received the Nobel Prize in Economics.

13. Thaler and Sunstein, *supra* note 12, at 31–33.

14. Russell Korobkin interprets the status quo bias as resulting primarily in contracting parties sticking with default background rules. *See*

Russell Korobkin, *The Status Quo Bias and Contract Default Rules*, 83 CORNELL L. REV. 608 (1998). As I think he recognizes, however, this is not true of firms that develop boilerplate alternative legal universes. *Id.* at 621. They do not stick with the default background rule of jury trial; instead they deploy arbitration clauses. They do not stick with the default background rules of liability for negligent harm and consequential damages; instead they deploy exculpatory clauses and limitations of remedy. Firms do stick with boilerplate once they have developed it, however; the status quo can easily proliferate in the guise of industry-wide identical forms. And recipients do stick with being recipients once they are used to doing so.

15. *See* Robert A. Hillman and Ibrahim Barakat, *Warranties and Disclaimers in the Electronic Age*, CORNELL LEGAL STUDIES RESEARCH PAPER No. 1154121 (June 2008); *See also*, Simon Bradshaw, Christopher Millard, and Ian Walden, CONTRACTS FOR CLOUDS: COMPARISON AND ANALYSIS OF THE TERMS AND CONDITIONS OF CLOUD COMPUTING SERVICES, Centre for Commercial Law Studies, Queen Mary, University of London (2010) (finding strict limitations of liability and other onerous clauses in various Terms of Service schemes of cloud computing providers); Florencia Marotta-Wurgler, *What's in a Standard Form Contract? An Empirical Analysis of Software License Agreements*, 4 J. EMPIRICAL LEGAL STUDIES, 677–713 (2007); *see also* Scott Adams, DILBERT STRIP (January 14, 1997) http://dilbert.com/strips/comic/1997-01-14/, satirizing Microsoft, and the later Dilbert strip satirizing software EULAs generally: Scott Adams, DILBERT STRIP (February 23, 2011) http://dilbert.com/strips/comic/2011-02-23/. (The 2011 strip is the frontispiece of this book.)

16. You might find examples of this kind of boilerplate by checking the online terms of service (TOS) of financial firms.

17. *See*, e.g., Nikki Schwab and Katy Adams, *'Covert Affairs' Not Covert About Filming in D.C.*, THE EXAMINER (Aug. 31, 2011, 12:10 PM), http://washingtonexaminer.com/blogs/yeas-nays/2011/08/covert-affairs-not-covert-about-filming-dc; *You Are Being Photographed*, FLICKR, http://www.flickr.com/photos/navymailman/5521471277/ (last visited Nov. 14, 2011). (For another example, see page 115.)

18. *See*, e.g., Stephen Ware, *The Case for Enforcing Arbitration Agreements—With Particular Consideration of Class Actions and Arbitration*

Fees, 4 J. AM. ARB. 251, 278 (2006) ("The deal implicit in an arbitration agreement with a prohibition on class adjudication becomes: an even better price or wage than would have been achieved by an arbitration agreement without such a prohibition, plus greater leverage on non-aggregatable, small-yet-meritorious claims in exchange for reduced leverage on claims that could lead to a big-dollar jury award and on aggregatable claims."). For a discussion of the US Supreme Court's affirmance of clauses denying any form of aggregative relief, see chapter 7.

Chapter Three

1. It is possible to reinterpret the public/private distinction as pragmatic rather than formal or conceptual. (See discussion below.) To the extent that World B becomes run-of-the-mill, however, it undermines the liberal ideal of private ordering and contributes to democratic degradation.

2. *See also* Margaret Jane Radin, *Reconsidering the Rule of Law*, 69 B.U. L. REV. 781 (1989).

3. *See* Lon L. Fuller, THE MORALITY OF LAW (rev. ed. 1969); John Rawls, A THEORY OF JUSTICE 206–13 (1971); Joseph Raz, *The Rule of Law and Its Virtue*, in THE AUTHORITY OF LAW: ESSAYS ON LAW AND MORALITY 210 (1979); Margaret Jane Radin, *Can the Rule of Law Survive Bush v. Gore?* in BUSH V. GORE: THE QUESTION OF LEGITIMACY 110 (Bruce Ackerman, ed., 2001).

4. Fuller, *supra* note 3, 81–91.

5. *Eldred v. Ashcroft*, 537 U.S. 186 (2003).

6. Liberals and conservatives alike were dismayed by this; it is something a liberal, Lawrence Lessig, and a conservative, Richard Epstein, could agree on, because they are both committed to the ideal of the rule of law. Richard A. Epstein, *The Dubious Constitutionality of the Copyright Extension Act*, 36 LOY. L.A. L. REV. 123 (2002); Lawrence Lessig, *How I Lost the Big One*, LEGAL AFF., Mar.–Apr. 2004, at 57.

7. See below, "Copycat Boilerplate," page 41.

8. Suggested to me by Kim Krawiec. I would guess that well-funded lobbying interests are more likely to realize this than their public-interest opponents; consider copyright industries vs. libraries and user groups, for example.

9. Someone might well argue that there are worse democratic degradations, such as the increasing role of corporate money in all aspects of US political structure.

10. *See generally* Albert O. Hirschmann, Exit, Voice and Loyalty: Responses to Decline in Firms, Organizations, and States (1970). Hirschmann argues that people can react to dissatisfaction with an entity either by withdrawing from the relationship (exiting) or attempting to improve the relationship through communication (using their voice). In some markets there can be voice if consumers push back hard against the scheme deployed by the firm. This happens sometimes with online firms whose consumers are concerned about privacy; for example. Miguel Helft and Jenna Wortham, *Facebook Bows to Pressure over Privacy*, New York Times, May 27, 2010, at B1. See discussion in chapter 10 of situations in which consumer pushback might occur.

11. Heuristic biases include our tendency to feel that misfortune or serious difficulties will befall other people but not us. When buying a product, no one expects that she may later need to sue the manufacturer because the product has seriously injured her. See discussion in chapter 2.

12. Of course, tacit collusion is hard to prove. Firms will argue that each arrived independently at the most efficient solution needed for effective competition. *See*, e.g., *Starr v. Sony BMG Music Ent.*, 592 F.3d 314, 322 (2d Cir. 2010) ("[A]llegations of parallel conduct must be placed in a context that raises a suggestion of a preceding agreement, not merely parallel conduct that could just as well be independent action.") (internal citations and quotations omitted).

13. It is often argued, and might sometimes be true in some markets, that industry-wide standardization indicates that the terms have "won out" in a competitive market. But less propitious results are also possible. See chapter 6 for discussion of various possibilities.

14. *See*, e.g., Marcel Kahan and Michael Klausner, *Standardization and Innovation in Corporate Contracting (or "The Economics of Boilerplate")*, 83 Va. L. Rev. 713, 726 (1997) ("Contractual network benefits include higher quality and lower cost legal and professional services in the future, as lawyers and accountants gain (and retain) expertise by encountering questions or disputes regarding a particular contract term.").

15. For an explanation and discussion of welfare-maximization (economic) theory and its treatment of boilerplate, see chapters 4 and 6.

16. This concept, which allows individual plaintiffs to rely on constitutional rights to sue another individual for violating those rights is known as *Drittwirkung*. For a discussion of the development of *Drittwirkung, see generally* Kenneth M. Lewan, *The Significance of Constitutional Rights for Private Law: Theory and Practice in West Germany*, 17 Int. & Comp. L. Q. 571 (1968). *See also* Helen Herskoff, *Just Words: Common Law and the Enforcement of State Constitutional Social and Economic Rights*, 62 Stan. L. Rev. 1521, 1548 (2010) ("Examples from abroad usually draw from Germany, where the principle of *Drittwirkung* has been applied to accord the Basic Law—which, among other rights, protects as 'inviolable' the 'dignity of man'—an 'impact on third parties' in a court's interpretation of private law doctrine.") (footnotes omitted).

17. For a discussion of the inconsistent treatment of the state action doctrine over time, *see* Martin A. Schwartz and Erwin Chemerinsky, *Dialogue on State Action*, 16 Touro L. Rev. 773 (2000). *See generally* Geoffrey R. Stone et al., Constitutional Law 1543–1608 (6th ed. 2009).

18. This point was well recognized by Frank Michelman in an article published decades ago. Frank I. Michelman, *Ethics, Economics, and the Law of Property*, in Nomos xxiv: Ethics, Economics, and the Law (J. Roland Pennock and John W. Chapman, eds., 1982), reprinted in Frank I. Michelman, *Ethics, Economics, and the Law of Property*, 39 Tulsa L. Rev. 663, 673 (2004).

19. If only some legislation is to be considered as purely rent-seeking (maximizing welfare for one actor or a particular interest group), whereas some legislation is to be considered in the public interest (maximizing welfare for society as a whole), then the political economy theorist needs some method of distinguishing rent-seeking measures or regimes from public interest measures or regimes. I am not aware of any theory that satisfactorily lays out such a distinction. It is my impression that many political economy theorists do not advert to the problem with justification of the state if all decisions are taken to be driven by rent-seeking. Margaret Jane Radin, Comment, *Positive Theory as Conceptual Critique: A Piece of a Pragmatic Agenda?* 68 S. Cal. L. Rev. 1595, 1601–02 (1995). Steven Croley uses the existence of important instances where public-interest rulemaking triumphed over rent-seeking to argue that public choice theory is a failure because it cannot explain how the US regulatory system actually works. Steven Croley, Regulation and Public Interests: The Possibility of Good Regulatory Government 241–57 (2008).

20. WIPO Copyright Treaty, art. 11, Dec. 20, 1996; *see also* Digital Millennium Copyright Act, 17 U.S.C. §§ 1201–1205 (2006).

21. *See,* e.g., *Sega Enters. Ltd. V. Accolade, Inc.,* 977 F.2d 1510 (9th Cir. 1992) (indicating that copying for purpose of reverse engineering is likely to be fair use); *see also The Chamberlain Group, Inc. v. Skylink Technologies, Inc.,* 381 F.3d 1178 (Fed. Cir. 2004) (holding that maker of replacement garage door openers (GDOs) did not violate the antitrafficking provisions of the Digital Millennium Copyright Act (DMCA), because owners of GDOs were authorized to access Plaintiff's GDO software). *But cf. Bowers v. Baystate Techs.,* 320 F.3d 1317 (Fed. Cir. 2003) (holding that a party breached a contractual restriction on software reverse engineering although such copying is permitted by the Copyright Act).

22. It would not be possible, for example, for a boilerplate rights deletion scheme to delete all legal remedies, at least not explicitly, but a TPM implements the firm's will by machine and forecloses all legal remedies for the recipient.

23. A defender of TPMs could argue that the user chooses whether or not to purchase the content-plus-TPM package, and that this decision is an agreement, or at least consensual, an appropriate contractual transaction. This could be true under some market circumstances. But it should not be held true as a matter of abstract general theory. The question becomes analogous to the question whether in the contract-as-product view the buyer of the *functional* part of the product can be held to have consented to the *terms* part of the product. (I will explain and evaluate the contract-as-product view in chapter 6.) In order to conclude that a recipient of a TPM has chosen to be bound by the package purchased, including the automatic injunction, we must ask empirical questions about the market: whether the recipient is aware of the operations of the TPM, whether the same content is available in the market without the TPM, and so on. I believe that favorable assumptions about competition, information, and product availability are not warranted in a large number of cases; or at least cannot be presumed to be true, absent information about market circumstances. Moreover, even if one accepts this argument, the question remains whether all user entitlements may properly be treated as default rules defeasible by purchase of a product containing a machine that defeats them. (See chapter 9.)

24. *See,* e.g., Symposium, *Property Rights on the Frontier: The Economics of Self-Help and Self-Defense in Cyberspace,* 1 J.L. ECON. & POL'Y 1 (2005).

25. With real property, one may gain rights to use another's property—i.e., a prescriptive easement—by using the land adversely (e.g., walking across the land without permission) beyond a designated period of time. Consequently, an owner of land may attempt to prevent this result by erecting a fence or some other barrier to keep others from using her land. For an explanation of easements by prescription, *see* William B. Stoebuck and Dale A. Whitman, THE LAW OF PROPERTY 451–56 (3d ed. 2000). In the case of trade secrets, one must take "reasonable measures to keep such information secret" in order for the information to qualify as a trade secret. 18 U.S.C. § 1839(3)(a) (2006).

26. *See also* Bruce W. Frier and James J. White, THE MODERN LAW OF CONTRACTS 666–749 (3d. ed. 2012) (self-help during performance).

27. Indeed the ideal of the rule of law may be the main reason that the law moved to disallow spring guns. Under the ideal of the rule of law, the law of the state (the rules of tort and property) should be the sole authority to hold intruders liable, or not, and the law of the state (the remedies for trespass to land) should have sole charge of the level and applicability of remedy available. (You are not permitted to kill someone who breaks in to steal your cabbages or to warn you that your house is on fire.)

28. *Tapscott v. Cobbs*, 52 Va. (11 Gratt.) 172, 177 (1854).

29. See note 20, *supra*.

Chapter Four

1. There is a philosophical disagreement about when the redistribution takes place. It is possible to view the contractual promise as transferring to the other party an entitlement to performance—or to damages if not performed—as soon as the contract is entered—*see,* e.g., Peter Benson, *Contract as a Transfer of Ownership*, 48 WM. & MARY L. REV. 1673, 1703 (2007)—provided that the contract is one that the legal system recognizes as enforceable. *See also* Stephen A. Smith, CONTRACT THEORY 72–78 (2004); Andrew Gold, *A Property Theory of Contract*, 103 NW. U. L. REV. 1 (2009). It is also possible to view the transfer of entitlement as not taking place until actual performance, so that if the party who has promised performance breaches the contract and doesn't perform, the entitlement to whatever a court decrees as remedy does not become an entitlement of the nonbreaching party until the stage of enforcement. Either

way, contract formation or contract enforcement involves the transfer of an entitlement from one private party to another.

2. These two theoretical clusters are summarized in Michael J. Trebilcock, THE LIMITS OF FREEDOM OF CONTRACT 1–10 (1997).

3. *See,* e.g., RESTATEMENT (SECOND) OF CONTRACTS § 1 (1981) ("A contract is a promise or a set of promises for the breach of which the law gives a remedy, or the performance of which the law in some way recognizes as a duty.")

4. A few writers do not choose sides between autonomy theory and welfare theory. It is possible to try to amalgamate them, perhaps along with "reliance theory." Trebilcock, *supra* note 2 at 248; Jody S. Kraus, *Reconciling Autonomy and Efficiency in Contract Law: The Vertical Integration Strategy,* in 11 PHIL. ISSUES 420, 422 (2001); Melvin A. Eisenberg, *The Theory of Contracts,* in THE THEORY OF CONTRACT LAW: NEW ESSAYS 206, 223–35 (Peter Benson, ed., 2001). Or it may be said that both autonomy and welfare theories are inadequate and that trying to amalgamate them won't help much. Peter A. Alces, *The Moral Impossibility of Contract,* 48 WM. & MARY L. REV. 1647, 1661 (2007). (If both are inadequate and we don't have a more satisfactory theory of justification of contract enforcement to supplant them, then we may be in a more wholesale normative difficulty than just the one that I am addressing in this book.)

5. Randy E. Barnett, *A Consent Theory of Contract,* 86 COLUM L. REV. 269 (1986). Although Barnett intends his theory to be based on consent only, perhaps it is a variant of autonomy theory. Consent is indeed an aspect of autonomy. But a theory based solely on consent tends to focus only on one party, the one who is asked to give up something, without focusing inquiry so much on the reciprocal obligation of the other, so this theory lacks the reciprocity characteristic of traditional autonomy theory. Barnett's consent theory is designed explicitly as a libertarian theory, and as we shall see in chapter 5, it makes room for consent to be bound to unknown terms, perhaps more readily than does mainstream autonomy theory. Barnett can accomplish this by focusing primarily on the consent of the recipient of boilerplate without focusing on obligations of the party deploying the boilerplate, because consent is a one-sided inquiry. (Nevertheless, Barnett is considered an autonomy theorist by other scholars, such as Melvin Eisenberg, because his is a rights theory based upon liberty (freedom). Eisenberg, *supra* note 4, at 233.)

Barnett starts from the premise that we have "a system of entitlements where manifested rights transfers are what justify the legal enforcement of agreements," and for him it follows that "any such manifestation necessarily implies that one intends to be legally bound." Randy E. Barnett, *A Consent Theory of Contract*, 86 COLUM L. REV. at 304–306. If the inference about parties' intent when consenting assumes existence of the institution of contract, then the theory presupposes an institution that already decides which promises can be legally binding; so that if parties promise with (implied) intent to be legally bound if and only if the institution of contract provides that they will be bound, they must already know whether or not the institution will provide for legal bindingness; in which case we can't use their consent to validate or delineate the contours of the institution. This theory thus may be question-begging. Perhaps Barnett only means that our system of property entitlements gives people rights to transfer their property rights, so that when we see them transferring their rights, we should assume they intend to be legally bound. This tends to locate contract within the definition of property. (This move has some historical precedent in J. S. Mill's view of property.) *See* Margaret Jane Radin, CONTESTED COMMODITIES chapter 3 (1996) (discussing Mill's view of property and contracts).

Even if Barnett's theory isn't question-begging, it does not help us decide which types of attempted transfers actually are or should be legally binding. (Selling oneself into slavery? Selling babies? etc.) The theory also has a problem with adopting the objective theory of contract, which our system does adhere to, since, as Barnett realizes, it is paradoxical in a theory relying on actual consent as its basis to impute such an intent when it doesn't actually exist. Barnett concludes that this imputed consent is not inconsistent with liberty, however, because the rights and liberty interests of others are (more?) important. *Cf.* Eisenberg, *supra* note 4, at 233. For more on the objective theory of contract, see chapter 5.

6. Entitlements that are justly held in the first place are often referred to as "baseline" entitlements. Arguments about the nature and extent of baseline entitlements are part of the property half of the legal infrastructure of the system of private ordering, contracts being the other half.

7. *See*, e.g., RESTATEMENT (SECOND) OF CONTRACTS § 1 (1981). The philosophical premise that promising is the basis of contract has come under attack by American writers of the welfare school of thought. *See* Richard Craswell, *Contract Law, Default Rules, and the*

Philosophy of Promising, 88 MICH. L. REV. 489 (1989). From a moral philosopher's perspective, Seana Shiffrin has also questioned the use of the concept of promising as the basis of contract law. *See* Seana Valentine Shiffrin, *The Divergence of Contract and Promise*, 120 HARV. L. REV. 708 (2007). Shiffrin argues that the moral concept of promising does not fit contract law in practice, because various aspects of contract law dishonor the moral concept, and her perspective is indeed that it would be better for contract law to conform to the moral concept more than it does. She does not suggest that promising should be replaced by a premise that does not require autonomy or related concepts such as free will, choice, and voluntariness.

8. Charles Fried, CONTRACT AS PROMISE: A THEORY OF CONTRACTUAL OBLIGATION (1981). Although the idea that contract is rooted in the institution of promising is dominant, *see*, e.g., RESTATEMENT (SECOND) OF CONTRACTS § 1 (1981), it is not monolithic. Other cultures may consider contract to be rooted in the concept of agreement. *See*, e.g., PRINCIPLES, DEFINITIONS AND MODEL RULES OF EUROPEAN PRIVATE LAW: DRAFT COMMON FRAME OF REFERENCE (DCFR) 183 (Christian von Bar et al., eds., 2009), available at http://ec.europa.eu/justice/contract/files/european-private-law_en.pdf. This difference in conceptual underpinning may show up in some differences in doctrines and practices. But the difference does not matter at the level of abstraction I am addressing here, because voluntariness, in the sense of freedom of choice, is implicated both in promising and in agreement, and for that matter also in consent.

9. Another important criticism of Fried is that his theory seems too unilateral in the sense of focusing primarily on the promisor's intent while not taking into account the proper attitude of the promisee and the circumstances under which the proper attitude of the promisee can be rightfully inferred. *See*, e.g., Peter Benson, *Contract as a Transfer of Ownership*, 48 WM. & MARY L. REV. 1673, 1681–83 (2007). Thanks to Arthur Ripstein for helpful discussion on this point.

10. Charles Fried, *supra* note 8, at 17.

11. For example: Why does Fried endorse expectation damages as the remedy for breach? Why not specific performance, in which the court orders the breaching party to deliver what was promised? Or, why not allow autonomous parties to provide in their contract for whatever remedy they want, including none? *See*, e.g., Craswell, *supra* note 7, at 518 ("There is surely nothing in the idea of individual autonomy that requires the exact

degree of non-optionality [of performance] provided by the expectation measure.") Perhaps Fried would say that promising is a convention and would take as the moral basis of contractual promising the convention we already have; namely that the remedy for breach is expectation damages. But in rejecting utilitarian theory he has said that he wants a theory that is "deeper" than social utility, and he does not address why a particular existing convention is of the requisite superior depth. See Fried, *supra* note 8, at 17. *See also* Jody S. Kraus, *From Langdell to Law and Economics: Two Concepts of Stare Decisis in Contract Law and Theory*, 94 VA. L. REV. 157 (2008), who defends Fried by arguing that specific performance is not the same as promise keeping, and then apparently adopting a similar view of existing convention to justify expectation damages. It remains unclear how observation of existing convention can be part of a theory that is supposed to *justify* existing convention. See Peter Benson, *The Unity of Contract Law*, in THE THEORY OF CONTRACT LAW: NEW ESSAYS 118 (Peter Benson, ed., 2001); James Gordley, *Contract Law in the Aristotelian Tradition* in THE THEORY OF CONTRACT LAW: NEW ESSAYS 265 (Peter Benson, ed., 2001).

12. *See* Peter Benson, *The Unity of Contract Law*, *supra* note 11, at 127–28; *see also* Ernest J. Weinrib, *Punishment and Disgorgement as Contract Remedies*, 78 CHI.-KENT L. REV. 55 (2003); and Stephen A. Smith, CONTRACT THEORY *supra*, note 1; Andrew Gold, *A Property Theory of Contract*, *supra*, note 1.

13. Benson, *The Unity of Contract Law*, *supra* note 11, at 183.

14. *Id.* at 180–81 ("Now if contract, as the doctrine of offer and acceptance supposes, is to consist in a two-sided relation that is formed by two acts of will, it follows that at least one side must be a promise, with the other being either an act or a promise. . . . But the requirements introduced by the doctrine of consideration . . . articulate in the most elementary and encompassing terms the necessary conditions of just such a relation.")

15. *Id.* at 192. For a discussion of unconscionability, see chapters 7 and 8.

16. *Id.* at 188–91.

17. *Id.* at 191.

18. It should be noted that a newer model going by the name of "behavioral economics" blends economic reasoning with lessons learned from psychological findings regarding decisionmaking. Behavioral economics challenges some important aspects of economic reasoning. *See*,

e.g., BEHAVORIAL LAW AND ECONOMICS (Cass R. Sunstein, ed., 2003). Behavioral economics may eventually override some of the premises of the traditional model, especially its concept of "rationality," but in contemporary legal analysis the traditional premises are still dominant. *See* also note 23, *infra.*

19. *See* Louis Kaplow and Steven Shavell, FAIRNESS VERSUS WELFARE (2002); Robert C. Ellickson, *Adverse Possession and Perpetuities Law: Two Dents in the Libertarian Model of Property Rights,* 64 WASH. U.L.Q. 723 (1986). Some practitioners of the economic analysis of law have claimed not to espouse utilitarianism, or at least not unequivocally. Richard Epstein has claimed to be a utilitarian and a libertarian at the same time. Richard A. Epstein, PRINCIPLES FOR A FREE SOCIETY: RECONCILING INDIVIDUAL LIBERTY WITH THE COMMON GOOD 2–3 (1998) ("Laissez-faire [or libertarianism] is best understood not as an effort to glorify the individual at the expense of society, but as the embodiment of principles that, when consistently applied, will work to the advantage of all (or almost all) members of society simultaneously. . . . More concretely, my central mission here is to explain how a concern with the common good does not eviscerate the traditional protections otherwise provided to individual liberty and private property.") Richard Posner has claimed to be a normative economist without being utilitarian, espousing efficiency only in the positive sense. *See* Richard A. Posner, THE ECONOMICS OF JUSTICE 48 (1981) ("The important question is whether utilitarianism and [normative] economics are distinguishable. I believe they are and that the economic norm that I shall call 'wealth maximization' provides a firmer basis for ethical theory than utilitarianism does.").

Probably the core commitments of utilitarianism diverge greatly from the core commitments of libertarianism; and probably one can't coherently be normatively nonutilitarian and think that wealth maximization is what is morally required. *See* e.g., Anthony T. Kronman, *Wealth Maximization as a Normative Principle,* 9 J. LEGAL STUDIES 227, 229 (1980) ("Wealth maximization is not only an unsound ideal, it is an incoherent one which cannot be defended from any point of view.") *See also* Richard A. Posner, FRONTIERS OF LEGAL THEORY 98 (2001).

20. *See,* e.g., Richard A. Epstein, TAKINGS: PRIVATE PROPERTY AND THE POWER OF EMINENT DOMAIN 3–6 (1985). *See also* Ian Ayres and Robert H. Gertner, *Filling Gaps in Incomplete Contracts: An Economic Theory of Default Rules,* 99 YALE L. J. 87 (1989).

21. An important contemporary branch of welfare theory tries to figure out how to apply it to corporations and other business entities. I need not go into this here. (Other books have done this.)

22. Substituting revealed preference-satisfaction as the maximand arguably modifies the difficult notion that all human interests and desires can be arrayed and quantified on a single scale of "something" to be maximized.

23. A convincing body of psychological research in the past three decades has shown that human choices in fact deviate in many ways from the "rationality" of the economists' model. *See* Daniel Kahneman, THINKING, FAST AND SLOW (2011). Perhaps economic analysts will eventually modify the psychological version of this self-interest premise in light of this body of empirical work. Perhaps those who do not want to relinquish their theoretical model will retreat to the idea that the individual as self-interested maximizer is the proper premise to use when doing political or ethical theory even if it does not describe people in real life. The argument why this would be a useful model to use in that case is not self-evident.

24. This premise is known as "reductionism" by those who disagree with it—that is, by those who believe that valuation by humans involves different and incommensurable species of value that cannot be reduced to dollar-values. Basing theory on the maximization of subjective preference satisfaction rather than wealth arguably mitigates the problem of reductionism.

25. *See*, e.g., Michael J. Trebilcock, THE LIMITS OF FREEDOM OF CONTRACT, *supra* note 2, 58–77 (1993), who says that "the concept of externalities is one of the least satisfactory concepts in welfare economics." *Id.* at 59. As Trebilcock explains in this chapter, there are different accounts by economists, and none of them is satisfactory. The nature of the conceptual difficulty, he believes, is that "the problem of third-party effects from exchange relationships is pervasive and not aberrational." *Id.* at 58. Just about anything anyone does has some effect on others in the world: on their property, on their autonomy, on their scope of freedom; that is, in social welfare terms, on their total welfare. In Trebilcock's examples, "If I buy garish clothing that offends your sense of taste, or engage in unconventional sexual practices with a partner that offend your sense of decency, the transactions or interactions involved generate negative externalities." *Id.*

The question becomes, where do we draw the line in deciding the scope of the effects on the "utils" of others that should be counted in order to achieve efficiency, because, theoretically, in a system that is attempting to maximize social welfare, everyone's welfare counts. Another way of putting this problem would be that the decision where to draw the boundaries of the social welfare universe being considered is not one that yields to algorithmic formulations. Is it just the two parties to a transaction? Is it everyone who lives within two hundred yards of them? Is it everyone in their city? And so on . . . So when we propose to maximize welfare in the particular chosen universe, we can never be sure how the answer would change if we chose different boundaries for including effects on others.

26. P. S. Atiyah, *Essay 6: The Liberal Theory of Contract*, in ESSAYS ON CONTRACT 121, 133 (1986). See also Atiyah, *Essay 2: Contracts, Promises, and the Law of Obligations*, *supra*, at 33–40, in which Atiyah raises and refutes various arguments for enforcement absent reliance.

27. Atiyah, *Essay 6*, *supra* note 26, at 133–34. Other writers do defend the principle that entitlement to performance passes to the promisee at the moment the promise is made. *See* Peter Benson, *The Unity of Contract Law*, *supra* note 11, at 118; Stephen A. Smith, *supra* note 1 at 56–58; cf. James Gordley, *Contract Law in the Aristotelian Tradition*, in THE THEORY OF CONTRACT LAW: NEW ESSAYS 265, 327–32 (Peter Benson, ed., 2001). Acceptance of this principle may seem to require the remedy of specific performance rather than expectation damages, which makes the civil-law system more in accord with the justification of contract than the common-law system.

28. *See*, e.g., Atiyah, *Essay 6*, *supra* note 26, at 123.

29. Gordley, *supra* note 27.

30. *Id.*

31. *Id.* at 269.

32. *Id.* at 333.

33. *Id.* at 272–74 (discussing defects of welfare theory); *id.* at 274–80 (discussing defects of autonomy theory).

34. *See* Richard A. Posner, ECONOMIC ANALYSIS OF LAW (8th ed. 2011).

35. The economist who is seeking to maximize only aggregate welfare would not care, of course, that the entire profit from this move would

accrue to the breaching party. This theory has been well critiqued on various grounds. *See*, e.g., Mark Seidenfeld, MICROECONOMIC PREDICATES TO LAW AND ECONOMICS 56 (1996); Herbert Hovenkamp, *Positivism in Law and Economics*, 78 CAL. L. REV. 815, 847 (1990). At least practically speaking, damages are normally undercompensatory, since a plaintiff must employ attorneys to get them, and attorneys fees are normally not recoverable.

Moreover, theoretically speaking, if everyone has an incentive to breach (and pay off the other side) whenever they feel that it will be valuable to them to do so, everyone may also have lowered incentives to enter into contracts in the first place because of the expectation that others will breach; and this overall disincentive must be taken into account in efficiency calculus. *See*, e.g., Daniel Friedmann, *The Efficient Breach Fallacy*, 18 J. LEGAL STUD. 1, 7–8, 18–23 (1989).

36. *See* Richard Craswell, *Two Economic Theories of Enforcing Promises*, in THE THEORY OF CONTRACT LAW: NEW ESSAYS 19 (Peter Benson, ed., 2001).

37. Ian Ayres and Robert H. Gertner, *Filling Gaps in Incomplete Contracts: An Economic Theory of Default Rules*, 99 YALE L.J. 87 (1989).

38. Alan Schwartz, *The Case for Specific Performance*, 89 YALE L.J. 271 (1979).

39. Craswell, *supra* note 36, at 27–34.

40. One article that made a big splash reviews the literature and claims that economic analysis of contract law is a failure. Eric A. Posner, *Economic Analysis of Contract Law After Three Decades: Success or Failure?* 112 YALE L. J. 829 (2003). See Posner's conclusion:

"[E]conomics fails to explain contract law. It does not explain why expectation damages are the standard remedy, for example, or why liquidated damages are not always enforced. . . . And economics provides little normative guidance for reforming contract law. Models that have been proposed in the literature either focus on small aspects of contractual behavior or make optimal doctrine a function of variables that cannot realistically be observed, measured, or estimated. The models do give a sense of the factors that are at stake when the decisionmaker formulates doctrine, and might give that decisionmaker a sense of the trade-offs involved, but in the absence of information about the magnitude of these trade-offs—and the literature gives no sense of these magnitudes—the decisionmaker is left with little guidance."

Id. at 880.

41. *See,* e.g., Trebilcock, *supra* note 2, at 246.

42. Guido Calabresi and A. Douglas Melamed, *Property Rules, Liability Rules, and Inalienability: One View of the Cathedral,* 85 HARV. L. REV. 1089 (1972). This article spawned a very large literature; *see* Symposium, *Property Rules, Liability Rules, and Inalienability: A Twenty-Five Year Retrospective,* 106 YALE L. REV. 2081 (1997).

43. In their discussion of distributional goals, Calabresi and Melamed had in mind situations where we might want the government to facilitate coordination of relatively wealthy buyers to buy out poorer people (because this would be better for distributional goals, presumably, than a process whereby the wealthy simply use the legislative process to impose on the poor). The example Calabresi and Malamed used was a factory that employed lots of workers but used polluting cheap coal; they suggested that a legally structured liability rule could enable wealthier folks who desired clean air to compensate the factory and its workers. This argument, for a liability rule under certain circumstances in private ordering; i.e., for a species of private eminent domain, is controversial. It might suggest, for example, that we should enable neighbors to coordinate to condemn the right of an owner of vacant land to develop low-income housing; or it might suggest that workers should be enabled to condemn and buy out a firm that threatens to relocate its plant.

The argument is controversial precisely because "private eminent domain" is so difficult to countenance, at least while we are still under the influence of traditional liberal narratives of justification. Indeed, in their dialogue with a hypothetical naive first-year student about criminal law, Calabresi and Melamed explained that it would not do merely to charge thieves (or trespassers) damages equal to the value of what they took without the owner's consent, because that would allow them to change property rules into liability rules at will. Hence, an "indefinable kicker" was needed in order to deter such wholesale ability to make property rules lapse into liability rules.

44. That is, liability rules at best—if and only if the compensation is deemed adequate. A proponent of this scheme might argue that hypothetical consent of the recipient saves the scheme from being characterized as

simply a regime of liability rules. But hypothetical consent and liability rules coalesce in this case, because hypothetical consent is being inferred from the assumption that there is adequate compensation.

45. There are plenty of market circumstances in which passing-on does not occur. It is an empirical question which contracts in World B save money for consumers. It is a further empirical question whether the savings to recipients, if they exist, outweigh the costs of their loss of autonomy. For further discussion of these issues, see chapter 6.

46. Others writers have also ventured to find a limited place for liability rules in private ordering, but none has suggested that a blanket metamorphosis of people's baseline entitlements into liability rules defeasible at will by private firms through the use of mass-market boilerplate would be justifiable. For example, as I will discuss in chapter 7, courts sometimes rewrite the terms of contracts they find unconscionable, rather than merely declaring the contracts null and void. When they do this, they are implementing something other than a consented-to bargain, in their efforts to remedy something that was not a (freely, properly) consented-to bargain. Richard Craswell has contributed a thoughtful analysis of this practice; see note 47 *infra*, and accompanying text.

47. Richard Craswell, *Property Rules and Liability Rules in Unconscionability and Related Doctrines*, 60 U. CHI. L. REV. 1 (1993); Richard Craswell, *Remedies When Contracts Lack Consent: Autonomy and Institutional Competence*, 33 OSGOODE HALL L.J. 209 (1996).

48. HILTON HOTELS SITE USAGE AND INFORMATION AGREEMENT, http://www1.hilton.com/en_US/hi/customersupport/site-usage.do (last visited June 13, 2012).

49. A legislature might take the decision out of the courts' hands by validating a class of schemes that seemed open to question. But we might believe that legislation may have been put forward as rent-seeking on the part of some industry; that is, seeking to maximize that industry's return at the expense of social welfare as a whole. At least we might believe that it is very hard to tell when legislation is rent-seeking and when it is not, and thus we may believe that the legislature itself is not the best actor to be trusted with making this pronouncement. In other words, we may never find a way to know when Craswell's argument about institutional incompetence should apply and when it shouldn't.

Chapter Five

1. Karl N. Llewellyn, THE COMMON LAW TRADITION: DECIDING APPEALS 370 (1960).

2. This point of arrival will be discussed below, and in chapter 6.

3. We don't speak of "informed" consent in contract much; rather "informed" consent comes into play when we are considering consent to medical treatment or to sexual activity, etc. Could it be that the notion of being "informed" properly before one's capitulation is considered "consent" is absent from contract law? Although courts are willing to infer (or declare) assent or bindingness if they think there was an opportunity for the recipient to notice the terms—*see,* e.g., *Specht v. Netscape Commc'ns Corp.,* 306 F.3d 17 (2d Cir. 2004)—such reliance on judicially evaluated opportunities is nowhere near what is usually considered necessary for "informed" consent in other realms of law.

4. W. David Slawson, BINDING PROMISES: THE LATE 20TH CENTURY REFORMATION OF CONTRACT LAW 44–45, 64–65 (1996).

5. For interesting comments on the reasonable expectations doctrine in insurance cases, see Ethan J. Leib, *What is the Relational Theory of Consumer Form Contract? in* EMPIRICAL AND LYRICAL: REVISITING THE CONTRACTS SCHOLARSHIP OF STEWART MACAULAY (Bill Whitford et al., eds., forthcoming 2012).

6. Slawson, *supra* note 4, at 49–54. Such a move would have made all adhesion contracts enforceable only to the extent of that which the recipient expected to be there.

7. RESTATEMENT (SECOND) OF CONTRACTS § 211 cmt. f (1981). Section 211 reads: "Where the other party has reason to believe that the party manifesting such assent would not do so if he knew that the writing contained a particular term, the term is not part of the agreement."

8. Randy Barnett, *Consenting to Form Contracts,* 71 FORDHAM L. REV. 627, 637–43 (2002).

9. *See* Omri Ben-Shahar, *The Myth of the 'Opportunity to Read' in Contract Law,* 5 EUR. REV. CONT. L. 1, 9 (2009).

10. *Id.* at 12.

11. I will return to the problems facing courts in adjudicating unconscionability claims in chapters 7 and 8.

12. The reasonable person standard as applied to the victim may be a borrowing from the idea of assumption of risk in tort law. It is perhaps a confusion to apply it to contract law. Assumption of risk as applied in tort law involves a serious investigation and not the offhand assumptions put forward by apologists for contract boilerplate. See chapter 11.

13. It may be necessary to qualify the statement in the text with regard to the relationship of free will and autonomy to the community. It is fair to say that in a Kantian frame of reference, will is interior to a person, or indeed an attribute of personhood. But it should not be assumed that therefore the possibility of appropriate exercise of will or autonomy is entirely subjective in the sense in which a modern speaker might intend the term. In a Kantian frame of reference, the fruition, if not the existence, of autonomy of one person depends upon establishing reciprocal rights and obligations of every other person, in a total moral order.

14. Whether requiring detailed disclosures to patients can really achieve this goal is now seriously disputed. *See* Omri Ben-Shahar and Carl E. Schneider, MORE THAN YOU WANTED TO KNOW: THE FAILURE OF MANDATED DISCLOSURE (forthcoming 2012).

15. These heuristic biases are discussed in chapter 2.

16. Ethan J. Leib, *supra* note 5. Stewart Macaulay, along with Ian MacNeil, developed a theory of relational contract that is intended to replace the classical theory of contract. They wanted contract law and theory to be more cognizant of the fact that parties who enter into contracts may already be in relationships with each other, and, moreover, that entering into a contract (especially a long-term contract requiring cooperation) can create a relationship. *See*, e.g., Ethan J. Leib, *Contracts and Friendships*, 59 EMORY L.J. 649 (2010), excerpted in RANDY BARNETT, PERSPECTIVES ON CONTRACT LAW (4th ed., Aspen 2010). *But see* Melvin A. Eisenberg, *Why There Is No Law of Relational Contracts*, 94 Nw. U. L. REV. 805 (2000).

17. This is the sort of contract that under traditional theory would have been thought to be illusory, or at least too indefinite to be enforceable, because if one party can modify at will, it can modify its way out of the obligations that were supposedly basic to the deal. Today firms declare their boilerplate modifiable at will; see example on page 116. In *AT&T Mobility v. Concepcion*, 131 S. Ct. 1740, 1744 (2011), Justice Scalia mentions the unilateral modifiability of the contract as a fact in the case, with no hint that such modifiability might invalidate a contract.

18. *See* Barbara Herman, *Could It Be Worth Thinking About Kant on Sex and Marriage?* in A MIND OF ONE'S OWN 53 (Louise Antony and Charlotte Witt, eds., 2d ed. 2002). *But see*, Richard H.Thaler and Cass R. Sunstein, NUDGE: IMPROVING DECISIONS ABOUT HEALTH, WEALTH, AND HAPPINESS, 22–37 (2008) (proposing that marriage be withdrawn from state control; i.e. privatized).

19. See discussion of arbitration clauses and exculpatory clauses in chapter 7.

20. The word "constructive" signifies a legal fiction. See infra, note 29. Ben-Shahar takes aim at the opportunity-to-read fiction. He argues, along the lines of Barnett, that recipients who don't read form contracts, but who at least know that they may contain hidden terms or terms to come later that "might not be the nicest" can be covered by blanket assent. *See* Ben-Shahar, *supra* note 9, at 13–20. To my mind, there is a big difference between "not the nicest" and the loss of important legal entitlements, such as the right to sue for a legal remedy guaranteed by the state. See discussion of analytical framework in chapter 9. Moreover, it is extremely difficult for a court to determine whether a recipient "knows" anything. There is a tendency to slide to reasonable expectations, but that too has serious problems, as discussed earlier (pages 84–5).

21. *See*, e.g., *Specht v. Netscape Commc'ns Corp.*, 306 F.3d 17, 28–35 (2d Cir. 2002).

22. A constructive notice approach is adopted by the noted American contract scholar, Robert Hillman, and appears in the *Principles of the Law of Software Contracts*, published by the American Law Institute, for which Hillman is the primary Reporter (Am. Law Inst. 2010). Hillman has been a consistent advocate of the "opportunity to read" approach. *See*, e.g., Hillman, *Rolling Contracts*, 71 FORDHAM L. REV. 743 (2002); Hillman, *Online Boilerplate: Would Mandatory Website Disclosure of E-Standard Terms Backfire?* 104 MICH. L. REV. 837, 846 (2006). For further discussion of this approach, see chapter 8.

23. The basic precepts of the rule of law were summarized in chapter 3. *See*, e.g., Margaret Jane Radin, *Reconsidering the Rule of Law*, 69 B.U. L. REV. 781 (1986); *see also* Lon L. Fuller, THE MORALITY OF LAW (1964).

24. Indeed, as I argued in chapter 3 regarding democratic degradation, if our legal system is in practice deeming millions of transactions that are

not instantiations of freedom of contract to be enforceable divestments of entitlements, the justification of the underlying political state is thereby undermined.

25. In particular, what consent means in the context(s) of the background theories justifying contractual transfer of entitlements, which I have outlined in this and the previous chapter.

26. Brian Bix, *Contracts,* in THE ETHICS OF CONSENT 251 (Franklin G. Miller and Alan Wertheimer, eds., 2010).

27. *Id.* at 251.

28. *Id.*

29. Lawyers are familiar with constructive eviction, constructive trusts, and so forth. These are legal fictions permitting a legal doctrine to be made applicable to a situation in which courts believe it should apply, even though that situation does not fulfill the doctrinal requirements. The word "constructive" signifies a legal fiction. (For example, "constructive eviction" was invented when judges, in certain situations, wanted tenants who had departed from leased premises without actual eviction by the landlord to be treated legally as if the landlord had actually evicted them.)

Chapter Six

1. Arbitration clauses and their effects on remedies are further discussed in chapter 7.

2. *Hill v. Gateway 2000, Inc.,* 105 F.3d 1147, 1150 (7th Cir. 1997).

3. Another economic take on the problem is the literature on "reading costs." *See,* e.g., Alan Schwartz and Louis Wilde, *Imperfect Information in Markets for Contract Terms: The Examples of Warranties and Security Interests,* 69 VA. L. REV. 1387 (1983); Avery Katz, *Your Terms or Mine? The Duty to Read the Fine Print in Contracts,* 21 RAND J. ECON. 518 (1990); Yeon-Koo Che and Albert H. Choi, *Shrink-Wraps: Who Should Bear the Cost of Communicating Mass-Market Contract Terms?* (VA. LAW & ECON. RESEARCH PAPER No. 2009–15), *available at* http://ssrn.com/abstract=1384682. This literature takes account of the costs for recipients, or some subset of them, of reading and understanding the contract. (If those costs are too high, that is the economist's way of saying recipients will not read and understand the terms.) A recent entry

into this field by Abraham Wickelgren assumes that an efficient result—in terms of what recipients would demand if they read and understood the terms—can be achieved even if no one does actually read the terms, under circumstances where a subset *could* have read the terms, and where the terms that firms may offer are strictly limited to specific standardized sets. *See* Abraham L. Wickelgren, *Standardization as a Solution to the Reading Costs of Form Contracts*, 167 J. INSTITUTIONAL & THEORETICAL ECON. 30 (2011).

4. Douglas G. Baird, *The Boilerplate Puzzle*, 104 MICH. L. REV. 933 (2006), as reprinted in BOILERPLATE: THE FOUNDATION OF MARKET CONTRACT 131 (Omri Ben-Shahar, ed., 2007).

5. *Id.* at 933, 939.

6. Arthur Allen Leff, *Contract as Thing*, 19 AM. U. L. REV. 131 (1970).

7. Lewis A. Kornhauser, *Unconscionability in Standard Forms*, 64 CAL. L. REV. 1151 (1976).

8. Baird, *supra* note 4, at 934.

9. *Id.* at 933.

10. *Id.* at 949.

11. *See* Sunstein and Thaler's explanation of the distinction between "Humans" and "Econs." Richard H. Thaler and Cass R. Sunstein, NUDGE: IMPROVING DECISIONS ABOUT HEALTH, WEALTH, AND HAPPINESS, 6–8 (2008). Econs are "economically rational"; Humans are not. The contract-as-product theorists are not entitled to assume that Humans are Econs. The false assumption of economic rationality is also an important element of the economic theorists' purported justification for turning recipients' property rules into liability rules (that is, the idea that consumers, if economically rational, would choose compensation by the firm in the form of lower prices over retention of their right to sue).

12. *See*, e.g., Baird, *supra* note 4, at 936.

13. For a judge it cannot be a matter of a bright-line rule (which is how Judge Easterbrook and those who adopt his reasoning apparently wish to treat "legal-ware" bundled with software), but rather poses empirical questions of great difficulty, questions that courts cannot easily handle.

14. One prevalent economic theory of monopoly holds that a rational monopolist will take out all of its monopoly power in the price of the

product, and none of it in the quality of the product. *See*, e.g., A. Michael Spence, *Monopoly, Quality, and Regulation*, 6 BELL J. ECON. 417, 417 (1975). No doubt terms that are part of the product would be considered product quality issues rather than pricing issues. Thus, according to this theory, in cases of monopolization or collusion, we should see high-priced products with good terms. But when we add information impactedness to the mix, it is likely that we will see high-priced products with bad terms.

15. Abraham Wickelgren suggests, contrary to the prevailing contract-as-product view, that industry-wide standardization in a competitive market, if firms are free to set their own contract terms, will actually result in firms offering their worst contract, thus arriving at a "lemons equilibrium" result. Wickelgren, *supra* note 3. Wickelgren also suggests that industry-wide standardization can result in contracts containing good terms that consumers would choose, but only if the firms are restricted to certain particular sets of terms; and he suggests that this regime of standardization might have to be imposed by the government. *Id.* Thus he is suggesting a regulatory solution. See chapter 12.

16. Recall the PC Pitstop offer of $1000 to anyone who read far enough in the boilerplate (*supra* chapter 1, page 10, note *).

17. See sources cited in chapter 2 on heuristic bias. *See also* Yannis Bakos, Florencia Marotta-Wurgler, and David R. Trossen, *Does Anyone Read the Fine Print? Testing a Law and Economics Approach to Standard Form Contracts*, CELS 2009 4th Annual Conference on Empirical Legal Studies Paper (October 6, 2009); NYU Law and Economics Research Paper No. 09–40. Available at SSRN: http://ssrn.com/abstract=1443256.

Chapter Seven

1. *Williams v. Walker-Thomas Furniture Co.*, 350 F.2d 445, 449 (D.C. Cir. 1965).

2. Recipients could theoretically also invoke some species of duress (when presented with take-it-or-leave-it boilerplate in acquiring a necessity of life), or a version of failure to disclose (ignorance of the content of the boilerplate), or a version of no meeting of the minds (no intent to agree to what actually was in the boilerplate), or a version of misrepresentation. These traditional doctrines were in the past interpreted quite narrowly by the courts. The doctrine of unconscionability, of more recent

vintage, may have been intended to broaden consideration of these very concerns. *See*, e.g., UCC § 2-302, cmt. 1 ("mak[ing] it possible for a court to police explicitly against the contracts or terms which the court finds to be unconscionable instead of attempting to achieve the result by an adverse construction of language, by manipulation of the rules of offer and acceptance, or by a determination that the term is contrary either to public policy or to the dominant purpose of the contract").

3. Some writers who want to cut back on the scope of the unconscionability doctrine interpret it as functioning solely to police for duress or fraud in cases where those issues might be difficult to prove. *See*, e.g., Richard A. Epstein, *Unconscionability: A Critical Reappraisal*, 18 J.L. & ECON. 293, 302, 315 (1975).

4. *See*, e.g., *Wis. Auto Title Loans, Inc. v. Jones*, 714 N.W.2d 155, 165 (Wis. 2006) ("A determination of unconscionability requires a mixture of both procedural and substantive unconscionability that is analyzed on a case-by-case basis. The more substantive unconscionability present, the less procedural unconscionability is required, and vice versa").

5. *Williams v. Walker-Thomas Furniture Co.*, 350 F.2d 445, 450 (D.C. Cir. 1965) (quoting 1 ARTHUR L. CORBIN, CONTRACTS § 128 (1963)).

6. See discussion of this argument in chapters 2, 4, 7, and 9.

7. Epstein argues that what we see as oppressive contract terms actually operate to allow poor people to enter into contracts for items that would otherwise be priced too high for them. Epstein, *supra* note 3, at 305. How does he know this?

8. In order to reach consensus on its unconscionability provision, the UCC drafters arrived at positions within the same statute and accompanying official comments that are at odds with one another (one gets the impression of something for each side). For example, Comment 1 to this section says that "the principle is one of prevention of oppression and unfair surprise," but it goes on to say that the purpose is "not of disturbance of allocation of risks because of superior bargaining power." UCC § 2-302, cmt. 1 *See* Arthur Leff, *Unconscionability and the Code—The Emperor's New Clause*, 115 U. PA. L. REV. 485 (1967).

9. *See Cooper v. MRM Inv. Co.*, 367 F.3d 493, 503 (6th Cir. 2004), discussed in the prologue (*supra* prologue note 2 and accompanying text).

10. This has been California's position. *See*, e.g., *Discover Bank v. Super. Ct.*, 113 P.3d 1100, 1108 (Cal. 2005) (quoting *Little v. Auto Stiegler, Inc.*, 29 Cal. 4th 1064, 1071 (Cal. 2003)) (a contract of adhesion is one "which, imposed and drafted by the party of superior bargaining strength, relegates to the subscribing party only the opportunity to adhere to the contract or reject it.").

California did not adopt section 2-302 of the UCC but preferred to stand on its own doctrine of unconscionability, presumably because it was thought to be more helpful for recipients of form contracts and/or easier to apply. Harry G. Prince, *Unconscionability in California: A Need for Restraint and Consistency*, 46 HASTINGS L.J. 459, 495 (1999) ("[T]he common law in California was already well-developed enough to guard against unfair contracts.")

11. *See*, e.g., *A.Z. v. B.Z.*, 725 N.E.2d 1051 (Mass. 2000).

12. *See* David Adam Friedman, *Bringing Order to Contracts Against Public Policy*, 38 FLA ST. L. REV. (forthcoming) available at http://ssrn.com/abstract=1908026 (examining a sample of cases from 2009 and finding a roughly 2–1 success ratio of the "against public policy" defense to contract enforcement, if there was a legal rule or statute to rely on).

13. *See generally* Duncan Kennedy, *Form and Substance in Private Law Adjudication,* 89 HARV. L. REV. 1685 (1976); Louis Kaplow, *Rules Versus Standards: An Economic Analysis*, 42 DUKE L.J. 557 (1992). For a critique of this distinction, see Margaret Jane Radin, *Reconsidering the Rule of Law*, 69 B.U. L. REV. 781 (1989).

14. See examination of "reasonable expectations" in chapters 2 and 5.

15. As discussed below, the extremely proarbitration position of the US Supreme Court has made it more and more difficult to challenge arbitration clauses, because preemption by federal law under the Federal Arbitration Act, as that act is currently interpreted by the Court, means that states may not single out arbitration clauses for more stringent treatment than other contract terms. In light of the US Supreme Court's recent holdings, state legislatures' decisions to institute aggregative remedies for situations where otherwise no relief would be possible for injured parties are erased by boilerplate arbitration clauses, and state courts are prohibited from singling out such arbitration clauses in an attempt to remedy the situation. Prior state court decisions invalidating arbitration clauses probably are no longer precedential.

16. In fact, well into the nineteenth century the common-law courts of England invoked the doctrine of "ouster" to void arbitration clauses as unlawful circumventions of judicial jurisdiction and as denials of judicial justice. Philip J. McConnaughay, *The Risks and Virtues of Lawlessness: A "Second Look" at International Commercial Arbitration*, 93 Nw. U. L. REV. 453, 462 (1999).

17. Federal Arbitration Act, 9 U.S.C. § 2 (2006). Grounds for revocation of any contract would be, for example, coercion or fraud.

18. Paul D. Carrington and Paul Y. Castle, *The Revocability of Contract Provisions Controlling Resolution of Future Disputes Between the Parties*, 67 LAW & CONTEMP. PROBS. 207, 217 (2004).

19. *AT&T Mobility LLC v. Concepcion*, 131 S. Ct. 1740 (2011) (discussed later in this chapter). A different situation prevails in Canada, because Canada does not have a federal law analogous to the FAA. Individual provinces can govern the use of arbitration clauses. Ontario and Quebec have prohibited their use against consumers. S. O. 2002, ch. 30, Schedule A (Ont.); Consumer Protection Act, R.S.Q., ch. p-40.1, § 11.1 (Que.). British Columbia has adopted the position (as interpreted by the Canadian Supreme Court) that certain actions involving breach of consumer protection statutes (whose remedies include injunction against offending firms and public dissemination of adverse information about firms using bad practices) must be brought to court, but arbitration clauses will be valid otherwise. *Seidel v. TELUS Commc'ns Inc.* [2011], 1 S.C.R. 531 (Can.). *See also* Alberta's Fair Trading Act, R.S.A. 2000, ch. F-2, § 16 (Alta.).

20. Preemption stems from the US Constitution, U.S. CONST. art. VI, cl. 2 ("the Supremacy Clause"), stating that federal law is the supreme law of the land. Except in cases of direct conflict (if, for example, California were to try to enact its own patent law to replace the federal Patent Act), preemption is a difficult doctrine to apply. It is usually said that state law is preempted where Congress meant to occupy the field ("field preemption"), where Congress expressly states in the text of a statute its intention to displace state authority in the area ("express preemption") and where there is an actual conflict between state and federal law. *See*, e.g., Stephen A. Gardbaum, *The Nature of Preemption*, 79 CORNELL L. REV. 767 (1994).

21. *See Armendariz v. Foundation Health Psychcare Servs., Inc.*, 6 P.3d 669, 679 (Cal. 2000) ("[A]n arbitration agreement may only be invalidated for the same reasons as other contracts."). *See also* Susan Randall,

Judicial Attitudes Toward Arbitration and the Resurgence of Unconscionability, 52 BUFF. L. REV. 185 (2004). In the past, state courts have found arbitration clauses entirely or partly unconscionable because they unduly restrict the statute of limitations, provide inadequate opportunities for discovery, select inconvenient forums for arbitration, impose excessive confidentiality, and (most controversially) forbid class-wide arbitration. In *AT&T Mobility v. Concepcion*, the US Supreme Court ruled that California could not hold a clause forbidding class-wide arbitration to be unconscionable. *AT&T Mobility v. Concepcion,* 131 S. Ct. 1740 (2011). The various state court decisions that have in the past (sometimes) disallowed arbitration clauses should not be considered good precedent in view of the Supreme Court's ever-widening effort to preclude state remedies. *See e.g., Kilgore v. Key Bank, N.A.,* 673 F.3d 947 (9th Cir. 2012) (California consumer protection law prohibiting use of arbitration of "claims for broad, public injunctive relief" does not survive *Concepcion*).

Some state courts may try to find a way around *Concepcion*. One avenue is to limit *Concepcion* to its facts; *see Brewer v. Missouri Title Loans,* 364 S.W.3d 486 (Mo. 2012) (en banc); another avenue is to find another federal statute, such as the National Labor Relations Act, that would disallow requiring arbitration by employees; *see Herrington v. Waterstone Mortgage Corp.,* __ F.3d __ (Dist. Ct., W.D. WI, opinion issued March 16, 2012) (ban on collective action and concerted activity violates NLRA). As this book goes to press, the responses of state courts to *Concepcion* are rapidly unfolding; it remains to be seen whether or how the Supreme Court will revisit the issue.

22. *See, e.g., Hill v. Gateway 2000, Inc.,* 105 F.3d 1147, 1151 (7th Cir. 1997).

23. *Cooper v. MRM Inv. Co.,* 367 F.3d 493, 506 (6th Cir. 2004) (quoting *Bank One, N.A. v. Coates,* 125 F. Supp. 2d 819, 834 (S.D. Miss. 2001).

24. *Cir. City Stores, Inc. v. Adams,* 532 U.S. 105 (2001).

25. *See, e.g., Cooper v. MRM Inv. Co.,* 367 F.3d 493 (6th Cir. 2004), in which the appellate court held that in order to prove that an arbitration clause that a manager at a fast-food outlet (earning about $7,000 per year), had to sign in order to be employed was in a contract of adhesion, the worker would have had to prove that she did not have other employment opportunities where she could have been employed without having to sign the form containing the clause. Without this proof, it would not

be possible to argue that the clause was unconscionable under state law. Moreover, she would have to present evidence on "factors bearing on the relative bargaining position of the contracting parties, including their age, education, intelligence, business acumen and experience. . . ." *Id.* at 504. (The story of the plaintiff in this case was presented in the prologue.) In other words, the burden is on a civil rights plaintiff to prove that she is not very intelligent, not well educated, and not employable in some other job before she can escape a mandatory arbitration clause presented in a form contract and get her case before a jury of her peers. (We should note, once more however, that the court did allow the arbitration clause to be invalidated because the firm using the arbitration clause allowed the expenses to the plaintiff to appear too onerous. *Id.* at 509–13).

A number of bills have been introduced in Congress to reverse the use of mandatory arbitration, especially in civil rights cases and employment contracts, but so far none of them has made progress toward enactment. *See,* e.g., Arbitration Fairness Act of 2011, S. 987, 112th Cong. (2011); Arbitration Fairness Act of 2011, H.R. 1873, 112th Cong. (2011). An amendment inserted into the FY 2010 Defense Appropriations Bill denies defense contractors federal funding if they deploy mandatory arbitration clauses foreclosing suits by victims of sexual assault. *See* Sam Stein, *Franken Gets His First Amendment Passed By Roll Call Vote,* THE HUFFINGTON POST (Oct. 7, 2009, 10:47 AM, http://www.huffingtonpost.com/2009/10/07/franken-gets-first-amendm_n_312399.html).

26. *See* Theodore Eisenberg, Geoffrey P. Miller, and Emily Sherwin, *Arbitration's Summer Soldiers: An Empirical Study of Arbitration Clauses in Consumer and Nonconsumer Contracts,* 41 U. MICH. J.L. REFORM 871 (2008). The authors' survey of contracts drafted by large telecom, consumer credit, and financial corporations, provides evidence that avoiding class actions is the principal purpose of many arbitration clauses. Over 75 percent of the consumer contracts in these sectors contained arbitration clauses, whereas only 6 percent of the companies' substantial contracts with other businesses did.

27. *See,* e.g., *Am. Online, Inc. v. Super. Ct.,* 108 Cal. Rptr. 2d 699 (Ct. App. 2001).

28. Despite the additional burdens imposed on the judicial system as a result of the class action lawsuit, "the procedure may represent the only viable method for people with small claims to vindicate their rights or for

important social issues to be litigated." Jack H. Friedenthal et al., CIVIL PROCEDURE 758 (4th ed. 2005). As European markets become more deregulated and liberalized, proposals to introduce class-action-style lawsuits have become a subject of controversy. *See,* e.g., Samuel Issacharoff and Geoffrey P. Miller, *Will Aggregate Litigation Come to Europe?* NYU Law and Economics Research Paper No. 08-46 (2008), *available at* http://ssrn.com/abstract=1296843.

29. *AT&T Mobility LLC v. Concepcion*, 131 S. Ct. 1740 (2011).

30. *Id.* at 1748.

31. *Id.* at 1751.

32. *Id.* at 1752.

33. *Id.* at 1760–61 (Breyer, J. dissenting).

34. See chapter 9, note 19.

35. For a summary of rule of law precepts, see chapter 3.

36. *Carnival Cruise Lines, Inc. v. Shute*, 499 U.S. 585 (1991).

37. *See,* e.g., *Goodyear Dunlop Tires Operations, S.A. v. Brown*, 131 S. Ct. 2846, 2850-51 (2011). For extended commentary on due process and open courts in light of recent Supreme Court cases, *see* Judith Resnik, *Comment: Fairness in Numbers: A Comment on AT&T v. Concepcion, Wal-Mart v. Dukes, and Turner v. Rogers*, 125 HAR. L. REV. 78 (2011).

38. For a critique of this rationale, see chapter 4.

39. *See,* e.g., *Hill v. Gateway*, 105 F.3d 1147, 1148-49 (7th Cir. 1997) (invoking *Carnival Cruise* against purchasers who entered into a contract via a boxtop license). Note that a true economic analysis of this situation would have to consider not only the money saved by the firm but the extra costs incurred by consumers.

40. *See,* e.g., Edward A. Purcell, Jr., *Geography as a Litigation Weapon: Consumers, Forum-Selection Clauses, and the Rehnquist Court*, 40 UCLA L. REV. 423 (1992). *See also* Stephen J. Ware, *Arbitration Clauses, Jury-Waiver Clauses, and Other Contractual Waivers of Constitutional Rights*, 67 LAW & CONTEMP. PROBS. 167, 188–97 (2004).

41. *See generally* Martin H. Redish and William J. Katt, *Taylor v. Sturgell, Procedural Due Process, and the Day-in-Court Ideal: Resolving the*

Virtual Representation Dilemma, 84 NOTRE DAME L. REV. 1877 (2009) (discussing the history of due process rights to one's day in court).

42. While forum selection clauses generally are presumed *prima facie* valid, a forum selection clause may be unconscionable if the "place or manner" in which litigation is to occur is unreasonable taking into account "the respective circumstances of the parties." *Comb v. PayPal, Inc.*, 218 F. Supp. 2d 1165, 1177 (N.D. Cal. 2002) (citing *Bolter v. Super. Ct.*, 104 Cal. Rptr. 2d 888, 894 (Ct. App. 2001)). In *Bolter*, the court found that enforcement of a Utah forum selection clause along with a choice of law clause would be cost prohibitive in light of the fact that the potential claimants located around the country would be required to retain counsel familiar with Utah law. *Bolter*, 104 Cal. Rptr. 2d at 895. *See also Kawasaki Kisen Kaisha Ltd. v. Reqal-Beloit Corp.*, 130 S. Ct. 2433, 2448 (2010) (acknowledging that a forum selection clause which denies a party its day in court would be invalid).

43. *See*, e.g., David Adam Friedman, *Bringing Order to Contracts Against Public Policy*, 38 FLA ST. L. REV. (forthcoming) available at http://ssrn.com/abstract=1908026.

44. *See*, e.g., *Newton's Crest Homeowners' Ass'n v. Camp*, 702 S.E. 2d 41, 47 (Ga. Ct. App. 2010) ("As a general rule, a party may contract away liability to the other party for the consequences of his own negligence without contravening public policy, except when such an agreement is prohibited by statute.") (citations omitted).

45. *See*, e.g., *N. Sunrooms & Additions, LLC v. Dorstad*, No. A10-1217, 2011 WL 292160, at *2 (Minn. Ct. App. Feb. 1, 2011) ("Whether it contravenes public policy is determined by asking if there was a disparity in the parties' bargaining power and if the services being provided were essential services.").

46. *See Tunkl v. Regents of the Univ. of Cal.*, 383 P.2d 441, 445-46 (Cal. 1963) (finding the following factors relevant: (1) whether the type of business is one generally thought suitable for public regulation; (2) whether the party seeking exculpation is performing a service of great importance to the public; (3) whether the party holds himself out as willing to perform this service for any member of the public seeking it; (4) whether, as a result of factors 1–3, the party invoking exculpation has a decisive advantage of bargaining power; (5) whether the exculpation is in a standard adhesion contract with no provision for paying additional fees to obtain protection from negligence; and (6) whether, as a result of the

transaction, the purchaser, or his property, is under the control of the seller and subject to the risk of carelessness).

47. As I will discuss in chapter 11, the compromise is a mixture of contract and tort concepts.

48. But note that in the perhaps rare event that a firm does not reduce damages to the bare minimum allowable, section 2-715(2) adopts the tort concept of proximate cause to govern the extent of damages allowable. In chapter 11, I will take up the overlapping conceptions of contract and tort law.

49. *Prima facie* means "on its face." In this context it means that the attempt to limit consequential damages will be presumed unconscionable, but the firm deploying the term can try to prove otherwise.

Chapter Eight

1. H. W. Fowler, A DICTIONARY OF MODERN ENGLISH USAGE 573–74 (David Crystal ed., 2009); William Strunk, Jr. and E. B. White, THE ELEMENTS OF STYLE 39–65 (4th ed. 1999).

2. Irma S. Rombauer and Marion Rombauer Becker, JOY OF COOKING Vol. 2: APPETIZERS, DESSERTS & BAKED GOODS (1998 edition, at 475); first published, privately, in 1931, and continuously in print since 1936).

3. Because of preemption of state law by federal law in the field of arbitration (i.e., the US Supreme Court's interpretation of the Federal Arbitration Act, 9 U.S.C. §§ 1-16 (2006)), only federal law could accomplish this result. See discussion in chapter 7.

4. UCC § 2-719(2) (1977).

5. *Id.* § 1-103(b) (1977) ("Unless displaced by the particular provisions of [this Act], the principles of law and equity, including the law merchant and the law relative to capacity to contract, principal and agent, estoppel, fraud, misrepresentation, duress, coercion, mistake, bankruptcy, and other validating and invalidating cause supplement its provisions.").

6. *Carnival Cruise Lines, Inc. v. Shute*, 499 U.S. 585 (1991). As I recounted in chapter 7, the majority opinion by Justice Blackmun assumed that the plaintiffs had notice of the choice of forum clause, ostensibly on the ground that the plaintiffs had conceded the point during the litigation.

As the dissent by Justice Stevens makes clear, that plaintiffs had notice before purchase was very unlikely: the plaintiffs bought a cruise ticket which was nonrefundable, and only when they received the ticket could they possibly have seen the fine print on the face of the ticket which (had they read it) would have told them that there were legal terms on another page that they might have seen had they looked for them. *Id.* at 597–98 (Stevens, J., dissenting). Justice Blackmun's opinion reasoned that, given that the recipients had notice, the contract did not arise to a constitutional level of unfairness, because (Justice Blackmun assumed, without evidence) that the clause saved money for the firm and those savings would be passed on to consumers, thereby compensating them for the loss of their opportunity to sue in a forum convenient for them. Courts routinely cite this case without taking any notice of its limitation to a situation where the recipient had notice of the choice of forum clause before entering into the contract containing it. *See*, e.g., *ProCD, Inc. v. Zeidenberg*, 86 F.3d 1447, 1451 (7th Cir. 1996) (citing to *Carnival Cruise* as support for the Court's unqualified holding that "[t]o use the ticket is to accept the terms, even terms that in retrospect are disadvantageous.").

7. *Doe 1 v. AOL LLC*, 552 F.3d 1077, 1083–84 (9th Cir. 2009).

8. California developed a class-wide arbitration procedure to be used by recipients subject to arbitration clauses and therefore precluded from class actions. *See Ingle v. Cir. City Stores, Inc.*, 328 F.3d 1165, 1175 (9th Cir. 2003) (holding that under California law at the time, a provision in an arbitration agreement that prohibited class-action arbitrations was substantively unconscionable). In mid-2011, however, the Supreme Court struck down this aspect of California state contract law, when it held, in *AT&T Mobility LLC v. Concepcion*, 131 S. Ct. 1740 (2011), that the Federal Arbitration Act compels California courts to enforce arbitration agreements even if the agreement requires that consumer complaints be arbitrated individually. (See discussion of this case in chapter 7.)

9. *Compare Ferguson v. Countrywide Credit Indus., Inc.*, 298 F.3d 778, 782–87 (9th Cir. 2002) (holding an arbitration agreement in an adhesion contract unconscionable under California state law), *with Carter v. Countrywide Credit Indus., Inc.* 362 F.3d 294, 301 (5th Cir. 2004) (holding the identical arbitration clause valid under Texas state law).

10. *See*, e.g., Robert A. Hillman, *Online Boilerplate: Would Mandatory Website Disclosure of E-Standard Terms Backfire?* 104 Mich.L. Rev. 837 (2006).

11. Am. Law Inst., PRINCIPLES OF THE LAW OF SOFTWARE CONTRACTS (2010) ("ALI Principles").

12. *Id.* § 2.02(c)(1).

13. *Id* § 2.02, Summary Overview.

14. *Id.*

15. Hillman, *supra* note 10, at 845–56.

16. Omri Ben-Shahar, *The Myth of the 'Opportunity to Read' in Contract Law*, 5 EUR. REV. OF CONT. L. 1, 15 (2009).

17. *See,* e.g., Michael Trebilcock, THE LIMITS OF FREEDOM OF CONTRACT 78–101 (1993), which provides an astute survey of the ways the problem of coercion is approached by various theorists. *See also* Alan Wertheimer, COERCION (1987).

18. Richard Craswell, *Remedies When Contracts Lack Consent: Autonomy and Institutional Competence*, 33 OSGOODE HALL L.J. 209, 221–29 (1995).

19. On mass torts, *see* Am. Law. Inst., PRINCIPLES OF THE LAW OF AGGREGATE LITIGATION (2010); see discussion in chapter 11.

Chapter Nine

1. In my discussion of which rights may be waived, and how, I will be talking primarily about the rights of individuals, because the recipients of boilerplate are most often individuals. I will therefore leave for others the attempt to theorize which basic rights of our system also accrue to firms, and to what extent. It has been argued that freedom of contract does not apply to organizations in the same way it does to individuals. Todd D. Rakoff, *Contracts of Adhesion: An Essay in Reconstruction*, 96 HARV. L. REV. 1174, 1235–37 (1983). Firms and individuals both are entitled to redress of grievances. It was previously thought that freedom of speech is a right of human persons, but the US Supreme Court held, very controversially, that it is also a right of corporate "persons." *Citizens United v. Fed. Election Comm'n*, 130 S. Ct. 876 (2010). Firms have user rights under intellectual property regimes, probably the same as those of individuals. Whether or not firms have privacy rights in the same sense as individuals seems to me doubtful.

2. "Alienability" often involves the transfer of rights to someone else, rather than just deleting them, but in my view it describes either process. *See*, e.g., Margaret Jane Radin, CONTESTED COMMODITIES 16–29 (1996).

3. *Id.*

4. Nozick does say "yes" to selling oneself into slavery. Robert Nozick, ANARCHY, STATE AND UTOPIA 331 (1974) ("The comparable question about an individual is whether a free system will allow him to sell himself into slavery. I believe that it would."). *But see* John Stuart Mill, ON LIBERTY, THREE ESSAYS 126 (1975) ("The principle of freedom cannot require that [one] should be free not to be free. It is not freedom, to be allowed to alienate [one's] freedom.").

5. "Market-inalienability" is the term I coined for a situation in which a right is not waivable or transferable by contract, but could be transferred by a nonmarket transaction, such as a gift. Relinquishment of parental rights by a birth mother to adoptive parents is an example. Margaret Jane Radin, *supra*, note 2, at 18.

6. Much-debated cases of market-inalienability involve the sales of children, organs, and sexual services. *See id.*, chapters 6 and 10. These are the cases in which sale is disallowed, but nonsale divestments of rights are approved (such as relinquishing parental rights in an adoption proceeding). In cases of market-inalienability the universe of default rules is limited by concerns about commodification (market trading in objects that society considers off limits to commercial exchange or indeed not cognizable as entitlements separate from the person).

7. See chapters 2 and 4 (turning property rules into liability rules), and chapter 6 (assumptions of market information and passing-on not likely to be empirically true).

8. In our legal system, the right to jury trial would not be held inalienable if payment were not exchanged for the waiver, because litigants are permitted voluntarily to waive jury trial under appropriate legal safeguards and to have their case tried by a judge instead, as are accused persons, FED. R. CRIM. P. 23(a). Criminal defendants cannot waive jury trial in favor of binding arbitration. *Id.* 23(c) ("In a case tried without a jury, *the court* must find the defendant guilty or not guilty.") (*emphasis added*). It is unclear why American courts have seen fit to allow jury trial to be waived tacitly by boilerplate arbitration clauses, especially in light of the fact that the US Constitution's Seventh Amendment guarantees the right

to jury trial. Cases lack argument to explain why contract, and a fortiori boilerplate, can so readily trump the Constitution.

9. UCC § 2-719(3) (1977) ("Limitation of consequential damages for injury to the person in the case of consumer goods is prima facie unconscionable . . . ."). See discussion in chapter 7.

10. Some courts have been willing to validate browsewrap if they think the online user had the opportunity to find out the terms, even if the user did not in fact know about them. *See*, e.g., *Cairo, Inc. v. Crossmedia Servs., Inc.*, No. C 04-04825 JW, 2005 WL 756610, at *5 (N.D. Cal. Apr. 1, 2005), (finding a forum selection clause not unconscionable because, even if "Cairo's allegation that it did not explicitly agree to CMS's Terms of Use [is assumed to be true,] Cairo's use of CMS's website under circumstances in which Cairo had actual or imputed knowledge of CMS's terms effectively binds Cairo to CMS's Terms of Use and the forum selection clause therein."). *See* also *Specht v. Netscape Commc'n Corp.*, 306 F.3d 17 (2d Cir. 2002), where the court took pains to investigate how many clicks would have been required for the user to see the terms (and decided it was too many).

11. See chapter 5.

12. Randy E. Barnett, *Consenting to Form Contracts*, 71 FORDHAM L. REV. 627 (2002) (arguing that when consumers click "I agree," they agree to be legally bound to unread terms that are not "radically unexpected"). For a discussion and critique of this position, see chapter 5.

13. *See*, e.g., *Feldman v. Google, Inc.*, 513 F. Supp. 2d 229, 235-43 (E.D. Pa. 2007) (citing numerous cases where clickwrap contracts are enforced as long as their terms are not so unexpected as to be unconscionable).

14. Inquiry into the nature of the right could lead a legislature or court to make a decision that the right should be market-inalienable or partially market-inalienable. Recall that, as I argued in chapter 5, expectation can be normative, referring to the rights we have a right to expect in a just system, even if the current system is unjust. The ambiguity between positive and normative expectation is a great cause of confusion for the courts, confusion that could be ameliorated by replacing the expectation inquiry with inquiries into the nature of the right and the quality of consent.

15. In the memorable terminology of Richard Thaler, we must recognize that humans are Humans, and we are not entitled to assume that

they are "Econs" and treat them as if they were "Econs." *See* e.g., Richard H. Thaler and Cass R. Sunstein, NUDGE: IMPROVING DECISIONS ABOUT HEALTH, WEALTH, AND HAPPINESS 15–103 (2008). "Econs" are imaginary beings that make decisions like the economically "rational" individuals who inhabit economics textbooks. "Humans" are human individuals, who live in the real world and are subject to the pervasive heuristic biases that render economic "rationality" largely irrelevant.

16. These categories are somewhat arbitrary, but I hope they provide a useful heuristic. Freedom of speech is a legal right in the US because of its inclusion in the Constitution, and privacy is a legal right in some jurisdictions because of its enactment or inclusion in structural documents. I make the somewhat arbitrary distinction because (with the possible exception of freedom of speech under one interpretation of its source) the rights I am calling political rights are related more directly to the rule of law than the rights I am calling human rights. Also, the rights I am calling human rights are basic background rights whether or not enacted, and they may have force that exceeds the delineations of what is actually enacted (in other words, they are not exhausted by positive law).

17. Owing to the US Supreme Court's expansive interpretation of the preemptive effect of the Federal Arbitration Act, 9 U.S.C. §§ 1–16 (2006), it seems as though the practical effect of widespread use of arbitration clauses will be the loss of all remedy for large swaths of the public. Remedies available for small losses imposed on a large number of consumers are now arguably illusory. *See AT&T Mobility LLC v. Concepcion*, 131 S. Ct. 1740 (2011), 1760–61 (Breyer, J., dissenting).

18. *Discover Bank v. Super. Ct.*, 113 P.3d 1100 (Cal. 2005).

19. Some arbitration providers are for-profit entities that advertise themselves to firms, touting their ability to save firms money by their victories over consumers in arbitration. A particular example that hit the news a few years ago involved an entity called the National Arbitration Forum (NAF) that was employed by many banks and financial firms. The firm's own statistics showed that in the period from 2003 through March 21, 2007, it handled 18,075 arbitrations in California, only 30 of which were won by the consumer. This firm was the subject of testimony before the Senate Judiciary Committee by Harvard law professor Elizabeth Bartholet on July 23, 2008. Bartholet stated that she had been an arbitrator for this firm, but was essentially dismissed after ruling in favor of a consumer in one case. *See* Testimony of Elizabeth Bartholet, July 23, 2008, available

at http://www.judiciary.senate.gov/hearings/testimony.cfm?id=e655f9e28 09e5476862f735da13e81c7&wit_id=e655f9e2809e5476862f735da13e 81c7-1-2. NAF was also sued by the state attorney general in Minnesota, and by the City of San Francisco. See Nathan Koppel, *San Francisco Sues Provider of Arbitrators*, WALL ST. J., Apr. 7, 2008, at A3. Various banks decided to stop employing the firm after this bad publicity; and as this book goes to press, the new Consumer Protection Bureau is studying arbitration clauses in consumer boilerplate (under legislative mandate of the Dodd-Frank Wall Street Reform and Consumer Protection Act of 2010), Pub. L. 111-203, 124 Stat. 1376 (2010), and may issue regulations banning mandatory arbitration clauses in consumer financial contracts.

It is not clear that many arbitration providers are essentially in the business of debt collection, as NAF seems to have been, and it may be that those that do not serve primarily the financial industry are more even-handed. Cell phone arbitration clauses, and the arbitration firms that are hired by the cell phone companies, have also come in for criticism for systemic bias, and two senators introduced a bill in October of 2011, the Consumer Mobile Fairness Act, S. 1652, 112th Cong. (2011), that would ban imposing mandatory arbitration clauses in boilerplate accompanying cell phone service.

Certainly scholars have risen to the defense of arbitration, when properly neutral and duly respecting legal rights. *See*, e.g., Letter to the Editor by Michigan law professor Theodore J. St. Antoine, *Resolving Disputes Through Arbitration*, NEW YORK TIMES, March 7, 2012, available at http://www.nytimes.com/2012/03/19/opinion/resolving-disputes-through-arbitration.html?_r=1, who argues against banning arbitration clauses and instead for "legislation that would guarantee due process in arbitration, including neutral arbitrators, and ensure that grievants have a voice in their selection and all the remedies that could have been obtained in court." Some studies have found that imposing arbitration on employees results in a better recovery rate for employees, but those results are subject to some significant caveats, including the nature of the data sets used; see, *e.g.*, Alexander J.S. Colvin, *Empirical Research on Employment Arbitration: Clarity Amidst the Sound and Fury?* 11 EMP. RTS AND EMP. POL'Y J. 405 (2007). Before concluding that employees forced out of court are better off, we should also consider what rights they are trying to vindicate, and whether those rights (such as antidiscrimination rights, or the rights to organize and engage in collective action) cannot be vindicated by the occasional individual arbitration.

In spite of the defenses of arbitration in some industries, it is suspected by consumer advocates that firms have great advantages over consumers in arbitration: because firms are repeat players in arbitration and consumers are not, and because firms choose the arbitration entity they prefer (*see*, e.g., the example on page 111), and because arbitrators are not drawn from the ranks of consumers or consumer-protection advocates.

It is also widely suspected that many consumers are deterred from entering into arbitration because of the odds against winning, the hassle it would entail, and the small amount at stake. (I can report that as someone interested in these matters I thought about taking my cell-phone provider to arbitration when it blithely imposed an extra fee that I didn't learn about until it showed up on a whopping bill, which its representative assured me was valid because of its right to modify its contract unilaterally at any time. Yet I didn't do it: too much hassle, not worth it.) Occasionally a judge shares this suspicion. See Griffin v. Dell Canada, Inc., 2010 ONCA 29, 98 O.R. (3d) 481 (Court of Appeal for Ontario). In that case the lower court had ruled in favor of a class action that Dell's arbitration clause would have prohibited, stating that it was "fanciful to think that any claimant could pursue an individual claim in a complex products liability case" and that enforcing Dell's arbitration clause would have the effect of immunizing Dell "from accounting to class members for any wrong it may have caused." The appeals court agreed: "[T]here is a lack of reality to Dell's argument that the claim should proceed by way of arbitration. There will be no arbitration." The real choice, the court said, is "not between arbitration and class proceeding, but rather between "clothing Dell with immunity for liability for defective goods" and giving purchasers of its allegedly defective computers their day in court.

20. The current situation may be different from the historical situation in which the copyright industries, opposed only by libraries and perhaps universities, controlled the extent of copyright legislation (and, largely, also its interpretation by the courts). *See* Jessica Litman, DIGITAL COPYRIGHT 22–34 (2d ed. 2006).

21. So far, this attempted economic rejoinder is not validated in practice to any significant extent; that is, we do not observe widespread user-friendly terms available to those who dislike the terms in boilerplate waivers. As for another common economic rejoinder, that such mass waivers of rights are efficient even without the recipient's assent, the blanket assumption of efficiency (assuming competitive markets, perfect pass-through of cost savings, and so forth) amounts, as I hope my references to it in this

book have shown, to a breathtaking coup of armchair economics. See chapters 2, 5, and 6. Moreover, the underlying idea that system efficiency can substitute for individual consent in divesting entitlements is at odds with the traditional ideal of justifiable private exchange transactions, the narrative upon which our legal infrastructure of contracts is based.

22. I say "it seems" because the statutes do not actually provide that all provisions establishing ownership rights (and establishing user rights, often by omission from ownership rights) are alienable. U.S. copyright law restricts alienability in a few cases; e.g., by requiring a writing to effect transfer of rights; or (in the exceptional case of the termination of transfers provision) by requiring that certain transfers by the author be renegotiated after years. 17 U.S.C. § 203 (2006). Does the mention of such limited restraints on alienation mean that all other rights are freely alienable? An argument can be made that user rights—especially fair use, but also such things as the free use of unoriginal facts and material that amounts to idea rather than expression—should not be so easily waivable. *See*, e.g., Neil Weinstock Netanel, *Copyright and a Democratic Society*, 106 YALE L.J. 283, 372–74 (1996) (comparing fair use of hard-copy books with fair use of Internet content and determining that copyright protections must protect Internet content that would be fair use if it were a hard-copy book).

23. *See* Litman, *supra* note 20.

24. *See also* Guy A. Rub, *Contracting around Copyright: The Uneasy Case of Unbundling Rights in Creative Works*, 79 U. CHI. L. REV. 257 (2011) (arguing that contracting to exclude user rights is probably not defensible on efficiency grounds).

25. User rights in information also have aspects that place them arguably within the purview of noneconomic political, cultural, and human rights, which further argues against the common practice of minimalist review of the mass-market waiver of these rights in boilerplate schemes.

26. *Lovell v. Griffin*, 303 U.S. 444, 450 (1938). For example, *Intel Corp. v. Hamidi*, 71 P.3d 296 (Cal. 2003) involved the question whether a disgruntled exemployee could be allowed to send mass e-mails to Intel employees disparaging the corporation's labor practices. The opinions of the California Supreme Court in this case did not seriously consider freedom of speech, demonstrating contemporary courts' reluctance to consider freedom of speech between private parties (a giant corporation and an ex-employee). Instead the court rather unsatisfactorily struggled with the

doctrine of trespass to chattels, which assesses whether the person sending e-mail is illegally bombarding the corporation's computer with electrons. In my opinion, this sort of end run around what is really going on in the dispute makes the law look silly. *See* Margaret Jane Radin, *A Comment on Information Propertization and Its Legal Milieu*, 54 CLEV. ST. L. REV. 23, 37–38 (2006).

27. *See,* e.g., *Yahoo! Inc. v. La Ligue Contre Le Racisme et L'Antisemitisme*, 433 F.3d 1199 (9th Cir. 2006) (discussing the enforceability of a French court's order requiring Yahoo! to cease and desist making available certain Nazi websites in France).

28. For example, the Fifth Circuit ultimately allowed Papa John's advertising slogan "Better Ingredients. Better Pizza." because it did not find the slogan to be an objectifiable statement of fact upon which consumers rely. *Pizza Hut, Inc. v. Papa John's Int'l, Inc.*, 227 F.3d 489 (5th Cir. 2000). Thus, though the court never explicitly addressed First Amendment freedom of speech concerns, Papa John's was allowed to say whatever it chose as long as it fell short of the legal standard for false advertising.

29. Annalee Newitz, *Dangerous Terms: A User's Guide to EULAs*, ELECTRONIC FRONTIER FOUNDATION: DEFENDING YOUR RIGHTS IN THE DIGITAL WORLD (Feb. 17, 2005, 12:00 AM), https://www.eff.org/wp/ dangerous-terms-users-guide-eulas.

30. Constitutional scholars have attempted to harmonize the regime of speech ownership (copyright) with the regime of freedom of speech (First Amendment). *See* C. Edwin Baker, *First Amendment Limits on Copyright*, 55 VAND. L. REV. 891 (2002); Neil Weinstock Netanel, COPYRIGHT'S PARADOX (2008). This is a field that deserves further attention.

31. *See* Neil Weinstock Netanel, COPYRIGHT'S PARADOX *supra*, note 30; *see also* Neil Weinstock Netanel, *Locating Copyright Within the First Amendment Skein*, 54 STAN L. REV. 1 (2001) (discussing the historical interaction of the First Amendment with copyright law).

32. *See,* e.g., James Boyle, *The Second Enclosure Movement and the Construction of the Public Domain*, 66 LAW & CONTEMP. PROBS. 33 (2003); The Duke Center for the Study of the Public Domain, http:// www.law.duke.edu/cspd/about.html ("[The Center's] mission is to promote research and scholarship on the contributions of the public domain to speech, culture, science and innovation. . . ."); Jerome H. Reichman, Graeme B. Dinwoodie, and Pamela Samuelson, *A Reverse Notice and*

Takedown Regime to Enable Public Interest Uses of Technically Protected Copyrighted Works, 22 BERKELEY TECH. L.J. 981 (2007); Lawrence Lessig, *Re-Crafting a Public Domain*, 18 YALE J.L. & HUMAN. 56 (2006) (arguing that a failure to recraft the public domain will lead to its demise and describing the costs to society of losing it).

33. Although I am not discussing group and cultural "rights" here, personal identity is closely tied to group and cultural identity. Cultural human rights include aspects of information important to cultural identity. A system that allows the allocation of control of such information to be determined by mass-market boilerplate rather than by more dialogic means is at minimum not auspicious for democracy or for the participation of cultural groups in their own identity formation. A waiver of privacy rights in a widely disseminated boilerplate scheme may be a candidate for market-inalienability, as discussed below.

34. *See,* e.g., Lisa M. Austin, *Privacy and Private Law: The Dilemma of Justification*, 55 MCGILL L.J. 165 (2010) (proposing a justification for privacy rights that is rooted in the value of protecting identity interests, where identity is understood in terms of one's capacity for self-presentation).

35. Christine Jolls has examined the role of consent in common-law privacy cases. *See* Christine Jolls, *Rationality and Consent in Privacy Law* (Dec. 10, 2010), http://www.law.yale.edu/documents/pdf/Faculty/Jolls_ RationalityandConsentinPrivacyLaw.pdf.

36. *See* 45 C.F.R. pts. 160, 164 (2007).

37. See Controlling the Assault of Non-Solicited Pornography and Marketing Act of 2003 (CAN-SPAM Act of 2003), 15 U.S.C. 7701–7713 (2003).

38. The market factors summarized in this paragraph were examined in more detail in chapter 6.

39. If Microsoft has about 90 percent of the market for personal computers, and if there are about a billion personal computers in the world (*see* WIKIPEDIA: *Personal Computer*, http://en.wikipedia.org/wiki/ Personal_computers (last visited June 8, 2012)), that makes 900 million subject to the Windows EULA. How many are in the US? In the EU? In Canada? How many users for each computer on which Windows is installed? The number of personal computers may be rapidly rising as the twenty-first century progresses. (Wikipedia projects the second billion by

2014 (*id.*)) At the same time, perhaps Microsoft's market share is declining against Apple and Linux?

40. *See,* e.g., UTILITY CONSUMERS' ACTION NETWORK, http://www
.ucan.org/telecommunications/home (last visited Nov. 19, 2011) (offering
consumers helpful advice on what stock terms in a cell phone contract
mean and allowing them to file a complaint and ask questions).

41. Perhaps a starting point can be the procedures developed for adjudicating mass-market tort claims. See discussion in chapter 11.

42. UCC § 2-719(3) (1977).

43. UCC § 2-316(2)-(3) (1977).

44. Even Douglas Baird, who finds nothing problematic about boilerplate per se (so that he is not too troubled by the consent problem) does find that arbitration clauses and forum selection clauses should at least be regulated for disclosure: an arbitration clause is "problematic" both because it may prevent even sophisticated recipients from knowing what they are actually getting and because "an arbitration clause undercuts process rights that the law regards as particularly important." Douglas G. Baird, *The Boilerplate Puzzle,* 104 MICH. L. REV. 933, 950 (2006). It should be noted that even something so simple as what Baird proposes here, a legislative mandate that arbitration clauses be foregrounded rather than buried in fine print, *id.,* would be of doubtful validity if imposed by a state in light of the current stance of the Supreme Court that arbitration clauses must not be singled out for any treatment by a state court or legislature that does not apply to all other contractual terms. *See AT&T Mobility LLC v. Concepcion,* 131 S. Ct. 1740 (2011).

45. UCC § 2-719(2).

46. Magnuson-Moss Warranty Act, 15 U.S.C. §§ 2301-12 (2006), at § 2308.

47. UCC § 2-302(2) (1977).

48. See chapter 6.

Chapter Ten

1. Of course, we certainly might increase regulation of boilerplate by legislative or administrative legal entities, ranging from piecemeal interventions into particular markets to the EU's scheme of comprehensive regulation. Regulation of various kinds is well worth exploring, and I will

do so in chapter 12; but calls for regulation tend to receive a hostile reception in the US.

2. It is possible to use legislation to bolster this kind of reputational deterrence. For example, a statute can provide that if a firm is found to have engaged in actions that violate consumer protection law, part of the remedy is to publicize the firm's deviations from good practice. *See,* e.g., Business Practices and Consumer Protection Act, S.B.C. 2004, c.2 (Can.), discussed in *Seidel v. TELUS Commc'ns Inc.,* 2011 SCC 15, para. 24 (Can.).

3. Principles of the Law of Software Contracts § 2.02 (c) (Am. Law Inst. 2010). These Principles are discussed in chapter 8.

4. For a summary of Facebook's privacy problems, see *Criticism of Facebook,* Wikipedia, http://en.wikipedia.org/wiki/Criticism_of_Facebook (last visited Nov. 14, 2011).

5. *See,* e.g., Ronald J. Mann, Charging Ahead: The Growth and Regulation of Payment Card Markets Around the World 128–153 (2006).

6. At the time of preparing this book for publication, at least some competition based on contract provisions has arisen in the provision of cell phone service. A few service providers are advertising that there is no contract for their service, obviously attempting to take customers away from the providers that try to lock in customers for two years. No competition has arisen, however, with regard to provisions that deprive customers of remedies against the company. As a guess, heuristic biases make it much less likely that customers will ever experience enough dislike for the remedies deletion clauses to make them look for a provider without such clauses, but they might experience that level of dislike for the lock-in clauses. Tolerances for various clauses prevalent in boilerplate might vary with different segments of the market.

7. *See* Thomas J. Smedinghoff, Information Security Law: The Emerging Standard for Corporate Compliance ch. 3 (2008).

8. A cautionary tale from the environmental field of forest management can be gleaned from Governing Through Markets: Forest Certification and the Emergence of Non-State Authority (Benjamin Cashore et al., eds., 2004). It is evident from the authors' research that in many areas forestry firms themselves set up the rating agencies that certify them. (Thanks to Prof. Edward A. Parson for this reference.)

9. A system of "machine bargaining," in which computers belonging to one party with sets of acceptable terms could seek out contracting partners' computers with at least a set of terms in common, would eliminate the "battle of the forms," because it would result in actual agreement in the sense that each side ends up with terms that it has previously determined are acceptable to it.

10. Standard-setting by a trade association or by a group of firms can raise an antitrust issue of collusion. *See*, e.g., Erica S. Mintzer and Logan M. Breed, *How to Keep the Fox Out of the Henhouse: Monopolization in the Context of Standards-Setting Organizations*, 9 INTELL. PROF. & TECH. L.J. 5 (2007); Mark A. Lemley, *Intellectual Property Rights and Standard-Setting Organizations*, 90 CAL. L. REV. 1889, 1937–48 (2002).

11. *See* Electronic Privacy Information Center (EPIC) for a list and descriptions of technological privacy protection systems, http://epic.org/privacy/tools.html (last visited Oct. 31, 2011). *See*, e.g., http://internet-filter-review.toptenreviews.com/ (last visited Oct. 31, 2011) for some software tools that are supposed to screen out pornography.

12. Of course, a porn filtering technology is only as good as its accuracy in labeling sites as porn or not. Techniques for doing this either by machines or humans are not foolproof.

13. This idea has a possible serious drawback. Firms may offer the worst contract that would not turn away the bottom part of their demand curve, while allowing well-off recipients to buy their way to a better contract.

A related worry arises from the practice described or suggested by a number of law-and-economics writers, who argue that firms can maximize profit by deploying a seemingly rigid boilerplate contract, but in practice relaxing it in situations favorable to the firm. *See*, e.g., Lucian A. Bebchuk and Richard A. Posner, *One-Sided Contracts in Competitive Consumer Markets*, 104 MICH. L. REV. 827, 833 (2006); Clayton P. Gillette, *Rolling Contracts as an Agency Problem*, 2004 WIS. L. REV. 679, 680 (2004). It might turn out that firms can maximize profit by imposing onerous terms on poor people, while routinely relaxing them for wealthier people who might buy more and become repeat customers. Or it might turn out that the selective implementation of boilerplate can facilitate anticompetitive behavior by firms. *See* David Gilo and Ariel Porat, *The Hidden Roles of Boilerplate and Standard-Form Contracts: Strategic Imposition of Transaction Costs, Segmentation of Consumers, and Anticompetitive Effects*, 104 MICH. L. REV. 953, 964 (2006). Another possibility is that firms might practice racial or gender discrimination by routinely singling out people from a preferred group to benefit from the nonenforcement of its ostensibly strict rules. Such a practice could well be difficult to perceive and remedy.

14. At least, we shouldn't use justificatory theories that imagine that we are "Econs" (choosing on the basis of "rationality" as defined by economists, when actually we are "Humans" (who do not choose in this way). *See* Richard H. Thaler and Cass R. Sunstein, NUDGE: IMPROVING DECISIONS ABOUT HEALTH, WEALTH, AND HAPPINESS (2008). *See also* John E. Montgomery, *Cognitive Biases and Heuristics in Tort Litigation: A Proposal to Limit Their Effects Without Changing the World*, 85 NEB. L. REV. 15 (2006) (discussing the effects of biases and heuristics on legal systems and the remedies proposed by various scholars to deal with these biases). For more discussion of heuristic biases, see chapter 2.

Chapter Eleven

1. This statement is oversimplified in practice because of the large areas of overlap. Malpractice by accountants or lawyers is a tort against their client, with whom they are in a contractual relationship. But the statement does capture a prevalent "theory" underlying tort, and (as I have recounted in chapter 4) underlying contract. A different way to draw the distinction between tort and contract would be: Tort provides remedies for the breach of duties imposed (or recognized) by law; whereas contract provides the tools to create new duties and provides remedies for breach of those duties. This way of drawing the distinction will fit malpractice just as well as negligent harm, and has the advantage of explicitly taking into account that not all duties we are under as members of the polity depend on our contractual choices.

2. Samuel D. Warren and Louis D. Brandeis, *The Right to Privacy*, 4 HARV. L. REV. 193 (1890).

3. The legal system has developed methods for dealing with mass torts, such as environmental harm or large-scale pharmaceutical injuries. These methods include but are not limited to class actions. Courts have developed aggregation methods of their own, and also have developed methods of arriving at settlement agreements. *See* Am. Law Inst., PRINCIPLES OF THE LAW OF AGGREGATE LITIGATION (2010); *see also* Judith Resnik,

Compared to What? ALI Aggregation and the Shifting Contours of Due Process and of Lawyers' Powers, 79 GEO. WASH. L. REV. 628 (2011).

4. *See* Baird, *supra* chapter 6, note 4, and accompanying text. *See also* Lewis Kornhauser, *Comment, Unconscionability in Standard Forms*, 64 CAL. L. REV. 1151 (1976) (making the same point over thirty-five years ago, and recommending that this necessitates that legislatures address the issue).

5. See discussion in chapter 3.

6. Digital Millennium Copyright Act, 17 U.S.C. § 1201 (2006) (implementing the World Intellectual Property Organization Copyright Treaty).

7. *See* Daniel Schwarcz, *A Products Liability Theory for the Judicial Regulation of Insurance*, 48 WM. & MARY L. REV. 1389, 1435–62 (2007).

8. Grant Gilmore, THE DEATH OF CONTRACT (1st ed. 1974; 2d ed. 1995, Ronald K. L. Collins, ed.).

9. Grant Gilmore, *supra* note 8 (2d ed.), at 110.

10. *Id.* at 66 *et seq.*

11. "Perhaps what we have here is Restatement and anti-Restatement or Contract and anti-Contract. . . . The one thing that is clear is that these two propositions cannot live comfortably together: in the end one must swallow the other up." *Id.* at 68.

12. Restatement 2d extended recovery based on reliance, where and to the extent justice requires it, to third parties. RESTATEMENT (SECOND) OF CONTRACTS § 90 (1981). In a comment, Restatement 2d went so far as to say that in situations where section 90 is applicable, a one-sided promise is a contract. *Id.* § 90 cmt. d ("A promise binding under this section is a contract. . . .").

13. Implementation of relief for reliance on a one-sided promise varies from state to state, and some courts keep it within more minimalist bounds than those apparently envisioned by the Restatement. *See*, e.g., *Frost Crushed Stone Co. v. Odell Geer Constr. Co.*, 110 S.W.3d 41, 47 (Tex. App. 2002) (refusing to put promisee in a position as if the contract had been performed because "[d]amages recoverable in a case of promissory estoppel are not the profits that the promisee expected, but only the amount necessary to restore him to the position in which he would have been had he not relied on the promise.") (citations omitted).

14. *See generally* Curtis Bridgeman, *Default Rules, Penalty Default Rules, and New Formalism*, 33 FLA ST. U. L. REV. 683 (2006).

15. Gilmore, *supra* note 8, at 96.

16. *See* Atiyah, *supra* chapter 4, note 26.

17. It is vigorously debated among scholars whether malpractice is better treated under contract or under tort; *compare*, e.g., Richard A. Epstein, *Medical Malpractice: The Case for Contract*, 1976 AM. B. FOUND. RES. J. 87 (1976) (arguing for contract) *with* P.S. Atiyah, *Medical Malpractice and the Contract/Tort Boundary*, 49 LAW & CONTEMP. PROBS. 287 (1986) (arguing for tort).

18. RESTATEMENT (SECOND) OF CONTRACTS § 205 (1981). US doctrine has it that good faith obligation attaches only after a contract is formed, leaving an uncertain grey area regarding how much manipulative behavior (short of outright fraud, of course) parties can get away with in the negotiation phase. *See* Charles L. Knapp, *Enforcing the Contract to Bargain*, 44 N.Y.U. L. REV. 673 (1969). In civil-law countries, the doctrine of culpa in contrahendo makes bad faith in the negotiation process actionable. By and large the US rejects this doctrine. *See*, e.g., *Racine & Laramie, Ltd. v. Dep't of Parks and Recreation*, 14 Cal. Rptr. 2d 335 (Ct. App. 1992).

19. *Compare* Steven J. Burton, *Breach of Contract and the Common Law Duty to Perform in Good Faith*, 94 HARV. L. REV. 369 (1980) (attempting to rationalize bad faith doctrine via abuse of discretion) *with* Robert S. Summers, *The General Duty of Good Faith—Its Recognition and Conceptualization*, 67 CORNELL L. REV. 810, 821–24 (1982) (arguing there is no way to rationalize this doctrine into rule(s)).

20. *See* David G. Owen, *The Evolution of Products Liability Law*, 26 REV. LITIG. 955 (2007) (discussing the rise of strict liability in product defect law, as well as the decline of the privity requirement).

21. *See*, e.g., *Greenberg v. Lorenz*, 173 N.E. 2d 773 (N.Y. 1961) (extending the warranty of merchantability to allow recovery for a defective product despite the fact that the injured party was not the purchaser of the defective product). Note that the Uniform Commercial Code provisions on warranty, as enacted by US states, do not presently provide for liability extended through the chain of distribution. (Recall that the UCC is a model code promulgated and revised from time to time by an NGO, the National Conference of Commissioners on Uniform State Laws (NCCUSL). Revisions that would have extended warranties beyond the immediate

parties to a transaction were promulgated by NCCUSL in 2003, but they were not enacted.)

22. See discussion of economic loss doctrine, pages 214–216.

23. U.C.C. § 2-314 (1977).

24. On the history of the implied warranty of habitability, see David A. Super, *The Rise and Fall of the Implied Warranty of Habitability,* 99 CAL. L. REV. 389 (2011).

25. *See,* e.g., CAL. CIV. CODE § 1941.1 (West 2011); N.Y. REAL PROP. LAW § 235-b (McKinney 2011); KENT. REV. STAT. § 383.595 (West 2011).

26. RESTATEMENT (SECOND) OF PROP.: LANDLORD & TENANT § 11.1 (1977).

27. Of course, lawyers should plead both contract and tort causes of action when it is appropriate; but probably much of the time they hope the court will decide the case under the tort cause of action.

28. A classic example, *Cent. of Ga. Ry. v. Price,* 32 S.E. 77 (Ga. 1898), involved the negligence of a railroad company in failing to drop a passenger off at her correct stop. The railroad then paid for her to stay in a hotel, where a kerosene lamp accidentally caught the mosquito net on fire and the passenger suffered burns trying to put out the fire. The court held that the railroad's negligent act was not the proximate cause of her injuries, and therefore that the railroad was not liable. *See also* economic loss rule discussion, pages 214–216.

29. *Hadley v. Baxendale,* (1854) 156 Eng. Rep. 145 (Ex.); 9 Ex. 341.

30. Chief Judge Cardozo, in *Murphy v. Steeplechase Amusement Co.,* 166 N.E. 173 (N.Y. 1929), famously denied recovery for a plaintiff trying to recover damages because an amusement park ride, called "The Flopper" had jerked him. *Volenti non fit injuria.* (One who takes part in such a sport accepts the dangers that inhere in it so far as they are obvious and necessary . . .) *Id.* at 174 (internal citations omitted).

31. The objective theory of contract differs from the idea of assumption of risk. It relies on what a speaker of a shared language would reasonably be taken to have meant and focuses not on the recipient but the firm: it asks whether it would have been reasonable for a person in the position of the firm deploying the boilerplate (not the consumer receiving it) to understand that the recipient was consenting. See discussion in chapter 5.

32. *See also* P. S. Atiyah, *Essay 1: The Modern Role of Contract Law*, in ESSAYS ON CONTRACT 1, 8–9 (1986).

33. *See* Jean Braucher, *Deception, Economic Loss and Mass-Market Customers: Consumer Protection Statutes as Persuasive Authority in the Common Law of Fraud*, 48 ARIZ. L. REV. 829, 836–46 (2006) (discussing cases).

34. It is often held, however, that a contract obtained by fraud is "voidable" by the defrauded party, rather than "void," in order to allow the defrauded party voluntarily to affirm the contract after she has knowledge of the fraud, or in order to protect third parties to whom rights have been transferred. *See* RESTATEMENT (SECOND) OF CONTRACTS §§ 7, 8, 164 (1981).

35. If being the recipient of boilerplate initiates a relationship between me and the firm imposing it, it is not the sort of relationship imagined by relational contracts theorists, and not the sort of relationship that by its existence calls upon us to honor it. In cases of sheer ignorance, it is difficult to maintain that any relationship at all could be created. See discussion in chapter 5.

36. It seems that courts became worried about this tort takeover during the period when warranty law migrated to defective-product law in some quarters. *See*, e.g., P. S. Atiyah, *Essay 9: Judicial Techniques and the Law of Contracts*, in ESSAYS ON CONTRACT 244, 266–67 (2001) (discussing the rise of the tort of negligence as replacing contract-law theories of implied warranties).

37. A modern interpretation of warranty in contract would make an exception to the requirement of privity. See the revisions to the UCC warranty provisions promulgated in 2003 by NCCUSL but not enacted; available at http://www.law.upenn.edu/bll/archives/ulc/ucc2/annual2002.pdf.

38. See chapter 6.

39. Naming the tort "intentional deprivation of basic legal rights" invites the observation that if the defendant is found liable and the court invalidates its boilerplate, the plaintiffs do not end up being deprived of their rights. (Others whom the boilerplate has deterred from bringing suit are in a practical sense deprived of rights.) My colleague Scott Hershovitz has suggested that a more accurate name for the tort might be "attempted deprivation of basic legal rights" or "assault on basic legal rights." I think it is important to emphasize that this tort is intentional, which would give

us "intentional attempted deprivation, etc." or "intentional assault, etc.," perhaps not quite satisfactory.

Courts could also, by analogy with the implied warranty of habitability in residential leases, consider an implied warranty of reasonability in form contracts. I would not prefer this solution, because it seems too much like the doctrine of reasonable expectations, which courts have largely not been willing to apply to anything but insurance contracts. The doctrine of reasonable expectations (as I have said) leans anyway toward being tort-like, as does the implied warranty of habitability. I think it would be better to start anew and straightforwardly in a tort regime.

40. I mean this in the spirit of the Warren and Brandeis article on privacy, which led to the development of a complex of new torts. Warren and Brandeis, *supra* note 2.

41. *Private Attorney General*, WIKIPEDIA, http://en.wikipedia.org/wiki/Private_attorney_general (last visited Nov. 14, 2011). *See also* Labor Code Private Attorneys General Act of 2004, CAL LABOR CODE §§ 2698–99 (West 2011) (aggrieved employees who sue for labor violations may recover the civil penalty for the violation).

42. *See*, e.g., Todd D. Rakoff, *Contracts of Adhesion: An Essay in Reconstruction*, 96 HARV. L. REV. 1173, (1983). Rakoff suggested that all adhesion contracts should be prima facie unenforceable, which I think is overkill. As has been pointed out by Michael Trebilcock and others, we purchase many products under a contract of adhesion, at least in the sense that terms are not dickered, but the mere use of a non-dickered price term should not render a transaction prima facie unenforceable. *See*, e.g., Michael J. Trebilcock, THE LIMITS OF FREEDOM OF CONTRACT 119–20 (1993). My concern is not solely with issues raised by a lack of dickered terms, but rather with the normative and democratic degradations caused by some adhesion contracts, particularly those that amount to mass-market rights deletion schemes.

43. *See*, e.g., Robert L. Rabin, *Respecting Boundaries and the Economic Loss Rule in Tort*, 48 ARIZ. L. REV. 857, 869 (2006); *see also* Dan B. Dobbs, *An Introduction to Non-Statutory Economic Loss Claims*, 48 ARIZ. L. REV. 713 (2006).

44. Courts may also be inclined to declare that such losses belong to the realm of contract, and that therefore relief must be obtained under the law of warranty, if at all. I am suggesting that some of these purported

contracts should not be adjudicated as contracts. As I pointed out earlier in this chapter, and in chapter 7, the UCC subjects warranty disclaimer to specific disclosure requirements, but subjects to no such requirement drastic curtailments of remedy, including exclusion of consequential damages other than for personal injury. The UCC should be read in light of underlying commitments of legal infrastructure, however, including such things as redress of grievances. *See*, e.g., UCC § 1-103 (listing the underlying principles of the UCC). I think courts have ample grounds to make more than they do of the notion of "failure of essential purpose" in UCC § 2-719(2).

45. *See* Dobbs, *supra* note 43, at 721–22.

46. It could be argued that the loss of the right to redress of grievances amounts to economic loss, because the injured party who cannot sue might in fact have received money damages if allowed to sue. That would be a fallacious argument, because the right to a remedy cannot be equated with the actual remedy that would have been available. The argument also would not apply to deprivation of the right to jury trial, for example; nor to the remedy I am tentatively advocating, which amounts to a form of injunctive relief.

Chapter Twelve

1. *See* Bernard E. Harcourt, THE ILLUSION OF FREE MARKETS: PUNISHMENT AND THE MYTH OF NATURAL ORDER 1–52 (2011) (interesting comparison between Paris market in 1739 and the Chicago Board of Trade in the contemporary era).

2. Health Insurance Portability and Accountability Act, Pub. L. No. 104-191, 110 Stat. 1936 (codified as amended in scattered sections of 26 U.S.C.).

3. Truth in Lending Act, 15 U.S.C. §§ 1601–1667f (2006).

4. Family Education Rights and Privacy Act, 20 U.S.C. § 1232g (2006).

5. Children's Online Privacy Protection Act of 1998, 15 U.S.C. §§ 6501–6506 (2006).

6. Gramm-Leach-Bliley Act, Pub. L. No. 106-102, 113 Stat. 1338 (codified as amended in scattered sections in Titles 12, 15, and 16 of the United States Code).

7. *See*, e.g., CAL. BUS. & PROF. CODE §§ 22575–22578 (West 2011) (requiring an operator of a commercial website to post a conspicuous privacy policy on its website and comply with that policy).

8. *See*, e.g., DEL. CODE. ANN. tit. 19, § 705 (2011) (prohibits employers from monitoring or intercepting electronic mail or the Internet access or usage of an employee, unless the employer has first given a one-time written or electronic notice to the employee).

9. *See* RESTATEMENT (SECOND) OF TORTS §§ 652C and 652D (1977).

10. *See*, e.g., *People v. Nesbitt*, 938 N.E. 2d 600 (Ill. App. Ct. 2010) (holding that there is a right to privacy in bank records contained in the Illinois constitution). *See also* CAL. CONST. art. 1, § 1 (granting citizens the "inalienable right" to pursue and obtain "privacy").

11. *See*, e.g., *Eisenstadt v. Baird*, 405 U.S. 438, 453 (1972) ("If the right of privacy means anything, it is the right of the individual, married or single, to be free from unwarranted governmental intrusion into matters so fundamentally affecting a person as the decision whether to bear or beget a child.")

12. *See*, e.g., *Griswold v. Conn.*, 381 U.S. 479, 484 (1965) ("The Fourth and Fifth Amendments were described . . . as protection against all governmental invasions 'of the sanctity of a man's home and privacies of life'" (quoting *Boyd v. United States*, 116 U.S. 616, 630 (1886)).

13. Omri Ben-Shahar and Carl E. Schneider, *The Failure of Mandated Disclosure*, 159 U. PA. L. REV. 647 (2011); Omri Ben-Shahar and Carl E. Schneider, MORE THAN YOU WANTED TO KNOW: THE FAILURE OF MANDATED DISCLOSURE (forthcoming 2012). There is also an ironic subtext to the use of disclosure. It is (at least ostensibly) meant to protect people who are naïve and uninformed, but it seems that only those who are well educated might actually read it and understand it. For example, mandatory disclosure of ingredients on food labels is much valued by well-educated and well-off people, but probably fails to do anything for those who must eat whatever is available cheaply.

14. Used Motor Vehicle Trade Regulation Rule, 16 C.F.R. § 455 (2011). The Rule requires clear disclosure through a window sticker, called the "Buyers Guide," of any warranty coverage and the terms and conditions of any dealer-offered warranty, including the duration of warranty coverage and the percentage of total repair costs that the dealer will pay. *Id.*,

§ 455.2. The sticker must also warn against reliance on spoken promises that are not confirmed in writing and list the fourteen major systems of an automobile and defects that can occur in these systems. *Id.* Dealers must as well place a specific, two-sentence disclosure in the sales contract informing the purchaser that the information on the Buyers Guide will govern if there is an inconsistency between the Buyer's Guide and the sales contract. *Id.* § 455.3. This regulation doesn't apply to states that regulate used-car dealers by state law. 16 C.F.R. § 455.6.

15. 15 U.S.C. §§ 2301–2312 (2006). The Magnuson-Moss Act also goes beyond mandating disclosure by prescribing substantive structure and limits on contract law. Regulations pursuant to the Act provide that once a firm gives any kind of written warranty, the warranty must contain certain content (*see* 16 C.F.R. § 701.3), thus preempting (overriding) state law allowing the disclaimer of warranties, if the recipient is a consumer. *See* U.C.C. § 2-316 (2002).

16. For example, to find out how each state treats the return of security deposits, see THE NATIONAL LANDLORD TENANT GUIDES, http://www.rentlaw.com/securitydeposit.htm (last visited Nov. 14, 2011).

17. When I taught first-year property law, I asked my students to bring in their leases. Many of them contained illegal clauses. Students were able to read the clauses, but (without a lawyer or their as-yet-to-come legal training) they had no way of knowing which ones were unenforceable. Landlords might be able to threaten tenants with enforcement in many cases without much risk of pushback. Occasionally a state will enact a remedy for this sort of behavior, such as a fine for implementing illegal clauses, but this is rather rare. *See,* e.g., CAL. CIV. CODE § 1950.5(L) (landlord who in bad faith refuses to return tenant's security deposit may be liable for statutory damages up to twice the amount of the deposit, in addition to actual damages).

18. As noted, landlords must follow rules different from those followed by others purveying products and services to the public; so must door-to-door sales companies and used-car dealers and a number of other specific industries. US courts hold that for insurance contracts only (with very rare exceptions), the terms will be not what the policy *says* but what the court thinks the reasonable expectations of the insured were. US courts hold that for subcontractor bids in the construction industry only, the subcontractor will be bound to its bid when the general contractor

uses it in bidding on the main contract; whereas normally bids are offers subject to revocation at any time before the offeree accepts.

The members of the American Law Institute seem to have been uncomfortable with these piecemeal rules in the common law. In the Second Restatement of Contracts, the ALI attempted to make these piecemeal rules apply to all contracts when justice or the circumstances require. RESTATEMENT (SECOND) OF CONTRACTS §§ 87(2) & 211 cmt. f (1981). Nevertheless, courts have resolutely not taken up the Restatement's invitation to generalize.

19. U.C.C. § 1-103(a)(2) (2001) ("The [UCC] must be liberally construed . . . [t]o permit the continued expansion of commercial practice through custom, usage, and agreement of the parties. . . ."). *See* Lisa Bernstein, *Merchant Law in a Merchant Court: Rethinking the Code's Search for Immanent Business Norms*, 144 U. PA. L. REV. 1765 (1996) (critiquing this UCC strategy of incorporating usages of trade into contracts). As I argued in chapter 5, it may be possible to relate trade usage to the objective theory of contracts.

20. A case in point might be the US CAN-SPAM Act of 2003, 15 U.S.C. § 7701, et seq., whose original thrust may have been to protect consumers from unsolicited commercial e-mail, but which, by the time it was enacted, had become an opt-out regime granting free rein to much unsolicited e-mail, and preempting state laws with stricter standards.

21. *Southland Corp. v. Keating*, 465 U.S. 1 (1984). Various bills have been introduced in Congress to amend the Federal Arbitration Act to overrule the US Supreme Court's expansive interpretation of it. As of this writing, these bills have died in committee. See chapter 7. Such proposals aim to curtail the use of arbitration clauses against civil rights plaintiffs, such as those claiming race or gender discrimination in employment, and against certain other classes of plaintiffs that legislative advocates believe should be able to get their cases before a court and a jury of their peers. It is also possible for courts to interpret other federal laws, such as the National Labor Relations Act, to preclude mandatory arbitration clauses. See chapter 7, note 21.

22. After *AT&T Mobility LLC v. Concepcion*, 131 S. Ct. 1740 (2011), discussed in chapter 7, it seems inevitable that this will be the case, unless federal legislation precludes it.

23. Such as rules imposed by the Federal Trade Commission, and to be imposed in the future by the Consumer Financial Protection Bureau

that was created by the financial reform legislation of 2010; as well as state consumer protection agencies, etc. *See* Dodd-Frank Wall Street Reform and Consumer Protection Act, Pub. L. 111–203, 124 Stat. 1376–2223 (2010).

24. *See* PRINCIPLES OF THE LAW OF SOFTWARE CONTRACTS § 2.02 (c) (1) (Am. Law Inst. 2010) (discussed in chapter 8).

25. See chapter 8 (electronic disclosure as proposed best practice).

26. Clayton P. Gillette, *Pre-Approved Contracts for Internet Commerce*, 42 HOUS. L. REV. 975 (2005).

27. *Id.* at 1012-13.

28. For explanation of this terminology, see chapter 4. It essentially means that firms are privately "condemning" recipients' entitlements.

29. *See*, e.g., David Gilo and Ariel Porat, *The Hidden Roles of Boilerplate and Standard-Form Contracts: Strategic Imposition of Transaction Costs, Segmentation of Consumers, and Anticompetitive Effects*, 104 MICH. L. REV. 983 (2006).

30. *See*, e.g., N.Y. GEN. OBLIG. LAW § 5-501 (McKinney 2011) (forbidding usurious interest rates).

31. Generally, the implied warranty of habitability, whether imposed by statute or common law, cannot be waived. Some jurisdictions allow more wiggle room; *see*, e.g., *Centex Homes v. Buecher*, 95 S.W.3d 266 (Tex. 2002) (noting that the implied warranty of habitability can be waived to the extent that defects are adequately disclosed so that the buyer has full knowledge of any defects that affect habitability).

32. See discussion in chapter 9.

33. The opposite, minimal scrutiny, occurs when a judge approves the term without evidence other than his own sense of fairness or efficiency. For example, sometimes a judge will just assume that a firm's practice of imposing a certain clause on a buyer is economically efficient. In one case it seemed obvious to the judge that the clause was part of a strategy of price discrimination, and therefore efficient, because price discrimination is efficient according to economic theory. *See ProCD, Inc. v. Zeidenberg*, 86 F.3d 1447 (7th Cir. 1996).

34. *See*, e.g., Richard Craswell, *Remedies When Contracts Lack Consent: Autonomy and Institutional Competence*, 33 OSGOODE HALL L.J. 209 (1996); Clayton P. Gillette, *supra*, note 26.

35. *See generally* Frederick Schauer, PLAYING BY THE RULES: A PHILO-SOPHICAL EXAMINATION OF RULE-BASED DECISION-MAKING IN LAW AND IN LIFE (1991); Duncan Kennedy, *Form and Substance in Private Law Adjudication*, 89 HARV. L. REV. 1685 (1976); Louis Kaplow, *Rules Versus Standards: An Economic Analysis*, 42 DUKE L.J. 557 (1992).

36. I discussed these in chapter 7.

37. For example, some jurisdictions make recipients jump through hoops trying to meet multiple burdens of proof to demonstrate that a contract is actually adhesive. *See*, e.g., *Cooper v. MRM Inv. Co.*, 367 F.3d 493 (6th Cir. 2004). *See supra* chapter 7, note 25.

38. Council Directive 95/46, 1995, O.J. (L 281) 31-39 (EC) available at http://eur-lex.europa.eu/LexUriServ/LexUriServ.do?uri=OJ:L:1995:281:0031:0050:EN:PDF.

39. Council Directive 93/13, 1993 O.J. (L 95) 29 (EC), available at http://eur-lex.europa.eu/LexUriServ/LexUriServ.do?uri=OJ:L:1993:095:0029:0034:EN:PDF. For a different comprehensive approach, see the Unfair Contract Terms Law, part of the Australian Consumer Law of 2010, sections 23–28; *see* also the Australian Securities and Investments Commission Act of 2001, section 12BH.

40. The EC Commission issued *A More Coherent European Contract Law: An Action Plan* in 2003, launching an initiative to consider (inter alia) whether commercial and consumer contract law could be brought together under more general principles. Commission of the European Communities, Communication, *A More Coherent European Contract Law: An Action Plan,* at 22 para. 86, COM (2003) 68 final (Dec. 2, 2003), available at http://eur-lex.europa.eu/LexUriServ/LexUriServ.do?uri= COM: 2003:0068:FIN:EN:PDF. As part of this harmonization discussion, the promulgation of specific pan-EU-approved contract clauses is being considered, to be developed in conjunction with firms and interested parties. In other words, it seems that the EU is considering a hybrid white list at the EU level rather than relying on a general black list that has to be implemented by each member state separately. In fact this list became known as "the grey list" because it was couched so vaguely and presented so many opportunities for variance by member states.

41. Indeed, some economists of high stature have said that more comprehensive regulation could have prevented the difficulty. *See*, e.g., Joseph E. Stigliz, FREEFALL: AMERICA, FREE MARKETS, AND THE SINKING OF THE

WORLD ECONOMY (2010) (arguing for increased regulation and governmental involvement in the economy).

42. Council Directive 93/13, 1993 O.J. (L95) 29, 29 (EC). Note that the Annex in its Article 2 also lists exemptions from certain of these proscriptions, particularly for firms in the financial sector.

43. It is fair to assume that many of the boilerplate schemes that are unquestioned or found legally valid in the US would not pass muster in the EU. *See* Jane K. Winn and Mark Webber, *The Impact of EU Unfair Contract Terms Law on U.S. Business-to-Consumer Internet Merchants*, 62 BUSINESS LAWYER 209, 209–14 (2006) (discussing a French case in which the court fined AOL for abusive and illegal contracts, *AOL France v. UFC Que Choisir*, R.G. N_ 04/05564, Cour d'appel [CA][regional court of appeal] Versailles, 1e ch., Sept. 15, 2005, J.C.P. IV 150905).

44. "Whereas, for the purposes of this Directive, the annexed list of terms can be of indicative value only and, because of the cause of the minimal character of the Directive, the scope of these terms may be the subject of amplification or more restrictive editing by the Member States in their national laws . . ." Council Directive 93/13, *supra* note 42.

45. Hugh Collins, *The Directive on Unfair Contract Terms: Implementation, Effectiveness and Harmonization*, in STANDARD CONTRACT TERMS IN EUROPE: A BASIS FOR AND A CHALLENGE TO EUROPEAN CONTRACT LAW 1, 4 (Hugh Collins, ed., 2008). For a report on the various ways that member states implemented the directive, see Hugh Collins, *Implementation of the EU Directive on Unfair Terms in Consumer Contracts in Member States*, 8 CONTEMP. ISSUES IN LAW 99 (2007). This special issue contains reports on the Czech Republic, France, Germany, Greece, Ireland, Italy, Portugal, Spain, the United Kingdom, the Baltic States, Hungary, and Poland. See also EC, Report on the Implementation of Council Directive 93/13/EC of 5 April 1993 on Unfair Terms in Consumer Contracts (2000), available at http://eur-lex.europa.eu/LexUriServ/LexUriServ.do?uri=COM :2000:0248:FIN:EN:PDF.

46. Hans Schulte-Nolke, ed., in cooperation with Christian Twigg-Flesner and Martin Ebers, EC CONSUMER LAW COMPENDIUM: COMPARATIVE ANALYSIS, 327–418 (prepared for the European Commission) (2007), available at http://ec.europa.eu/consumers/cons_int/safe_shop/acquis/comp_ analysis_en.pdf.

47. Christian von Bar and Eric Clive, eds., PRINCIPLES, DEFINITIONS AND MODEL RULES OF EUROPEAN PRIVATE LAW: DRAFT COMMON FRAME

OF REFERENCE (DCFR), prepared by the Study Group on a European Civil Code and the Research Group on EC Private Law (Acquis Group), 6 vols. The prologue by the general editors states: "This full edition of the Principles, Definitions and Model Rules of European Private Law is a document of pan-European co-operation. It is the collaborative work of jurists from thirty European jurisdictions." *Id.* at v.

48. The proposed Consumer Rights Directive is described and analyzed in MODERNISING AND HARMONISING CONSUMER CONTRACT LAW (Geraint Howells and Reiner Schulze, eds., 2009).

49. DCFR, *supra* note 47, II–9: 404.

50. *Id.* II-1:110.

51. *Id.* II-9:409.

52. *Id.* II-9:410.

53. *Id.*

54. See Jules Stuyck, *Unfair Terms*, in MODERNISING AND HARMONISING CONSUMER CONTRACT LAW 115, 134–136 (analyzing the proposed Consumer Rights Directive as it relates to unfair terms in contracts between business and consumers). This article provides a summary of the similarities and differences between the 1993 Directive, the DCFR, and the proposed Consumer Rights Directive.

55. *Id.* 128.

56. For example, the Dodd-Frank Wall Street Reform and Consumer Protection Act of 2010 (H.R. 4173), Pub. L. 111–203, 124 Stat. 1376–2223 (2010), prohibits mandatory arbitration in mortgage and home equity loans. The Act requires the new Bureau of Consumer Financial Protection to study and report to Congress on the use of mandatory arbitration clauses in consumer financial services, and this may lead to regulatory prohibitions on mandatory arbitration in other consumer credit contexts.

57. *See generally* Gregory Shaffer, *Globalization and Social Protection: The Impact of EU and International Rules in the Ratcheting Up of U.S. Privacy Standards*, 25 YALE J. INT'L LAW 1 (2000).

58. *See Id.*

59. *AOL France v. UFC Que Choisir*, R.G. N_ 04/05564, Cour d'appel [CA][regional court of appeal] Versailles, 1e ch., Sept. 15, 2005, J.C.P. IV 150905.

60. United Nations Convention on the International Sale of Goods, Apr. 11, 1980, 19 I.L.M. 668 (CISG). The CISG, however, does not deal with exclusion of warranties or unconscionability or limitation of remedies. Moreover, firms trading internationally may opt out of its provisions and use the national law of one of the parties instead.

acceptance, procedures construed as, 29–30

Adams, Katy, 254n17

Adams, Scott, 254n15

adhesion contracts: blanket assent and, 82–83; careful scrutiny of, 147; "exit" vs. "voice" in, 40; industry-specific regulation and, 222–23; insurance contracts, adhesion and, 83–84; origin of term, 250n5; standardized form contracts, traditional, 10; tort law and, 210, 302n42; unconscionability in, 127–28, 277n10. *See also* boilerplate; contract of adhesion; take-it-or-leave-it contracts

adhesive label on software, sample, 118

advertising rights, freedom of speech and, 175, 292n28

aggregate welfare, maximization of: welfare theories and, 63, 266n35. *See also* economic analysis of contract law; economic theory of law

aggregation, economic theory of law and, 63–64

agreement: clicking "I agree," 13, 25–26, 88–89; devolution of voluntary, 29–32; as talismanic word, 14

Alces, Peter A., 260n4

ALI. *See* American Law Institute (ALI)

alienability: continuum from market-inalienability to full alienability,

157; full alienability, 155–56; partial market-inalienability, 158–61. *See also* market-inalienability; partial market-inalienability

alienable rights: range of alienability, 157; rights deletion schemes, evaluation of, 155, 286n2

American Law Institute (ALI), 84, 252n4, 253n9; international harmonization and, 241; *Principles of the Law of Software Contracts*, 149, 190, 220, 225, 244; Restatement of Contracts (first), 200; Restatement of Contracts (second), 84, 200, 298n12, 305–6n18; suggestion for boiler-plate project by, 244

"anchor point," 27–28. *See also* heuristic biases

Aquinas, Thomas, 67

arbitration: by agreement, commercial parties, 131; Federal Arbitration Act (FAA), intent of, 131; for-profit entities, arbitration providers, 288–90n19

arbitration clauses, 130–35; *AT&T Mobility v. Concepcion* and, 133–35; bilateral arbitration, switch to class arbitration, 133; in British Columbia, 278n19; in Canada, 278n19; class actions and, 132–34, 280–81n28; common law courts, nineteenth century, 278n16; exculpatory clauses and, 138–40; Federal Arbitration Act (FAA) and, 130–33, 277n15,

arbitration clauses (*cont.*)
278n19; mandatory arbitration
and, 132, 134, 280n25; mass-
market deletion schemes and,
183–84; normative degradation
and, 254–55n18; preemption
of state law by federal law and,
131, 278n20 (*see also* Federal
Arbitration Act [FAA]); reasons
for use by firms, 132–33; state
court past invalidation of, 278–
79n21; state court responses to
US Supreme Court validation of,
279n21; unconscionability and,
278–79n21, 279n25; US Supreme
Court and, 131–32, 224, 277n15
Aristotle, 67–68
"armchair" economics, 232, 290–
91n21
Ashcroft, Eldred v., 39
assent, 82–83
assumption of risk: contracts and
torts, fuzzy "line" between, 208;
objective theory of contract and,
300n31; reasonable expectations
and, 208
AT&T Mobility v. Concepcion,
133–34
Atiyah, Patrick, 66–67, 266nn26–28,
299nn16–17, 301n32, 301n36
Austin, Lisa M., 293n34
automated filtering, private reform
and, 189, 193–96
autonomy (rights) theories, 58–62,
260n4; "browsewrap," question
whether contractual, 62; doctrine
of consideration and, 263n14;
doctrine of unconscionability and,
61; entitlements and, 59, 261n6;
libertarianism and, 264n19; re-
jection of, 81; rights deletion,
justifications of, 82–98; variant of,
260–61n5; voluntariness in, 59,

62; welfare school of thought and,
261–62n7
autonomy, tension between objective
theory of contract and, 89–90. *See
also* objective theory of contract
Ayres, Ian, 71, 264n20, 267n37

background rights, waiver of,
105–6
bad faith: contracts and torts, fuzzy
"line" between, 202–3, 299nn18–
19; normative degradation and,
20, 252n4
"bailment," 25
Baird, Douglas G., 100–101, 106,
198, 274nn5–4, 274nn8–10,
274n12, 294n44, 298n4
Baker, C. Edwin, 292n30
Bakos, Yannis, 275n17
Barakat, Ibrahim, 254n14
Barnett, Randy E., 84–86, 163,
260–61n5, 270n8, 287n12
Bartholet, Elizabeth, 288–89n19
Baxendale, Hadley v., 206
Bebchuk, Lucian A., 296n13
Becker, Marion Rombauer, 283n2
behavioral economics, 263–64n18
Ben-Shahar, Omri, 84, 149–50, 219,
270nn9–10, 271n14, 272n20,
285n16, 304n13
Benson, Peter, 60–62, 259n1, 262–
63nn11–17, 266n27
Bentham, Jeremy, 63–66
Bernstein, Lisa, 306n19
"best practices," oversight
improvement and, 147
bilateral arbitration, switch to class
arbitration, 133
Bix, Brian, 96–97, 273n26
black lists: in European Union, 240;
hybrid regimes and, 227, 229–31,
233; warranty of habitability and,
230, 307n31

blanket assent, 30; devolution of voluntary agreement and, 82–84

blended tort and contracts principles, 201–6

boilerplate: analytical framework for evaluating, application of, 181–86; business argument for, 15–16; circumstances in which boilerplate is received, 87–88; consent and (*see* consent; nonconsent; problematic consent); contract formation and, 12–15; copycat, 41–42; definition of, xvi–xvii; democratic degradation and (*see* democratic degradation); devolution of voluntary agreement and, 82; "exit" vs. "voice" in, 40, 105–6; freedom of contract and, 14, 19, 285n1 (*see also* freedom of contract); industry-wide, 41, 107–8; law and economics view of, 99–109; market-inalienability and, 156, 158–61 (*see also* market-inalienability; partial market-inalienability); normative degradation and (*see* normative degradation); objective theory of contract and, 86–89; poor people and, 76, 127, 150–52, 296n13; relational theory of contract and, 91–92; samples of, 111–19; sheer ignorance and, 21–23; social dissemination of (*see* social dissemination of boilerplate); suggestions for improvement of, 243–48; sui generis legal regime and, 217–18, 233, 242; tort law, reconceptualizing under, 197–99; varieties of (typology), 10–12; why we do not read, seven reasons, 12. *See also* adhesion contracts; boilerplate rights deletion schemes; evaluation of boilerplate, improving; information asymmetry; judicial oversight of contract law, evaluating

boilerplate rights deletion schemes, 16–17, 33, 130–42; democratic degradation and, 39–45. *See also* rights deletion schemes, evaluation of

boilerplate samples, 111–19; adhesive label on software, 118; cellular telephone contract, arbitration clause, unilateral modification, 116; concert ticket, broad exculpatory clause, 118; equitable remedies, deletion of court's discretion, 112; event in public park, sign displayed, expansive rights deletions, 114; financial services contract, arbitration clause, "agreement" to terms not presented, 111; mountaineering device, instructions for use, 113; online services contract, rights in user-generated content, 119; online services contract, warranty disclaimer, 119; parking garage tickets, responsibility disclaimers, 117; placard addressed to passersby, right to control use of likeness, 115

"bottom-up," private ordering as: exchange transactions and, 34; public/private distinction and, 43; standardization and, 42. *See also* private law

"bounded rationality," 26–27. *See also* heuristic biases

Boyle, James, 292n32

Bradshaw, Simon, 254n15

Brandeis, Louis D., 198, 297n2, 302n40

Braucher, Jean, 301n33

breach of contract: remedies for, 4, 70, 95, 140–41, 184 (*see also* redress of grievances); rule of law and, 39, 55

Breed, Logan M., 296n10

Bridgeman, Curtis, 299n14

British Columbia, arbitration clauses in, 278n19

"browsewrap," 12, 22; autonomy (rights) theories and, 62; consent and, 162, 287n10; imputed knowledge of terms, 287n10; suggestions for better oversight of, 246–47; tort law and, 211. *See also* varieties (typology) of boilerplate

Bureau of Consumer Financial Protection, 221, 310n56

Burton, Steven J., 299n19

Calabresi, Guido, 72–76, 268nn42–43

California: choice of forum clauses in, 138; class-wide arbitration procedure in, 284n8; *Moore v. Regents of University of California*, 21, 252–53n6; unconscionability, approach to, 146–47, 277n10, 284n9

Canada, arbitration clauses in, 278n19, 290n19

Cardozo, Benjamin N. (Chief Judge), 300n30

Carnival Cruise Lines v. Shute, 6, 31, 135–37, 146, 283n6

Carpio, Myla Vicenti, 252–53n6

Carrington, Paul D., 278n18

cartelization, contract-as-product theory, market structure assumptions, 105

Cashore, Benjamin, 295n8

Castle, Paul Y., 278n18

cell phone service providers: consumer pushback and, 191–92; heuristic bias and, 295n6; remedies deletion clauses and, 295n6

cellular telephone contract, arbitration clause, sample, 116

certifications, private reform and, 192–93

Che, Yeon-Koo, 273n6

Chemerinsky, Erwin, 257n17

children, sales of, market-inalienability and, 286n6

Choi, Albert H., 273n6

choice of forum (forum selection) clauses, xv, 6, 135–38, 246, 250n2; in California, 137–38; consent and, 137, 282n42; constitutional due process and, 136–37; in Utah, 282n42

CISG. *See* Convention on the International Sale of Goods (CISG)

class actions: arbitration clauses and, 132–34, 280–81n28; in California, 284n8; in Virginia, 25

clicking "I agree," 13, 25–26, 88–89

Clive, Eric, 252n4, 262n8, 309n47

coercion, 20, 123, 151. *See also* duress; nonconsent

Collins, Hugh, 237, 309n45

Colvin, Alexander J.S., 289–90n19

commensurability, economic theory of law and, 65

common-law courts: creation of new torts by, 198; improvement of standard oversight measures by, 144–52; in nineteenth century, arbitration clauses and, 278n16. *See also* judges; judicial oversight of contract law, evaluating

common-law economic loss doctrine: "intentional deprivation of basic legal rights" and, 215–16; tort law and, 214

community language/behavior socialization, objective theory of contract and, 89

competitors shown in disparaging light, freedom of speech and, 175, 292n28 comprehensive regulation in European Union, 233–39

Concepcion, AT&T Mobility v., 133–34

congruence, rule of law and, 39

consent, 15, 19, 84, 86, 161–62; "browsewrap" and, 162, 287n10; choice of forum clauses and, 137, 282n42; clear consent to clear nonconsent, continuum, 157–58; constructive (as-if), 93 (*see also* hypothetical consent); contract-as-product theory, role in, 101–3; devolution of concept of voluntariness and, 30–31, 82–83; expectation and, 163; (mere) opportunity to consent or assent, 93; nonconsent, effect of, 162–64; objective theory of contract and, 84–87, 90; oversight improvement and, 151; privacy and, 293n35; problematic consent, 162–65; quality of, 161–62; silence and, 23. *See also* assent; coercion; duress; hypothetical consent; informed consent; nonconsent; problematic consent

consequentialism: economic theory of law and, 63; utilitarianism and, 63

"consideration," contract doctrine of. *See* contract

constitutional rights: standardization and, 43, 257n16; stricter scrutiny and, 246. *See also* due process of law; freedom of speech; jury trial, right to; privacy; redress of grievances

constructive (as-if) consent, 93–96; constructive notice approach and, 272n22; definition of constructive, 272n20; opportunity to read and, 93. *See also* hypothetical consent

constructive notice approach, 149, 272n22

consumer contract terms, regulation of: in European Union, 234–39, 308n40; by federal administrative agency, 227–29

Consumer Law Compendium (EC Commission), 237–38

consumer pushback, private reform and, 190–92

contract: bargained-for exchange and, 3; breach of, 4; choice of forum (forum selection) clauses, xv, 6, 135–38, 246, 250n2; consideration, doctrine of, 61, 251n1; defined, 3; escape from fault, 6–7 (*see also* exculpatory clauses); escaping (*see* escaping contract); exchange (basic premise), 31; formation of, 12–15; forms, alternative legal universes created by, 7–8; "freedom of contract," 14, 96 (*see also* freedom of contract); indefiniteness, doctrine of, 232, 251–52n1; integration, doctrine of, 25; liberal theory of the state and, 34–35, 55 (*see also* justification of political state; liberal theory); merger, doctrine of, 25; modification of, 271–72n17; necessity of remedy, 4; objective theory of (*see* objective theory of contract); purported contracts (*see* purported contracts); reasonable expectations and, 83–85; reciprocal promises and, 251n8; relational theory of (*see* relational theory of contract); subsets of, 250n6; unconscionability, doctrine of (*see* unconscionability); "wild-card" doctrines and (*see* "wild-card" doctrines). *See also* boilerplate; contract of adhesion;

contract (*cont.*)
contract, philosophy of; liberal theory; take-it-or-leave-it contracts
contract, liberal theory of. *See* liberal theory
contract, philosophy of, 55–81; agreement-based theory and, 58, 262n8; autonomy (rights) theories and, 58–62, 260n4; contract-as-product theory and, 56; economic theory of law, basic premises and, 63–66; entitlement and, 67, 266n27; equivalence of exchange theory and, 58; fissure between autonomy theory and objective theory and, 89–90; gift transfers and, 67–68; involuntary contract, contradiction in terms, 56; "just price" and, 68; liberal theory and, 55–56; libertarian premises and, 58; neo-Aristotelian theory and, 67–68; promise-based theory and, 57–58, 261–62n7; property-like entitlement and, 67; property rights, redistribution of, 55, 259n1; reliance theory and, 66–67, 260n4; "unfree" contract, contradiction in terms, 56; voluntariness and, 57, 80–81; welfare theories and, 57, 69–80, 260n4. *See also* objective theory of contract; relational theory of contract
contract-as-product theory, 99–109; background rights, waiver of, 105–6; "bundling of hardware and legal-ware," 99; cartelization and, 105; choice, role of, 101–3; consent and, 101–3; "contract as thing," 100; "Econs and Humans," distinction between, 274n11; EULA ("End User License Agreement"), 106–7; heuristic bias, role of, 103, 105; information asym-metry, role of, 103; "lemons equilibrium" and, 108, 275n15; market assumptions, role of, 103–9; monopolization and, 105, 274n14; passive behavior as consent, 102; reading costs and, 273–74n3; welfare branch of contract theory, 99
Contract as Promise (Fried), 59–60
"contract as thing," 100
contract of adhesion: origin of term, 250n5. *See also* adhesion contracts
contract remedies, boilerplate and: evaluation of boilerplate, improving (analytical framework), 154–86; traditional judicial oversight, evaluating, 123–42; traditional oversight, improvement of, 143–53; Uniform Commercial Code (UCC), 126–27, 140–41, 145–46 (*see also* "failure of essential purpose" [UCC]; limitation of remedy). *See also* redress of grievances
contracts and torts, fuzzy "line" between, 200–216; assumption of risk, remedies and, 208, 301n32; bad faith and, 202–3, 299nn18–19; blended tort and contracts principles, 201–6; breach of contract and, 203; comparison and interaction of remedies, 206–9; estoppel, promissory, 298n13; extended warranty and, 203–4; fraud and, 201–2; good faith and fair dealing and, 202, 299n18; malpractice and, 202, 299n17; misrepresentation and, 201; mistake and, 202; negligence and, 202, 300n28; one-sided promises, enforcement of, 200–201, 298n13; privity and, 203; proximate cause, remedies and, 206; reasonable

expectations, remedies and, 207–9; remedies and, 206–9; warranty and, 203–6, 299n21

contract theory, boilerplate and: contract, philosophy of (*see* contract, philosophy of); introduction to contract theory, 57–66; rights deletion, attempted justification (autonomy theory), 82–98; rights deletion, attempted justification (economic theory), 99–109. *See also* boilerplate

contractual network benefits, standardization and, 256n14

Convention on the International Sale of Goods (CISG), 241

Cooper v. MRM Investment Co., 279–80n25

COPPA (children's information on the Internet), 219

copycat boilerplate, democratic degradation and, 41–42

Copyright Act, 248

copyright law: coordination problem and, 171; "defection" from legislative "bargain" and, 172; freedom of speech and, 176, 292n30; "holes" in, 172; political economy and, 170–73; political rights and interests and, 168, 171–73, 290n20; user rights and, 168–69

Corbin, Arthur L., 276n5

courts, role of, suggestions for improvement, 246–49

Craswell, Richard, 64, 71–80, 153, 261–62n7, 267n36, 267n39, 269nn46–48, 285n18, 307n34

Croley, Steven, 257n19

DCFR. *See* Draft Common Frame of Reference (DCFR)

The Death of Contract (Gilmore), 200–201, 209

default rule. *See* legal default rules

defective goods, and harm done by, oversight improvement and, 145–46

defective product, boilerplate as. *See* contract-as-product theory

deletion schemes as "sturdy indefensibles," 143–44

democratic degradation, 16–17, 33–51; boilerplate and, 33–34; causes of, 33–34; copycat boilerplate and, 41–42; distinction between public and private ordering and, 35; heuristic biases and, 256n11 (*see also* heuristic biases); legal directives and, 38–39; legal rights, erasing, 39–42; political debates and procedures and, 39–40; political economy theory and, 44–45; private law and, 34–37; private ordering and, 45–46; public/private distinction and, 36–37; reverse engineering and, 258n21; rule of law and, 37–38, 50; standardization and, 42–46, 256n13; tacit collusion and, 41–42, 256n12; take-it-or-leave-it contracts and, 40; technological protection measures (TPMs) and, 46–51

devolution of voluntary agreement, 29–32

digital rights management (DRMs). *See* technological protection measures (TPMs)

Dinwoodie, Graeme B., 292n32

Directive of 1993 on Unfair Terms in Consumer Contracts (EC Commission), 234–36, 238, 245–46, 309nn44–45

disclosure regimes, legal infrastructure of US and, 219–20, 304n13

Discover Bank v. Superior Court, 133, 288n18

divested right or interest, nature of, 165–78; Federal Arbitration Act (FAA) and, 288n17; freedom of speech and, 166, 288n16; human rights and interests and, 175–78; mass-market delivery of boilerplate and, 165–66; National Arbitration Forum (NAF) and, 288–90n19; political rights and interests and, 166–74

Dobbs, Dan B., 302n43, 303n45

"doctrinal borderline," tort law and, 199, 201

doctrine of consideration, autonomy (rights) theories and, 263n14

doctrine of privity, contract law, tort law and, 203, 210

Doctrine of Right (Kant), 59

doctrine of unconscionability. *See* unconscionability

Dodd-Frank Wall Street Reform and Consumer Protection Act of 2010, 246, 310n56

Draft Common Frame of Reference (DCFR), 238–39

due process of law: choice of forum clauses and, 135–37; constitutional right of, 135–37; fair play and substantial justice and, 136; proposed stricter scrutiny of waivers, 246; right to one's day in court and, 4, 135

Duke Center for the Study of Public Domain, 292–93n32

duress: judicial oversight, evaluating, 123, 275–76n2, 276n3; oversight improvement and, 151. *See also* coercion; economic duress; nonconsent; problematic consent

Easterbrook, Frank H. (Judge), 99, 274n13

eBay, 191

economic analysis of contract law: "default rules" and, 71; remedies and, 70; role of incentives and, 69–70; theory of efficient breach and, 71, 266n35; welfare theories and, 71–72, 267–68n40. *See also* economic theory of law

economic duress, 20, 151–52

economic efficiency, economic theory of law and, 65–66

economic loss doctrine, tort law and, 214–16; inapplicability to intentional boilerplate tort and, 215–16

economic theory of law, 63–66; aggregation and, 63–64; basic premises of, 63–66; commensurability and, 65; consequentialism and, 63; "distributional considerations" and, 64; economic efficiency and, 65–66; empiricism and, 65; externality and, 65–66, 265–66n25; human choices and, 265n23; individualism and, 64; individual psychology and, 65, 265n23; maximization of the sum of welfare ("size of pie") and, 63–64; preference satisfaction and, 63, 65, 265n22; "rationality" and, 65, 263–64n18, 265n23; reductionism and, 265n24; rule-utilitarianism and, 66; self-interest and, 64–65; subjectivism and, 64; utilitarianism and, 65, 264n19

"Econs" and "Humans," distinction between, 274n11; evaluation of boilerplate and, 287n15; private reform and, 297n14

efficiency: contract law and, 71–72; economic theory of law and, 65–66; "efficient breach" and, 71, 266n35

"efficient breach," 71, 266n35

Eisenberg, Melvin A., 260nn4–5, 271n16

Eisenberg, Theodore, 280n26

Eldred v. Ashcroft, 39

Electronic Frontier Foundation, 292n29; private reform and, 189

Electronic Privacy Center, private reform and, 189

Ellickson, Robert C., 264n19

eminent domain, 74. *See also* private eminent domain

empiricism, economic theory of law and, 65

"endowment effect," 27

entitlements: autonomy (rights) theories and, 59, 261n6; contract, philosophy of, 67, 266n27; "liability rules" and, 269n46; private law, democratic degradation and, 36

Epstein, Richard A., 255n6, 264nn19–20, 276n3, 276n7, 299n17

equitable remedies, deletion of court's discretion, sample, 112

equivalence of exchange theory, 58

escape from fault, 6–7. *See also* exculpatory clauses

escaping contract: private reform, ideas for, 189–96; regulatory solutions for, 217–42; tort law and, 197–216

estoppel, promissory: reliance on one-sided promise and, 298n13; Restatement of Contracts (first) section 90, 200; Restatement of Contracts (second) section 90, 200. *See also* reliance theory

EULA ("End User License Agreement"), 11; contract-as-product theory, market assumptions, 106–7; democratic degradation and, 169–70; reform suggestion and, 248; social dissemination of boilerplate and, 170, 180, 292n29

European Community Commission (EC Commission), 233–34; Consumer Law Compendium, 237–38; Directive of 1993 on Unfair Terms in Consumer Contracts, 234–36, 238, 245–46, 309nn44–45; Draft Common Frame of Reference (DCFR), 238–39; Proposal for a Consumer Rights Directive, 238

European Union: black lists in, 240; consumer contract terms, regulation of, 234–36, 308n40; EC Commission (*see* European Community Commission [EC Commission]); grey lists in, 240; harmonization, international and, 239–42; private reform and, 189; regulation of boilerplate in, 218; US as trading partner with, 240

evaluation of boilerplate, improving, 154–86; analytical framework for, 181–83; "browsewrap," consent and, 162, 287n10; consent, quality of, 161–65; divested right or interest, nature of, 165–78; "Econs" and "Humans," distinction between, 287n15; elements of analysis, 155–65; expectation, consent and, 163; expectation vs. exploitation and, 163; freedom of contract and, 285n1; grievances, redress of, 173–74, 183–86; heuristic biases and, 163; "I agree" (terms of service), 162, 287nn12–13; Magnuson-Moss Federal Warranty Act and, 185; market-inalienability, effect of, 158–65; mass-market deletion schemes and, 183; negligence, exculpatory clauses for, 184–85; nonconsent, effect of, 162–64; partial market-inalienability evaluation of boilerplate (*cont.*) and, 183; problematic consent and, 162–65; redress of grievances and, 173–74, 183–86; rights deletion schemes, questions for evaluating, 154–55; social dissemination of boilerplate and, 178–81; unconscionability and, 186; Uniform Commercial Code (UCC) and, 183, 185–86; validity of waiver and, 181; warranty disclaimers and, 185. *See also* boilerplate; boilerplate rights deletion schemes

event in public park, sign displayed, expansive rights deletions, sample, 114

eviction, constructive, 273n29

exchange transactions: commitment to the market and, 35; freedom of contract and, 35; freedom of individuals to engage in, 35; liberal theory and, 34–35; private law and, 34; private ordering and, 34–35

exculpatory clauses, xv–xvi, 7, 138–40; adhesion contracts and, 283n46; boilerplate and, 138–39, 140; in California, 139; freedom of contract and, 140; heightened scrutiny and, 184–85; insurance and, 139–40, 245–46; judicial limits on enforcement and, 25, 138; moral hazard and, 139; negligence and, 139, 184–85, 282n44; public policy and, 139, 282–83n46. *See also* void as against public policy

expectation: ambiguity of (positive vs. normative), 85, 163; consent and, 163; exploitation versus, 151; oversight improvement and, 151; reasonable (*see* reasonable expectations)

exploitation: ambiguity and, 85, 163; expectation versus, 151;

oversight improvement and, 151–52, 163

extension of warranty beyond immediate buyer: contracts and torts, fuzzy "line" between, 203–4. *See also* warranty

externality, economic theory of law and, 65–66, 265–66n25

FAA. *See* Federal Arbitration Act (FAA)

Facebook, 191

"failure of essential purpose" (UCC), 141, 145–46, 184, 207, 224–25, 302–3n44. *See also* limitation of remedy

fair dealing, implied obligation of good faith and, 252n4

fairness, industry-specific regulation and, 223

Federal Arbitration Act (FAA): amendment of, 145, 306n21; arbitration clauses and, 130–33, 277n15, 278n19; disclosure rules of, 220–21; expansion of, 246, 288n17; original intent of, 131, 184; oversight improvement and, 145, 146, 283n3; piecemeal "fixes" and, 224; preemption and, 131, 278n20, 283n3; redress of grievances and, 183–84; US Supreme Court interpretation of, 131–34, 288n17. *See also* arbitration clauses

federal statutes, patchwork legal infrastructure of US and, 219

Federal Trade Commission, 220, 241; hybrid regimes and, 306n23; oversight improvement and, 147

FERPA (educational information), 219

financial services contract, arbitration clause, "agreement" to terms not presented, sample, 111 firms currently imposing boilerplate: possible reputational harm to, 245; suggested reconsideration for, 245; transaction costs savings for, 245

First Amendment violations, 175; "state action" and, 291–2n26

forms, alternative legal universes created by, 7–8

for-profit entities, arbitration providers, 288–90n19

forum selection clauses. *See* choice of forum (forum selection) clauses

Fowler, Henry Watson, 143, 283n1

"framing," 27. *See also* heuristic biases

fraud: contracts and torts, fuzzy "line" between, 201–2; doctrinal border area, contract and tort, 202; nonconsent and, 20; tort law and, 201–2, 209, 301n34

freedom of contract: consent and (*see* consent); as core value, 19, 56; exculpation from tort liability and, 140; individual freedom and, 35; organizations and, 285n1; private ordering and, 19, 34; "unfree" or "involuntary" contract (contradiction in terms), 19, 56. *See also* autonomy (rights) theories; justification of political state; legal infrastructure; liberal theory

freedom of speech: advertising rights and, 175, 292n28; competitors shown in disparaging light and, 175, 292n28; copyright law and, 176, 292n30; divested right or interest, nature of, 166, 288n16; Electronic Frontier Foundation and, 292n29; First Amendment violations and, 175; "hate speech" and, 175; human rights and interests and, 175–77

Fried, Charles, 59–61, 262–63nn8–11

Friedenthal, Jack H., 280n28

Friedman, David Adam, 277n12, 282n43

Friedmann, Daniel, 266n35

Frier, Bruce W., 259n26

Fuller, Lon L., 39, 255nn3–4, 272n23

Gardbaum, Stephen A., 278n20

Gateway 2000, Hill v., 99

Gelles, Jeff, 10

Gertner, Robert H., 71, 264n20, 267n37

gift transfers, 67–68

Gillete, Clayton P., 227–29, 296n13, 307nn26–27

Gilmore, Grant, 200–201, 208–9, 298nn8–11, 299n15; *The Death of Contract*, 200–201, 209

Gilo, David, 296n13, 307n29

Gold, Andrew, 259n1, 263n12

good faith and fair dealing: bad faith breach of contract, 202; border area between contracts and torts and, 202; fraud and, 202; implied obligation of, 202, 252n4; inalienability and, 202; US doctrine vs. civil law doctrine of, 252n4, 299n18

Google, 191

Gordley, James, 66–68, 262–63n11, 266nn29–33

Gramm-Leach-Bliley Act, 219

grey lists: in European Union, 240; "heightened scrutiny" and, 231; hybrid regimes and, 227, 231–32; partial market-inalienability and, 231; piecemeal grey listing, 232; as "treatment with suspicion," 231; Uniform Commercial Code (UCC) and, 231

grievances, redress of. *See* redress of grievances

Hadley v. Baxendale, 206
Harcourt, Bernard E., 303n1
hardware, design and marketing of, 244
harmonization, international, 239–42; European Union and, 239–42
"hate speech," freedom of speech and, 175
Hegel, Georg Wilhelm Friedrich, 59, 61
heightened scrutiny (strict scrutiny): definition of, 157; hybrid regimes and, 231; partial market-inalienability and, 157; presumption against validity and, 231; suggestions for boilerplate review, 246–47
Helft, Miguel, 256n10
Herman, Barbara, 272n18
Hershovitz, Scott, 301–2n39
Herskoff, Helen, 257n16
heuristic biases, 26–29; anchoring, 27–28; cell phone service providers and, 295n6; clicking "I agree" and, 163; consent and, 29; democratic degradation and, 180; framing, 27–28; status quo bias, 27; stubborn nature of, 28–29, 247; underestimation of risk, 12, 26–27, 29, 103, 256n11. *See also* "bounded rationality"
heuristic reasoning, 95
Hillman, Robert A., 148–49, 254n15, 272n22, 284n10, 285n15
Hill v. Gateway 2000, 99
HIPAA (medical information), 219
Hirschmann, Albert O., 256n10
home equity loans, Bureau of Consumer Financial Protection and, 310n56
Hovenkamp, Herbert, 266n35
Howells, Geraint, 310n48
human choices, economic "rationality" and, 265n23

human rights and interests, 175–78; freedom of speech and, 175–77; privacy and, 177–78
hybrid regimes, 225–33; black lists and, 227, 229–31, 233; burdens of proof and, 308n37; Federal Trade Commission and, 306n23; grey lists and, 227, 231–32; heightened scrutiny and, 231; mass-market rights deletion schemes and, 233; minimal scrutiny and, 307n33; piecemeal adjudication and, 232–33; *Principles of Software Contracting* (American Law Institute), 225; public support and, 225; "rules" vs. "standards" and, 232–33; white lists and, 227–29
hypothetical consent: constructive (as-if) consent, 93, 97; justifying political state and, 93–95; normative degradation and, 96–98; vs. real contractual consent, 95–96

"I agree" (terms of service), 9, 13; "clickwrap," 11; evaluation of boilerplate and, 162, 253n8, 287nn12–13; objective theory of contract and, 88–90. *See also* clicking "I agree"
ignorance: normative degradation and, 21–23. *See also* sheer ignorance
illegal contracts, unenforceability of, 251–52n1
implied warranty of habitability in residential leases, 204–5
incentives: "default rules" and, 71; economic theory of law and, 69–71; prediction of effect of, 70; remedies for breach of contract and, 70–71; rule-utilitarianism and, 69–70
"indefiniteness," contract doctrine of. *See* contract

individualism (economic theory of law), basic premise, 64

individual psychology (economic theory of law): motivation for maximization and, 65; self-interest and, 65, 265n23

industry-specific regulation, 221–23; adhesion contracts and, 222–23; boilerplate and, 222; fairness and, 223; interest-group lobbying and, 223; legal generality and, 222–23; piecemeal regulation and, 223; reconceptualization under tort law and, 222; rule of law and, 222; transparency and, 223; usage of trade (UCC) and, 222

information asymmetry, 24–26; assumption of economic "rationality" and, 103; consent and, 25–26; contract-as-product theory and, 105; definition of, 24, 103; information failure and, 105, 107; prevalence in boilerplate context of, 103; suggestion for judicial review and, 247; vitiation of free choice and, 108

information failure, 105, 107; "lemons equilibrium" and, 108, 109; race to the bottom and, 108

informed consent, 21; autonomy theory and, 89–90; in contract law, lack of prevalence of, 253n7, 270n3; extent of information known by a person, 21; lack of informed consent, 22–23

institutional (in)competence of courts, 79–80, 153, 269n49

insurance contracts, reasonable expectations doctrine and, 83–84. *See also* reasonable expectations

integration, contract doctrine of. *See* contract

intellectual property regimes, federal, political rights and interests, 168–70

intentional deprivation of basic legal rights, proposed tort of, 211–12, 301–2n39; liability, determination of, 211–12; market-inalienability and, 212; rights deletion schemes and, 212; tort law and, 211–12, 301–2n39

interest groups: capture by, 193, 223; industry-specific regulations and, 223; politically weak rights and interests and, 167–68; standardization and, 45; US CAN-SPAM Act of 2003 and, 306n20

Internet privacy, legal infrastructure of US and, 219

involuntary contract (as contradiction in terms), 19, 56

Issacharoff, Samuel, 250n6, 280–81n28

joint socialization, and alleged consent of recipients, 87. *See also* objective theory of contract

Jolls, Christine, 293n35

Joy of Cooking (Rombauer), 143

judges: possibilities for future review of boilerplate, 246–49

judicial oversight of contract law, evaluating, 123–42; arbitration clauses and, 130–35; boilerplate and (*see* evaluation of boilerplate, improving); choice of forum clauses and, 135–38; current legal situation and, 130–42; doctrinal grey areas and, 124; duress and, 123, 275–76n2, 276n3; invalid contract formation and, 124; limitation of remedies and, 140–42 (*see also* limitation of remedy); oppressive contract terms and, 127–28, 276n7; traditional judicial oversight doctrines, 123–30; unconscionability and, 124–28, 275–76n2; undue influence and,

judicial oversight of contract
law (*cont.*)
123; Uniform Commercial Code
(UCC) and, 126–27, 140, 276n8;
void as against public policy, 128;
"wild-card" doctrines and, 128–30
(*see also* "rules" vs. "standards";
"wild-card" doctrines)
jury trial, right to: market-
inalienability and, 160, 286–87n8;
vanishing of, xiv, 4–6, 16, 108,
131
justification of political state, 45, 55,
95; democratic degradation and,
34–37; liberal theory and, 21, 34–
35, 44, 46 (*see also* liberal theory);
normative degradation and, 19–
21; public/private distinction and
(*see* public/private distinction)
"just price," 68

Kahan, Marcel, 256n14
Kahneman, Daniel, 253n12, 265n23
Kant, Immanuel, 57, 59–60, 271n13
Kaplow, Louis, 264n19, 277n13,
308n35
Katt, William J., 281n41
Katz, Avery, 273n3
Kennedy, Duncan, 277n13, 308n35
Kessler, Friedrich, 250nn5–6
Klausner, Michael, 256n14
Knapp, Charles L., 299n18
Koppel, Nathan, 288–89n19
Kornhauser, Lewis A., 100, 274n7,
298n4
Korobkin, Russell, 253–4n14
Kraus, Jody S., 260n4, 262–63n11
Krawiec, Kim, 255n8
Kronman, Anthony T., 264n19

landlords, US preference for market
solutions and, 220, 305nn17–18
Lat, David, 251n7

law-and-economics view of
boilerplate, 99–109
lawyers, role in boilerplate
improvement, 248
leases: implied warranty of habitability in residential leases, 204–5;
US preference for market solutions
and, 220, 305nn17–18
Leff, Arthur Allen, 100, 274n6,
276n8
legal default rules, 28, 71, 145, 154,
159–61, 213, 248, 253–54n14
legal directives, rule of law precepts
applicable to, 38–39. *See also* rule
of law
legal infrastructure, xvi, 20; of
contract law, 34; definition of, 34;
disclaimed by firms, 174; liberal
ideal thought and, 44 (*see also*
liberal theory); private ordering
and, 34, 36, 150; privatization of,
36; as solution to coordination
problem, 107; substantive
regulation and, 217; threat posed
by TPMs to, 46; underlying basis
of contract and, 36
legal infrastructure of US, patchwork, 218–23; American Law
Institute (ALI) and, 241; Bureau
of Consumer Protection and, 221;
comprehensive regulation and,
233–39; Convention on the International Sale of Goods (CISG)
and, 241; COPPA (children's information on the Internet) and,
219; disclosure regimes and, 219–
20, 304n13; Federal Arbitration
Act (FAA) and, 220–21, 224;
federal statutes and, 219; Federal
Trade Commission and, 220, 241;
FERPA (educational information)
and, 219; Gramm-Leach-Bliley
Act and, 219; HIPAA (medical

information) and, 219; hybrid regimes and, 225–33 (*see also* hybrid regimes); industry-specific regulation in, 221–23; insurance contracts and, 305–6n18; international harmonization and, 239–42; Internet privacy and, 219; landlords and, 220, 305nn17–18; leases and, 220, 305nn17–18; "lemon law" 220, 304–5n14; Magnuson-Moss Federal Warranty Act and, 220, 305n15; National Labor Relations Act and, 278–79n21, 306n21; piecemeal "fixes" and, 223–25; *Principles of Software Contracting* (American Law Institute), 220; TILA (loan terms) and, 219; Uniform Commercial Code (UCC) and, 221, 241; United Nations Commission on International Trade Law and, 241; "usage of trade" and, 221, 306n19; Used Car Rule (Federal Trade Commission) and, 220, 304–5n14

legal rights, erasing: democratic degradation and, 39–42. *See also* boilerplate rights deletion schemes

legal scholars, role of, 248

legislative "bargain," defection from: copyright user rights as example, 170–73; deployment of boilerplate rights deletion schemes and, 170–73

legislatures, suggestions for boilerplate oversight, 246

Leib, Ethan J., 270n5, 271n16

Lemley, Mark A., 296n10

"lemon law," 220, 304–5n14

"lemons equilibrium," 108, 275n15

Lessig, Lawrence, 255n6, 292–93n32

Lewan, Kenneth M., 257n16

liability: "intentional deprivation of basic legal rights," tort liability for, 211–12. *See also* liability, denial of; "liability rules"; welfare theories

liability, denial of: tort law and, 215, 302–3n44

"liability rules": economic defense of boilerplate and, 72–76; economic theory of law and, 72–74, 268–69nn43–44; expanded use of, 76–80, 269n46; private eminent domain and, 74; and "property rules," explanation of, 72; turning recipients' property rules into liability rules, 75

liberal theory, 34–35, 37, 46, 154; contract and, 3, 21, 55, 58, 68, 95; definition of, 3; justification of political state and, 21, 34–35, 44–46, 55, 95; public/private distinction and, 35 (*see also* public/private distinction)

libertarians, 252n5; autonomy (rights) theories and, 264n19; premises, contract theory validating, 58; utilitarianism and, 264n19

limitation of remedy: judicial oversight, evaluating, 140–42; mass-market contracts and, 174; rule of law and, 137, 160, 166–67. *See also* "failure of essential purpose" (UCC)

LinkedIn, 191

Litman, Jessica D., 290n20, 291n23

Llewellyn, Karl, 82–84, 270n1

lottery analogy, 84–85

Macaulay, Stewart, 270n5, 271n16

MAC EULA, 180

machine bargaining, private reform and, 189, 193–96, 296n9

"machine rule," 47. *See also* technological protection measures (TPMs)

MacNeil, Ian, 271n16

Magnuson-Moss Federal Warranty Act, 185, 220, 305n15

malpractice: contracts and torts, fuzzy "line" between, 202, 299n17; tort law and, 202, 209, 297n1, 299n17

mandatory arbitration: arbitration clauses and, 132, 134, 280n25; enforcement of, 146–47, 284n8. *See also* arbitration clauses

Mann, Ronald J., 295n5

market, free market vs. anarchy, 55

market assumptions, contract-as-product theory and, 103–9

market conditions, recipients' escape from boilerplate and, 179–80

market-inalienability: clear alienability, continuum from market-inalienability to, 156; consequential damages and, 161, 287n9; definition of, 155, 286n5; discrimination and, 159; effect of, 158–65; element in analysis of rights deletion schemes, 155, 286n3, 286n6; "intentional deprivation of basic legal rights" and, 212; jury trial, right to, 160, 286–87n8; partial market-inalienability (*see* partial market-inalienability); privacy and, 293n33; slavery, selling oneself into, 159, 286n4; as trump of other elements of analysis, 158

Marotta-Wurgler, Florencia, 254n15, 275n17

mass contracts: lack of aggregate remedy and, 198; tort law legal infrastructure and, 198, 297n3

mass-market contracts, limitation of remedies and, 174

mass-market deletion schemes, evaluation of boilerplate and, 183–84

mass-market delivery of boilerplate, divested right or interest, nature of, 165–66

mass waivers of rights, efficiency argument and, 290–91n21

maximization of aggregate social welfare, economic theory of law and, 63–64

McConnaughay, Philip J., 278n16

medical records, privacy of, 177

Melamed, A. Douglas, 72–76, 268nn42–43

merger, contract doctrine of. *See* contract

Michelman, Frank, 257n18

Microsoft: Windows EULA, 29. *See also* EULA ("End User License Agreement")

Mill, John Stuart, 286n4

Millard, Christopher, 254n15

Miller, Franklin G., 273n26

Miller, Geoffrey P., 280n26, 280–81n28

minimal scrutiny: assumption of efficiency and, 307n33. *See also* heightened scrutiny (strict scrutiny)

Mintzer, Erica S., 296n10

misrepresentation, contracts and torts, fuzzy "line" between, 201

mistake, contracts and torts, fuzzy "line" between, 202

"money-now-terms-later," 11; tort law and, 211. *See also* "rolling contracts"

monopolization, 105, 274n14; political rights and interests and, 170

Montgomery, John E., 297n14

Moore, John, 21; *Moore v. Regents of University of California*, 252–53n6 moral premises, relationship of contract law to, 251n9

mountaineering device, instructions for use, sample, 113

National Arbitration Forum (NAF), for-profit arbitration providers and, 288–90n19

National Conference of Commissioners on Uniform State Laws (NCCUSL): Uniform Commercial Code (UCC) and, 126–27, 241, 299n21, 301n37

National Labor Relations Act, 278–79n21, 306n21

negligence: contracts and torts, "fuzzy" line between, 202, 300n28; exculpatory clauses for, 184–85 (see also exculpatory clauses)

neo-Aristotelian theory, 67–68

Netanel, Neil Weinstock, 291n22, 292nn30–31

Newitz, Annalee, 292n29

NGOs, 243–44

nonconsent: effect of, 162–64; rights deletion schemes, evaluation of, 158–65; varieties of, normative degradation and, 20–23

nonstranger relationships, tort law and, 210

normative degradation, 15–16, 19–32; arbitration agreements and, 254–55n18; bad faith and, 20, 252n4; "browsewrap" and, 22; deletion of rights and, 31; explanation of, 15; fraud and, 20; freedom of contract and (see freedom of contract); good faith and, 252n4; "I agree" (terms of service) and, 253n8 (see also clicking "I agree"); ignorance and, 21–23; illegal contracts and, 251–52n1; informed

consent and, 21–22, 253n7; justification of political state and (see justification of political state); liberal theory of contract and (see liberal theory); nonconsent, varieties of, 20–23 (see also nonconsent); problematic consent and, 23–29 (see also problematic consent); "sheer ignorance" and, 21–23; social dissemination of boilerplate and, 179; unconscionability and, 20, 252n3 (see also unconscionability); voluntary agreement, devolution of, 29–32

Nozick, Robert, 252n5, 286n4

objective theory of contract, 86–92; autonomy theory, tension between objective theory and, 89–90; clicking "I agree" and, 88–90; community attribution and, 89, 271n13; inapplicability to boilerplate and, 87; reasonable person standard and, 86–89, 271n12; socialization into particular form of life and, 86–89

offsite terms, 10

one-sided promises: obligation based on, 200–201, 298n13; Restatement of Contracts, section 90, 200. See also estoppel, promissory; reliance theory

online services contract, rights in user-generated content, sample, 119

opportunity to assent: vs. actual notice of terms, 93; constructive (as-if) consent and, 93

oppressive contract terms, judicial oversight, evaluation of, 127–28, 276n7

organs, sales of, rights deletion schemes and, 286n6

"original position," 95

oversight, improvement of, 143–53; adhesion contract and, 284n9; "best practices" and, 147; coercion and, 151; consent and, 151; defective goods, and harm done by, 145–46; deletion schemes as indefensible, 143–44; duress and, 151; expectation and, 151 (*see also* expectation; reasonable expectations); exploitation and, 151–52 (*see also* exploitation); Federal Arbitration Act (FAA) and, 145, 146, 283n3; Federal Trade Commission and, 147; mandatory arbitration clauses, enforcement of, 146–47, 284n8; possibilities for future review of boilerplate, 246–49; rights deletion schemes, dilemma posed by disallowance of, 150–53 (*see also* poor people, onerous clauses and); standard oversight measures and, 144–48; traditional oversight methods and, 148–50; Uniform Commercial Code (UCC) and, 145–46, 152, 283n4 (*see also* Uniform Commercial Code [UCC]). *See also* judicial oversight of contract law, evaluating

Owen, David G., 299n20

ownership rights in intellectual property, alienability of, 170, 291n22

parking garage tickets, responsibility disclaimers, samples, 117

Parson, Edward A., 295n8

partial market-inalienability: definition of, 161; effect of, 161; level of review and, 161, 183; range of alienability continuum and, 157; social dissemination of boilerplate and, 178

passing-on to recipients of savings by firms, 31, 75, 79, 80, 127, 136, 213, 269n45, 283n6, 290n21

passive behavior as consent, 102. *See also* sheer ignorance

patchwork regulation. *See* legal infrastructure of US, patchwork

PC Pitstop, 10

Philosophy of Right (Hegel), 59

piecemeal adjudication, "rules" vs. "standards" and, 232–33. *See also* "rules" vs. "standards"

piecemeal "fixes," 223–25; case-by-case adjudication and, 232–33; normative and democratic degradation and, 223

piecemeal grey listing, 232. *See also* grey lists

placard addressed to passersby, right to control use of likeness, sample, 115

political economy (public choice) theory: democratic degradation and, 45; dissolution of public/private distinction and, 44 (*see also* public/private distinction)

politically weak rights and interests, 167–68. *See also* interest groups

political rights and interests, 166–74; coordination problem and, 171; copyright and, 168, 171–73, 290n20 (*see also* copyright law); divested right or interest, nature of, 166–74; EULA ("End User License Agreement") and, 169–70; intellectual property regimes, federal, 168–70; legislative "bargain," defection from, 170–73; mass-market contracts and, 174; mass waivers of rights and, 290–91n21; monopolization and, 170; ownership rights and, 291n22; "prisoner's dilemma" and, 171; redress of grievances, 173–74 (*see also* redress of grievances); trademarks and, 169; trespass, doctrine of, 291–92n26; user rights and, 168–70, 172–73, 291n25

political state, justification of. *See* justification of political state

poor people, onerous clauses and, 76, 127, 150–52, 296n13

Porat, Ariel, 296n13, 307n29

pornography, websites containing, private reform and, 194, 296n12

Posner, Eric A., 267–68n40

Posner, Richard A., 251n7, 264n19, 266n34, 296n13

preemption of state law by federal law, 131, 278n20. *See also* Federal Arbitration Act (FAA)

preference satisfaction, economic theory of law and, 63, 65, 265n22

prima facie, defined, 283n49

Prince, Harry G., 277n10

Principles of the Law of Software Contracts (American Law Institute), 149, 190, 220, 225, 244

"prisoner's dilemma," 171; defection from legislative "bargain" and, 170–71

privacy: consent and, 177–78, 293n35; cultural identity and, 293n33; default rules and, 177–78; heuristic biases and, 177; human rights and interests and, 177–78; market-inalienability and, 293n33; medical records and, 177; problematic consent and, 177; socially widespread waiver and, 177–78

private condemnation. *See* private eminent domain

private eminent domain: dissolution of public/private distinction and (*see* public/private distinction);

economic theory of law and, 74, 268n43; normative degradation and, 15. *See also* turning recipients' property rules into liability rules

private law, 34–37; "bottom-up," private ordering as, 34; democratic degradation and, 35; entitlements and, 36; exchange transactions and, 34; private ordering, defined, 35; privatization of functions and, 36; public and private ordering, undermining distinction between, 35–36; public/private distinction, destabilizing, 36–37; vs. "top-down," public ordering as, 34, 35. *See also* justification of political state; liberal theory

private ordering: as "bottom-up," 34, 42; defined, 35; private law, democratic degradation and, 35; public and private ordering, undermining distinction between, 35–36; standardization and, 44–45; vs. "top-down" (public) ordering, 34, 35, 42

private reform ideas for boilerplate: automated filtering and, 189, 193–96; cell phone service providers, consumer pushback, 191–92; certifications and, 192–93; choice systems and, 193–96; consumer pushback and, 190–92; "Econs" and "Humans," distinction between, 297n14; Electronic Frontier Foundation and, 189; Electronic Privacy Center and, 189; ideas for, 189–96; machine bargaining and, 189, 193–96, 296n9; pornography, websites containing, 194, 296n12; *Principles of the Law of Software Contracts* (American Law Institute), 190; rating agencies private reform ideas for boilerplate (*cont.*)

and, 189, 192–93; reputation and, 190–92, 295n2; seals of approval and, 192–93; social networking sites, consumer pushback, 191; standard software packages and, 194, 296n10; telephone service providers, consumer pushback and, 191

privatization of public functions, private law, democratic degradation and, 36

privity of contract, 203, 210

problematic consent, 23–29, 162–65; heuristic biases and, 26–29 (*see also* heuristic biases); information asymmetry and, 24–26; market-inalienability and, 164; normative degradation and, 23–29; risk assessment and, 26

promise-based theory, 58, 261–62n7

property-like entitlement, 67

property rights: in California, 21, 252–53n6; redistribution of, 55, 259n1

"property rules": economic theory of law and, 72–74; liability rules, collapse of property rules into, 74–76 (*see also* "liability rules")

Proposal for a Consumer Rights Directive (EC Commission), 238

proximate cause, 206

psychology, economic theory of law and, 65, 263–64n18, 265n23

public and private ordering, undermining distinction between, 35–36. *See also* public/private distinction

public choice theory: democratic degradation and, 45; purchase of legislation and, 44. *See also* political economy (public choice) theory

public ordering: boilerplate transactions and, 45–46; excessive privatization of, 36; public functions in care of polity, 35–36, 174, 210, 212; relationships in care of polity, 91; "top-down" ordering, 34

public policy, void as against. *See* void as against public policy

public/private distinction: destabilizing of, 36–37; pragmatic interpretation of, 45–46, 217, 255n1; undermining of, 43–45

public support, legal infrastructure for market initiatives, 225

Purcell, Edward A., 281n40

purported contracts, 8, 10–12, 302n44; coercion or fraud and, 15; consent and, 20, 22, 30, 158; effect of labeling as contract, 10; juridical structure and, 47; market-inalienability and, 158; normative degradation and, 144; unconscionability and, 20; varieties of purported contracts, 10–12

Rabin, Robert L., 302n43

radical unexpectedness, 84–85. *See also* reasonable expectations

Rakoff, Todd D., 285n1, 302n42

Randall, Susan, 278n21

rating agencies, private reform and, 189, 192–93

Rawls, John, 94, 94n, 95n

Raz, Joseph, 255n3

reading costs, economic theory of law and, 273–74n3

real consent, settling for less than, 96–98

real property, self-help and, 49, 259n25

reasonable expectations, 129, 163, 185, 186; adhesion contracts and, 84, 270n6; insurance policies and, 83–84; receipt of boilerplate characterized as actual consent, 84–85, 270n5; Restatement of Contracts and, 84, 207n5, 305–6n18; tort interpretation of, 207–9. *See also* radical unexpectedness

reasonable person standard: objective theory of contract and, 86–89; tort law and, 208–9, 271n12. *See also* objective theory of contract

reciprocal promises, 251n8

reconceptualization, industry-specific regulation and, 222

Redish, Martin H., 281n41

redress of grievances, 4, 145, 147, 160, 167, 173–74, 183–86, 247–48; democratic degradation and, 167; infrastructure of legality and, 247–48 (*see also* legal infrastructure); liberal theory of contract and (*see* liberal theory); market-inalienability and, 160, 167; opportunities for improvement of, 247–48; per se or prima facie unconscionability and, 145; political rights and interests and, 173–74; public legal infrastructure and, 35–36, 174, 210, 212; rule of law and, 173–74, 183, 247 (*see also* rule of law); technological protection measures (TPMs) and, 48. *See also* remedies

reductionism, economic theory of law and, 265n24

reform, private. *See* private reform ideas for boilerplate

regulation of boilerplate, 217–42; in European Union, 218; legal infrastructure of US and, 218–23 (*see also* legal infrastructure of US, patchwork); private solutions and, 218; technological protection measures (TPMs) and, 217

regulatory agencies, suggestions for, 245–46

Reichman, Jerome H., 292n32

relational theory of contract, 91–92, 271n16; boilerplate and, 91–92; juridical limits of, 91

reliance theory, 66–67, 260n4

remedies: contract remedies, boilerplate and (*see* contract remedies, boilerplate and); contracts and torts, fuzzy "line" between, 206–9; tort law and, 206–9, 212–13. *See also* limitation of remedy; redress of grievances

remedies deletion clauses, cell phone service providers and, 295n6

rentals: implied warranty of habitability in residential leases, 204–5; self-help and, 49, 259n25; standards of habitability for, 205; substandard apartments and, 205

rent-seeking, 170, 257n19, 269n49; economic theory of law and, 269n49

reputation, private reform and, 190–92, 295n2

Resnik, Judith, 281n37, 297n3

Restatement of Contracts (first), 200

Restatement of Contracts (second), 84, 200, 298n12, 305–6n18

Restatements of contract law (American Law Institute), 252n4

reverse engineering: contractual restriction on, 258n21; fair use (copyright law) and, 258n21

rights deletion: black listing, "rules" vs. "standards" and, 233; disallowance of, dilemma caused by, 150–53; evaluation of (*see* rights deletion schemes, evaluation of); "intentional deprivation of basic legal rights" and, 212; normative degradation and, 31. *See also*

rights deletion (*cont.*)
boilerplate rights deletion schemes; rights deletion schemes, evaluation of
rights deletion, attempted justification (autonomy theory), 82–98; actual consent and, 86–92; constructive (as-if) consent and, 93–96; eviction, constructive, 273n29; objective theory of contract and, 86–92; real consent, settling for less than, 96–98; voluntary agreement and, 82–85
rights deletion, attempted justification (economic theory), 99–109; contract-as-product theory and, 99–109; law-and-economics view of boilerplate, 99–109
rights deletion schemes, evaluation of, 154–55; alienable rights and, 155, 286n2; children, sales of, 286n6; consent, range of quality of, 157–58; market-inalienability and, 155, 158–65, 286n3, 286n6; nature of right being relinquished, 163, 287n14; nonconsent, effect of, 158–65; organs, sales of, 286n6; partial market-inalienability and, 157; range of alienability and, 157; sexual services, sales of, 286n6; social dissemination, range of, 158
Ripstein, Arthur, 262n9
risk assessment, problematic consent and, 26
"rolling contracts," 11, 247
Rombauer, Irma S., 143, 283n2
Rub, Guy A., 291n24
rule of law, 15, 33, 37–39; vs. anarchy, 38; vs. arbitrary rule, 38; boilerplate divestment of legal rights and, 15, 143; boilerplate rights deletion schemes, tort law and, 216; boilerplate undermining of, 33; commitment to law itself and, 39; democratic degradation and, 37–38, 49, 183 (*see also* democratic degradation); foreclosure of remedies and, 137, 160, 166–67; law of the state and, 259n27; legal generality and, 222; legal infrastructure and, 218, 247; liberal political thought and, 37–38, 45–46, 94–95; political rights and interests and, 288n16; precepts of (enumeration of), 38–39; redress of grievances and, 173–74, 183, 247 (*see also* redress of grievances); replacing precedent system with ad hoc decisions and, 135; technological protection measures (TPMs) and, 49–50, 51, 199
"rules" vs. "standards": case-by-case adjudication and, 232–33; jurisprudential dilemma of, 128–29
rule-utilitarianism, economic theory of law and, 66

Samuelson, Pamela, 292n32
Scalia, Antonin (Justice), 133–35
Schauer, Frederick, 308n35
Schneider, Carl E., 219, 271n14, 304n13
Schulte-Nolke, Hans, 309n46
Schulze, Reiner, 310n48
Schwab, Nikki, 254n17
Schwarcz, Daniel, 298n7
Schwartz, Alan, 71, 250n6, 267n38, 273n3
Schwartz, Martin A., 257n17
Scott, Robert E., 250n6
seals of approval, private reform and, 192–93
Seidenfeld, Mark, 266n35
self-help, technological protection measures (TPMs) and, 48–49

self-interest, economic theory of law and, 64–65

sexual services, sales of, market-inalienability and, 286n6

Shaffer, Gregory, 310n57

Shavell, Steven, 264n19

sheer ignorance, 21–23. *See also* nonconsent

Sherman Antitrust Act, 41

Sherwin, Emily, 280n26

Shiffrin, Seana Valentine, 251n9, 261–62n7

"shrink-wrap" licenses, 10–11. *See also* varieties (typology) of boilerplate

Shute, Carnival Cruise Lines v., 6, 31, 135–37, 146

slavery, selling oneself into, market-inalienability and, 159, 286n4

Slawson, W. David, 270n4, 270n6

Smedinghoff, Thomas J., 295n7

Smith, Stephen A., 259n1, 263n12, 266n27

social dissemination of boilerplate, 178–81; analytical framework and, 182; EULA ("End User License Agreement") and, 180, 292n29; evaluation of boilerplate, 178–81; heuristic biases and, 180; MAC EULA and, 180; market factors and, 179–80; normative degradation and, 179; number of recipients and, 180–81; partial market-inalienability and, 178; rights deletion schemes, evaluation of, 158

social networking sites, consumer pushback, private reform and, 191

software: adhesive label on (sample), 118; design and marketing of, 244; *Principles of the Law of Software Contracts* (American Law Institute), 129, 190, 220, 225, 244; standard software packages, 194, 296n10

Spence, A. Michael, 275n14

spring guns, 48, 259n27

standardization, 42–46, 106–7, 256n13; adhesion contracts, traditional, 10; "bottom-up," vs. "top-down" emergence of, 42–43; consumer choice and, 107–8; democratic degradation and, 43; "lemons equilibrium" and, 108; network benefits and, 42, 256n14; privatization of social ordering parameters and, 43

standards of habitability, 205

standard software packages, private reform and, 194, 296n10

St. Antoine, Theodore J., 288–89n19

"state action" (US), application of constitutional values and, 43, 257n17

status quo bias: problematic consent and, 27. *See also* heuristic biases

Stein, Sam, 279–80n25

Stigliz, Joseph E., 308n41

Stoebuck, William B., 259n25

Stone, Geoffrey R., 257n17

stranger relationships, tort law and, 209

Strunk, William, Jr., 283n1

"sturdy indefensibles," 143–44

Stuyck, Jules, 310n54

subjectivism, economic theory of law and, 64

sui generis legal regime, boilerplate and, 248

Summers, Robert S., 299n19

Sunstein, Cass R., 250n4, 253nn12–13, 263–64n18, 272n18, 274n11, 287n15, 297n14

Super, David A., 300n24

tacit collusion, boilerplate proliferation and, 41–42, 256n12

take-it-or-leave-it contracts, 40, 94. *See also* adhesion contracts

technological protection measures (TPMs), 46–51; defenders of, 258n23; democratic degradation and, 46–51; "machine rule" and, 47, 217; real property and, 49, 259n25; rentals and, 49, 259n25; rule of law and, 49–51; self-help and, 48–49; spring guns and, 48, 259n27; as successor to boilerplate, 46–47; tort law and, 199

telephone service providers, consumer pushback, private reform and, 191

termination of transfers (copyright law), alienability restriction and, 291n22

"terms of service" (TOS), 11, 17

Thaler, Richard H., 250n4, 253nn12–13, 272n18, 274n11, 287n15, 297n14

TILA (loan terms), 219

"top-down," private ordering as: standardization and, 42. *See also* private ordering

tort law: adhesion contracts and, 210, 302n42; blended tort and contracts principles, 201–6; "browsewrap" and, 211; contract justification and, 210; contracts and torts, fuzzy "line" between, 200–216 (*see also* contracts and torts, fuzzy "line" between); creation of new torts, 198; "doctrinal borderline" and, 199; doctrine of privity and, 203, 210; economic loss doctrine, inapplicability of, 214–16; escaping contract, 197–216; explained, 197–99; fraud and, 201–2, 209, 301n34; "intentional deprivation of basic legal rights" and, 211–12, 301–2n39; legal default rules and, 213; liability, denial of, 215, 302–3n44; malpractice and, 202, 209, 297n1, 299n17; mass contracts and, 198, 297n3; "money-now-terms-later" and, 211; new tort, considering, 209–16; nonstranger relationships and, 210; normative degradation and, 23, 253n11; pharmaceutical injuries and, 297n3; redress of grievances and, 216, 303n46; remedies and, 206–9, 212–13; stranger relationships and, 209; technological protection measures (TPMs) and, 199; warranty and, 203–4, 301n37

TOS. *See* "terms of service" (TOS)

TPMs. *See* technological protection measures (TPMs)

trademarks, political rights and interests and, 169

transparency, industry-specific regulation and, 223

Trebilcock, Michael J., 260n2, 260n4, 265–66n25, 268n41, 285n17, 302n42

trespass to chattels, 291–92n26; freedom of speech and, 291–92n26

Trossen, David R., 275n17

Tsotsis, Alexia, 251n7

turning recipients' property rules into liability rules, 75

UCC. *See* Uniform Commercial Code (UCC)

unconscionability: in adhesion contracts, 127–28, 277n10; application of doctrine, 129; of arbitration clauses, 278–79n21, 279n25; autonomy (rights) theories and,

61; boilerplate as primary field of application of, 124; case-by-case adjudication and, 129; classical contract doctrine and, 125; definition of, 18, 20, 124; determination of, 125–26, 276n4; duress and, 275–76n2, 276n3; evaluation of boilerplate (analytical framework) and, 186; of forum selection clauses, 137–38, 282n42; judicial interpretations of, 127–28; judicial oversight and, 124–28, 275–76n2; normative degradation and, 20, 252n3; oppressive contract terms and, 127–28, 276n7; "procedural" unconscionability, 125; "substantive" unconscionability, 125; Uniform Commercial Code and, 126–27; as "wild card" doctrine, 128–29

undue influence, coercion or duress and, 123

"unfree" contract (contradiction in terms), 19, 56

Uniform Commercial Code (UCC): evaluation of boilerplate (analytical framework), 183, 185–86; "failure of essential purpose" of remedy, 141, 145–46, 184, 207, 224–25, 302–3n44; grey lists and, 231; industry-specific regulation and, 222, 224–25; international harmonization and, 241; judicial oversight, evaluating, 126–27, 140, 276n8; limitation of remedy and, 140–41 (*see also* limitation of remedy); oversight improvement and, 145–46, 152, 283n4; piecemeal "fixes" and, 224–25; "usage of trade" and, 221, 306n19. *See also* National Conference of Commissioners on Uniform State Laws (NCCUSL)

United Nations Commission on International Trade Law, 241

unwitting contract, 11–12. *See also* sheer ignorance

"usage of trade," 221, 306n19

US CAN-SPAM Act of 2003, possibility of capture and, 306n20

Used Car Rule (Federal Trade Commission), 220, 304–5n14

user rights in intellectual property, 168–70, 172–73, 291n25. *See also* copyright law

Utah, forum selection clauses in, 282n42

utilitarianism, economic theory of law and, 65, 264n19

validity of waiver, evaluation of boilerplate (analytical framework) and, 181–82

varieties (typology) of boilerplate, 10–12; "browsewrap," 12; "clickwrap," 11; offsite terms, 10; "rolling contracts," 11; "shrinkwrap licenses," 10; "shrinkwrap of the second kind," 11; standardized adhesion contracts of the traditional variety, 10; "unwitting contract," 11

Vienna, Convention on the International Sale of Goods (CISG), 241

void as against public policy: common-law courts and, 128; difficulty of alleviating normative and democratic degradation and, 144; examples of, 128, 156; exculpatory clauses and, 138–40, 250n7; explanation of, 18. *See also* exculpatory clauses; "wildcard" doctrines

voluntariness: autonomy (rights) theories and, 59, 62, 262n8; as

voluntariness (*cont.*)
  basic premise of philosophy of
    contract, 57, 80–81; economic
    theory and, 72; gerrymandering
    of the word "agreement" and,
    30; ineradicability of, 56; lack of,
    normative degradation and, 57
voluntary agreement. *See* voluntary
    agreement, devolution of; volun-
    tary agreement, rights deletion
voluntary agreement, devolution of:
    normative degradation and, 29–32
voluntary agreement, rights deletion,
    82–85; adhesion issue and, 83;
    blanket assent and, 82–84; in-
    formed consent and, 83, 270n3;
    insurance contracts and, 83; lot-
    tery analogy, 84–85; radical un-
    expectedness and, 85; reasonable
    expectations doctrine and, 84–85,
    270n5
von Bar, Christian, 252n4, 262n8,
    309n47

waivers: of background rights, 105–6;
    of consequential damages, 25;
    extent of social dissemination of
    waiver, 158; mass waivers of rights,
    290–91n21; nature of recipient's
    right waived, 157; privacy and,
    177–78; quality of recipient's con-
    sent to waiver, 158; validity of, 181
Walden, Ian, 254n15
Ware, Stephen J., 254–55n18, 281n40
warranty: contracts and torts, fuzzy
    "line" between, 203–6, 299n21;
    disclaimers, evaluation of boiler-
    plate, 185; of habitability, black
    lists and, 230, 307n31; implied
    warranty of habitability in resi-
    dential leases, 204–5; standards
    of habitability and, 205; tort law
    and, 301n37; Uniform Commer-
    cial Code (UCC) and, 204

Warren, Samuel D., 198, 297n2,
    302n40
weak rights and interests. *See* in-
    terest groups; politically weak
    rights and interests
Webber, Mark, 309n43
Weinreb, Ernest J., 263n12
welfare branch of contract theory,
    99
welfare theories, 57, 62–66, 69–80,
    260n4, 262–66; aggregate welfare,
    maximization of, 63–64, 266n35;
    basic premises of economic analy-
    sis of law, 63–66; collapse of
    property rules into liability rules,
    74–76; commensurability and,
    65; consequentialism and, 63;
    economic analysis of contract
    law and, 71–72, 267–68n40; eco-
    nomic efficiency and, 65–66; eco-
    nomic theory of law and, 63–66;
    efficiency and contract law and,
    71–72; eminent domain and, 74,
    268n43; empiricism and, 65; en-
    titlements, liability rules and,
    269n46; expanded use of liability
    rules and, 76–80; externality and,
    65–66, 265–66n25; human choices
    and, 265n23; incentives, role of,
    69–71, 266n35; individualism
    and, 64; individual psychology
    and, 65, 265n23; institutional
    (in)competence and, 79–80, 153,
    269n49; "liability rules" and, 72–
    74, 268–69n44; maximization of
    the sum of welfare, 63–64; pref-
    erence satisfaction and, 63, 65,
    265n22; private eminent domain
    and, 74, 268n43; "property rules"
    and, 72–74; reductionism and,
    265n24; rent-seeking and, 170,
    257n19, 269n49; rule-utilitarianism
    and, 66; self-interest and, 64–65;
    subjectivism and, 64; utilitarian-

ism and, 65, 264n19. *See also* economic theory of law

Wertheimer, Alan, 273n26, 285n17

White, E.B., 283n1

White, James J., 259n26

white lists: hybrid regimes and, 227–29; international harmonization and, 241–42

Whitman, Dale A., 259n25

why we do not read boilerplate, seven reasons, 12

Wickelgren, Abraham L., 273–74n3, 275n15

"wild-card" doctrines, 124, 229, 232; function of, 155; jurisprudential problem of, 128–30; "rules" vs. "standards" and, 129. *See also* unconscionability; void as against public policy

Wilde, Louis, 273n3

Windows EULA. *See* EULA ("End User License Agreement")

Winn, Jane K., 309n43

Wortham, Jenna, 256n10

Yahoo!, 191